VANF

Abraham Lincoln

The Image of His Greatness

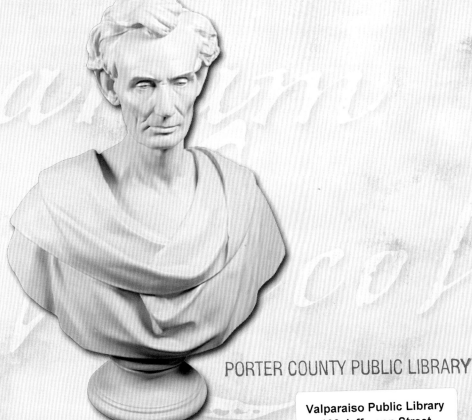

FRED REED

Whitman
Publishing, LLC
PUBLISHING SINCE 1934

Atlanta, Georgia

Abraham Lincoln
The Image of His Greatness

www.whitman**books**.com
© 2009 Whitman Publishing, LLC

3101 Clairmont Road · Suite C · Atlanta GA 30329

Correspondence concerning this book may be directed to the publisher, Attn: Abraham Lincoln, at the address above.

ISBN: 0794827047

Printed in China

This book was prepared to document the biography of Abraham Lincoln and the public's perception of his image. It includes a wide variety of promotional materials used in historical political campaigns along with cartoons, advertisements, magazine covers, and other popular-media materials that provided commentary and publicized Lincoln's popular image. The reader will find commentary and analyses of the included materials, which allow the historian and collector to perform their own analysis and form their own opinions. We hope this book is helpful in your study of Abraham Lincoln and his public image over the past 160-plus years.

> About the cover: Abraham Lincoln, an oil on canvas portrait by Italian-American muralist and illustrator Vincente Aderente, was likely created to celebrate the Lincoln Centennial a century ago. It is based on the same Anthony Berger photograph that the cent designer, Lithuanian-American sculptor Victor David Brenner, used that year. The photograph was taken February 9, 1864, for Lincoln's 55th birthday, showing Lincoln at the zenith of his powers. This image came to represent the popular view of Lincoln, the idol to both newly arrived immigrants and to their generation of all Americans.

If you enjoy *Abraham Lincoln: The Image of His Greatness,* you will also enjoy *100 Greatest American Medals and Tokens* (Jaeger and Bowers), *A Guide Book of Lincoln Cents* (Bowers), *A Guide Book of Confederate Currency* (Shull), and other books by Whitman Publishing. For a complete catalog of numismatic reference books, supplies, and storage products, visit Whitman Publishing online at www.whitman**books**.com.

❧ CONTENTS ❧

Dedication and Acknowledgments iv

Foreword by Thomas R. Turner...vi

Introduction...vii

CHAPTER 1.

Abraham Lincoln: 1809–1865 1

CHAPTER 2.

Lincoln the Ideal: 1865–1909...92

CHAPTER 3.

Lincoln the Idol: 1909–1959...174

CHAPTER 4.

Lincoln the Icon: 1959–2009...220

Chapter 5.

Lincoln the Irrelevant? 2009–future...252

Notes...256

Bibliography...259

About the Author...264

Photo Credits...266

Index...267

⅜ Dedication ⅜

To Dr. LeRoy Fischer, Matt Rothert, and Lloyd Ostendorf,
who sparked my Lincoln interest,
and
Pat, Becky, and Fred IV,
who patiently supported my Lincoln mania for many years.

⅜ Acknowledgments ⅜

As one might well imagine I have benefited from the insights of a great many individuals, organizations, and archives over the past decades. D. Wayne Johnson, *Coin World's* founding editor, generously supplied me with his unpublished compendium of signed Lincoln medals, an extract of his forthcoming monumental encyclopedic dictionary of medalists, coiners, and die sinkers. Dick also supplied the photo of his wonderful beardless Lincoln bust by cent designer Victor David Brenner. Through his representation at various auction sales over the years, Hugh Shull has enabled me to purchase many of the rarest Lincoln items in my collection. Well done, Hugh! Retired reference librarian Karl Kabelac supplied research and Lincolniana, and as well as answering my questions in several areas. Historian Stephen Mihm proofed my discussions relating to counterfeiting. My able editors Beth Deisher, Bill Gibbs, Michele Orzano, Barbara Gregory, Dave Kranz, and Robert Van Ryzin assisted me in preparing many previously published Lincoln works. Dr. Thomas R. Turner and Steve Wilson, editor and managing editor of the *Lincoln Herald,* their scholarly publication to the Lincoln community, presented my article on the effect of Lincoln money images in secondary media. I am also indebted to Dr. Turner for reviewing my manuscript and penning the fine Foreword contained herein. Additionally, Steve was very helpful to me during my week of research at the Abraham Lincoln Library and Museum at Lincoln Memorial University. I would also thank the dean of Lincoln image historians Harold Holzer for his support and critique of my humble efforts.

I am greatly indebted to Steve Ivy and Jim Halperin, who provided me unfettered access to Heritage Auctions' incomparable archives. I've known Steve for more than 30 years and Jim only slightly less long. They are both visionary and generous, and their great success attests to their business acumen and hard work. I would also like to thank friends Paul Minshull, Mark Van Winkle, Frank Clark, Tom Slater, Len Glazer, and Allen Mincho at Heritage.

Dean of professional numismatists Q. David Bowers, another colleague of more than 30 years, provided me a great many Lincoln exonumia images and several very rare Lincoln obsolete note images. Thirty-three years ago I edited Dave's *Coin World* column, and over many years his research and collegiality have been invaluable inspiration to me. His firm Stack's also supplied several images.

Alan Weinberg, the consummate Lincoln numismatic connoisseur, unselfishly shared many of his rare Lincoln ferrotypes, medals, and additional material for this book. Whitman photographer Tom Mulvaney provided the excellent images of a number of Lincoln items from the Weinberg and Reed collections. Emily Cowin, Spink Smythe, provided several images. John Zuckerman, Siegel Auction Galleries, also provided several images. Dr. Robert Schwartz, H.R. Harmer, did likewise. *Rail Splitter* editor Donald Ackerman supplied the image of the Lincoln fractional currency *CDV.* Mastro Auctions supplied images of several very desirable items. Ira Goldberg supplied images of several exceptional Lincoln cent rarities. Dana Linett, Early American History Auctions, supplied images of several choice Lincoln items, most exceptionally the Lincoln land grant shown. Ed Dauer supplied images of very rare Lincoln Demand and Legal Tender notes.

Dr. Richard Doty, numismatic curator at the Smithsonian Institution, supplied an image of a rare hand-drawn counterfeit note by Emmanuel Ninger from the National Numismatic Collection. Dennis Forgue enabled me to acquire an exceptional Lincoln philatelic collection. Mark Vorhies made possible my acquisition of his dad Jack's collection of Lincoln engravings. Cindy Van Horn, Louis A. Warren Lincoln Library and Museum, enabled me to complete my collection of the periodical *Lincoln Lore*. Jessica Rossner helped me fill gaps in my collection of the magazine *Lincoln Herald*. Jonathan Brecher supplied images of his silver Brenner "Preserve, Protect and Defend" medal. David Beach supplied very high-quality images of a number of very rare Lincoln tobacco labels. Jim Kerns, University of Wyoming, supplied a photo of sculptor Robert L. Russin and his monumental Lincoln bust. Katherine Jaeger provided exonumia photos. Terry Bryan supplied several Lincoln engravings from his collection.

Gene Hessler, the greatest living scholar on U.S. currency and a friend for more than 30 years, supplied photos, answered questions, and critiqued various parts of my research over the years. Gene's paper-money books should be on the shelves of every academic and public library. Chris Nelson generously shared his extensive collection of Lincoln cartoon *CDVs*. Galen Frysinger supplied his personal images from Lincoln's tomb and home in Springfield, Illinois. Steve Morawiec, Dolphin Photos, supplied the exceptional close-up photo of the Lincoln bust at Mount Rushmore. Roger Best and Seth Bienstock supplied photos of Lincoln plaques in their collections. Mark Tomasko answered many questions based on his intimate knowledge regarding 19th-century security engraving. Larry Adams and Ron Horstman supplied images of various Lincoln paper items in their collections. Additionally Horstman supplied excellent research on Demand Notes which was very helpful in writing this book.

Claudia Dickens of the Bureau of Engraving and Printing Office of External Relations provided helpful information on numerous occasions. Members of the BEP Historical Resource Center, including Dr. Franklin Noll, Barbara Bither, and Margaret Richardson, were also very responsive. Dr. Noll researched various Lincoln bond remnants. Ms. Richardson compiled a draft listing of all Lincoln security portrait work done by the BEP especially at my request. Over the years, Jeanne Howard of the BEP Public Affairs Section was also very helpful. Michael White at the U.S. Mint supplied images of the proposed 2009 Lincoln commemorative coins. Art Paradis and David Treter shared their research on counterfeit Lincoln 50-cent fractional notes. Delbert Wallace supplied an image of his very rare Lincoln-Washington ribbon. The leading authority on U.S. national currency, Peter Huntoon, shared his manuscript of Lincoln National Banks. Ray Herz provided images of his 1959 Lincoln Assay Commission medal. Joe Levine supplied several Lincoln exonumia photos. Richard Rosenthal provided me the 1910 Lincoln historical pageant photo. Daniel Dolfi supplied the image of the Ohio veterans badge. Robert Laper provided an image of the Volk Lincoln life mask to accompany the one I owned. Saul Teichmann provided images of the so-called Lincoln $3 gold pattern, sometimes attributed to Joseph Merriam. Peter Schwartz provided the image of the rare 3-cent Lincoln Emancipation Proclamation stamp essay. Steve W. Lee supplied a photograph of the Lincoln statue at the San Francisco City Hall.

Over the years Mark E. Neely Jr. supplied me with many images, answered many questions, and facilitated my research in various ways. Howard Shoemaker created for me a hilarious original Lincoln cartoon illustrated in chapter 4. Sergio Sanchez and Freddy Wolfe supplied images of rare Series of 1869 Rainbow Notes. Fred Schwan supplied the image of the Series 1870 $500 Gold Certificate. Austin Sheheen shared his rare high-grade contemporary Lincoln fälschgeld. Wayne Homren furnished a copy of the rare Zabriskie Lincoln medal pamphlet. Eric Amend assisted by imaging various items. Others supplying photos or assisting my research over the years included Arlie Slabaugh, Neil Shafer, Eric Jackson, Robin Ellis, Dan Weinberg, Joe Lepczyk, Daniel Pearson, Bob Kerstein, William S. Nawrocki, Terri Williams, Lea Morton, Angus Lincoln, Robert Unfug, Michael Baadke, Richard Jones, Keith Littlefield, Colin Bruce, David Ganz, Bob Cochran, Roger W. Burdette, David W. Lange, Michael Turoff, Steve Whitfield, Matt Hansen, Richard Hershberger, Larry Schuffman, John Herzog, William Hallam Webber, Tom Denly, and the White House Historical Association.

I would also like to express my appreciation for the staff of Whitman Publishing, whose vision for this book and hard work translated my work into readers' hands.

Fred Reed
Oklahoma City, Oklahoma

⊰ Foreword ⊱

In most academic fields—and the Lincoln field is no exception—it is possible to be very familiar with scholars through their publications and to correspond easily by email even if you have never met. While Fred Reed and I have never met in person, I first became acquainted with his work in my capacity as editor of the *Lincoln Herald,* when we decided to reprint his article "Did Abraham Lincoln's Icon Image on Money Influence His Public Perception?", which first appeared in *Paper Money* (September/October 2006).

Reed had utilized the archives of the Abraham Lincoln Library and Museum on the campus of Lincoln Memorial University, the university that publishes the *Herald,* to conduct his research. This link to Lincoln Memorial University was obviously one reason we were interested in the article, but what really drew me to it was the provocative question that Reed raised in his title. Certainly there is no shortage of written words about Abraham Lincoln, with only Jesus of Nazareth and William Shakespeare standing ahead of him in the number of related books published. With almost 20,000 books written about Lincoln's life and career, fourth-place Napoleon Bonaparte (who has a mere 5,700 books about him) pales in comparison.

There is no denying that the written word has had a strong influence in shaping public perceptions about our 16th president. However, Reed argues that since a piece of currency can change hands literally thousands of times, currency images had a larger impact on public perceptions about Lincoln both in the United States and abroad than any other source. It struck me that, in a common-sense way, Reed was on to something important, a unique way to examine the shaping of Lincoln's image. Since we all handle currency and coins every day, in a certain sense the evidence to test his hypothesis had been hiding in plain sight.

While an examination of currency might be unusual for American historians, historians of the ancient world, for example, have always studied coinage to gain insight into that historical period. The ancient world was very used to seeing the ruler's image on its coinage; Roman emperors were shown on their coins to awe and inspire their subjects. Our image of Cleopatra may be the beautiful Liz Taylor who portrayed her in the famous movie. However, on her coins she looks more like a man (some scholars have even noted a resemblance to Lincoln), perhaps to convey to her subjects that she was tough enough to rule Egypt.

One of my colleagues at Bridgewater State College is an expert on Greek and Roman coins, and I am constantly amazed at the insights to Greek and Roman history that they provide. Since the manuscript records are not always complete in the ancient world, the historian of this period is instinctively drawn to artifacts, which in some cases are all that he has to rely on. The American historian, faced with such a voluminous written record, has apparently not felt a need to delve into similar sources. But if historians can gain insights about Julius Caesar by examining coinage and other images, then why wouldn't the same hold true for Abraham Lincoln?

This is not to say that Lincoln scholars have entirely avoided the study of Lincoln images. There are a number of excellent books about Lincoln photographs, prints, and cartoons, and several of our most noted Lincoln scholars (such as Gabor Boritt, Harold Holzer, and Mark Neely Jr.) have written about this topic. There are also works about Lincoln medals, sculpture, coins, stamps, and films, but many of these appear in such specialized journals that they are not widely known in the Lincoln and Civil War communities.

Reed's *Herald* article reinforced his thesis about the relationship between currency images and perceptions about Lincoln, but admittedly his study was based on a rather small sample. What he attempts to do here, in *Abraham Lincoln: The Image of His Greatness,* is to greatly expand his research to include not only currency but also stamps, prints, photographs, and even advertising. He utilizes these images to try and understand how the Lincoln image has changed over time.

Reed divides his study into four time periods: Abraham Lincoln (1809–1865), Lincoln the Ideal (1865–1909), Lincoln the Idol (1909–1959), and Lincoln the Icon (1959–2009). While today the honoree generally needs to be safely deceased before appearing on a coin or stamp, during the Civil War Treasury Secretary Salmon P. Chase chose his boss's image for a $500 bond issue, with Lieutenant General Winfield Scott on the $100 denomination, and Chase himself on the $50 note. This was not simply a matter of ego but a shrewd move to assure investors that with the chief of state, the ranking general, and the paymaster on the bonds, their investment was secure.

These bonds were not meant to circulate, however, so even more significantly Lincoln's image appeared on the Treasury Notes that would pass from hand to hand. While prior generations of historians have sometimes stressed Lincoln's unpopularity until his 1865 assassination, Hans Trefousse in *First Among Equals* has clearly demonstrated that Lincoln was actually quite popular in the Union during his lifetime. The president who was portrayed as resolute and patriarchal would reassure the public that their cause was just and would triumph in the end.

After Lincoln's death, there was a desire to memorialize the "Great Emancipator" who had passed from the realm of mere mortals to sainthood. Congress held a special ceremony on February 12, 1866, attended also by the president, cabinet, and other dignitaries. Charles Burt, who had designed the original Lincoln currency image, designed a new Lincoln image for the $100 Legal Tender Note. (This image ultimately would appear on the $5 bill, one of the most common denominations of currency in circulation.) While Burt was the engraver most responsible for creating the original Lincoln image, his name would be unknown to most Americans.

The centennial of Lincoln's birth witnessed a celebratory mood that is once again with us as we approach the bicentennial on February 12, 2009. Between 1909 and the sesquicentennial in 1959, the Lincoln image and brand had become so well established that Lincoln was used to sell everything from cigarettes to life insurance and automobiles. Lincoln was an advertising executive's dream, since everyone knew his image and the traits they believed were associated with him, such as honesty, good value, character, and thrift.

During the last 50 years that trend has continued. It was no accident that Barack Obama launched his presidential campaign in Springfield, Illinois, on the steps of the Old State Capitol, the building where Lincoln gave his "House Divided" speech. Obama was only the latest in a long line of politicians, both Republican and Democrat, who have attempted to wrap themselves in Lincoln's mantel.

The use to which Lincoln's image has been put has also broadened to include the selling of whiskey, football fields, tombstones, and comic books. I confess that on a shelf in my office sits an unopened bottle of "Flatlander's Abe's Honest Ale," which occasionally generates discussion with my students and colleagues. One obviously can't go wrong drinking an ale with Lincoln's image on the label.

Reed hints that ultimately the old cliché that familiarity breeds contempt is true. Lincoln has been satirized and even ridiculed on television in situation comedies and commercials. Bookstores feature anti-Lincoln diatribes by neo-Confederate authors who want to return him to the rank of a mere mortal (and not a very good one at that). Even the Lincoln image on the revised $5 bill shows a Lincoln with a twinkle in his eye, a mod Lincoln more hip and in touch with the 21st century than the melancholy Lincoln of 1865.

One of the easiest phrases for any foreword or review writer to utter is "This book is a unique study and makes a significant contribution to the field." Despite this, I trust that *Abraham Lincoln: The Image of His Greatness* will gain the audience that it rightly deserves since it highlights an additional way of interpreting the life, death, and changing image of Abraham Lincoln over a period of time, through sources other than the written word. The rich illustrations that accompany the text will also provide readers with many hours of enjoyment as they seek to draw their own conclusions about the changing nature of Lincoln's image.

During this bicentennial year the Lincoln enthusiast will be bombarded with many more Lincoln books, new currency and coinage, stamps, and a variety of other images. It will be interesting to see what these new sources may reveal about the future direction of Lincoln studies. I am not naïve enough to think that simply by reading Fred Reed's book millions of Americans will pause to examine their currency or other images they possess to determine what they might reveal about changing perceptions. Hopefully however, American historians may conclude, like our colleagues in other fields, that while we have learned a great deal about Lincoln from manuscript sources, there are other ways of approaching our 16th president. If Fred Reed's book moves the study of currency and other images away from the realm of specialists and makes it more available to mainstream Lincoln studies, then his book will provide a definite service.

Dr. Thomas R. Turner
Bridgewater State College
Editor, *Lincoln Herald*

Dr. Thomas R. Turner is the longtime editor-in-chief of the *Lincoln Herald,* the oldest continuously published journal devoted to the life and career of Abraham Lincoln. In addition, Dr. Turner is a professor of history at Bridgewater State College in Bridgewater, Massachusetts. He is the author of *Beware the People Weeping: Public Opinion and the Assassination of Abraham Lincoln* (1991); *Many Faces of Lincoln: Selected Articles from the Lincoln Herald* (with C. Hubbard and S. Rogstad, 1997); and *The Assassination of Abraham Lincoln* (1999).

Introduction

Seven score and four years deceased, Abraham Lincoln's face is still familiar to his fellow Americans. The reason, of course, is that he remains omnipresent. His image has appeared on more than 450 billion cents and an additional 40 billion notes (mostly $5 bills) over the last century and a half. Lincoln references permeate pop culture. Lincoln kitsch is ubiquitous. Lincoln consciousness is largely universal.

In our hectic present age, media is the message. Today we are barraged with images: computer terminals flash multiple activities simultaneously; multiplex cinemas project dozens of movies concurrently; television screens pander programming separated only by the click of a button; cable channels cover late breaking events with split screen technology; screen crawls supplement this stream of consciousness. Events cascade live from the other side of the globe and the far-flung reaches of space. Yet much of our information is gleaned from brief encounters via visual and sound bites. Setting aside for a moment our 21st century conception of the visual, paper money can teach us a great deal about our forebears' situation a century and a half ago. For them, the media was the message, too. Money played a pivotal role in shaping public visual perception. When the federal government created paper currency to wage the Civil War, it branded its notes with patriotic motifs and the portrait of the president, Abraham Lincoln, to consolidate public support. Money was mass media long before George Lucas, Ted Turner, Bill Gates, or even Johann Gutenberg drew breath. The Caesars knew a thing or two about media and message when they stamped their own images and special messages on coins of their realms.

Numismatists are fortunate in holding windows to our past in their hands. In February 2009, no citizen of the world is unfamiliar with Lincoln's looks. Money is *still* mass media. Those several hundreds of billions of Lincoln cents over the past century have carried Lincoln's image to everyone everywhere as the world's most popular coin design ever. When U.S. soldiers liberated Afghanistan several years ago, American GIs distributed Lincoln cents to local children as a message of freedom and good will. The kids in the streets received these modest gifts enthusiastically. The additional billions of small-size $5 notes with Lincoln portraits have increased the world's perception of Lincoln's significance as Yankee dollars have changed hands around the globe.

It might surprise readers just how beloved a figure "Father Abraham" is around the world. His likeness has appeared on the stamps of several dozen countries, and the coinage of nations as disparate as Cuba, Liberia, and the Cook Islands. Lincoln biographies have been published in the native tongues of many lands. Monuments to his greatness have been erected in Europe, Scandinavia, Africa, Latin America, and Asia.

Marketing practitioners have invented a yardstick called a "Q-rating" to measure a person's popularity (usually defined as the quotient "Q" of familiarity and favorable opinion). This information is important for media buyers, talent agencies, PR firms, and the like. Over the year's Abraham Lincoln has reaped a lot of press and his favorables are substantial. Year-in and year-out for a century and half Lincoln has remained a mainstay on our paper money, and for a century now, also on the country's most widely circulated coin. According to the Federal Reserve, five-dollar bills circulate on average a year and a half. The Mint reports that the life expectancy of a penny is about 30 years. Each time one handles a cent or a $5 bill, one receives an impression. Lincoln awareness is reinforced. Think about how many five-dollar bills and pennies each of us has handled over the last year. Surely that number is in the hundreds, maybe thousands. The cumulative effect of all this money handling is reinforcement of Lincoln consciousness.

But money images are not our only source of Lincoln impressions, of course. We may pick up a book or a magazine, watch an historical program or movie, view one of the innumerable Lincoln monuments, or meet up with Mr. Lincoln in various other ways. This book is a study in "Lincoln consciousness," what did people know of Abe Lincoln, and when and how did they know it? This purview is broad and I hope will delight the reader.

Lincoln is believed to be—excepting Jesus of Nazareth and William Shakespeare—the most written about historical figure of all time. (A distant fourth is Napoleon.) In 1939 when Jay Monaghan compiled the most comprehensive Lincoln bibliography to that time, he listed just short of 4,000 volumes on Lincoln. Twenty years later Carl Sandburg contended the number had grown to 6,000. In 1984 George Tice pegged the number of Lincoln volumes at 10,000. In 2002 historian Gerald Prokopowicz reported his worldwide catalog search had found about 15,000 works on Lincoln.

Other bibliographic specialists tell us that the number should be more, as many as 16,000 separate books and monographs published on our country's Great Emancipator. That was the number Lincoln authority Merrill Peterson told C-Span's Brian Lamb more than a decade ago in 1994. If historian Peterson was correct, the number should be larger now, but a similar figure has been cited over the years by various authors, including recently by a spokesman for the Abraham Lincoln Presidential Library. Today these figures can be more easily corroborated than formerly. A search of WorldCat (www.worldcat.org), a cooperative electronic database of books in 10,000 libraries worldwide, is revealing. A search for "Abraham Lincoln" returns nearly 20,000 book records (19,848 as of July 26), including works as diverse as David Herbert Donald's monumental 1996 biography *Lincoln,* which won the Lincoln prize, and Gore Vidal's 1984 controversial best-selling novel *Lincoln,* which has been adapted for stage and screen.

The report includes collections and/or commentaries for which Lincoln is listed as author, government publications by the United States and Illinois, works of fiction, and academic dissertations. Nearly a thousand titles are classified as juvenile literature. Prolific Lincoln authors include Emanuel Herz, Carl Sandburg, Louis A. Warren, Paul Angle, Ida Tarbell, Benjamin P. Thomas, Harry Pratt, George Bancroft, R. Gerald McMurtry, Harold Holzer, Ralph G. Newman, and Walt Whitman. Lincoln interest is worldwide. More than 200 books have been published on Lincoln in German and in Spanish, nearly 150 in Japanese, more than 100 in Chinese and in French, and dozens each in countries such as Sweden, Russia, Korea, Italy, Portugal, Holland, and Denmark. Lincoln books in Burmese, Hindi, Arabic, Vietnamese, Indonesian, Hebrew and Yiddish, Croatian, Persian, and Native American dialects have also been published. Retired reference librarian Karl Kabelac, a longtime friend, urges a measure of caution in interpreting these results, since changing cataloging rules conceivably could have created some small duplication in computer records.

By comparison, more than 100,000 books have been written about Jesus Christ, 56,000 about William Shakespeare (more than 10,000 of which are editions of his own writing), and a comparatively paltry 5,700 books on Napoleon Bonaparte. A great deal of scholarly interest has also been shown in the lives and accomplishments of people like Queen Victoria, the Apostle Paul, and George Washington. Still, it's clear there has been a lot of interest in Abraham Lincoln. As the bicentennial of Lincoln's birth dawns, many more books on him will doubtless appear.

Of course, Abraham Lincoln has been commemorated in ways other than money and printed literature. Hundreds of accounts have appeared theatrically. Lincoln has graced innumerable stamps. His likeness has adorned everything from sugar packets and matchbooks to large corporations, impressive buildings, and granite mountain tops. When I was a youth coming up in public schools in upstate New York, Lincoln's picture was on the front wall along with Washington's. Seeing that image day-after-day, year-after-year emblazoned his visage on my mind's eye. Lincoln appeared stern, formal, somber, elevated, solid, and capable. This image dramatized his character, if not personality. Aptly, both Lincoln's and Washington's pictures were the same images appearing then on our five and one dollar bills. If this repeated exposure could make such an impression on me, I felt it must also have impressed other baby boomers. After all, repeated exposure is the tenet of advertising in all media. Billions of dollars are risked on this principle. And this branding must work because people hum commercial jingles and salivate when they see golden arches.

I have endeavored to present a coherent, chronological survey of the Lincoln image over time. This present work is a book about Lincoln image in the broadest sense. Most aspects of Lincoln and his heritage have already been written about many times over. This is especially true of his image. Books on Lincoln photos, Lincoln prints, and Lincoln cartoons abound. Specialized works on Lincoln medals, sculptures, postcards, films, and representations in various other media also exist. These microscopic but narrow studies are important, of course. A great many of them have been accessed for their special insights. It seems, however, that no other author had attempted the panoramic view of Lincoln image that this present work considers. Another shortcoming the present work attempts to remedy is that the historical mainstream has paid only lip service to the impact of Lincoln's image on our government money. Although Lincoln's images on our notes and coins have been ubiquitous from his own lifetime to the present, little is said in mainstream publications about Abe's numismatic legacy. In fact, Abe's money images are the 800-pound gorilla in the room of Lincoln awareness.

Over time I realized that money is a powerful medium of indoctrination. I found that Lincoln's brand literally emerged from his depictions on coins and currency. The ancients indeed knew a thing or two about putting their graven images on their coinage, and the effects are no less pronounced today. Abe's appearances on our money over time created a public persona, an icon image, which was reflected in subsidiary ways in other popular media, creating a powerful brand in public consciousness.

The icon Lincoln in public consciousness mirrored his money images. Over several decades I have endeavored to call attention to this in more than 50 articles in the leading numismatic periodicals. These articles have traced the development of Lincoln money images and their impact on secondary media such as advertising, book, and periodical illustrations. Unfortunately, this was largely preaching to the choir.

One of the articles, however, which measures the impact of Lincoln money images on key book illustrations (book covers and frontispieces), has appeared recently in the prestigious *Lincoln Herald.* That article and the present book will hopefully turn the tide. The present work is not an attempt to duplicate earlier efforts. Those articles are listed elsewhere, if readers have an interest.

My preoccupation with Lincoln images traces directly to 1955, when I began collecting Lincoln cents from circulation around the dinner table with my Dad. Over the decades as my sophistication and budget grew, all kinds, photos, prints and other media attracted my interest. My early mentor on Civil War money was "Mr. In God We Trust" Matt Rothert, who was responsible for that motto appearing on this nation's paper money, and indirectly for its adoption as our national motto. In the 1970s I was introduced to Lloyd Ostendorf, a cousin of *Coin World's* photographer Paul Agnew. Early on I determined to collect thematically, in other words classifying images in all media by their photographic models, and over the years Lloyd—the preeminent Lincoln photo authority—was very helpful to me. By 1980 I was exhibiting my Lincoln collection. At the Tri-County Coin Show in Wapakoneta, Ohio, my five-case exhibit took "Best of Show" honors. My biggest prize that day however, became the memory of my display's affect on my young son, Fred IV. He was less than two at the time. Carrying him past the display over to where his mother and sister were standing, young Fred gleefully piped up, "See a Lincoln! See a Lincoln! See a Lincoln!" to the pleasure of his family and wonderment of the rest of the crowd in the bourse room. Train up a child in the way he should go, and when he is old, he will not depart from it. His mom and I were successful, as several of Fred's Lincoln illustrations in my Lincoln Room attest.

In 1985, I received a large and unprecedented $5,000 research grant from the American Numismatic Association to research Civil War money. While in Washington, I discovered Winfred Porter Truesdell's *Engraved and Lithographed Portraits of Abraham Lincoln* at the Rare Book Room of the Library of Congress. Truesdell was a man after my own heart. His exquisitely crafted volume classifies Lincoln engravings and prints just the way I had been collecting them—based on their original photographic models. I spent an enervating afternoon in cramped, hot quarters transcribing many entries from Truesdell's magnificent "second" volume, unfortunately the only one of a projected series that was published prior to his death. On one wintry afternoon several years later, Dan Weinberg allowed me to accompany him searching out treasures in his Abraham Lincoln Book Shop warehouse. We found several I couldn't live without. Shortly thereafter Dan was able to find a copy of the Truesdell book for me at a fancy price, which I gladly paid.

My Lincoln collection grew apace. I obtained an oil portrait of Lincoln painted early in the 20th century by Italian-American muralist and illustrator Vincente Aderente. This portrait hung in a New Jersey attorney's office for many decades. I have always suspected this painting, which adorns this book's cover, was created for a magazine cover illustration, but diligent search has failed to reveal when this might have been. Thus before this present volume it may have been unpublished. I was especially pleased to fill out my set of all 1,894 issues of *Lincoln Lore* to date through fortuitous purchases of several original accumulations from the heirs of the previous owners, and the assistance of Cindy VanHorn at the Lincoln Museum in Fort Wayne. However, my most significant acquisition has been the original steel intaglio die engraved in 1861 by Charles Burt for the American Bank Note Company, and the steel cylinder, roller die by which Burt's Lincoln portrait was translated to currency plates for the first $10 federal government greenbacks, which are special highlights of the present volume. Along the way I frequently exhibited items from my growing collection at the Memphis International Paper Money Show, which has been the major gathering for collectors of paper money since 1977. These have included lavish displays of Lincoln checks, Lincoln non-federal currencies, and similar material. Several times, I have beat the proverbial drum for redesigned Lincoln currency utilizing the so-called "Gettysburg Lincoln" portrait—considered by many the finest depiction of the Savior of the Nation—on our paper money. I also have written articles promoting this to no effect, but several examples are displayed here.

Pursuit of my Lincoln study has materially benefited from two research grants that I received from the Society of Paper Money Collectors, and for which I am most grateful. These grants allowed me to travel to Lincoln Memorial University and other archives to research Lincoln imagery in periodicals and books, and what effects (if any) Lincoln money imagery has had on these secondary mass media. Founded in 1961, SPMC is the major focus group for those interested in collecting paper money in the United States, with membership in many lands abroad too. The organization has a website (www.spmc.org) and a wonderful, slick award-winning bimonthly journal of 80-pages, of which I am proud to say I have been editor and publisher for nearly a decade.

In short, I have been pursuing the subject matter detailed here in one way or another for a half century. Pop philosopher and my lifelong hero Yogi Berra taught me "You can observe a lot by watching." From what

I've seen, Lincoln's image has not been fixed over time. The Lincoln icon is not just a picture, form without content. Lincoln has meaning too, which has also evolved. This illustrated narrative outlines that transition. As a lifelong journalist, my task, not unlike that of the professional historian—whom I am most decidedly not—is to examine the historical record and report coherently what I find. Facts and interpretation. Research and analysis. As my graduate school history professor, Civil War historian Dr. LeRoy Fischer, once told me, "History is nothing but . . . facts and interpretation." Dr. Fischer's *Lincoln's Gadfly: Adam Gurowski* won a Civil War book prize in 1964 roughly equivalent in present-day dollars to the fabulous Lincoln Prize of today. There are facts aplenty in the pages that follow, and interpretation surely.

A key resource that I have tapped are the physical objects from past eras. To archaeologists material culture is more than simply the objects themselves. There is also a psychological component of meaning they hold within the culture. Examining and handling objects such as those shown here is exciting because one can see history come alive in one's hands. It's not just the numismatist, but collectors of all stripes who benefit from reflection upon objects great and small. These relics were not created in a vacuum. They have a context and bear meaning. Discovering this meaning is the thrill I have enjoyed for many years, and hope that I can share with the reader through this book. I'm not the first to find special joy in the collection of Lincolniana in all its myriad aspects. Lincoln contemporary and pioneer Lincolnphile Andrew Boyd expressed it so well nearly 140 years ago. "It is not without reason we preserve even the slightest memorial of the great and good who have passed away," he wrote in 1870. "The merest trifles may have a distinct value of their own in history, as it is from this *we* reproduced in *our* minds the character of the great and noble men who have passed away in the long years and centuries gone by." [emphasis in original] The American Numismatic Society preaches the same creed. "Parva ne pereant" (Let not the little things perish) is that organization's motto.

Although this is an illustrated narrative, it is not a catalog. It traces Lincoln commemoration and ongoing development of Lincoln consciousness in myriad media from his own time down to ours. The selection was more eclectic than scientific. If George Washington was "First in War; First in Peace; and First in the Hearts of His Countrymen" (words from a eulogy for Washington adopted by Congress immediately after his death), Abraham Lincoln is certainly second to no one else in the volume of remembrances of his fellow citizens.

As recently as this past February a Harris Interactive poll found Americans consider Lincoln our best president in this nation's history. "When asked to choose the best presidents in U.S. history from a list including all recent presidents and some of the other most famous presidents, a 20 percent plurality choose Abraham Lincoln and a further 13 percent pick him as the second best," the pollsters reported. Lincoln's favorability rating is nearly twice that of his nearest rivals: Ronald Reagan, Franklin Roosevelt, and John Kennedy. America's first chief executive, soldier/patriot George Washington, lags in fifth place, although 11% still regard the "Father of His Country" as the best president of all time.

When Lincoln was a youth he scratched out this doggerel: "Abraham Lincoln, // His hand and pen: // He will be good // But God knows When." On the greatest national stage Lincoln the man was both idolized and vilified. Contemplating Abraham Lincoln's life and acts has become a source of continual national inspiration. With the coming commemorations of the Lincoln bicentennial, many will echo Julia Ward Howe's "praise to God who gave him for our need." However, this was not always so, and Lincoln, himself, would be much surprised by the elevated saintliness attributed to him by devotees. In his own life, Lincoln the man knew the sting of loss, defeat, and harsh criticism. Much of the invective directed against him and shown in this work may surprise readers. Racially insensitive images may offend some. However, I have endeavored to be neither cheerleader nor mudslinger, merely true to the historical record in words and pictures.

Abraham Lincoln: The Image of His Greatness is presented in four chronological eras: (1) Abraham Lincoln (1809–1865); (2) Lincoln, the Ideal (1865–1909); (3) Lincoln, the Idol (1909–1959); and (4) Lincoln, the Icon (1959–2009). Consider these divisions shorthand categories, not exclusive precincts. These designations have considerable overlap to be sure, but do present the dominant transitional historical view of the evolving Lincoln image during those eras, according to my research.

I have been a collector of Lincolniana for a half century, so I naturally concur with late Illinois governor Henry Horner's conviction: "A man can have no finer hobby than an interest in Lincoln and all that he stood for." Through the years I have become the fortunate conservator of nearly 4,000 Lincoln items, so the choice of illustrations for this volume has been difficult. Always I was faced with a daunting balancing act judging what to include and what not. Nevertheless, no one owns "everything," so I have endeavored to check my ego at the door and am indebted to many colleagues for their outstanding contributions to this work.

Chapter 1
Abraham Lincoln
1809–1865

The image of Abraham Lincoln in the minds of his fellow countrymen has been anything but static. Rather, his persona has been an evolving drama in several acts unfolding over two centuries. Lincoln's story has been shaped by political partisan press and fanned by zealots who have raised Lincoln consciousness to the level of a civil religion. To be sure, Lincoln lived a remarkable life. Born on the frontier, self-educated, he made himself into an able, experienced lawyer, married up, entered politics, and was elected the nation's president on the eve of the Civil War.

On March 4, 1861, Lincoln took the oath of office to become the 16th president of the United States. Before then, however, while still in Springfield, Illinois, planning his cabinet appointments, working on his inaugural address, and growing the beard that was to reshape his presidential image, Lincoln posed for a cameraman. The resulting photos were almost immediately translated into twin engravings, which appeared on U.S. securities—first bonds and then currency—and became the predominant, accepted portrait of Lincoln while he lived. Their wide publication and broadcast on these official government media meant repetition and continuous reinforcement. For most people, the Abe Lincoln on the money was the Abe Lincoln in the White House. These images in turn were widely copied by commercial printmakers. The official Lincoln and the popular Lincoln became one and inseparable.

At the commencement of Lincoln's administration, his political adversary, Salmon P. Chase, whom Lincoln wisely brought to the capital as his Treasury secretary, deferentially chose his boss to appear on $500 bonds, which were the largest of three denominations issued. The Lincoln vignette is a large full bust based on the Springfield photographs. Chase also selected himself for the $50 denomination and the Army general-in-chief, Lt. Gen. Winfield Scott, for the $100 certificates. Selection of these three figures was important. It sent a positive message to the capital marketplace: Lincoln was captain; Scott, the military leader, was first mate; and, Chase, the paymaster, was bosun of the nation's ship of state in the critical times ahead. Capital loaned was still in good hands. The Union and the marketplace would be preserved and the bondholder would get his vigorish, to

Fig. 1.1. Lincoln's birth cabin has iconic value in Lincoln lore, serving as the inspiration for a child's toy, a maple syrup, and a political movement. Die V48868 (originally 264), imprint of Homer Lee Bank Note Co., New York, circa 1880.

The dominant Lincoln image during his presidency was a photograph taken by Christopher S. German in Springfield, Illinois, on January 13, 1861 (Ostendorf-41), shown opposite on a cabinet card by McNulty, 1883. It was widely replicated on *cartes de visite (CDVs)*. However, it was from its translation to security engravings employed on government bonds and Treasury Notes that most people came to know Lincoln's image during his lifetime.

Fig. 1.2. The birth cabin on foreign postage: *(a)* Honduran 25-centavo stamp (Scott C296), Waterlow & Sons, Ltd., 1959; *(b)* Cuban 1-centavo stamp (Scott 952), 1965.

boot. Tables turned when hostilities began with the firing on Fort Sumter on April 12. The ante was upped a hundredfold. Congress authorized $250 million in six-percent, 20-year bonds, which appeared for sale that summer. These high-value bonds were printed by the National Bank Note Co. (NBNCo), New York. Again Lincoln appeared on the largest denomination. More government bonds with Lincoln's portrait, and other patriotic motifs, would follow as the government sought to satisfy the demands of its creditors.

That summer, to provide cash, Congress authorized the issue of $50 million non-interest-bearing Treasury Notes receivable for all government dues and payable in specie on demand. Six months later, on February 12, 1862 (Lincoln's 53rd birthday), Congress extended this issue to $60 million. A similar Lincoln portrait, this time engraved for the American Bank Note Co. (ABNCo), which had obtained the contract to print the notes, was prepared from the same photographic model by Charles Burt (pictured later in this chapter). These two portraits were so similar, in fact, that their distinctiveness was probably lost on most observers at the time and by many other commentators since. With the nation splintering following Lincoln's inauguration in 1861, it was important for people to see their new president. The choice of presidential portraiture for the money markets was an important one, but the choice of portraits for the Treasury Notes was even more important. The former would be squirreled away by capitalists and bankers; the latter would be carried by the man in the street. Patriotism was necessary to bind popular will to the war effort. Chase selected Lincoln to appear on the $10 bill—the now-familiar Demand Notes that became the first U.S. "greenbacks." The following year, the same image was extended to the $10 Legal Tender Notes. Late in the war the NBNCo bond portrait was adapted for use on $20 Interest-Bearing Treasury Notes. It was originally intended that Navy secretary Gideon Welles was to appear on the notes, but Treasury Secretary Chase insisted that Lincoln's portrait appear instead.

The importance of all this imagery on official government emissions must not be underestimated. Not only did these Lincoln images bear official government sanction throughout the war, but their repeated use on subsequent large emissions created constant reinforcement for its acceptance by the public and popular culture. No amount of private use of competing images could displace this view of Lincoln in the popular mind. And in fact it did not. This is an important point recorded by Lincoln engraving historian Winfred Porter Truesdell, who itemized a disproportionately large number of engravings and lithographs based on the Springfield photographic model. The same portrait subsequently appeared on bank notes and a host of commercial work for the New York bank-note companies.

The practical effect was to spawn a host of copies in all the other graphic-arts media as well. The cumulative effect of this was to flood the populace with a contemporary iconic Lincoln image of powerful persuasion. Significantly, no other Lincoln image appeared on government-issued media prior to Lincoln's death. During Lincoln's own time, these government security portraits were normative. In the short span of four years, Abraham Lincoln's portrait had gone from an unknown face of a relatively obscure Western lawyer to "the best-known face" of his age, in the words of Harold Holzer, eminent Lincoln pictorial scholar. Lincoln's presidential image on official federal obligations had represented him splendidly as resolute and patriarchal. During the war years and those immediately following, Burt's Lincoln portrait was doubtless the most prevalent presidential image avail-

Fig. 1.3. The birth cabin as represented at Lincoln Memorial Hall, Lincoln Farm, Hodgenville, Kentucky.

able to the public. Circulated on U.S. currency by the millions of impressions, it crystallized perception of Lincoln in the public's mind. As poet and Lincoln biographer Carl Sandburg recalled years later: "On the $10 bill a steel engraving representing Lincoln's face became familiar to all who looked at it." These engravings had performed their work well.

The original intaglio steel die created by Charles Burt in March 1861 for currency use still exists. It is doubtless the most important Lincoln engraving from his own lifetime, a true national treasure. It resides in the collection of the author.

Abraham Lincoln was born February 12, 1809, near Hodgenville in Hardin County, Kentucky. In a cartoonist's take on that day, one local farmer inquires of another, "Any news, Eb?" and hears the response, "Nothing much doin', Zeke. Caught a cold. Mail arrived last week. Heard Tom Lincoln's wife had a kid out by Sinkin' Spring. You?" To which the less garrulous one replies, "Nope. No news either."

Rather than try to duplicate any of the excellent biographies of our 16th president, since this present work is not a biography per se, Lincoln's own description of his station in life will suffice here. In response to inquiries while a presidential candidate, Lincoln penned three short autobiographies during the run-up to his selection for the highest seat in the land. To friend Jesse W. Fell, on December 20, 1859 (as recorded in *The Collected Works of Abraham Lincoln*[1]), he wrote the following:

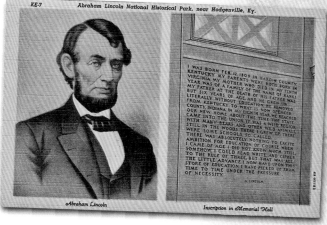

Fig. 1.4. Curt Teich linen postcard featuring Abraham Lincoln National Historical Park.

> Herewith is a little sketch, as you requested. There is not much of it, for the reason, I suppose, that there is not much of me.
>
> If any thing be made out of it, I wish it to be modest, and not to go beyond the materials. If it were thought necessary to incorporate any thing from any of my speeches, I suppose there would be no objection. Of course it must not appear to have been written by myself. . . .
>
> I was born February 12, 1809, in Hardin County, Kentucky. My parents were both born in Virginia, of undistinguished families—second families, perhaps I should say. My mother, who died in my tenth year, was of a family of the name of Hanks, some of whom now reside in Adams, and others in Macon counties, Illinois. My paternal grandfather, Abraham Lincoln, emigrated from Rockingham County, Virginia, to Kentucky, about 1781 or 2, where, a year or two later, he was killed by indians, not in battle, but by stealth, when [where?] he was laboring to open a farm in the forest. His ancestors, who were quakers, went to Virginia from Berks County, Pennsylvania. An effort to identify them with the New-England family of the same name ended in nothing more definite, than a similarity of Christian names in both families, such as Enoch, Levi, Mordecai, Solomon, Abraham, and the like.

Fig. 1.5. Postcard advertising the replica of Lincoln's boyhood home (1811–1816) on Knob Creek.

> My father, at the death of his father, was but six years of age; and he grew up, literally without education. He removed from Kentucky to what is now Spencer county, Indiana, in my eighth year. We reached our new home about the time the State came into the Union. It was a wild region, with many bears and other wild animals still in the woods. There I grew up. There were some schools, so called; but no qualification was ever required of a teacher, beyond "readin, writin, and cipherin," to the Rule of Three. If a straggler supposed to understand latin, happened to so-journ in the neighborhood, he was looked upon as a wizzard. There was absolutely nothing to excite ambition for education. Of course when I came of age I did not know much. Still somehow, I could read, write, and cipher to the Rule of Three; but that was all. I have not been to school since. The little advance I now have upon this store of education, I have picked up from time to time under the pressure of necessity.
>
> I was raised to farm work, which I continued till I was twenty two. At twenty one I came to Illinois, and passed the first year in Macon county. Then I got to New-Salem (at that time in Sangamon, now in Menard county), where I remained a year as a sort of Clerk in a store. Then came the Black-Hawk war; and I was elected a Captain of Volunteers—a success which gave me more pleasure than any I have had since. I went the campaign, was elated, ran for the Legislature the same year (1832) and was beaten—the only time I ever have been beaten by the people. The next, and three succeeding biennial elections, I was elected to the Legislature. I was not a candidate afterwards. During this Legislative period I had studied law, and removed to Springfield to practice it. In 1846 I was once elected to the lower House of Congress. Was not a candidate for re-election. From 1849 to 1854, both inclusive, practiced law more assiduously than ever before. Always a Whig in politics, and generally on the Whig

Fig. 1.7. Raymond Massey as militia captain in *Abe Lincoln in Illinois*, RKO Radio Pictures, 1940.

Fig. 1.8. Dominican $5 souvenir sheet (Scott 2459), picturing Norman Rockwell's *Lincoln for the Defense.*

LINCOLN AS A CAPTAIN IN THE BLACK HAWK WAR (1832)

Fig. 1.6. Sculptor Leonard Crunelle's statue of Lincoln as a 23-year-old militia captain in the Black Hawk War; statue dedicated at Dixon, Illinois, on August 23, 1930.

electoral tickets, making active canvasses. I was losing interest in politics, when the repeal of the Missouri Compromise aroused me again. What I have done since then is pretty well known.

If any personal description of me is thought desirable, it may be said, I am, in height, six feet, four inches, nearly; lean in flesh, weighing, on an average, one hundred and eighty pounds; dark complexion, with coarse black hair, and grey eyes—no other marks or brands recollected.

Yours very truly A. LINCOLN

Fell had requested Lincoln's personal story for use in a Pennsylvania newspaper account, which was widely copied in the Republican press of the day.

Much of what we would come to know about Lincoln's early days, apart from legal documents, press accounts—especially during the U.S. Senate campaign against Stephen A. Douglas in 1858—and recollections of colleagues and acquaintances, were compiled, embellished, and disseminated by Lincoln's longtime law partner, William Henry Herndon. Herndon was affiliated with Lincoln for two decades in Springfield prior to Lincoln's removal to Washington. Their office occupied a second floor opposite the State House.

After Lincoln's death, Herndon set out to contact Lincoln's friends and acquaintances to compile from oral history a "true biography." On November 16, 1866, he delivered a lecture in Springfield on Lincoln and Ann Rutledge.[2] According to Boyd, Herndon had published five of his lectures on Lincoln by 1870. Herndon was engaged in this project for many years, during which time, for a fee, he set up shop as something of a Lincoln interpreter. Herndon's efforts finally found a more concrete form with the collaboration of Jesse W. Weik in the book *Herndon's Lincoln: The True Story of a Great Life,* published in 1888. That book has been subject to much scrutiny and criticism from Herndon's day and since, yet it reflects upon the "Lincoln image" considered in this present work in important ways.

Herndon and Weik dedicated their work to "the men and women of America who have grown up since his tragic death, and who have yet to learn the story of his life." For the two decades after Lincoln's untimely demise, Billy Herndon lived off that association by writing and speechifying for the benefit of his own purse. Most of the "colorful" notions that have become so familiar to schoolchildren and moviegoers over the years can be traced to Herndon's research and/or imagination. Here are several of the common themes in *Herndon's Lincoln:*

Lincoln was a voracious reader, day, night and all hours in between.

His chief delight during the day, if unmolested, was to lie down under the shade of some inviting tree to read and study. At night, lying on his stomach in front of the open fireplace, with a piece of charcoal he would ciphler [*sic*] on a broad, wooden shovel.

[W]hile clerking in the store or serving as postmaster he would apply himself as opportunity offer to his studies, if it was but five minutes time—would open his book which he always kept at hand, study it, reciting to himself; then entertain the company present or wait on a customer without apparent annoyance from the interruption.

Lincoln's athletic prowess gave him social standing in the community.

All New Salem adjourned to the scene of the wrestle. Money, whiskey, knives, and all manner of property were staked on the result [of a challenge match between a local bully, Jack Armstrong, and a new store clerk by the name of Lincoln]. . . . Everyone knows how it ended; how at last the tall and angular rail-splitter, enraged at the suspicion of foul tactics, and profiting by his height and the length of his arms, fairly lifted the great bully by the throat and shook him like a rag; how by this act he established himself solidly in the esteem of all New Salem, and secured the respectful admiration and friendship of the very man whom he had so thoroughly vanquished.

Fig. 1.9. Etching depicting a beardless Lincoln as a young lawyer after Samuel Sartain's mezzotint from a life portrait by John Henry Brown.

Fig. 1.10. Henry Fonda as attorney Lincoln in *Young Mr. Lincoln,* 20th Century Fox, 1939.

Fig. 1.11. "The Boy Lincoln," Immortal American sticker, R.L. Parkinson, 1938.

Fig. 1.12. Lincoln (Henry Fonda) reads a book in *Young Mr. Lincoln.*

Fig. 1.13. Raymond Massey's Lincoln reading in *Abe Lincoln in Illinois*.

Lincoln was devastated by his star-crossed love affair with Ann Rutledge.

The courtship with Ann Rutledge and her untimely death form the saddest page in Mr. Lincoln's history. . . . I knew Miss Rutledge myself, as well as her father and other members of the family, and have been personally acquainted with every one of the score or more of witnesses whom I at one time or another interviewed on this delicate subject. From my own knowledge and information thus obtained, I therefore repeat, that the memory of Ann Rutledge was the saddest chapter in Mr. Lincoln's Life.

Lincoln's sorrow over Rutledge's early death was manic.

The most astonishing and sad sequel to this courtship was the disastrous effect of Miss Rutledge's death on Mr. Lincoln's mind. . . . As he returned from the visit to the bedside of Miss Rutledge, he stopped at the house of a friend, who relates that his face showed signs of no little mental agony. "He was very much distressed," in the language of this friend, "and I was not surprised when it was rumored subsequently that his reason was in danger."

Fig. 1.14. The most endearing and enduring of the Herndon fabrications was Lincoln's romantic involvement with Ann Rutledge. It played out on the silver screen repeatedly; invariably, Ann was played by the most vivacious female in the cast: *(a)* George Billings as Lincoln the storekeeper with Ruth Clifford in *The Dramatic Life of Abraham Lincoln*, Rockett-Lincoln Film Co., 1924; *(b)* Walter Huston as Lincoln the railsplitter and Una Merkel in *Abraham Lincoln*, D.W. Griffith Productions, 1930; *(c)* Raymond Massey and Mary Howard in *Abe Lincoln in Illinois*; *(d)* Pauline Moore and Henry Fonda in *Young Mr. Lincoln*; *(e)* Joseph Henabery and Mae Marsh (as Flora Cameron) in *The Birth of a Nation*, D.W. Griffith Corp., 1915; and *(f)* Grace Kelly and Stephen Courtleigh in the Philco Television Playhouse drama *Ann Rutledge*, NBC, 1950. According to Herndon, Ann Rutledge's death was traumatic for her young beau: *(g)* Henry Fonda at her graveside in *Young Mr. Lincoln*.

Lincoln reveled in vulgar conversation.

It has been denied as often as charged that Lincoln narrated vulgar stories; but the truth is he loved a story however extravagant or vulgar, if it had a good point. If it was merely a ribald recital and had no sting in the end, that is, if it exposed no weakness or pointed no moral, he had no use for it either in conversation or public speech; but if it had the necessary ingredients of mirth and moral no one could use it with more telling effect.

Lincoln was not in love with his wife Mary, and he suffered interminably at her hand.

The sober truth is that Lincoln was inordinately ambitious. He had already succeeded in obtaining no inconsiderable political recognition . . . but . . . [c]onscious, therefore, of his humble rank in the social scale, how natural that he should seek by marriage in an influential family to establish strong connections and at the same time foster his political fortunes! This may seem an audacious thing to insinuate, but on no other basis can we reconcile the strange course of his courtship and the tempestuous chapters in his married life.

To me it has always seemed plain that Mr. Lincoln married Mary Todd to save his honor, and in doing that he sacrificed his domestic peace. He had searched himself subjectively, introspectively, thoroughly; he knew he did not love her, but he had promised to marry her! . . . [He] stood face to face with the great conflict between honor and domestic peace. He chose the former, and with it years of self-torture, sacrificial pangs, and the loss forever of a happy home.

Lincoln was an infidel, and antagonistic to the principles of Christianity.

My own testimony, however, in regard to Mr. Lincoln's religious views may perhaps invite discussion. The world has always insisted on making an orthodox Christian of him, and to analyze his sayings or sound his beliefs is but to break the idol. It only remains to say that, whether orthodox or not, he believed in God and immortality; and even if he questioned the existence of future eternal punishment he hoped to find a rest from trouble and a heaven beyond the grave.

Lincoln's experiences in New Orleans presaged his abolition of slavery.

In New Orleans, for the first time Lincoln beheld the true horrors of human slavery. He saw "negroes in chains—whipped and scourged." Against this inhumanity his sense of right and justice rebelled, and his mind and conscience were awakened to a realization of what he had often heard and read. No doubt, as one of his companions has said, "Slavery ran the iron into him then and there."

The whole thing was so revolting that Lincoln moved away from the scene [a slave auction of a "vigorous and comely mulatto girl"] with a deep feeling of "unconquerable hate." Bidding his companions follow him he said, "By God, boys, let's get away from this. If ever I get a chance to hit that thing [meaning slavery], I'll hit it hard."

Fig. 1.15. Hollywood's portrayal of Lincoln's relationship with his wife Mary Todd Lincoln frequently suffered from William Herndon's jaundiced presentation. Neither Henry Fonda in *Young Mr. Lincoln* (a) nor Raymond Massey in *Abe Lincoln in Illinois* (b) appeared to enjoy his wife's affections.

Fig. 1.16. George A. Billings (standing) as Lincoln on flatboat in *The Dramatic Life of Abraham Lincoln*.

Fig. 1.17. Lincoln (Billings) observes a New Orleans slave market in *The Dramatic Life of Abraham Lincoln*.

Most people have the impression that Lincoln came from very poor circumstances, and in fact he did live the life of many hardscrabble, 19th-century young men in the West. But his circumstances were certainly not novel. His father was practically illiterate. His mother died when he was young. He had an older sister, who would die in childbirth at the age of 20, and a younger brother, who died in infancy. Young Abe and Sarah briefly attended schools in Kentucky that were kept by Zachariah Riney and Caleb Hazel. History records the Lincoln family's relocation from Kentucky to frontier Indiana in December 1816; the death of his mother, Nancy Hanks Lincoln, on October 5, 1818; and the remarriage of his father, Thomas, to a widow lady, Sarah Bush Johnston, on December 5, 1819. Lincoln's stepmother had three children of her own.

Thereafter Lincoln had little time for formal education. The family's new environment in Spencer County, Indiana, came with a price. They settled "in an unbroken forest," Lincoln recalled later, "and the clearing away of surplus wood was the great task ahead." Although Abe was just a boy, he said, his father handed him an ax "at once, and from that till within his twenty-third year he was almost constantly handling that most useful instrument . . . less, of course, in plowing and harvesting seasons."

Fig. 1.18. Lincoln's boyhood home in Farmington, Kentucky.

Fig. 1.19. *Lincoln the Rail Splitter,* by Jean Leon Gerome Ferris, circa 1909.

1818 DECEMBER 13. Future first lady Mary Todd Lincoln is born.

1830S. During Lincoln's early adulthood, there occur several incidents to which his nickname "Honest Abe" is later ascribed. Frequently it is linked to the period that Lincoln was a store clerk, as is recorded in *Lincoln Lore.* Supposedly, on one occasion Lincoln became aware that he had short-weighted a woman on a purchase by putting the wrong weight on the scale. He subsequently made it up to her. On another, he allegedly discovered an extra half bit (6-1/4 cents) in the till, which he returned to a purchaser with considerable effort. Lincoln also is said to have enhanced his reputation by paying off his debts. He earned his sobriquet early in life, and never forfeited it.[3]

1833 MAY 7. Abraham Lincoln is appointed postmaster of Salem, Illinois. When the post office closed, Lincoln settled his accounts with the government to the penny. "I never use any man's money but my own," Lincoln scholar Louis A. Warren reports Lincoln as saying.[4]

1833 MARCH 8. Lincoln and partners William F. Berry and Bowling Green post bond for a tavern license to serve liquor by the drink at the Berry-Lincoln store.

1835 AUGUST 25. Ann Rutledge dies. The Ann Rutledge story humanized Lincoln, capturing the public imagination in a way that the wrestling story with Jack Armstrong and stories of his off-color humor couldn't quite do. (Lincoln historian Paul Angle would expose the Lincoln–Ann Rutledge love-letter forgeries of Wilma Minor in about 1930.)

1846 APRIL 18. "I would give all I am worth, and go in debt, to be able to write so fine a piece as I think that [the poem 'Mortality'] is," Lincoln writes to "Friend Johnston." At the time, Lincoln was 37; early in his life he had tried his hand writing poems, one of which is given in the introduction.

Fig. 1.20. The duality of Lincoln's life and legend has always been part and parcel of Old Abe's appeal. He was both the sensitive and the ruffian. *(a)* George A. Billings showed his strength by hefting a sawhorse in *The Dramatic Life of Abraham Lincoln.* Billings was 53 years old when he played the young Lincoln; he also portrayed Lincoln in three other films; *(b)* Alice Brady as Abigail Clay joined Henry Fonda in *Young Mr. Lincoln.*

Fig. 1.21. Immortal American stickers by R.L. Parkinson, 1938: *(a)* "Lincoln and Ann Rutledge, 1834"; *(b)* "Lincoln the Rail Splitter."

Fig. 1.22. "Abraham Lincoln and Ann Rutledge in their Courting Days," postcard, H.N. Shonkwiler, Springfield. Shonkwiler made a cottage industry producing Lincoln-related postcards.

Fig. 1.23. Abe's stovepipe hat is another Lincoln icon: *(a)* worn by Henry Fonda in *Young Mr. Lincoln; (b)* worn on stage by Raymond Massey in Robert Sherwood's play *Abe Lincoln in Illinois,* 1938—in this De Merjian publicity photo, the height of the hat has been exaggerated by a retoucher.

1846 DECEMBER 3. Abraham Lincoln defends Ammai Merill, charged with passing counterfeit coin. The defendant was found guilty and sentenced to three years' imprisonment.

1849 MAY 22. Lincoln patents a device for "buoying vessels over shoals" (number 6469). The patent was filed March 10, 1849 (fig. 1.26). Historians have found several occasions during which Lincoln was on a vessel that had run aground, only to occasion much difficulty in its removal. His solution was to equip a flatboat with buoyant chambers "that can be expanded so as to hold a large volume of air when required for use, and can be contracted, into a very small space and safely secured as soon as their services can be dispensed with." In Lincoln's mind this would prove much easier than the tug-of-war then necessary. His solution was inventive, to be sure. Lincoln was the only U.S. president to obtain a patent. He was passionate about the application of technology and about the uniqueness of the patent laws of this country. The establishment of the U.S. patent system secured the advantage of a new invention to the inventor himself, thus adding in Lincoln's own words "the fuel of interest to the fire of genius in the discovery and production of new and useful things."[5] In recognition of Lincoln's inventive genius, he appears on the medal of the National Inventors Hall of Fame, which is shown and discussed in chapter 4 (in the 2007 May 5 entry in the timeline).

1853 MARCH 1. Abraham Lincoln opens a bank account at the Springfield Marine and Fire Insurance Co.[6]

1853 AUGUST 22. Lincoln, Illinois, in the central part of the state 30 miles east of Springfield, is named after Abe Lincoln because he had filed the legal paperwork necessary for its founding. Lincoln also reportedly "christened it" with watermelon juice. According to the *Springfield Register* of August 22, 1853, "The town was named by

Fig. 1.24. Lincoln's circuit-riding legal career as portrayed by Henry Fonda in *Young Mr. Lincoln*. In this film, Lincoln rode a jackass because he could not afford a horse.

Fig. 1.26. Lincoln patent drawing "Manner of Bouying [*sic*] Vessels," patent number 6,469, May 22, 1849.

Fig. 1.25. The prairie lawyer Lincoln was the most experienced trial lawyer of any of the presidents. *(a)* The earliest extant photograph of Lincoln, this daguerreotype (Ostendorf-1) was taken in Springfield by N.H. Shepherd in 1846 when Lincoln was 37 years old. *(b)* A painting by Robert Marshall Root, mistitled *June 15, 1856* (the events pictured actually took place August 9 of that year). *(c)* A scene with Hal Holbrook lawyering in *Sandburg's Lincoln*, David L. Wolper Productions, 1974.

the proprietors of whom our enterprising citizen, Virgil Hickox, is one, in honor of A. Lincoln, esq., the attorney of the Chicago and Mississippi Railroad Company." Lincoln, Illinois, was the only U.S. town named for Lincoln before his presidency with his knowledge and cooperation. Posthumously, Lincoln's name sprung up on mailboxes in more than a dozen states, and even in foreign countries. Three times wheels were put in motion to carve out of the plains region of the country a Lincoln Territory, which would in due course have become the state of Lincoln.

1856. The first Republican convention to nominate a candidate for president of the United States selects John C. Fremont. Lincoln is described as "a prince of good fellows and an old line Whig." Lincoln's politics owed a great deal to the tradition of Henry Clay. A lifelong Whig, Lincoln favored the interests of the central government over the constituent states, promoted centralized banking from the days of the Bank of the United States onward, favored large federal public-works expenditures, and generally preferred top-down economic control and development. Eastern abolitionists attached themselves to the progressive new political party.

1856 DECEMBER 10. Lincoln and 300 of his fellow Republicans attend a banquet at the Tremont House in Chicago. The crowd was jubilant over Republican gains in Illinois, but licking their wounds over the loss by their party's candidate, John C. Fremont, to James Buchanan for the presidency of the United States. Chicago attorney Jonathan Scammon delivered the first toast of the celebration: "First The Union—the North will maintain it—the South will not depart there from," Lincoln rose and addressed the crowd in response; he was greeted resoundingly when he stressed the equality of all men, and the resolve of his party to change public opinion on this matter.

1858 JULY 9. Lincoln was again in Chicago, this time for the U.S. District Court session. He listened to Stephen Douglas deliver the opening salvo of his senatorial campaign from a Tremont House balcony. The following evening from the same balcony, Lincoln responded to Douglas before a large and enthusiastic audience. Lincoln said, in part: "I have always hated slavery, I think as much as any Abolitionist. . . . I have always hated it, but I have always been quiet about it until this new era of the introduction of the Nebraska Bill began. I always believed that everybody was against it, and that it was in course of ultimate extinction . . . and that such was the belief of the framers of the constitution itself." Then Lincoln recalled the Fourth of July celebrations of the previous week. "I should like to know," he said, "if taking this old Declaration of Independence, which declares that all men are equal upon principle and making exceptions to it where will it stop. If one man says it does not mean a negro, why not another say it does not mean some other man?"

1858 AUGUST 21–OCTOBER 15. The Lincoln-Douglas debates take place. Over a period of eight weeks, the U.S. senatorial contenders travel a thousand miles and face off against one another seven times, defining their views on the issues of the day, including slavery. What is not generally remembered is that these debates, however stirring, were essentially an entertainment for the public. Although the Republicans out-polled the Democrats in the popular vote, the Democratically controlled Illinois state legislature had gerrymandered the districts so they retained control. Senators were chosen not by popular vote but by the legislature. Douglas went to Washington to represent the people of Illinois; Lincoln stayed in Springfield. These debates, however, did aid Lincoln's political career in important ways. He articulated important precepts and became widely known. An outsider to most of the nation, he earned a degree of popular recognition through his debates with Judge Douglas.

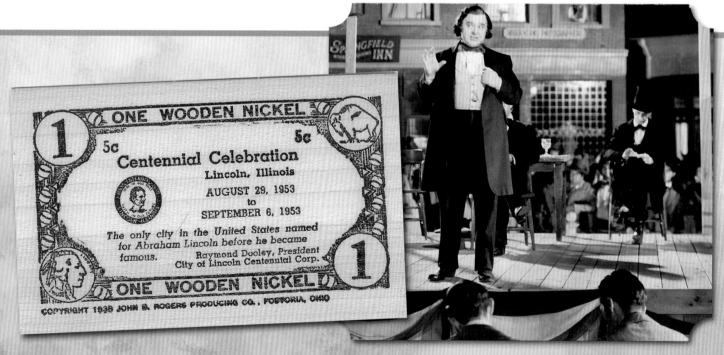

Fig. 1.27. Lincoln, Illinois, "the only city in the United States named for Abraham Lincoln before he became famous," celebrated its centennial with a series of wooden nickels in 1953.

Fig. 1.28. Gene Lockhart as Stephen Douglas presses home a point as Lincoln (Raymond Massey) takes notes at the back of the platform in *Abe Lincoln in Illinois*.

1860 FEBRUARY 27. In a single day, Lincoln poses for what will be an iconic and image-changing portrait and delivers a speech to the Eastern wing of his party. Still smarting from his senatorial loss to Douglas, Lincoln had received a golden opportunity in October 1859 when a small group of young Republican leaders in New York City invited him to give an address. The location was to be Henry Ward Beecher's church in Brooklyn, and the subject something of Lincoln's own choosing. The speech was part of a series of events the Republican club had arranged to hear out potential candidates.

When Lincoln arrived, he was unaware that the venue for the speech had been changed from the church to the grand hall of the Cooper Union. Cooper Union for the Advancement of Science and Art had recently been founded by idiosyncratic inventor and philanthropist Peter Cooper as a free school for New York's masses. Lincoln's Cooper Union speech and the portrait made earlier that day are said to have made him president. Before the event, Lincoln was introduced to historian George Bancroft at the Mathew Brady gallery, where his handlers had taken him for a photo opportunity. (It was Bancroft who would deliver a memorial address on Lincoln to Congress after the assassination. "I am on my way to Massachusetts," Lincoln told Bancroft, "where I have a son [Robert] at school [Harvard], who, if report be true, already knows much more than his father."[7])

Brady was the preeminent professional photographer of his day. He had the long fellow turn slowly several times while he sized up how best to project this gaunt and gangly customer on a two-dimensional glass negative. Mentally determining what features to emphasize and how to highlight them, Brady opted against a close-up, seated portrait, his usual stock in trade. Instead, he posed Lincoln standing, and pulled in a prop column to lend dignity and provide scale. Brady also set a table with books, so the gentleman could rest his hand and appear less simian. Furthermore, Brady moved his camera farther away to emphasize Lincoln's noble stature and soften his craggy features. Brady asked permission to arrange Lincoln's collar, the better to shorten the model's turtle neck, and he had Lincoln open his coat to increase the size of his chest.

In printing the image, the photographer further and subtly refined Lincoln's features. The cameraman's retouching redrew Lincoln's protruding ears, tamed his leathery facial features, smoothed his unruly and recently cropped hair, and further prettified his image. Brady's artistry made Lincoln look distinguished and presidential rather than like a gangling, shabbily dressed backwoodsman. Lincoln scholar Harold Holzer, who recently published a best-seller on the Cooper Union event, praises the result. "Brady," he wrote, "succeeded in making Lincoln look dignified, resolute and powerful."[8] This image (fig. 1.31) is certainly a striking one and presents Lincoln most favorably. Lincoln's rough-hewn image is transformed into one of a rather elegant, thoughtful gentleman ready to take on the heady issues of the day. Lincoln photo historians have estimated that 100,000 copies of this photograph were circulated. Its impact cannot be overstated.

Lincoln's speech, however, was what really marked the Western lawyer as a man to be reckoned with. Lincoln rightly regarded the speech as a presidential audition before the Eastern wing of his party and the national media centered in Gotham. This was Lincoln's opportunity to grab the brass ring and give wings to his presidential aspirations. He planned his speech as a refutation of Douglas's doctrine of popular sovereignty, which would have allowed the spread of slavery into the territories. Lincoln—although not an abolitionist per se—was firmly committed to the principle of "no extension of slavery." His speech was electric. Its resounding concluding sentiment to the 1,500 assembled there that night still rings down the halls of liberty: "Let us have faith that RIGHT makes MIGHT, and in that faith let us, to the end, dare to do our duty, as we understand it." It was reprinted widely

Fig. 1.29. Three photos of Lincoln taken around the time of the Lincoln-Douglas debates: *(a) CDV* after an ambrotype attributed to Roderick M. Cole, Peoria, Illinois, circa 1858 (Ostendorf-14); *(b)* cabinet card attributed to C.S. German, Springfield, September 26, 1858 (Ostendorf-9); and *(c)* CDV by Samuel M. Fassett, Chicago, October 4, 1859 (Ostendorf-16).

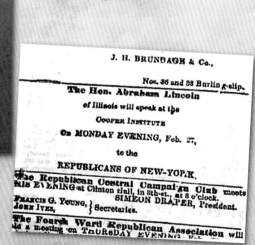

Fig. 1.30. A notice that "The Hon. Abraham Lincoln of Illinois will speak at the Cooper Institute . . . to the Republicans of New York," which appeared in the *New York Tribune*, February 23, 1860.

in the periodical press, and the *New York Tribune* published Lincoln's speech as number four among its tracts on national politics.

1860 MARCH 3. The group called the Hartford Wide Awakes—a pro-Lincoln patriotic organization—is organized, according to a legend on the group's political token. This Republican organization was formed to welcome Lincoln to Hartford on March 5, following his highly successful speech at New York City's Cooper Union. In the Charter Oak City, Lincoln was met by a jubilant crowd. "It was a larger infusion of young men than was usually the case in ante-bellum political assemblies," according to the *New York Times*.[9] In his speech, Lincoln referred to himself as a "dirty-shirt" Republican, emphasizing his working-class roots. Lincoln's "gaunt, homely figure, unpretending manner, conversational air, careless clothing, and dry humor made him at once a favorite with the audience, who felt that he was indeed a man of the people." At a large banquet in his honor at Hartford, Lincoln declined the proffered champagne politely. The following morning he met Gideon Welles, his future secretary of the Navy. Lincoln was overjoyed by his reception, and jokingly referred to the raucous crowd: "The boys are wide awake. Suppose we call them the 'Wide-awakes.'" Organizers followed his suggestion, and the marching Republican club came to be known as the Wide Awakes. Other groups followed suit. The Wide Awakes of Albany, New York, circulated several leaflets pumping the Lincoln campaign in mid-June. Wide Awake groups became notable for their torch-light parades. These groups gathered en masse at Hartford July, 26, 1860, at which original rails and mauls used by Lincoln were on display.[10]

1860 MARCH 31. Lincoln sits for a "life mask" by Chicago artist Leonard Wells Volk, a relative by marriage of Stephen A. Douglas. The latter had, in fact, financed Volk's study abroad, and in 1857 Volk had created a life mask of Lincoln's soon-to-be rival. In 1858 Volk set up a studio in Chicago, where he first met Lincoln during the time of the Lincoln-Douglas debates. In late March 1860 he convinced Lincoln to sit for a life mask, which is a cast from a mold taken directly from the sitter's face. According to art historians, Volk prepared a thick plaster, which he applied directly to Lincoln's face. In 1881, Volk said, "It was about an hour before the mold was ready to be removed, and being all in one piece, with both ears perfectly taken, it clung hard, as the cheek bones were higher than the jaw at the lobe of the ear. He bent his head low and took hold of the mold, and gradually worked it off without breaking or injury; it hurt a little, as a few hairs of the tender temples pulled out with the plaster and made the eyes water." Lincoln later recalled that the session "was anything but agreeable."

The mask (see fig. 1.33) shows Lincoln at age 51, two months prior to his nomination as Republican candidate for president. Volk used this cast to carve a bust (fig. 1.34). None other than Lincoln scholar Louis A. Warren has called the Volk mask "the most outstanding contribution to a correct reproduction of Lincoln's features." Volk also made plaster casts of Lincoln's hands, his right hand clutching a cut-off broom handle (fig. 1.33-b). Volk had Lincoln clutch the object to see what his hand would look like and how his fingers would be placed if he were clutching a rolled-up document. Lincoln returned to the artist's studio several times while Volk was sculpting

his bust. At one point, Lincoln is said to have proclaimed, "There is the animal himself." On May 18, Volk journeyed to Lincoln's home in Springfield and presented him with a smaller replica of the bust as a present. Lincoln was very pleased to see Volk and pleased with the result. As they shook hands, Volk recalled saying, "I am the first man from Chicago, I believe, who has the honor of congratulating you on your nomination for President."

Lincoln's personal secretary, John Hay, said that Volk's life mask "has a clean firm outline; it is free from fat, but the muscles are hard and full; the large mobile mouth is ready to speak, to shout, or laugh; the bold curved nose is broad and substantial, with spreading nostrils; it is a face full of life, of energy, of vivid aspiration." Volk's mask from life occupies a storied place in the annals of Lincoln lore and art history. Artists of all stripes have consulted it as a definitive source for Lincoln's physiognomy. Gutzon Borglum, whose clean-shaven bust of Lincoln is displayed in the U.S. Capitol, was especially impressed by Volk's mask. "I have never found a better head than his," Borglum related, "and I have never seen a face that was so mature, so developed, in its use of his expression." Volk's mask is as close to Lincoln as possible, and in fact is *the* image of the pre-presidential Lincoln. (The Borglum bust is shown and discussed in chapter 2.)

1860 APRIL 7. Candidate Lincoln writes Harvey Gridley Eastman, a Republican partisan, abolitionist, and business-college proprietor in Poughkeepsie, New York, in response to a request for a photograph (fig. 1.35). "Yours of March 18th addressed to me at Chicago, and requesting my photograph is received. I have not a single one now at my control; but I think you can easily get one at New York [City]. While I was there I was taken to one of the places where they get up such things, and I suppose they got my shadow and can multiply copies indefinitely. Any of the Republican Club men their can show you the place. Yours truly, A. Lincoln." Lincoln was referring to the Brady photo (see fig. 1.31).

1860 MAY 16–18. The Republican convention to pick the party's second candidate for the president of the United States is auspiciously held in Chicago. Lincoln did not go before the convention as the favorite, only as the favorite son of the local political machine. The clean-shaven, gangly rail-splitter proved to be a stealth candidate, however, when he captured the nomination on the third ballot against formidable rivals who included William Seward of New York and Salmon P. Chase of Ohio.

The convention was held in a newly constructed building called the Wigwam. Lincoln's campaign was managed from the Tremont House, a local hotel where Lincoln was an intimate of proprietors David A. and George W. Gage and John B. Drake. The Gage brothers purchased Tremont House in 1853, and Lincoln apparently first visited the establishment in 1854. Drake, formerly steward at the famous Burnet House in Cincinnati, bought a quarter-ownership in 1855. Under its new management the Tremont had developed a fashionable style, hosting sporting, civic, and society functions. By this time, John B. Drake had become famous for his sumptuous spreads. According to a contemporary newspaper account, "Every luxury which the most fastidious palate could desire . . . was present in bounteous profusion and enjoyed with peculiar unction."

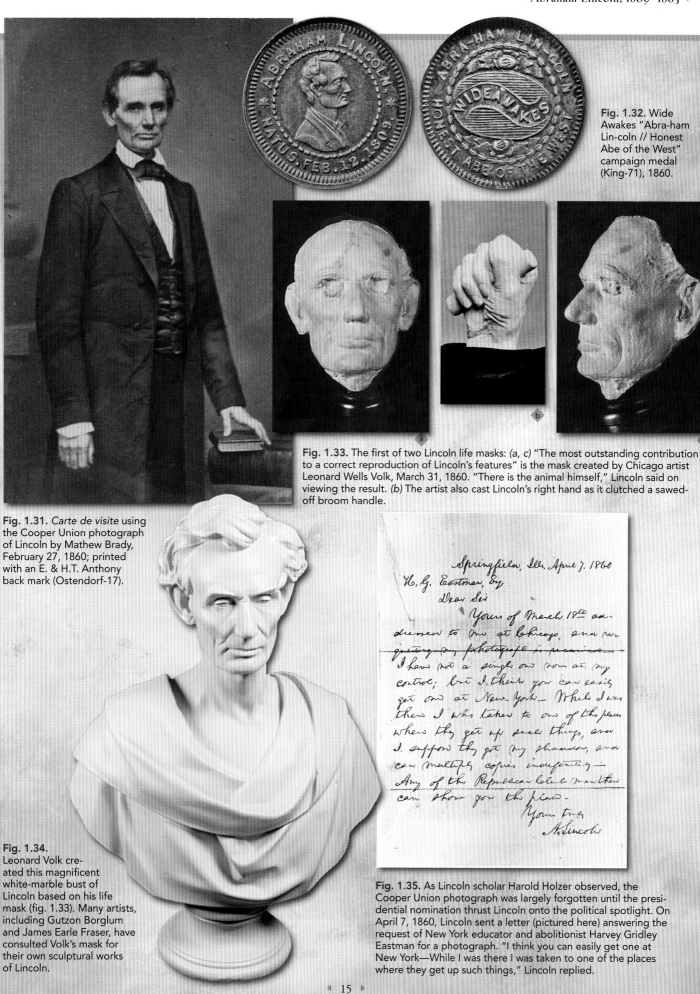

Fig. 1.32. Wide Awakes "Abra-ham Lin-coln // Honest Abe of the West" campaign medal (King-71), 1860.

Fig. 1.33. The first of two Lincoln life masks: *(a, c)* "The most outstanding contribution to a correct reproduction of Lincoln's features" is the mask created by Chicago artist Leonard Wells Volk, March 31, 1860. "There is the animal himself," Lincoln said on viewing the result. *(b)* The artist also cast Lincoln's right hand as it clutched a sawed-off broom handle.

Fig. 1.31. *Carte de visite* using the Cooper Union photograph of Lincoln by Mathew Brady, February 27, 1860; printed with an E. & H.T. Anthony back mark (Ostendorf-17).

Fig. 1.34. Leonard Volk created this magnificent white-marble bust of Lincoln based on his life mask (fig. 1.33). Many artists, including Gutzon Borglum and James Earle Fraser, have consulted Volk's mask for their own sculptural works of Lincoln.

Fig. 1.35. As Lincoln scholar Harold Holzer observed, the Cooper Union photograph was largely forgotten until the presidential nomination thrust Lincoln onto the political spotlight. On April 7, 1860, Lincoln sent a letter (pictured here) answering the request of New York educator and abolitionist Harvey Gridley Eastman for a photograph. "I think you can easily get one at New York—While I was there I was taken to one of the places where they get up such things," Lincoln replied.

Tremont House also developed an illustrious clientele. Abraham Lincoln became not only a frequent visitor but a close friend of the proprietors. George W. Gage, especially, became an intimate of the prairie lawyer. A New England abolitionist, the elder Gage quickly identified with the Republican Party and became active in its circles. His hotel became Lincoln's Chicago home when the latter was in town to attend to the District Court, as he was when he sat for Leonard Volk. It also increasingly became a political rallying point for Lincoln's successive campaigns. Lincoln addressed a large crowd there during his 1858 congressional campaign. During the 1860 Republican convention, the Tremont was Lincoln's campaign headquarters. Judge David Davis and Lincoln's other "handlers" roamed its halls wresting the nomination from the grasps of the other Republican contenders. Following Lincoln's nomination, the National Republican Committee assembled there. A cannon atop the hotel was fired "one hundred times, while Chicago [turned] itself upside down with rapture" as a grand parade followed. After his election, Lincoln and his family lived at the hotel for a week before going on to Washington for the inauguration. A few years later, George W. Gage, in his capacity as a member of the Chicago Light Guards military organization, would serve as honorary pall bearer for Lincoln's coffin when it passed through Chicago on the way to burial in Springfield.

1860 MAY 18. Lincoln is told that he has been chosen as the Republican presidential candidate. A legend says that he was informed of the nomination while playing ball, and a great deal of speculation has arisen about the exact game the future president may have been engaged in that day. Before the Civil War, several competing ball-and-stick games were played in cities and hamlets across the North, with varying origins and different rules. If Lincoln was indeed engaged in a ball game that day, the best current hypothesis is supplied by 19th-century baseball historian Richard Hershberger. Hershberger told this author that there are no contemporary or near-contemporary sources that connect Lincoln with baseball "in the sense of the New York game" that has evolved into the game we play today. However, "there is legitimate evidence of his playing town ball as an adult in Illinois, though the contemporary account of him playing a game when he received word of his nomination is probably campaign propaganda."[11] The near-contemporary evidence to which the sports historian refers is the anecdote collected by Lincoln's former law partner, William Herndon, from a James Gurley, who knew Lincoln from his 20s on.[12] Speculation over Lincoln's role in a ball game on that momentous day has given rise to several interesting depictions over time.

1860 MAY 19. In the evening, Lincoln is formally notified of his nomination by a delegation at his home.

Fig. 1.36. A Currier & Ives print, based on Roderick M. Cole's circa-1858 Lincoln photograph (Ostendorf-14), was the basis of several 1860 campaign ferrotypes, including these three outstanding examples: *(a)* an unlisted example, *(b)* a type of Sullivan AL 1860-114A, and *(c)* a Sullivan AL 1860-121.

Fig. 1.37. Abraham Lincoln is known to have played "townball," an early variant of America's national pastime, and according to a legend was engaged in that recreational pursuit in Springfield when a delegation arrived to inform him of his 1860 nomination for president in Chicago. In this illustration Lincoln tells the delegation chairman, "Tell the gentlemen they will have to wait a few minutes until I get my turn at bat."

Fig. 1.38. Hon. Abraham Lincoln of Illinois and Hon. Hannibal Hamlin of Maine, "The Republican Banner for 1860," Currier & Ives, New York, 1860.

1860 MAY 26. Easterners are curious about this frontier candidate; *Harper's Weekly, a Journal of Civilization* in New York City introduces "Hon. Abram [*sic*] Lincoln, of Illinois Republican Candidate for President" with a woodcut (fig. 1.39) based on the Cooper Union photo by Brady. It fills the front page.

1860 MAY. A correspondent for the *New York Post* interviews the candidate and his wife in Springfield following the convention, reporting favorably. "His integrity is proverbial; and his legal abilities are regarded as of the highest order," this account read. "The soubriquet of 'Honest old Abe,' has been won by years of upright conduct, and is the popular homage to his probity. He carries the marks of honesty in his face and entire deportment."

1860 JUNE 12. Sculptor Leonard Volk patents a life-size nude bust of Lincoln based on his life mask. The patent was much infringed upon.

1860 JUNE 13. First portrait of the candidate from life is painted by Thomas Hicks of New York (it sold at Parke-Bernet Galleries, New York City, November 23, 1940). Orville Browning, a fellow attorney and Lincoln friend, "spent a portion of the day with Lincoln talking to him whilst Mr. Hicks worked upon his portrait. . . . [Hicks] completed it this P. M. In my judgment it is an exact, life like likeness, and a beautiful work of art. It is deeply imbued with the intellectual and spiritual, and I doubt whether any one ever succeeds in getting a better picture of the man."[13]

1860 JUNE 27. J.E. Hurlbut sends Abraham Lincoln a campaign medal.[14]

1860 JULY 4. Orville Browning writes Lincoln to tell him he will be conferred an LLD from Knox College the following day. "You will, therefore, after tomorrow consider yourself a 'scholar' as well as a 'gentleman,' and deport yourself accordingly," Browning wrote.[15]

1860. The excellent New York engraver J.C. Buttre creates a popular image of Lincoln during this pitchman's paradise. Vendors in cities across the country hawked campaign biographies, ribbons, medallions, and other mementoes. The Cooper Union photograph by Brady was a popular campaign image (fig. 1.42). In addition to the tintype and other photo images, Buttre's excellent likeness of Lincoln, after the Cooper Union image, circulated as *cartes de visite (CDVs)* and was also printed on silk badges. Lithographs, like that of New York City printmakers Currier & Ives, were framed and mounted on parlor walls.

1860. Campaign biographies include D.W. Bartlett's authorized *Life and Public Services of Hon. Abraham Lincoln,* with a portrait on steel and a biographical sketch of Lincoln's running mate, Hannibal Hamlin of Maine. The portrait, engraved by R.S. Jones, was based on the Cooper Union photo. Bartlett also offered a 25¢ abridged

Fig. 1.39. *Harper's Weekly* presented a woodcut of the "Hon. Abram [*sic*] Lincoln, of Illinois, Republican Candidate for President," in its May 26, 1860, issue. The portrait was based on Brady's Cooper Union image.

Fig. 1.40. Lincoln's nomination for president brought a host of requests for photo shoots. Springfield photographer Alexander Hessler created this wonderful likeness of candidate Lincoln on June 3, 1860 (Ostendorf-26).

Fig. 1.41. This 1860 campaign ribbon, based on the circa-1858 Roderick Cole photo (see fig. 1.36), also represents the candidate as "Abram [*sic*] Lincoln," with his running mate, Hannibal Hamlin (Sullivan-Fischer AL-9).

paperback version. A German-language edition was also created. Journalist William Dean Howells contributed a Lincoln biography for Follett, Foster & Co.'s *Lives and Speeches of Abraham Lincoln and Hannibal Hamlin.* The frontispiece is Buttre's engraving of Brady's Cooper Union photo. According to the William Dean Howells Society Web site, his campaign biography of Lincoln "earned him enough money to travel to New England and meet the great literary figures of the day—Nathaniel Hawthorne, Ralph Waldo Emerson, Henry David Thoreau, James Russell Lowell, and Walt Whitman among them." When Lincoln won the election, he awarded Howells with the post of U.S. consul to Venice, where Howells remained for the next four years. Howells wrote several novels, including *The Rise of Silas Lapham,* after the war. New York publisher Rudd & Carleton published a Wigwam edition of its *Life, Speeches, and Public Services of Abraham Lincoln, together with a Sketch of the Life of Hannibal Hamlin, Republican Candidates for the offices of President and Vice President of the United States.* In Boston, Thayer & Eldridge circulated a Wide Awake edition of its *Life and Public Services of Hon. Abraham Lincoln, of Illinois, and Hon. Hannibal Hamlin, of Maine.* Compilations of the Lincoln-Douglas debates were also published in New York City, Boston, Chicago, Detroit, and Columbus, Ohio.[16]

1860. Although many of the campaign biographies bear portraits of the candidates, one of the most elaborate of this species of literature is prepared by J.C. Buttre. His contribution to campaign literature was the brief (32-page) *Portraits and Sketches of the Lives of all the Candidates for the Presidency and Vice Presidency, for 1860, comprising Eight Portraits engraved on Steel, Facts in the life of each, the Four Platforms, the Cincinnati Platform, and the Constitution of the United States.*

Fig. 1.43. This splendid ambrotype pin shows Brady's Cooper Union image. It was manufactured by Geo. Clark Jr. & Co, Ambrotype Artists, No. 59 Court Street, Boston.

Fig. 1.44. Lincoln's running mate, Hannibal Hamlin, a former congressman, senator, and governor of the state of Maine, as pictured on the back of a ferrotype campaign badge (see fig. 1.42d for the front).

Fig. 1.42. Once the campaign began in earnest, the Cooper Union photo decorated a plethora of campaign paraphernalia, including the following: *(a)* a silk ribbon (Sullivan-Fischer AL-8 variant), *(b)* a Currier & Ives lithograph, *(c)* a campaign biography by D.W. Bartlett, and *(d)* a ferrotype badge (Sullivan AL 1860-97).

Fig. 1.45. A torchlight rally for candidate Lincoln (Raymond Massey) in *Abe Lincoln in Illinois.*

1860. Campaign songsters include such melodically titled booklets as *The Lincoln and Hamlin Songster, or, the Continental Melodist, comprising a choice collection of Original and Selected songs, in honor of the People's Candidates, Lincoln and Hamlin, and illustrative of the enthusiasm everywhere entertained for "Honest Old Abe," of Illinois, and the noble Hamlin of Maine.* The songbook was published in New York by Wm. J. Bunce, and in Philadelphia and Baltimore by Fisher & Bros. (fig. 1.46). Sheet music also touted "Honest Old Abe" and "Hon. ABRM Lincoln."

1860. One of the earliest of the campaign tokens supporting Lincoln's candidacy is put out locally by Jensch & Meyer, Chicago, emblazoned with the verbose legend "Our Policy Is Expressly The Policy Of The Men Who Made The Union No More, No Less" (fig. 1.47). Chicago had a vigorous tradition of token issues, but Lincoln issues were hardly confined to the Midwest. Other vendors, like

Joseph Merriam (Boston), J.D. Lovett (New York), and B.F. True (Cincinnati), all cranked out these medals with slogans like "No More Slave Territory," "Let Liberty Be National & Slavery Sectional," and "Liberty Union And Equality." (See fig. 1.48)

1860. Campaign covers (fig. 1.49) are circulated in a great variety of styles by several dozen printers. Magnus in New York, Magee in Philadelphia, and Car Bell in Hartford, Connecticut, produced a wide variety. Many portrayed Lincoln as a rail-splitter. Like the small campaign medals, they frequently bore political or patriot slogans. Used covers are especially prized by collectors.

1860. Among the many campaign prints published by Currier & Ives, "The National Game, Three 'Outs,' and one 'Run'" capitalizes on the growing popularity of baseball. It depicts Lincoln besting his three political opponents, John Bell, Stephen Douglas, and John C. Breckinridge. Lincoln claims home base with a bat in the form of a

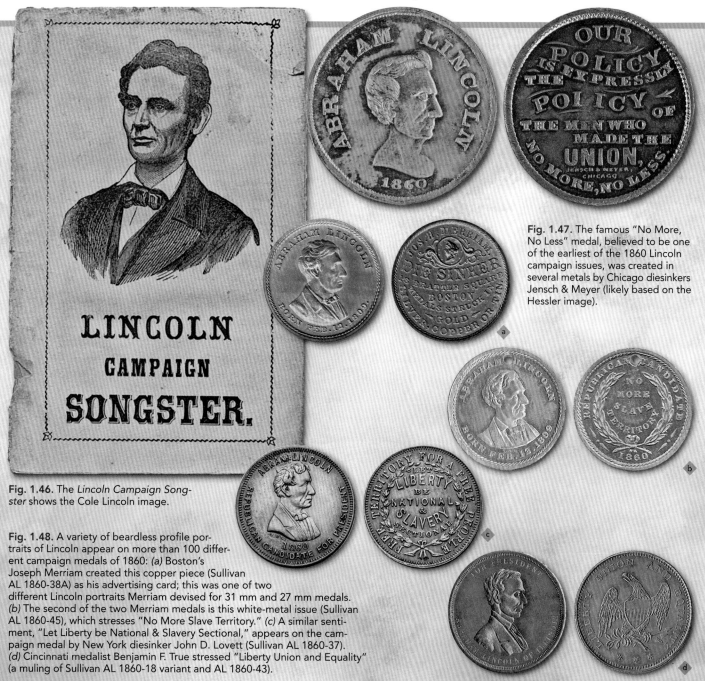

Fig. 1.47. The famous "No More, No Less" medal, believed to be one of the earliest of the 1860 Lincoln campaign issues, was created in several metals by Chicago diesinkers Jensch & Meyer (likely based on the Hessler image).

Fig. 1.46. The *Lincoln Campaign Songster* shows the Cole Lincoln image.

Fig. 1.48. A variety of beardless profile portraits of Lincoln appear on more than 100 different campaign medals of 1860: (a) Boston's Joseph Merriam created this copper piece (Sullivan AL 1860-38A) as his advertising card; this was one of two different Lincoln portraits Merriam devised for 31 mm and 27 mm medals. (b) The second of the two Merriam medals is this white-metal issue (Sullivan AL 1860-45), which stresses "No More Slave Territory." (c) A similar sentiment, "Let Liberty be National & Slavery Sectional," appears on the campaign medal by New York diesinker John D. Lovett (Sullivan AL 1860-37). (d) Cincinnati medalist Benjamin F. True stressed "Liberty Union and Equality" (a muling of Sullivan AL 1860-18 variant and AL 1860-43).

rail emblazoned with "Equal Rights and Free Territory"; Bell and Douglas complain from the sidelines, while a skunked Breckinridge slinks back to Kentucky (fig. 1.51).

1860 AUGUST 13. A half-dozen ambrotypes of Lincoln are taken by Springfield photographer Preston Butler for the benefit of artist John Henry Brown. These were the last photographs of a beardless, clean-shaven Lincoln, according to Lincoln photo historian Lloyd Ostendorf.

1860 OCTOBER. *Household Journal* in New York publishes "A Presidential Poet" in its October 1860 issue. According to Boyd, "this journal published the poem 'Immortality,' crediting Mr. Lincoln with its authorship, prefacing it with a note about the great rulers who had written poetry, and among them mentioning Mr. Lincoln as a Poet." The publication was mistaken. Lincoln was not the author of this poem, sometimes also known as "Mortality,"

which was written by the promising Scots poet William Knox, who in fact died young. The first quatrain of this poem is the most famous.

> Oh! Why should the spirit of mortal be proud?
> Like a swift-fleeting meteor, a fast-flying cloud
> A flash of the lightning, a break of the wave
> He passeth from life to his rest in the grave."

In his 20s Lincoln had memorized the poem and was said by acquaintances to recite it out loud, but he only found out late in life its true author.

1860 NOVEMBER 6. Abraham Lincoln is elected the 16th president of the United States.

Fig. 1.49. Specialists have cataloged more than 100 different beardless 1860 Lincoln campaign covers, including the following: (a) Milgram AL-84, postally used October 10, 1860, has a Series 1857–1861 stamp, as does (b) Milgram AL-66, used September 3, 1860. (Note that the federal government demonetized stamps that were current at the start of the war to deprive the Confederacy of the benefit of U.S. stamps on hand.) (c) Milgram AL-94, a patriotic showing Lincoln-Hamlin, was sent to a soldier with a new Series 1861 three-cent stamp and manuscript cancel March 15, 1862.

Fig. 1.50. Three contemporary pictorial views of the 1860 presidential election: (a) the candidates "Dividing the National Map" by ripping the country asunder in a print published in Cincinnati; (b) Lincoln balancing the delicate constitutional question of slavery à la the Niagara River gorge tightrope walker Blondin, attributed to Jacob Dallas and published in *Harper's Weekly* August 25, 1860; and (c) Frank Leslie's caustic depiction of "Dis-Union," wherein the drum beater is keeping the presidential candidates (at left) and others wide awake, while wondering out loud "who dat passenger is who 'spects to git out at de Wite House?" which appeared in the September 1, 1860, issue of *Budget of Fun*.

1860 NOVEMBER 10. *Harper's Weekly* publishes a standing, nearly full-page illustration (also based on the Cooper Union photo) on its cover (fig. 1.57).

1860 NOVEMBER 21. President-elect Lincoln meets his vice-president elect, Hannibal Hamlin, at Chicago's Tremont House hotel. This meeting, according to contemporary newspaper accounts, was "cordial to the highest degree." The following day, Lincoln and his wife escorted Hamlin and his party around Chicago, visiting the Wigwam, custom house, courthouse, and post office before returning to the hotel. On Friday morning, November 23, the Tremont House was the location of a grand public reception for the future president and vice president. "Until noon, a steady stream of visitors poured in at the Lake Street entrance of the Tremont House," the newspapers reported. According to an account, Lincoln, Hamlin, and Mrs. Lincoln greeted and shook the hands of all comers. At night Lincoln and Hamlin dined with Lyman Trumbull at the hotel.

1860 NOVEMBER 25. The first bearded image of Lincoln is taken by Samuel G. Alschuler in Chicago.

1860 NOVEMBER 26. Before leaving the Tremont House, Lincoln pens a note to a friend on Tremont House stationery about a photographic request: "Your note in behalf of Mr. Alshuler was received. I gave him a sitting."[17] This photo, the one taken by Alshuler the previous day, is most historic, since it is the first to record Lincoln with chin whiskers—the first bearded photograph of the president-elect.[18]

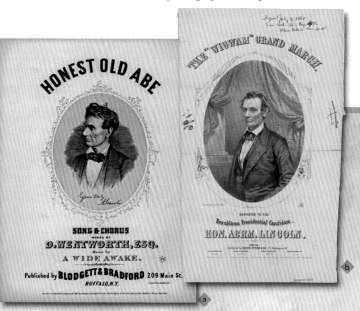

Fig. 1.52. Campaign music played a prominent role in public gatherings. These two examples were published in 1860. *(a)* "Honest Old Abe," by D. Wentworth, was published by Blodgett & Bradford in Buffalo; *(b)* "The Wigwam Grand March," by Oliver Ditson & Co. in Boston.

Fig. 1.53. Lincoln & Hamlin Republican ticket, Ward 5, Boston, printed by Wright & Potter, 1860.

Fig. 1.51. Another baseball analogy for the 1860 presidential canvas is made in this Currier & Ives print, "The National Game. Three 'Outs' [John Bell, Stephen Douglas, and John C. Breckinridge] and One 'Run' [Lincoln]." "Gentlemen," Lincoln says, "if any of you should ever take a hand in another match at this game, remember that you must have 'a good bat' and strike a 'fair ball' to make a 'clean score' & a 'home run.'"

Fig. 1.54. Cincinnati diesinker Benjamin F. True circulated a great variety of small 1860 campaign medals. He depicted Lincoln and the "President's House" on this one (Sullivan AL 1860-61).

Fig. 1.55. Lincoln's image as "The Rail Splitter of the West" was a powerful one, dramatized on this 1860 campaign medal by Ellis (Sullivan AL 1860-41).

Fig. 1.56. This 1860 Rail Splitter medal by S.D. Childs & Co. of Chicago (Sullivan AL 1860-10) appeared very early in the campaign. What progress Lincoln achieved since he reached majority in 1830 can be seen fully realized by bright dawn at right and the White House on the horizon at left.

THE NATIONAL GAME. THREE "OUTS" AND ONE "RUN".
ABRAHAM WINNING THE BALL.

Fig. 1.57. *Harper's Weekly* announced Lincoln's election in its November 10, 1860, issue, revisiting the Cooper Union image and spelling Lincoln's given name correctly.

1860 December 1. As publications are seeking their own angles on the newly elected president, *Scientific American* goes for Lincoln-as-inventor. Its December 1, 1860, story on the president-elect reports on Lincoln's patent for buoying ships (fig. 1.58).

1861 circa January. In early 1861 or perhaps late 1860, ABNCo's Alfred Sealey engraves a beardless Lincoln portrait for use on currency, basing his design (fig. 1.59a) on Brady's Cooper Union portrait, which had been so popular during the presidential campaign. Several (one report says six) proofs of the engraving were sent to Lincoln, who was still at home in Springfield meeting with advisors and hopeful appointees, accepting engagements for his impending trip East, and settling his affairs. Lincoln had a number of these proofs in his possession during the journey to Washington. He autographed several. He presented one to William M. Kasson when his train stopped in Buffalo, New York. According to Kasson's daughter, Lincoln is said to have described the engraving when he retrieved it from his carpet bag as his favorite picture of himself.[19]

Another of the proofs was autographed for his longtime friend John B. Drake, the bon vivant co-owner and steward of Chicago's famous luxury hotel Tremont House, where Lincoln and his family frequently stayed when they were in town. According to Lincoln print specialists, this is "the only print portrait Lincoln is known to have autographed."[20] In 1965 it appeared at auction with an inscription on the back stating it was received in February 1861, but misidentifying the recipient as J.R. Drake. A third autographed copy of the vignette was sold in a private transaction in 1976.[21]

The only known currency use of this portrait is on a $5 note of the Bank of Winsted, Connecticut (fig. 1.59b), issued April 1, 1862—by which time this likeness was thoroughly anachronistic.

1861 January 13. Christopher S. German takes two almost-identical photographs of a newly bewhiskered Abe Lincoln in Springfield. This was the first image of the presidential Lincoln to capture the public's attention, for it was soon reproduced on *CDVs* (fig. 1.60), and translated into prints. Caught short, some printmakers merely added beards

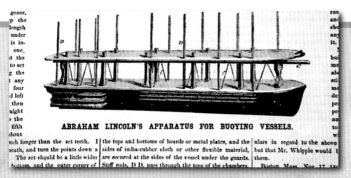

Fig. 1.58. In its December 1, 1860, issue, *Scientific American* reported on the president-elect's 1849 patent for buoying grounded vessels.

WM. HICKINBOTHAM, Artist 75 Federal St. Allegheny City, Pa.

ABRAHAM LINCOLN

Fig. 1.59. Further use of the Cooper Union image: *(a)* Between late 1860 and early 1861, engraver Alfred Sealey rendered the Cooper Union image as a security engraving for the American Bank Note Co., New York, die no. 123. *(b)* Because the president-elect grew out his beard just prior to the inauguration, Sealey's excellent likeness was an anachronism, and used on only one bank note, the $5 issue of the Winsted Bank, Connecticut.

Fig. 1.60. The famous Christopher S. German photo (shown at the beginning of this chapter) was the model for this engraved *CDV* by William Hickinbotham of Allegheny, Pennsylvania.

to their clean-shaven portraits and circulated the doctored images as "new" pictures of Old Abe (fig. 1.61).

1861 FEBRUARY 1. President-elect Abraham Lincoln acknowledges receipt of a bronze medal honoring Henry Clay, whom "during my whole political life, I have loved and revered as a teacher and leader."[22]

1861 FEBRUARY 11. President-elect Abraham Lincoln withdraws $400 from his account in Springfield for expenses on his trip to Washington, D.C., for his inauguration. That same day Lincoln takes leave of his fellow citizens of Springfield, boards a train with his wife and family, and travels to Indianapolis, Cincinnati, Columbus, Pittsburgh, Cleveland, Buffalo, Syracuse, Albany, New York City, and Trenton, arriving in Philadelphia February 21 on the eve of Washington's birthday. It was disclosed by Allan Pinkerton, head of a national police agency, that a plot to assassinate him during his sojourn through Baltimore was afoot. Ignoring caution, the next day in a scheduled event Lincoln raised the American flag over Inde-

pendence Hall (fig. 1.63) and addressed the Pennsylvania legislature. He then put himself in the hands of his bodyguards.

1861 FEBRUARY 23. Under the threat of assassination as he travels through Maryland, Lincoln proceeds instead on a direct train from Philadelphia to Washington, D.C. Lincoln's "sneaking" into the nation's capital to be inaugurated was lambasted by his political foes, especially Adalbert Volck, also known as V. Blada (fig. 1.64).

1861 FEBRUARY 24. Lincoln goes to Mathew Brady's gallery in Washington and poses for photographs. It is significant that this was one of the first things Lincoln did when he arrived at the national capital. The photo shoot was for the benefit of *Harper's Weekly*. Store manager Alexander Gardner took a series of seated photographs with a multiple-lens camera (fig. 1.66). The session was managed by artist George Story, who posed the president-elect with his elbow and top hat resting on a table next to the chair. Reportedly, Lincoln had become so exhausted by his hectic schedule on his nearly 2,000-mile trek from Illinois that he seemed dazed. Lincoln photo historian

Fig. 1.61. Lincoln's new chin whiskers caught printmakers short. Philadelphia engraver Samuel Sartain and many others updated their beardless Lincoln portraits (a) with deft strokes of the graver (b).

Fig. 1.64. Lincoln was under threat of assassination on the final leg of his journey to Washington, D.C. Baltimore illustrator Adalbert Volck lampooned Lincoln's alleged disguise passing through Baltimore in a freight car.

Fig. 1.62. President-elect Lincoln (Raymond Massey) boards the train for his trip to his inauguration in *Abe Lincoln in Illinois*.

Fig. 1.63. Lincoln's raising the Stars and Stripes on Washington's birthday, February 22, 1861, in Philadelphia en route to the inauguration under threat of assassination, was a defiant patriotic act. This illustration appeared in *Harper's Weekly* on March 9, 1861. Similar views were published as separate lithographs.

Fig. 1.65. *Harper's Weekly's* humor was less sharp edged. "Winding off the tangled skein" showed the unraveling Union President Buchanan handed off to his successor Lincoln in its March 30, 1861, issue.

Fig. 1.66. One of the first things Lincoln did on arriving at Washington, D.C., was go to Mathew Brady's gallery on Sunday, February 24, 1861. There, Alexander Gardner took several photographs, including this pose, which reveals Lincoln's swollen right hand, nearly crippled by the over-eager handshakes of well-wishers during his trip from Illinois.

Lloyd Ostendorf has pointed out that Lincoln's right hand was so swollen from accepting the congratulations of the party faithful across seven states that in the photos he intentionally "kept [it] closed or out of sight."[23]

1861 MARCH 1. Lincoln canvases Republican senators' preferences for secretary of the Treasury. He receives picks from 19 senators. Eleven chose Salmon P. Chase. Three each opted for Simon Cameron and Wm. L. Dayton. Others mentioned were William Pitt Fessenden and John Sherman. Lincoln picked Chase and convinced him to accept the post. Cameron became secretary of war; Dayton, minister to France; and Fessenden and Sherman Treasury secretaries at later dates.

1861 MARCH 4. Abraham Lincoln is inaugurated as the 16th president of the United States on the east portico of the incomplete U.S. Capitol building (fig. 1.67).

1861 MARCH 4. Ohio governor Salmon P. Chase takes his Senate seat, but resigns two days later to become Lincoln's Treasury secretary.

1861 MARCH. A frantic race ensues among the private bank-note companies to commit the newly bewhiskered visage of the president-elect to cold steel for use on bank notes, and for securing government printing work where the real money is to be made. National Bank Note Co. got a jump start when George Baldwin (likely) pro-duced a stunning miniature engraved portrait (fig. 1.69a) based on the new, January 13 photograph (pictured facing page 1) by Spring-field cameraman C.S. German. NBNCo immediately used this image on $500, six-percent, 20-year bonds (fig. 1.69b) authorized under the Act of March 2, 1861.

Congress had authorized $2.8 million in the bonds to pay expenses from suppression of Indian hostilities in the Oregon and Washington territories in 1855 and 1856. The Treasury also ordered $50 and $100 bonds from NBNCo; 2,000 of the bonds ($1 million face value) were to be of the $500 denomination. Bonds were first issued in the first fiscal quarter of 1862 (i.e., July through September 1861). Presidential portraiture on U.S. government bonds was usual. Ex-president James Buchanan, for instance, had appeared on the previous series of bonds. Portraits of George Washington, Andrew Jackson, Millard Fillmore, and Zachary Taylor had also been called for such duty. This vignette proved very versatile, as NBNCo's Lincoln portrait graces a succession of government bonds and Interest-Bearing Notes issued to finance the war effort. According to original research by the present writer, supplemented by records of Bureau of Engraving and Printing Historical Resource Center contract historian Franklin Noll, this image of Lincoln appeared on the following bonds printed by NBNCo:

$500 six-percent bond, Act of March 2, 1861 (to finance the Oregon war debt)

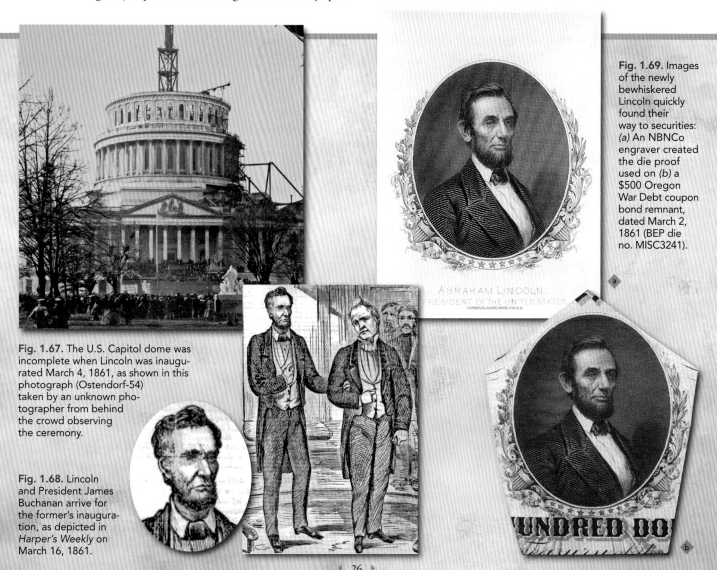

Fig. 1.67. The U.S. Capitol dome was incomplete when Lincoln was inaugurated March 4, 1861, as shown in this photograph (Ostendorf-54) taken by an unknown photographer from behind the crowd observing the ceremony.

Fig. 1.68. Lincoln and President James Buchanan arrive for the former's inauguration, as depicted in *Harper's Weekly* on March 16, 1861.

Fig. 1.69. Images of the newly bewhiskered Lincoln quickly found their way to securities: *(a)* An NBNCo engraver created the die proof used on *(b)* a $500 Oregon War Debt coupon bond remnant, dated March 2, 1861 (BEP die no. MISC3241).

ABRAHAM LINCOLN.
PRESIDENT OF THE UNITED STATES.
NATIONAL BANK NOTE CO.U.S.A.

UNDRED DO

$100 six-percent bond, acts of July 17, 1861, and August 5, 1861 (registered and coupon bonds)

$10,000 six-percent bond, same authorization as previous (registered and coupon bonds)

$10,000 five-percent, 20-year bond, Act of February 25, 1862 (registered bond)

$500 bond, same authorization as previous (registered and coupon bonds, Third Series)

$50 bond, same authorization as previous (registered and coupon bonds, Fourth Series)

$500 bond, same authorization as previous (registered and coupon bonds, Fourth Series)

The company then turned over the dies to the Treasury Department, which used the image on the following:

$20 five-percent, one-year Interest Bearing Treasury Note, Act of March 3, 1863

$20 six-percent, three-year Compound Interest Treasury Note, same authorization as previous

$20 six-percent, three-year Compound Interest Treasury Note, Act of June 30, 1864

$100 six-percent bond, Act of March 3, 1863 (registered and coupon bonds)

$50 six-percent bond, Act of June 30, 1864 (registered and coupon bonds)

Andrew Boyd listed several additional uses on bonds of this period, but these have not been seen and cannot be confirmed.[24]

1861 MARCH 30. American Bank Note Co. die number 141 (fig. 1.70), by Charles Burt (pictured in fig. 1.71), is approved for use in the lucrative printing of government securities. For competitive reasons, ABNCo needed to produce a bearded image of Lincoln as quickly as possible. Burt's design was the result. The engraver based his image on a large pen-and-ink drawing by Louis Delnoce, which in turn had been based on the same C.S. German photographic images that NBNCo's engraver had used. Since both dies are based on the same models, Burt's engraving is superficially similar to the NBNCo portrait. The style of the hair varies slightly, but the principal difference is the cut of Lincoln's right lapel: the vent is much larger on the ABNCo engraving. This die's first known use was on a $50 Commonwealth of Pennsylvania bond dated June 1, 1861.

Fig. 1.70. It is extremely rare for dies that were actually used to print U.S. currency to reside in a private collection, as these do. These national treasures were purchased from the ABNCo archives dispersal and are now in the collection of the author: (a, b) Two views of Charles Burt's engraving, the original ABNCo die number 141; (c) cylinder roller die number 2792, used to impress Lincoln's image on the plates.

Fig. 1.71. Charles Burt, self-portrait. Burt is the Lincoln portrait engraver for U.S. currency, having produced four likenesses of Old Abe used on various federal currency over a period of 138 years!

1861 APRIL 5. President Abraham Lincoln deposits his first salary warrant at Riggs & Co., Washington bankers.

1861 APRIL 19. Minnesota sculptor Salathiel Ellis files for a patent for a medallion of President Lincoln. It is unclear whether this piece was issued.

1861 APRIL 19. Lincoln supporter Carl Schurz organizes the First New York Cavalry Regiment in New York City. On April 15, in response to the attack on Fort Sumter, Lincoln had issued a call for 75,000 men to protect the capital. Almost immediately, Schurz sought to fulfill part of that call. While most of the troops came from downstate New York, others came from Syracuse and as far away as Wisconsin. The unit took the name of the "Lincoln Cavalry" in honor of Abraham Lincoln, who took a personal interest in its formation.[25]

On June 15 Col. Andrew T. McReynolds succeeded Schurz as regimental commander, following special authorization issued by President Lincoln two days earlier. This changeover was necessary due to Lincoln's appointment of Schurz as minister to Spain. The unit was mustered into U.S. service, beginning July 16, for three years. It served in the Army of the Potomac and later in the West. When its three-year term of service was nearing expiration, the regiment reenlisted as veteran volunteers on January 1, 1864. This unit was engaged in many of the important battles of the war, including Antietam and Sheridan's Shenandoah Valley campaign, and was present at Appomattox Court House April 9, 1865, for the surrender of Lee's army. The First New York Veteran Volunteer Cavalry participated in the Grand Review on May 23, and was mustered out on June 27, 1865. It had suffered 168 casualties.[26]

1861 APRIL 24. Lincoln presents a $20 gold piece encased in a silver Maltese cross to Sarah C. Ford, seven-year-old daughter of Capt. John A. Ford. The young lady had impressed the president with her

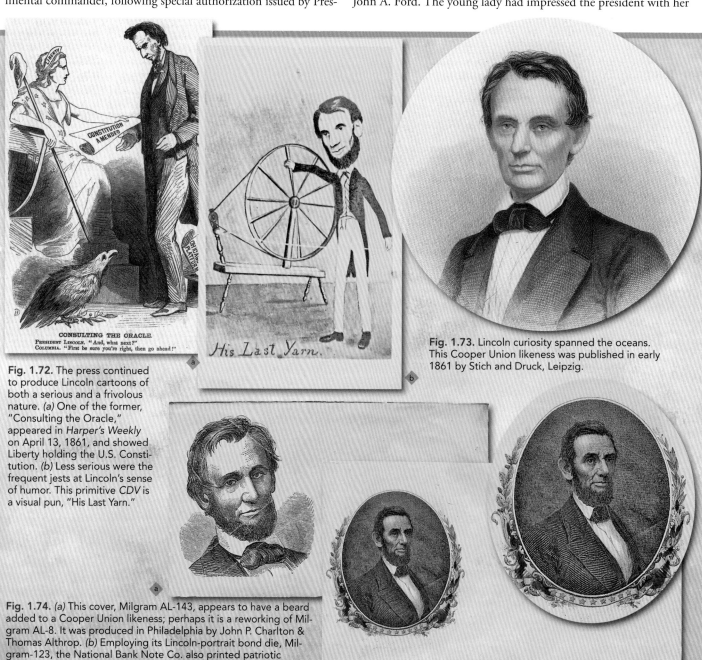

Fig. 1.72. The press continued to produce Lincoln cartoons of both a serious and a frivolous nature. *(a)* One of the former, "Consulting the Oracle," appeared in *Harper's Weekly* on April 13, 1861, and showed Liberty holding the U.S. Constitution. *(b)* Less serious were the frequent jests at Lincoln's sense of humor. This primitive *CDV* is a visual pun, "His Last Yarn."

CONSULTING THE ORACLE.
PRESIDENT LINCOLN. "And, what next?"
COLUMBIA. "First be sure you're right, then go ahead!"

His Last Yarn.

Fig. 1.73. Lincoln curiosity spanned the oceans. This Cooper Union likeness was published in early 1861 by Stich and Druck, Leipzig.

Fig. 1.74. *(a)* This cover, Milgram AL-143, appears to have a beard added to a Cooper Union likeness; perhaps it is a reworking of Milgram AL-8. It was produced in Philadelphia by John P. Charlton & Thomas Althrop. *(b)* Employing its Lincoln-portrait bond die, Milgram-123, the National Bank Note Co. also printed patriotic envelopes in 1862. These are the only known Civil War envelopes with an engraved design. This example was hand colored.

patriotism while seated in Lincoln's lap during a conversation Lincoln had with her father two weeks earlier.[27]

1861. Responding to the curiosity of many Europeans about this new American president, numerous companies publish Lincoln images. Sampson, Low & Co. in London published an engraving; Bacon & Co. in London and Otto Spamer in Leipzig did likewise. In Berlin, J. Hagelberg published a large, tinted lithograph portrait of Lincoln, and Berg & Porsch a large engraved portrait. In Leipzig Stich & Druck published a fine line-and-stipple engraving based on the Cooper Union image (fig. 1.73).

1861. Once it becomes known that Lincoln has grown chin-whiskers, printers scramble to update their bare-chinned campaign covers and prints by applying beards to the old images (fig. 1.74). One of the most elaborate new series of envelopes produced at this time was printed by J.H. Tingley, New York City, who issued a series

of five envelopes with all-over designs styled "Champion Prize Envelope Lincoln & Davis in 5 Rounds." The sequence starts with Lincoln and Davis in the ring, then proceeds to Lincoln ripping Davis's clothes, putting him in a headlock, and winning the championship belt. In Round Four (fig. 1.76), Gen. Winfield Scott and secretary of state William Seward occupy center ring, while Lincoln stands off to the side giving a stump speech. "I have taken the world by surprize [*sic*]," Lincoln says.

1861. Fort Lincoln is constructed on the northeast side of Washington, D.C., along the Baltimore and Ohio Railroad line, as part of the ring of defensive positions guarding the nation's capital (see fig. 1.78). Others include Fort Cameron, Fort Scott, Fort Totten, Fort Stanton, and Fort Bunker Hill. Fort Lincoln participated in the artillery salute, ordered by Secretary of War Edwin Stanton, that marked the installation of Thomas Crawford's statue *Freedom* atop

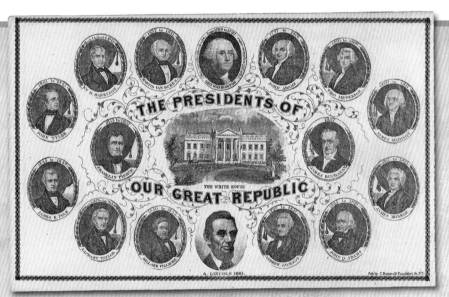

Fig. 1.75. New York lithographer Charles Magnus added an image of Lincoln based on the $10 model, and issued this print, "The Presidents of Our Great Republic," in 1861. He used this same Lincoln portrait on a wide variety of covers.

Fig. 1.77. Northern publications urged Lincoln to take hold of the situation with the South. *Harper's Weekly* likened it to (a) Jeff Davis stealing apples off a tree, in "the National Apple Orchard" (issue of May 18, 1861), and (b) robbing the U.S. Treasury (issue of July 13, 1861).

Fig. 1.76. "Champion Prize Envelope Lincoln & Davis in 5 Rounds," published by J.H. Tingley, New York City, in 1861, depicted a mythical champion prize fight between Lincoln and his counterpart, Jefferson Davis. In Round 4 (Milgram AL-295), General Winfield Scott and William Seward take center ring, while Lincoln, holding the prize belt at left, crows "I have taken the world by surprize [*sic*]."

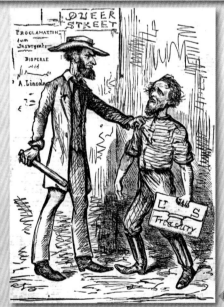

a

Fig. 1.78. The Union army and Fort Lincoln: *(a)* A photo of the fort, which was constructed in 1861 for the defense of Washington, D.C. *(b)* "The Union Soldier's Address to the Flag," written by John Y. Wren, Battery G, Second Artillery, Pennsylvania, while at Fort Lincoln in 1863. *(c)* In 1865, members of Company E, Fourth U.S. Colored Troops, were stationed there.

THE UNION SOLDIERS ADDRESS

TO THE FLAG.

The following Poem was composed and written by JOHN Y. WREN, of Battery G. Second Artillery, Pennsylvania Volunteers, while acting Canonier, at one of the 32 pound Guns at Fort Lincoln, D. C., December 2d, 1863, and Firing the National Salute, in Honor of the Godess of Liberty being raised upon the Dome of the National Capitol of The United States of America:

When freemens' hearts, with one accord,
Are bound by Freedom's claim,
Like torrents down the mountain gorge,
They sweep both hill and plain.
To guard the sire girds on the sword,
The boy becomes the man,
And mothers join with them the pledge
That bound men in Lang Syne.

CHORUS—

For old Lang Syne true hearts
Will ne'er forget Lang Syne,
We love the flag our fathers left
For us in old Lang Syne.

That dear old flag amidst her folds,
We see the dawning day,
The red, the white, the Blue, those stars
They speak to us and say
Man's heaven born rights may be assailed,
By brothers of our kind,
But heaven smiles while we defend
Our Union of Lang Syne.

CHORUS—

Why will the traitors dare pull down,
Our Nation's God given shield,
Why strike! with rebels hands that flag,
On bloody battle field.
Our Union is our Nation's strength.
Makes noble deeds to shine;
Republics died but ours will live,
We have a loved Lang Syne.

CHORUS—

Foes from abroad for gold or power,
May join with foes within,
Our Constitution based on truth,
Defy them all combined.
Our Union's laws the rights of man,
From shore to shore will shine,
As brothers fall, we'll fill the ranks,
And keep pure old Lang Syne.

CHORUS—

God speed our army in the field,
Our navy on the sea,
With hearts of steel strong may they wield,
The blows that make men free.
To meet the foes, and drive them back,
And raise our flag enshrined,
O'er every State we swear 'twill float
In honor of Lang Syne.

CHORUS—

God bless our noble President,
And Governors of our land,
Give strength to our brave officers,
Who lead our Union band.
Be kind to dear ones around our home,
Who will brave soldiers join,
When peace proclaimed our country rings
With joys of old Lang Syne.

CHORUS—

Now comrades dear, with armor on,
Let's not forget the prize,
That warmed the heart of Washington
Like him immortalize.
Our Nation's honor sovereign rights,
With hearts and hands combined,
To raise aloft through seas of blood
Our flag of old Lang Syne.

CHORUS—

And now amidst our cannon's boom,
We raise our emblem high,
Long may she grace our Nation's dome
The Godess of Liberty.
Our noble dead thy motto loved.
When dying did resign,
Immortal words unsullied keep
Our flag of old Lang Syne.

CHORUS—

The loyal hearts who sleep in death
And those in ranks resigned,
The braves reward a world's thanks
Will cause to be enshrined.
Your glorious battles fought and won,
Expands the scroll of fame,
Yes, children yet unborn will sing
Your brave deeds of old Lang Syne.

CHORUS—

Heaven guard our Union, bless her sons,
With feelings all sublime,
Feelings of Christian, patriot, friend,
Companions of brave men.
Draw mother's hearts by chords of love
Around the throne entwine,
Bless, bless, while we Redeem our flag,
Our flag of old Lang Syne.

CHORUS—

For old Lang Syne true hearts,
Will ne'er forget Lang Syne,
We love the flag our fathers left
For us in old Lang Syne.

Sold only by W. W. PELL, Camden, N. J.
PRICE THREE CENTS.

b

c

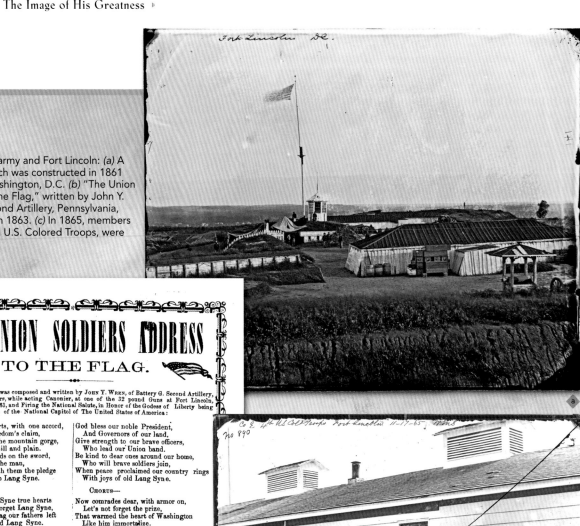

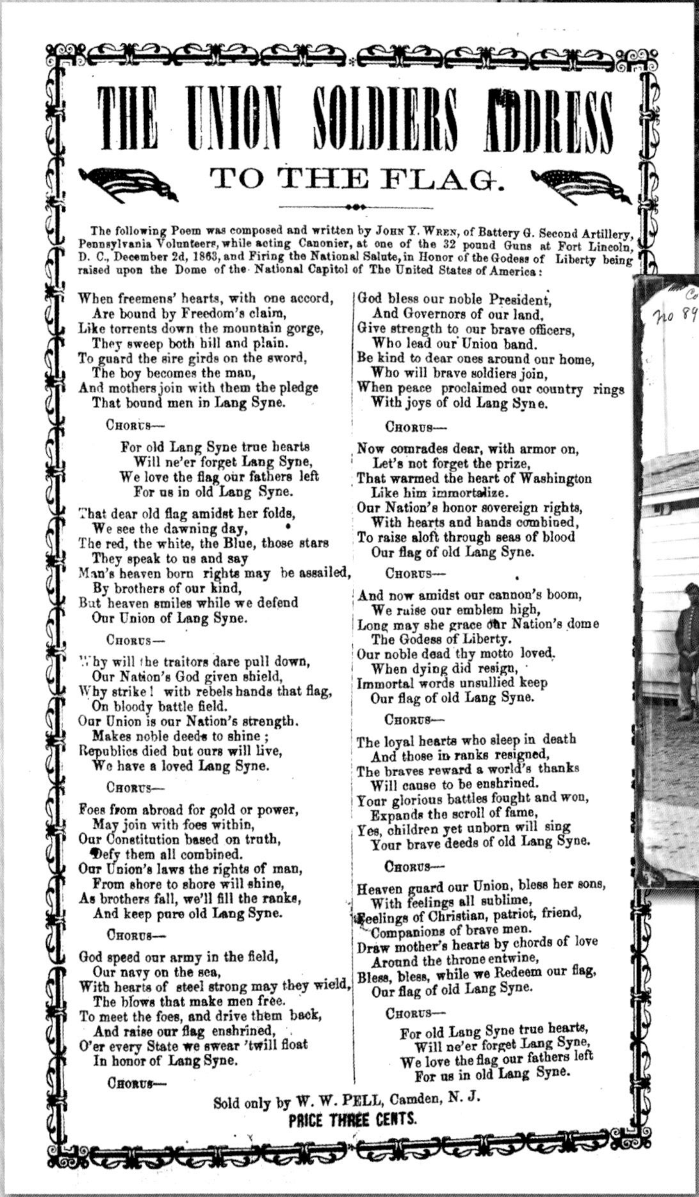

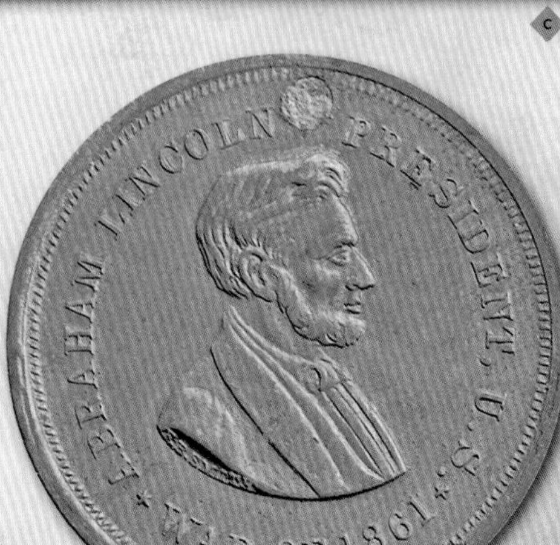

Fig. 1.79. New York diesinker F.B. Smith and others produced private-issue identification badges ("dog tags") in 1861. Soldiers could have their names inscribed on the reverse. This example (King-182) was holed for suspension but later plugged.

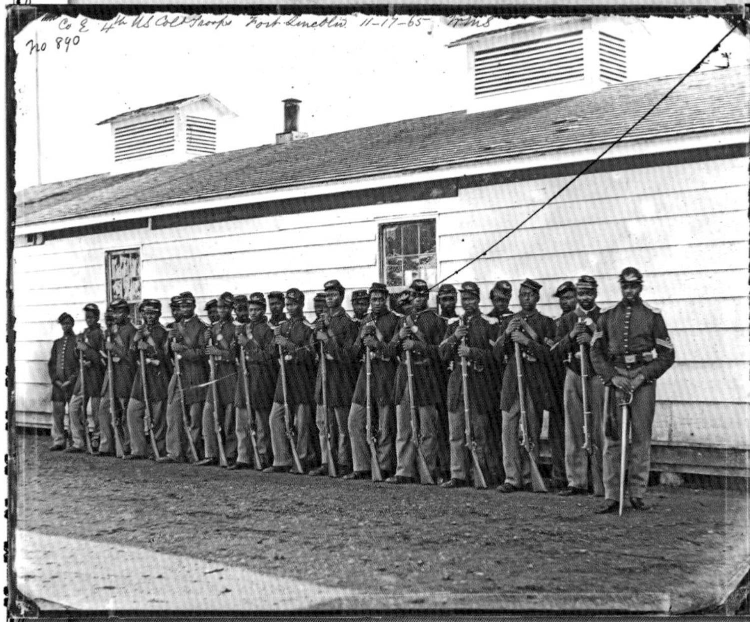

the completed U.S. Capitol dome on December 2, 1863. Following a 35-gun salute from a field battery on Capitol Hill at 20 minutes past noon, the ring of forts resounded with additional salutes in a sequence specified by special orders.[28]

1861 MAY 7. Lincoln accepts honorary citizenship number one from the Republic of San Marino, which offered the honor to the president-elect on January 22. "Although your dominion is small your state is nevertheless one of the most honored in all history," he wrote.

1861 MAY 14. Lincoln appoints James Pollock to be Mint director.

1861 JULY 4. Lincoln convenes Congress, and requests 400,000 men and $400 million dollars. Congress responded by giving the president more than he'd asked for.

1861 JULY 11. Treasury Secretary Chase writes Lincoln and reminds him that he promised to come "to the Treasury Building and let our artist take your photograph. He thinks he can beat any body; and I wish to have him try. Your countenance must do its part towards making our Treasury note current."[29]

1861 JULY 17. Congress authorizes $50 million in Treasury Notes, in denominations of $10 to $50, payable on demand. Realizing its mistake, Congress amended this legislation quickly, authorizing also $5 Demand Notes on August 5.

1861 JULY 25. The Treasury contracts with ABNCo to print Treasury Notes.[30]

1861 AUGUST 3. Josiah Perham forwards to Lincoln a specimen of the medal presented at Boston to Sixth Regiment Massachusetts Volunteers two days previously.[31]

1861 AUGUST 6. The *New York Times* reports that the plates for the $5, $10, and $20 Demand Notes are "in preparation by the American Bank Note Company of this City; but it will be a fortnight, perhaps before the work is completed."

1861 AUGUST 9. Treasury Secretary Chase writes President Lincoln that Chase is "obliged to go to New York today to arrange for loan."[32]

1861 AUGUST 24. First Demand Note, a $10 note with Lincoln's portrait, is issued by the Treasury Department in Washington, D.C., to Treasury Secretary Chase, who then delivers it to financier Jay Cooke.

1861 AUGUST 26. Charles Burt's Lincoln image (fig. 1.80) cascades through the marketplace on the faces of the newly introduced $10 greenbacks payable on demand in coin. Due to an oversight (the register and the treasurer could not really hand-sign all those notes), clerks hired for this purpose wrote "For the" with their signatures on the notes (fig. 1.81a). As soon as new plates could be prepared, "For the" was printed on the bills (fig. 1.81b). Notes were payable by assistant

Fig. 1.80. Charles Burt's Abraham Lincoln security portrait for ABNCo, die number 141 (approved March 30, 1861), is *the* most important engraving of Lincoln. Burt's engraving circulated on millions of $10 Demand Notes and Legal Tender Notes during and after the Civil War. Its importance, however, is more than a matter of numbers of impressions. This is the official government portrait of Lincoln observed by the man and woman on the street and passed hand-to-hand repeatedly in the marketplace for nearly a decade. Moreover, this is the picture of Lincoln that the president himself carried in his pocket. As Lincoln historian Carl Sandburg has observed, "on the $10 bill a steel engraving representing Lincoln's face became familiar to all who looked at it." Burt's Lincoln was *the* Lincoln.

Fig. 1.81. Lincoln came to be known to the American public primarily on the face of the $10 Demand Notes: *(a)* note with hand-signed "For the" (the rarest of the Demand Notes, denoted Friedberg 6-A); and *(b)* with "For the" printed in the signature blocks (Friedberg-7).

treasurers of the United States at Boston, New York City, Philadelphia, Cincinnati and St. Louis. Some 2,003,000 of these $10 notes with Lincoln's portrait were circulated. All Demand Notes are scarce; only about 140 of the $10 denomination are believed extant, and those with the handwritten "For the" are particularly rare.

1861 AUGUST 28. Hiram Prather sends President Lincoln examples of the new "Confederate" currency. Prather's original letter and the notes have apparently been lost, but the insert that contained the notes is among the Lincoln papers at the Library of Congress. Prather wrote: "PS inclosed [*sic*] find some of Gen. [Robert Selden] Garnetts [*sic*] currency which was take [*sic*] from his safe after we killed him at Carrick's ford VA HP Respectfully transmitted to the President War Dept Aug. 25/61."[33] Apparently these notes were wrapped in the letter for an extended period, because the image of the face of a $1 note of the Fairmont Bank, Fairmont, Virginia (now West Virginia) was offset on the letter sheet. According to research by authors Keith Littlefield and Richard Jones, all the $1 notes of this issue were evidently captured in the raid by Colonel Prather and his Indiana troops and carted

off as souvenirs. All the circulated notes seen today were signed by someone not connected with the bank. "It was apparently popular to put your own name, or some kind of made up name on them. A few years ago a large quantity of uncut sheets of them turned up," Jones wrote to this author. According to Littlefield, General Garnett was killed in mid-July, 1861.

Hiram Prather was a career army officer. On February 14, 1873, a Mr. Pratt of the Senate Committee on Claims submitted Report No. 437, accompanied by S1591, a bill "for the relief of Hiram Prather, late lieutenant-colonel of the Sixth Regiment Indiana Volunteer Infantry." The bill was for back pay from August 2, 1861, to September 20, 1861, for services in the reorganization of the regiment.[34] This claim kicked around House and Senate committees for a year until the Senate Committee on Military Affairs turned thumbs down and reported it adversely on May 2, 1874. Born the same year as Lincoln (1809), Colonel Prather had died March 27, 1874 of pneumonia.[35]

1861 OCTOBER 3. Lincoln inscribes a photograph to Mrs. Lucy G. Speed, mother of his friend Joshua F. Speed, "from whose pious hand

Fig. 1.82. Colorful red-and-blue patriotic covers were published in abundance at the beginning of the war: *(a)* Philadelphia printer J. Magee's cover (Milgram AL-300), depicting Lincoln and General Scott carving up meat while old dog "Jeff" begs for table scraps; *(b)* G.M. Whipple and A.A. Smith's very clever, ornate cover (Milgram AL-301) depicting Lincoln as an alchemist (note the "Jeff. Davis Seasoning" at upper left, with the traitor being hanged); *(c)* another Magee cover (Milgram AL-287), depicting Lincoln holding the Constitution as he consults with Generals McClellan and Scott.

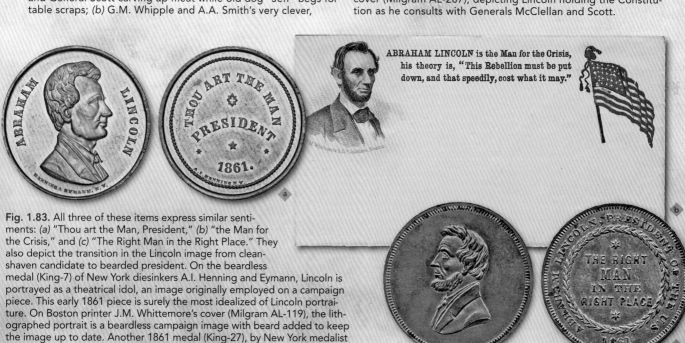

Fig. 1.83. All three of these items express similar sentiments: *(a)* "Thou art the Man, President," *(b)* "the Man for the Crisis," and *(c)* "The Right Man in the Right Place." They also depict the transition in the Lincoln image from clean-shaven candidate to bearded president. On the beardless medal (King-7) of New York diesinkers A.I. Henning and Eymann, Lincoln is portrayed as a theatrical idol, an image originally employed on a campaign piece. This early 1861 piece is surely the most idealized of Lincoln portraiture. On Boston printer J.M. Whittemore's cover (Milgram AL-119), the lithographed portrait is a beardless campaign image with beard added to keep the image up to date. Another 1861 medal (King-27), by New York medalist George H. Lovett, shows a fully bearded Lincoln.

I accepted the present of an Oxford Bible twenty years ago." This photograph (known as the "Speed" photo; fig. 1.84) was likely taken by James E. McClees of Philadelphia, and was duplicated widely.

1861 NOVEMBER 20. In addition to its use on federal bonds, the NBNCo Lincoln portrait first appears on state-chartered bank notes on the $1 note of Merchants Bank of Trenton, New Jersey (fig. 1.85a; Wait 2342A/B). On April 8, 1862, it appeared on $1, $2 (fig. 1.85b), and $3 notes of the Lincoln Bank, Oneida County, New York (Haxby-NY655); circa 1862 on $2 notes of Bank of Pottstown, Pennsylvania (fig. 1.85c; Hoober-333–2); and from early May 1862 on $1 notes of Bank of Commerce, Georgetown, D.C. (fig. 1.85d; Haxby-DC70).

1861 DECEMBER 21. President Lincoln signs a law authorizing the Navy Medal of Valor, thus permitting 200 medals to be prepared.

1862 FEBRUARY. To familiarize the public with the newly introduced federal paper money, *Harper's Monthly* publishes a detailed, illustrated article on how the new notes are engraved and printed. Included is an illustration of a $10 Demand Note depicting Lincoln (see fig. 1.87).

1862 FEBRUARY 10. Assayer Conrad Wiegand reports to Abraham Lincoln on patronage affairs at the San Francisco Mint.[36]

1862 FEBRUARY 12. The Act of February 12, 1862[37] (coincidentally, Lincoln's birthday) is signed. At the end of the previous year, the government coffers were bare. More money was required, and Congress considered an additional issue of $50 million and then $100 million in Demand Notes.[38] But in the end, legislators added only another $10 million by the act, while legislation to provide for Treasury Notes with legal-tender status was being formulated.[39] In addition, a cash shortage resulted in the recirculation of 3,000 Demand Notes in the $10 denomination. In all, 2,003,000 ten-dollar Demand Notes were issued. However, the question of authorizing additional issues of Demand Notes persisted even after the authorization of the Legal Tender Notes. Due to arrearages in payment to the soldiers, the House Military Committee pushed for an additional authorization of Demand Notes exclusively for troop payments as late as January 1863.[40] In the interim, a $5 Demand Note essay by NBNCo (possibly engraved by George Baldwin) was prepared. This essay note

Fig. 1.84. The "Speed photo" (Ostendorf-55) is among the most enigmatic of the Lincoln photographs. The original photo, taken in late spring 1861 by an unknown photographer, derived its nickname from a copy Lincoln inscribed to Lucy Speed, mother of Lincoln's friend Joshua Speed. Some examples, such as this *CDV (a)*, bear the backmark of James E. McClees, Philadelphia. The basis of the somewhat similar engraved image *(b)* was an 1863 photograph by Thomas Le Mere at Brady's Washington gallery on April 17, 1863 (Ostendorf-69). In it, Lincoln holds the Constitution and tramples secession. Boston lithographer J.H. Bufford used McClees's image to serve as the basis of his emancipation print *(c)*. Note Lincoln's hand rests on the table on the top of his Emancipation Proclamation.

employed a vignette of Lincoln quite similar to, but still distinct from, that which the company was using on the bonds it printed for the government. Ironically, this currency portrait was also based on the C.S. German photograph, although the engraver flopped it so that Lincoln faces to the observer's left (fig. 1.88).

1862 FEBRUARY 25. Congress authorizes $150 million in Legal Tender Notes, $50 million of which are to be in lieu of the Demand Notes previously issued. As may be seen, the design on the face of the $10 Legal Tender Note is very similar to that on the $10 Demand Note, except that the words "on demand" are omitted and the signatures of the register and treasurer are engraved. Legal Tender Notes also bear a red Treasury seal. These notes were not receivable in payment of duties on imports, nor were they payable by the government for interest upon its obligations, which remained payable in coin. The back of the first issue authorizes holders to exchange notes for six-percent bonds.

1862 MARCH 4. The American Bank Note Co., using the Lincoln image from the $10 federal bills, prints specimen $5 notes for Eagle Bank, Providence, Rhode Island, with issue date March 4 186__ (Durand 1263; see fig. 1.91a). Before the war, paper money in the United States was generally issued by state- or federally chartered banks, private banks, and other corporations. Bankers wanted this important Lincoln picture to adorn their banknotes, too, to make their notes appear as valid as government paper. This particular attempt by ABNCo, however, was thwarted (the heavy boot of the U.S. Treasury appears to have been the reason); no notes in this denomination were issued, although other denominations in the same series by ABNCo were circulated.

Fig. 1.85. Shut out of printing Demand Notes, NBNCo used its excellent Lincoln bond portrait on commercial work for state-chartered banks. The first such bank note was issued on November 20, 1861, for the Merchants Bank, Trenton, New Jersey, $1 note, plates A and B (Wait-2342A-B). This is the most common nonfederal note with Lincoln's portrait, as more than 5,000 notes were printed. A numbered but unissued remainder with plate-registration mark in selvedge (a) is shown. Meanwhile, NBNCo continued unfettered use of its Lincoln-portrait die on state bank notes. It produced $1, $2, and $3 notes for Lincoln Bank, Oneida County, New York, dated April 8, 1862. The $2 note (Haxby-NY655G4) is shown (b), as is a $1 note (c) for the Bank of Commerce, Georgetown, D.C. (Haxby-DC70G12b). The D.C. note issue was large; the Lincoln Bank issue very large. Presumptively the last commercial bank note printed by NBNCo using its Lincoln-portrait bond die was this $2 bill (d) created for the Bank of Pottstown, Pennsylvania (Hoober-322-2). The bank converted to a national bank in 1864, and virtually all its notes were redeemed. Haxby reports all denominations "SENC" (surviving example not confirmed), but this cancelled, partially filled-in remainder was in a Heritage Auctions sale.

Fig. 1.86. Special effects did not begin with George Lucas, nor image manipulation with Adobe Photoshop. Composite photos like this fabulous 1861 *CDV* of Lincoln and his officer corps were in great demand. This outstanding example shows the president and 41 officers, most of them generals or admirals (e.g., Scott is number 2, McClellan 3, Burnside 9, and Butler 10). Although it is difficult to read the legend, it appears to state "Photographed by J. Macy and published by C. Magnus, New York."

Fig. 1.87. *Harper's New Monthly Magazine* described the new federal currency in its February 1862 issue.

The same circumstances are evident with $10 proof notes of the Rutland County Bank, Vermont, issue-dated July 15, 1862 (Coulter 42; see fig. 1.91b). None were issued, although other denominations of this series were indeed circulated. If issued, this note would have been the latest-dated known Lincoln state-bank note.

Lincoln was the first U.S. president to appear on federal paper money issued in this country. His selection was a patriotic act, and also a political one. Impressing the image of the ruler on the coin of the realm was as old as the ancient empires, who knew a thing or two about money as a medium of indoctrination. Because it was official government portraiture, the Charles Burt ABNCo engraving of Lincoln on greenbacks ($10 Demand Notes) was increasingly becoming the most important image of the nation's president in everyday view, and thus in the minds of the public. Even prominent Lincoln biographer Carl Sandburg, in his 1940 Pulitzer Prize–winning Lincoln biography, *Abraham Lincoln: The War Years,* reproduced the image of Lincoln die number 141 from a $10 Demand Note and offered this insightful opinion: "On the 50-cent greenbacks and on the $10 bill a steel engraving representing Lincoln's face became familiar to all who looked at it."

The effects of the $10 note image on secondary media can be measured in other ways, as well. Engravings, prints, and *CDVs* based on the same model proliferated. For the man and woman on the street, Lincoln was the man on the $10 bill.

1862 MARCH 5. The issue of Demand Notes ends, according to U.S. treasurer James Gilfillan.[41]

1862 MARCH 6. Lincoln sends up to the Hill a special message to Congress urging a joint resolution to compensate all states for abolition of slavery as a war measure and to ensure public safety. Such a resolution was passed by both houses, and signed by Lincoln. When the states failed to act, Lincoln drafted an executive order to free slaves in rebellious districts, but had to wait impatiently for the right political and military climate to announce his purposes.

1862 MARCH 15. President Abraham Lincoln makes his first purchase of government bonds: $14,200 in seven-percent, 30-year Treasury Notes.[42]

1862 MARCH 31. The *New York Times* reports that "the Bank Note Companies of this City are understood to have completed the engraved plates for the new Notes of the U.S. for Circulation as lawful money under the Act of Feb. 25th."[43]

1862 APRIL 13. Newspaper headlines read: "Big Haul of Counterfeiters." Within months of the issue of $10 Demand Notes, counterfeiters (or "koniackers," in the parlance of the time) had jumped on them, engraving and printing their own bogus copies. Counterfeit $10 Demand Notes were discovered in St. Louis in April 1862.

1862 APRIL 16. President Abraham Lincoln purchases $2,000 more seven-percent, 30-year Treasury Notes.[44]

1862 APRIL 24. President Lincoln taps George Boutwell for the position of commissioner of internal revenue—an important post, since it was up to Boutwell to implement the internal revenue acts, secure revenue stamps, and promulgate regulations on the many items that fell under the tax code. Additionally, it was Boutwell whom Treasury Secretary Salmon P. Chase later designated to remedy the difficulties the Treasury Department was experiencing with the Post Office Department (in July of that year, Congress monetized postage stamps in a moment of panic over the shortage of small change in the country). Further, it was Boutwell who considered John Gault's plan for the U.S. Treasury to issue Encased Postage under his patent, but who instead chose to issue the Postage Currency recommended by U.S. treasurer Francis E. Spinner.[45]

1862 JUNE 7. Treasury Secretary Chase reports to House Committee on Ways and Means that virtually all Demand Notes are held because of their premium value and not in circulation.[46] He recommends a further issue of $150 million in Legal Tender Notes.

1862 JUNE 11. Congress authorizes another $150 million in Legal Tender notes, including notes of small denominations (under $5). Notes of the $1, $2, and $3 denominations are anticipated, but only the first two are issued. Several authors have made a great deal of the fact that Lincoln's rival, Salmon P. Chase, appears on the $1 note, a more prolific denomination than the $10 note on which Lincoln appears. It is true that about 2.5 times as many $1 notes as $10 notes were issued, but the case for devious motives on Chase's part seems flimsy at best. After all, both Lincoln and Chase appeared on various denominations.

1862 JUNE 23. Lincoln vetoes an act repealing the prohibition on banks' issuing small-denomination notes in Washington, D.C., to imminently alleviate the small-change crunch. Congress had just authorized small Legal Tender Notes, and eventually would authorize notes for fractional parts of the dollar as well.

1862. Lincoln's appearance, demeanor, and motives are vilified in the press. The London *Punch* was especially vitriolic toward Lincoln personally and his motives for fighting the war. Across the pond the conflict was viewed as almost entirely about slavery, and Britain's columns and cartoons reflect this view. Other publications, such as *Vanity Fair, Leslie's Illustrated,* and *Budget of Fun,* also jumped on Lincoln's back. Baltimore political cartoonists L.H. Stephens and Adalbert Volck were savage. Lincoln, who has been called by one of his closest friends "a wiry, awkward giant," was a sitting duck for the jests and jibes of editorial writers and political cartoonists. He was nearly six feet, four inches tall, and most men came barely up to his shoulder. His arms dangled, giving rise to simian cartoons. His facial features, unruly hair, and ruffled clothing were all open to caricature. Lincoln's Western upbringing, off-putting humor, and personality also brought forth sharp jabs. Cartoon impressions of Lincoln were not limited to periodicals. *Cartes de visite* and drawings of various kinds were mass produced, sold cheaply, and reached all classes of society. The highbrow thought him beneath them. The reserved saw him as a clown. Political enemies consistently underestimated his savvy.

1862. Even Lincoln's physiognomy is open to interpretation. L.M. Smith issues a pamphlet on "The Great American Crisis," which in reality was a phrenological assessment of Lincoln's character.[47]

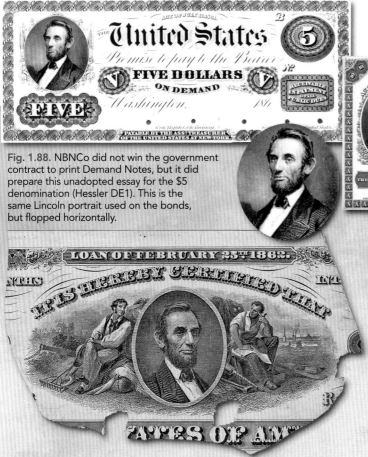

Fig. 1.88. NBNCo did not win the government contract to print Demand Notes, but it did prepare this unadopted essay for the $5 denomination (Hessler DE1). This is the same Lincoln portrait used on the bonds, but flopped horizontally.

Fig. 1.89. When more money was needed, Congress authorized Legal Tender Notes exchangeable for U.S. bonds, but not payable for duties on imports. Burt's Lincoln image continued on the $10 denomination (Friedberg-93).

Fig. 1.90. United States bonds continued to be the primary outlet for NBNCo's Lincoln portrait. Shown is a February 25, 1862, $10,000 five-percent, 20-year registered bond remnant (BEP die no. MISC3241/1268, cancelled in 1871).

Fig. 1.92. Boston medalist Joseph Merriam muled his small-size Lincoln campaign medal with a reverse commemorating the capture of Newbern, North Carolina, and struck from copper recovered from the turpentine works there (Bolen 212-372a).

Fig. 1.91. ABNCo attempted to use Charles Burt's Lincoln $10 portrait die on state-chartered bank notes, just as its competitor NBNCo was using its similar Lincoln-portrait bond die for commercial work. The ABNCo project, however, never got off the ground. The few known specimens consist of the following: (a) unissued specimens made in 1862 of a $5 note on Eagle Bank, Providence, Rhode Island (Durand-1263) dated March 4, 186(2); and (b) a $10 note proof on the Rutland County Bank, Vermont (Coulter-42) dated July 15, 1862.

Fig. 1.93. The ten-spot was the most widely counterfeited note. The present author has cataloged more than two dozen different $10 Legal Tender Note fakes. Shown are two that eventually were spotted: (a) Reed AL-CF93-13 was cut-cancelled four times as COUNTERFEIT, while (b) Reed AL-CF93-2 has "Counterfeit" hand-written across its face.

1862. "Lincoln hireling"—that is, a Northern soldier—becomes a term of derision by Southerners and Copperheads (anti-war Southern sympathizers).

1862. Lincoln finds a more restrained reception in the pages of *Harper's Weekly,* the largest of the illustrated periodicals. In the 1860 election, the publication had supported Douglas, but after Lincoln's election hitched itself to Lincoln's wagon. Many considered the tabloid a Republican tout sheet. It certainly was supportive.

1862. "Old Abe," a bald eagle named after President Lincoln, becomes the mascot of Company C, Eighth Wisconsin Regiment (fig. 1.99). He would accompany the troops into battle on three dozen occasions. "He enjoyed the excitement . . . In battle he was almost constantly flapping his wings, having his mouth wide open, and many a time would scream with wild enthusiasm," a historian recorded. Old Abe also participated in ceremonial events such as parades. In 1865 Joseph O. Barrett wrote the *History of "Old Abe," the Live War Eagle of the Eighth Regt. Wisconsin Volunteers.* The book

THE AMERICAN DIFFICULTY.

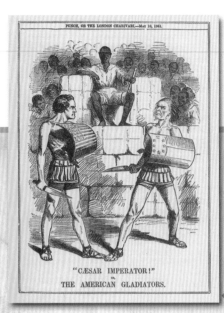

"CÆSAR IMPERATOR!"
THE AMERICAN GLADIATORS.

Fig. 1.94. Some periodicals saw the Civil War exclusively as a conflict over slavery. *Punch* was particularly brutal in its characterizations; *(a)* in its May 11, 1861, issue Lincoln—engulfed in smoke—ruminates before the fireplace: "What a nice White House this would be, if it were not for the Blacks." *(b)* In its May 18 issue *Punch* showed the American gladiators Lincoln and Davis in the arena before a Black audience. *(c)* Even

harsher was the October 12, 1861, *Frank Leslie's Illustrated* commentary, after General John C. Fremont had declared martial law in Missouri and freed the slaves of insurrectionists. In a choppy sea, Lincoln clings to his life preserver and pushes away a Black man, while Fremont's proclamation floats away in Lincoln's hat. Lincoln tells the slave "I'm sorry to have to drop you, Sambo, but this concern won't carry us both!"

THE NEW ORLEANS PLUM.

Fig. 1.95. The papers berated Lincoln over the loss of New Orleans. *(a)* The May 24, 1862, issue of *Punch* showed him as a simpleton—$250 million later, the plum of New Orleans fell into his hands. Major General Benjamin F. Butler's controversial administration in New Orleans was problematical for Lincoln, but Butler was thorough and effective before being relieved. *Harper's Weekly's*

January 17, 1863, issue *(b)* approved of Butler's "scrubbing," but showed Lincoln reaching for his general's implements. As usual, *Leslie's Budget of Fun* took the president to task on the race issue in its February 1863 issue *(c)*: Lincoln is inebriated on (Horace) "Greely's Abolition (T)onic," dreaming of minstrel entertainment, while Jeff Davis is musing about hanging Old Ben Butler.

was published in Chicago by Alfred L. Sewell and dedicated to the president after whom the bird was named. At the North Western Sanitary Fair, June 1865, an illustrated pamphlet titled *The Army of the American Eagle* was sold by children to earn "commissions" in the paper army. A child who collected a dollar became a corporal; $10, a captain; $400, a major general; with other ranks for other amounts in between.[48] Following the war, the eagle was presented to the State of Wisconsin, where he was provided special quarters in the basement of the state capitol. Old Abe died in 1881, and was stuffed

and displayed at the Capitol until a fire in 1904. Since then he has been represented by replicas.

1862 FEBRUARY. Lincoln writes composer Charles Rehm: "It gives me great pleasure to acknowledge the receipt of your favour of the 29th January, accompanying copies of your 'National Union March.' Permit me to thank you cordially for the honor done me, and the kind feeling evinced by you." The cover of Rehm's march (fig. 1.100) bears Lincoln's $10 bill portrait and stirring patriotic motifs.

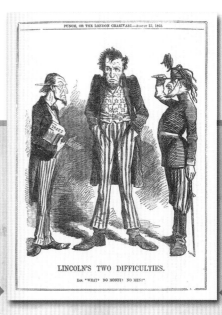

Fig. 1.96. *Punch's* invective continued in 1862, portraying Lincoln *(a)* as a treed coon in its January 11 issue; *(b)* negotiating for a little Black child in its April 5 issue; and *(c)* strapped for the sinews of war, men, and money, in its August 23 issue.

Fig. 1.97. Pressure on Lincoln's handling of the race issue continued unabated during 1862. In the February 1, 1862, issue of *Leslie's Budget of Fun*, Frank Bellew's front-page illustration shows Lincoln cuddling a white sheep while the bleating black sheep of slavery blares in his ear. "Oh, Thunder!" Long Abe moans, "Here's that darned black sheep again!"

Fig. 1.98. John Tenniel's illustration in the August 9, 1862, issue of *Punch* anticipated Lincoln's actions: "One Good Turn Deserves Another" shows minstrel Abe offering a resolute Black man a gun and a bayonet. "Why I du declare it's my dear old friend Sambo," Lincoln chirps. "Course you'll fight for us, Sambo, lend us a hand, old hoss, du!"

Fig. 1.99. An 1865 ballad published in Milwaukee by H.N. Hempsted memorializes the exploits of "Old Abe," the mascot of the Eighth Wisconsin Regiment.

Fig. 1.100. Charles Rehm's 1862 "Our National Union March" was dedicated to Lincoln, and the cover bears a similar portrait to the official Lincoln image on the $10 Treasury Note. Lincoln wrote the composer, thanking him for the honor.

1862 July 16. The *New York Evening Post* publishes the poem "We are Coming Father Abraham, Three Hundred Thousand More," with no author's name. Many presumed that it was written by William Cullen Bryant, the longtime editor of the *Post.* He was one of the founders of the Republican Party and a staunch supporter of Lincoln. The poem became popular and was set to music by a half-dozen composers, including Stephen Foster. On some sheet music (fig. 1.101) Bryant is credited with the lyrics.[49] A letter to the editor, written by James Herbert Morse and published in the *New York Times* on August 24, 1901, credits abolitionist James Sloan Gibbons and says that "about a month after the publication in the *Evening Post,* when the song was becoming well known, Mr. Bryant inserted a note in the *Post* giving the true authorship." Charles Grobe of New York published a variant of the song reading "Six Hundred Thousand More." By war's end, the version by L.O. Emerson had sold an estimated two million copies. Several greenback songs parodied this song.

Chicago publisher George F. Root issued "Father Abraham's Reply to the Six Hundred Thousand."

1862 July 22. Lincoln convenes his cabinet at the White House to hear him read his draft of the Emancipation Proclamation, which declares that all persons held as slaves in states still in rebellion as of January 1 "shall be then, thenceforward, and forever, free." This course of action differed from Lincoln's prewar concept of gradual, compensated emancipation and perhaps a repatriation to west Africa. As events turned out, though, Lincoln came to the conclusion that such a course was a military necessity and would be viewed in Europe favorably. Carpenter's painting *First Reading of the Emancipation Proclamation* was intended to capture that transitional moment in this nation's history.

1862 August 1. W.P. Carpenter, Utica, New York, issues 25¢ notes, the first dated merchant scrip with the image of current president

Fig. 1.101. Another 1862 musical composition, "We are coming Father Abra'am" (published in Boston by Oliver Ditson), set poet William Cullen Bryant's verse to music.

Fig. 1.102. Interest in Lincoln and his cabinet members is evidenced by this *Harper's Weekly* illustration from its July 13, 1861, issue (a), and by Milgram AL-171, Philadelphia printer Samuel C. Upham's overall cover design (b). Note the prominence allocated to Treasury Secretary Salmon P. Chase and Secretary of State William Seward, Lincoln's principal rivals for the Republican nomination. The periodical illustration shows Lincoln flanked by Chase (seated) and Seward (standing). Upham gives primacy to General Winfield Scott, but Chase and Seward occupy cardinal positions at 3 o'clock and 6 o'clock, respectively.

Abraham Lincoln (Harris 130/131). The notes were printed by Ferd. Mayer & Co. in New York City, and the portrait is strikingly similar to the $10 pose. Some later notes are overprinted in red. Ironically, August 1, 1862, is also the first day the Postage Currency circulated, and is the printed date on $1 and $2 Legal Tender Notes.

1862 CIRCA. Chicago lithographer Ed Mendel prints a 50¢ note for Quinby Market, Columbus, Kentucky (see fig. 1.103b). Presently only a single unissued remainder or essay of this issue, punch canceled, and a single issued note is known. The present author acquired the essay out of the Herb and Martha Schingoethe collection. Since it has Mendel's beardless Lincoln portrait, which appeared on Mendel's campaign covers, the note may date earlier than the small-change shortage of summer and fall 1862.

1862 AUGUST 12. Minnesota sculptor Salathiel Ellis receives design patent D1653 for his medallion of President Lincoln. It is likely that this is the same portrait employed on the official Abraham Lincoln peace medal (Julian IP-38). These silver medals were presented to principal chiefs of the various Native American tribes as tokens of friendship.

1862 SEPTEMBER 1. John Pipher, Manhattan, Kansas, issues $1, $2 (Whitfield 359/360), and possibly $3 scrip with Lincoln's image, printed by Middleton, Strobridge & Co., Cincinnati.

1862 SEPTEMBER. The Lincoln Indian peace portrait medal by Salathiel Ellis, who also engraved Indian peace medal portraits for James Buchanan, Franklin Pierce, and Millard Fillmore, is first struck at the U.S. Mint in Philadelphia (fig. 1.104; Julian IP-38). The reverse design is carried over from Joseph Willson's Buchanan medal. Silver medals were struck during the September 1862 to April 1863 time period, according to Mint-medal historian Bob Julian.[50] Bronze medals were restruck over time.

Fig. 1.103. A change shortage in 1862 resulted in a proliferation of merchant scrip, including several picturing Lincoln: *(a)* Quinby Market, 50 cents (Hughes-unlisted); *(b)* P. Vidvard, 15 cents (Harris-277); *(c)* W.P. Carpenter, 25 cents (Harris-132); *(d)* Parks House, Boston, 50 cents, variety payable in Bank Bills (unlisted); and *(e)* C. Dautremont, 50 cents, (Harris-4).

1862 SEPTEMBER 22. Following the Northern victory at Antietam, Lincoln reconvenes the cabinet on September 22 to refine his draft and issue a preliminary Emancipation Proclamation as an ultimatum for rebels to throw down their arms.

1862 SEPTEMBER 23. P. Vidvard, Utica, New York, issues 15¢ notes, printed by Ferd. Mayer & Co. and with Mayer's take on the $10 bill portrait (Harris 277; see fig. 1.103c).

1862 OCTOBER 3. Lincoln travels to Antietam to confront Maj. Gen. George McClellan and his slackness in following up his victory. A series of historic pictures taken that day by Alexander Gardner show the commander in chief in the field with "Little Mac" (fig. 1.105).

1862 OCTOBER 6. W.P. Carpenter, Utica, New York, emits a B Series second issue of his 25¢ scrip with Lincoln's portrait (see fig. 1-103a).

1862 NOVEMBER 1. A Massachusetts hotel, the Parks House in Boston, circulates 50¢ notes with Lincoln's portrait, lithographed by Louis Prang (see fig. 1.103d). Two varieties exist: redeemable in "Current Bank Bills" and redeemable in "U.S. Notes."

Fig. 1.104. The outstanding official medal of Lincoln's lifetime was his three-inch 1862 Indian Peace medal (Julian IP-38) produced at the U.S. Mint as gifts for Native American tribal allies. The overly ornate obverse portrait by engraver Salathiel Ellis was patented August 12, 1862, and the first pieces were struck in silver the following month. After eight impressions, Joseph Willson's reverse die (carried forward from the Buchanan medals) broke and a new reverse die was created without his name. More medals, such as this one, were struck in 1863. Ellis's portrait is justly criticized for Lincoln's soup-bowl haircut, aggressive beard, and smoking-jacket robes, but mostly for the unusual truncation that makes the bust look like a Weeble. Note that among the activities shown on the elaborate reverse is a stick-and-ball game, which many take to be an early version of baseball.

Fig. 1.105. The president's relationship with his commanding general George B. McClellan was a complex one that eventually devolved into McClellan's bid to unseat his commander in chief in the 1864 general election. Lincoln visited McClellan in the field at Antietam, Maryland, where they were photographed by Alexander Gardner on October 3, 1862 (image a, Ostendorf-62, and image b, Ostendorf-66).

1862 NOVEMBER 4. C. Dautremont, Angelica, New York, issues 50¢ notes (fig. 1.103e; Harris 4), printed by Ferd. Mayer & Co. with Mayer's Lincoln portrait.

1862 DECEMBER 1. Lincoln praises Congress for making Treasury Notes legal tender in his second State of the Union address. He also tells Congress that "suspension of specie payments by the banks make large issue of the U.S. notes unavoidable," and asks Congress to implement a national banking act. Lincoln's economic mentor was Philadelphia economist Henry Charles Carey (b. December 15, 1793; d. October 13, 1879).

1862 DECEMBER 29. Vinson Blanchard, Abington, Massachusetts, issues 50¢ notes with Lincoln's portrait; John J. Bohler, Charlestown, Massachusetts, issues 25¢ notes with the same portrait. Both are printed by Louis Prang.

1863 JANUARY 1. When the rebels refused to lay down their arms, Lincoln becomes "The Great Emancipator" with the force of his executive order freeing slaves in rebellious districts. Critics have pointed out that the proclamation by itself freed no slaves, and that it would take success on the battlefield and a constitutional amendment to do so—but church bells pealed in the North nevertheless.

On the January 4 at North Church, Salem, Massachusetts, minister Edmund B. Willson preached a sermon of the "Proclamation of Freedom." The next day, in Albany, New York, a grand demonstration was staged. Businesses were closed, and a 100-gun salute was fired.

1863 JANUARY 1. S. Cohn & Co., Boston, Massachusetts, issues 50¢ notes, lithographed by Louis Prang.

1863 JANUARY 24. *Harper's Weekly* lead illustrator Thomas Nast celebrates the Emancipation Proclamation with a double-truck (two-page) illustration in the January 24 issue (fig. 1.108). Titled *Emancipation,* Nast's central scene is a happy domestic gathering in a Black household. A portrait of "Pres. Lincoln" and a banjo hang on the wall near the hearth. According to the text accompanying the illustration: "On the wall hangs a portrait of President Lincoln, whom the family can not sufficiently admire and revere. They regard him with feeling akin to veneration, and in each heart there is honest love and gratitude for him." In the past, at left, are horrific scenes of slave life: capture, sale at public auction, flogging. At right are depictions of a hopeful future, including liberty, education, and wages. At bottom Father Time presents an infant to a joyful Negro father. The whole is surmounted by Thomas Crawford's statue representing freedom, which would soon adorn the U.S. Capitol dome.

Fig. 1.106. Charles Magnus's magnificent "Review of the Army" series cover (Milgram AL-220) didn't capture reality. In life, the 6-foot, 4-inch Lincoln towered over the diminutive general, but in Magnus's view McClellan is much the bigger man.

Fig. 1.107. *Punch* played the race card again in its issue of October 13, 1862, with John Tenniel's illustration "Abe Lincoln's Last Card." *Rouge et noir* (red and black) is a card game. Lincoln is playing a spade, a not-too-subtle commentary on Lincoln's explosive preliminary Emancipation Proclamation, issued September 22.

This print may seem insensitive to some today, but it was very popular at the time. The demand for Nast's drawing was so great that it was republished by a Philadelphia printer.[51] A large portrait of Lincoln was inserted at the bottom.

1863 CIRCA JANUARY. Continental Bank Note Co. forms in New York City in January to compete with ABNCo and NBNCo for U.S. Treasury printing contracts. The new company's first die is a portrait

of Abraham Lincoln (fig. 1.109a). Naturally, CBNCo, too, wanted its Lincoln to look like the C.S. German model, which was entrenched on both Wall Street and Main Street as the official imprimatur of the country's chief executive. The CBNCo engraver, possibly Joseph Ourdan, flopped the image and handled its details slightly differently, so that Lincoln faces the viewer's left, but the similarity of the pose is unmistakable. This portrait was employed on $100 Kansas Union military scrip from June 1, 1867 (fig. 1.109b; Whitfield 426),

Fig. 1.108. Lincoln's Emancipation Proclamation became effective January 1, 1863. *Harper's Weekly's* lead illustrator Thomas Nast contributed a double-truck (two page) illustration commemorating the event, which is discussed in detail in the text. *(a)* Philadelphia publisher S. Bott reprinted the popular illustration as a broadsheet with a large portrait of Lincoln replacing an allegorical scene at the bottom of the print. *(b)* In early 1863, a large steel die of an emancipated slave, his shackles broken, seated at the altar of Lincoln and Liberty, also celebrated the emancipation of a race. The die was produced by a bank-note company, presumably CBNCo in New York City.

and on the back of $1 City of Lincoln, Nebraska, municipal notes (illustrated in chapter 2) from about the 1870s. Of the latter, most printed were never legitimately issued because city officials were advised that they violated federal law. Sequestered for a period, they were "brought out" under false pretenses after having been signed and numbered fictitiously, with many artificially aged to appear as if they had been in circulation for an extended period of time. This vignette, paired with a portrait of young Queen Victoria, was also used on £50 first-mortgage bonds of the Great Republic Gold & Silver Mining Co. of Virginia, issue-dated July 25, 1867 (fig. 1.109c).

1863 JANUARY C. Almost as soon as it is formed, CNBCo (presumably) has die number 44 engraved to depict an emancipated slave family gathered around a virtual altar to the Great Emancipator himself. Early Lincoln collector and cataloger Andrew Boyd was very taken with this engraving. He owned an India-paper proof about which he wrote reverentially: "Size, 2 3/4 by 4 3/4. This is a proof on India paper of an exquisite little engraving, without title or engraver's name. . . . I call it 'Emancipation,' because a colored man sits upon the ground with clasped hands resting upon a portrait of Mr. Lincoln, at his feet lie broken shackles; opposite sits his wife and child and beside them two white doves. In the rear a female figure stands pointing to a Temple of Liberty, a sure promise of Freedom; while in the sky a rainbow is seen, suggestive of hope and a bright future."[52] The original large (by bank-note-company standards), six-inch by three-inch steel die for this engraving (renumbered V-38859 by ABNCo, which inherited the die when it bought out the originator) was sold June 20 and 21, 2007, in the Stack's auction of the Tory Prestera collection, from among items from the ABNCo archives. The cataloger wasn't off the mark in describing the lot as a desirable bit of Lincolniana. Even though this die was cracked in two places, it brought $2,530, a real bargain.

Fig. 1.109. CBNCo was formed in New York City in early 1863 to compete with the American and National bank-note companies for Treasury Department printing work. It's certainly no coincidence that this new company's very first security die (a) is based on the same model as NBNCo's bond die and ABNCo's Treasury Note die. The CBNCo engraver flopped the image so Lincoln faces left, but the resemblance is unmistakable. CBNCo's used its Lincoln-portrait die number 1 on (b) the $100 Union Military Scrip, Topeka, issue-dated June 1, 1867 (Whitfield-426); and on (c) an elaborate £50 Sterling bond for the Great Republic Gold & Silver Mining Co. of Virginia, incorporated January 25, 1867, along with a lovely vignette of the young Queen Victoria.

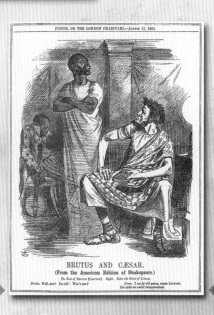

Fig. 1.110. Reaction to Lincoln's Emancipation Proclamation was mixed. (a) As might be expected, Baltimore secessionist Adalbert Volck attributed alcohol and demonic influences to Lincoln's trampling of the Constitution under foot in his print. (b) Somewhat similar is John Tenniel's *Punch* illustration in that periodical's August 15, 1863, issue. It likens the slain ghost of Caesar to "dy ebil genus," and predicts death for the "inimpressional" Black youth.

1863. Publishers of lithographs and engravings do not hesitate to express their sentiments toward the Emancipation Proclamation. For New York publisher of fine lithographs Currier & Ives, the religious significance of Lincoln's great freedom declaration is paramount. That firm's emancipation print boldly proclaimed the injunctive of Leviticus 35:10—"Proclaim liberty throughout all the land unto all the inhabitants thereof." In Baltimore, Southern sympathizer and Lincoln critic Adalbert Volck had a very different interpretation of the event. His engraving (fig. 1.110a) shows a demon-inspired, disheveled, and inebriated Lincoln stepping on the Constitution as he scribbles his proclamation.

1863 JANUARY. In addition to the day-by-day and month-by-month chronicles of the war's progress in the periodical press, publishers find a ready market for book-length histories. A large trade developed during the war in sequential volumes offering a broader perspective.

Two of the principal outlets were *Abbott's Civil War* and *Frank Moore's Rebellion Record* (fig. 1.111a). These volumes were illustrated by exquisitely engraved steel plates of "battle scenes . . . and portraits of distinguished men." Not surprisingly, the frontispiece of John S.C. Abbott's *History of the Civil War in America* (published in January 1863; fig. 1.111d), expertly engraved by J.C. McRae expressly for the book, was based on the same portrait as that on the $10 bill— by then very familiar to both artist and readers.

1863 MARCH 2. Abraham Lincoln receives $868 from a repentant thief. The born-again felon includes a message with his greenbacks: "Enclosed you will find eight hundred and sixty eight dollars which I came by in a dishonest manner and which I return to the United States through you. Being tempted, in an unguarded moment I consented to take it being very much in want of money but thanks be to my Saviour I was led by the influences of the Holy Ghost to see my

Fig. 1.111. Frank Moore's *Rebellion Record* was a popular compendium of anecdotes, poetry, and historical sagas published in 11 volumes from 1861 to 1868. *(a)* This hand-colored lithograph, based on the 1861 photo of the president-elect shown in figure 1.66, was the frontispiece of an early volume. *(b)* Actor Francis Ford strikes a similar pose in *The Heart of Lincoln*, Universal Gold Seal Co., which was released for Lincoln's birthday in February 1915. *(c)* Frank McGlynn Sr. looks askance in a not-dissimilar pose in *Abraham Lincoln*, Le DeForest Films, 1924. *(d)* The official $10 greenback portrait of Lincoln was mirrored by various commercial printmakers. In 1863 John C. McRae contributed this likeness as a frontispiece for John S.C. Abbott's very popular contemporary account *The History of the Civil War in America*. *(e)* This elegant Belgian silk portrait of Lincoln (Sullivan-Fischer AL-M2), mounted on card stock, was created in 1863 by Paul Durand from the same model as *The Rebellion Record's* frontispiece.

great sin and to return it to you as the representative of the United States." He continued: "Hoping you will pardon me in the name of the government you represent as I trust I will be pardoned by my Father who is in heaven (through the merits and mediation of Jesus Christ his son), I remain your penitent suppliant, Candide Secure." "Candide Secure" is Latin. It translates to "frankly fearless" or "openly fearless." The missive came from Brooklyn, New York, via Adams Express, marked "Private" and addressed to Lincoln himself. Lincoln forwarded the cash to U.S. treasurer Francis E. Spinner via his valet, William H. Johnson, with the notation "Stolen money returned" on the envelope. Lincoln requested acknowledgment from the treasurer. Spinner wrote: "Received, March 5, 1863, of A. Lincoln, President of the United States the sum mentioned within, in 'Green-backs.' F.E. Spinner."[53] This human-interest story was among the Abraham Lincoln papers that Robert Todd Lincoln turned over to the Library of Congress and the people of the United States. An archivist at the Library of Congress has made this comment on the letter and contents: "The origin of this document is as mysterious as that of any pseudonymous communication can be."

1863 MARCH 3. Congress authorizes an additional $150 million in Legal Tender Notes, totaling $450 million, and sets July 1 as the final day these notes can be exchange for bonds. This change in the law occasions a change in the clauses on the back of the Legal Tender Notes, which originally read, "This note . . . is exchangeable for U.S. six per cent twenty years [*sic*] bonds, redeemable . . . after five years." The new so-called Second Clause on the back of the Lincoln ten-spot (fig. 1.112) read, "This note . . . is receivable in payment of all

loans made to the United States." The highest amount in Legal Tender Notes actually outstanding occurred on January 3, 1864, when the total was $449,338,902.[54]

1863 MARCH 5. M.A. Meade, successor to Meade Bros. Daguerreotype Gallery, writes Lincoln:

> We are getting up medals in bronze 3-1/2 inches in diameter of the leading generals same style of the Clay & Webster medals in gold and bronze which we had the honor to present to Queen Victoria and Louis Napoleon. The Webster medal bears our name & the gold medals were presented to the families of Clay & Webster. We wish also to make a Medal of yourself & for that purpose would require a perfect profile of yourself[, but] we possess only a 3/4 face & front face. You will therefore if agreeable to you send us a profile taken on an Ambrotype plate one of the head about 2 inches in diameter at our expense & forward by express. When the Medal is finished we shall be most happy to forward one to you & are sure you will be well pleased with it. After a certain number of impressions are taken the Die will be destroyed so as to make the Medals rare and valuable. If you should conclude not to favour us we shall have to use the 3/4 face which will be rather difficult & we are afraid will hurt the likeness. Please reply by return mail & oblige.
>
> Yrs very respy-
>
> MA Meade, Successor to Meade Bros, 233 Broadway, New York, Established 1841[55]

This rather impertinent request apparently went unmet. Robert A. King's compendium *Lincoln in Numismatics* does not list such a medal.

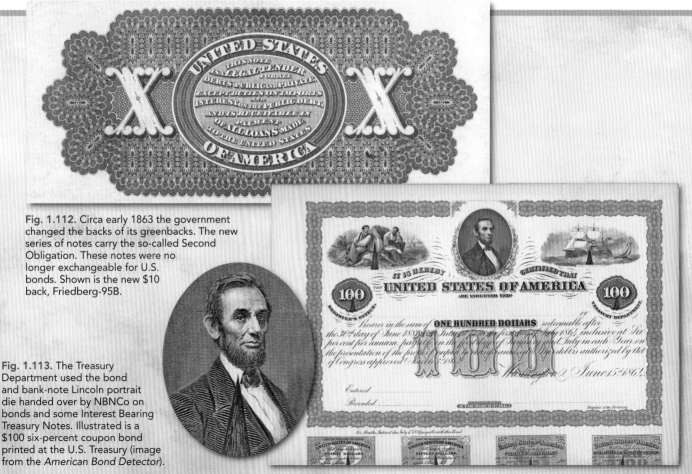

Fig. 1.112. Circa early 1863 the government changed the backs of its greenbacks. The new series of notes carry the so-called Second Obligation. These notes were no longer exchangeable for U.S. bonds. Shown is the new $10 back, Friedberg-95B.

Fig. 1.113. The Treasury Department used the bond and bank-note Lincoln portrait die handed over by NBNCo on bonds and some Interest Bearing Treasury Notes. Illustrated is a $100 six-percent coupon bond printed at the U.S. Treasury (image from the *American Bond Detector*).

1863 APRIL 14. M.A. Meade reiterates his request rather impatiently, requesting once again that President Lincoln sit for an artist so that a medal can be struck.[56] "We wrote you," Meade says, "in reference to a Profile for a Medal. Would you be so kind as to oblige us with a reply or say if you will sit to us if we come to Washington." Lincoln wrote on the envelope "on the Medallion business" and passed it on to his secretaries for filing.

1863 MAY 23. Treasury Secretary Chase requests that the president of ABNCo, George W. Hatch, turn over "dies, plates etc., from which the United States notes were printed," since in Chase's belief they belong to the U.S. government.[57] The Treasury Department was in the process of setting up its own security-printing bureau, and needed hardware. This was not the first request Chase had made to retrieve these currency dies. Hatch's predecessor, Tracy Edson, had already turned thumbs down. The plates and dies were the private company's stock in trade. Chase's request would certainly have included the original Lincoln currency portrait die, ABNCo die number 141 (presently in the hands of this author, and, according to experts on U.S. currency engraving Gene Hessler and Mark Tomasko, one of the few dies actually used for U.S. paper money to be in private hands). Hatch, too, said no to the Treasury secretary. ABNCo retained the Lincoln portrait and the cylinder die by which it transferred the original image, engraved by Charles Burt, to currency-production plates (also presently in the collection of this author). Together these historic 1861 security engravings of Lincoln enabled him to be the first U.S. president to appear on U.S.

federal paper money. These graven images produced the notes that Lincoln saw and carried in his own pocketbook. They influenced a myriad of other representations of Lincoln in his own time, and constitute the most important Lincoln engraving extant.

1863 MAY 28. Treasury Secretary Chase makes a similar request to the president of NBNCo to turn over dies, plates, and so forth from which U.S. notes and bonds were printed as property of the government. NBNCo complied. It transferred its bond-portrait die to the government, and the Treasury used it to print the $20 Interest-Bearing and $20 Compound Interest Notes (fig. 1.114).

1863 JULY 27. President Abraham Lincoln signs a holographic executive order appointing George Harrington "to discharge the duties of Secretary of the Treasury during the absence of Salmon P. Chase, the Secretary."[58]

1863 JULY 13–16. Riots break out in the streets of New York City, an anti-war Democratic hotbed, sparked by antagonism to the Conscription Act of March 3, 1863. The New York Seventh Regiment is recalled from service around Gettysburg to help quell the uprising. An anti-Lincoln *CDV* published at the time shows an effeminately garbed, clueless Lincoln reading about the draft riots in the newspaper with a magnifying glass. The myopic chief executive's clothes hark back to the female dress he purportedly donned to sneak unnoticed into Washington, D.C., for his inauguration. Some have seen a

Fig. 1.114. Similar Lincoln images began appearing simultaneously on both $10 and $20 U.S. Treasury Notes: *(a)* Treasury engraver James Duthie placed "secret marks" in the Lincoln portrait, and the Treasury printed Interest Bearing $20 Treasury Notes (Friedberg-197a, BEP die no. MISC3241). These notes bore 5 percent interest, and depicted religious affirmations in two shields on the face—the first such occurrence on U.S. coins or paper money. *(b)* Several months later, the same Lincoln portrait and same basic design were used to print $20 Compound Interest Treasury Notes, which bore 6 percent interest, compounded semi-annually and payable at maturity.

Fig. 1.115. Hall and Co. of New York lampooned Lincoln in 1863 on this *CDV*. They dressed him in nightclothes and slippers, and gave the clueless executive a magnifying glass so he could comprehend reports on the New York City draft riots of mid-July.

demonic representation in the shadow he casts. The clueless Lincoln looks up from his newspaper and magnifying glass and says, "That's what's the matter."

1863 AUGUST 1. President Lincoln purchases a five-percent Temporary Loan Treasury Certificate for $22,306.67.[59]

1863 AUGUST 18. President Lincoln purchases another five-percent Temporary Loan Treasury Certificate, this one for $3,874.73.[60]

1863 SEPTEMBER 30. George H. Boker of Philadelphia sends President Lincoln a medal by which Lincoln is made an honorary member of the Union League of Philadelphia.[61] The medal is intended to demonstrate the Union League's approval of Lincoln's conduct of the war. Lincoln was supposed to receive this gold medal in person during the Fourth of July celebration in Philadelphia. However, with the invasion of Gen. Robert E. Lee's Army of Northern Virginia, which culminated at the Battle of Gettysburg on July 1 through July 3, and the events at Vicksburg, Mississippi, Lincoln did not take the trip north. He acknowledged the gift in a return letter to Boker written by private secretary John Hay, signed by Lincoln, and dated October 24. Hay on Lincoln's behalf wrote:

> It is with heartfelt gratification that I acknowledge the receipt of your communication of the 30th of September, and the accompanying medal, by which I am made an honorary member of the Union League of Philadelphia. I shall always bear with me the consciousness of having endeavored to do my duty in the trying times through which we are passing, and the generous approval of a portion of my fellow-citizens so intelligent and so patriotic as those composing your Association, assures me that I have not wholly failed. I could not ask, and no one could merit, a better reward.
>
> Be kind enough, sir, to convey to the gentlemen whom you represent, the assurance of the grateful appreciation with which I accept the honor you have conferred upon me.
>
> I am very sincerely Your Obedient Servant A. LINCOLN.[62]

This medal was inherited by Robert Todd Lincoln. Following his death, his widow presented it to congressman George Dondero.[63]

1863. Copper-cent-sized tokens, produced by private diesinking firms in myriad designs, circulate as small change due to the scarcity of government coinage in circulation. One enigmatic die refers to Lincoln (Fuld 9/407; fig. 1.117). It shows "LINCOLN" around a star and the legend "Proclaim Liberty Through Out The Land," from Leviticus 30:10. This die is known only with one obverse, a Liberty Head with Phrygian cap indicating a freed slave. Of course, the token references Lincoln's Emancipation Proclamation. It is fairly scarce, and is attributed variously to the "Indiana Primitive" diesinker, Henry Darius Higgins, Mishawaka, Indiana.[64]

1863. Opposition to Lincoln stiffens. Ohio congressman Clement Vallandigham, who was against the war, denounces Lincoln as a tyrant, calling him "King Lincoln." The *New York Metropolitan Record*

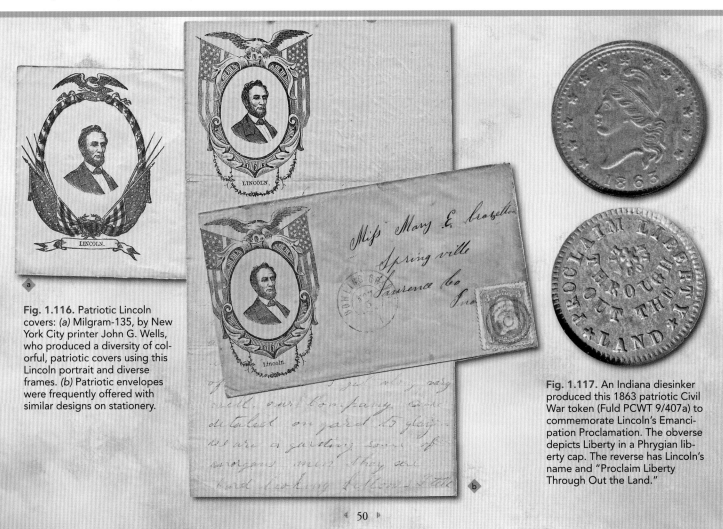

Fig. 1.116. Patriotic Lincoln covers: (a) Milgram-135, by New York City printer John G. Wells, who produced a diversity of colorful, patriotic covers using this Lincoln portrait and diverse frames. (b) Patriotic envelopes were frequently offered with similar designs on stationery.

Fig. 1.117. An Indiana diesinker produced this 1863 patriotic Civil War token (Fuld PCWT 9/407a) to commemorate Lincoln's Emancipation Proclamation. The obverse depicts Liberty in a Phrygian liberty cap. The reverse has Lincoln's name and "Proclaim Liberty Through Out the Land."

reports on a mock trial of the president "by the Great Statesmen of the Republic." In this representation of the "council of the past on the tyranny of the present," Lincoln is brought into the dock before judgment of the "Spirit of the Constitution" to answer for his crimes.

1863 October 3. Lincoln issues a Thanksgiving Day proclamation recommending that a day of general thanksgiving be observed on November 26, 1863. Lincoln recounts the many blessings that the country had experienced "in the midst of a civil war of unequaled magnitude and severity." He continues, "No human counsel hath devised nor hath any mortal hand worked out these great things. They are the gracious gifts of the Most High God." The president requests "citizens in every part of the United States, and also those who are at sea and those who are sojourned in foreign lands, to set apart and observe the last Thursday of November . . . as a day of Thanksgiving and praise to our beneficent Father who dwelleth in the heavens."[65] Lincoln's practice of Thanksgiving proclamations was followed by subsequent chief executives, until a law was passed in 1941 establishing the observance as a federal holiday.

1863 November 2. Judge David Wills of Gettysburg invites President Lincoln to dedicate the National Cemetery at Gettysburg on November 19 with a "few appropriate remarks."

1863 November 4. A *New York Times* article, dateline Chicago, reports, "The original draft of the emancipation, which was donated to the Northwestern Fair for the benefit of the Sanitary Commission, is now in the hands of the Commission who have charge of its sale." Private offers of up to $1,000 for the document were received, and a move was afoot to secure it for a historical society. Thomas B. Bryan ultimately purchased Lincoln's original holographic copy of the final Emancipation Proclamation for $3,000 in 1863 at the Northwestern Sanitary Fair in Chicago. Lincoln had donated the document to the fair to benefit Union soldiers. Bryan presented the document to the Chicago Soldier's Home. Chicago lithographer Ed Mendel published facsimile copies of the Emancipation Proclamation and of Lincoln's letter to the commission that accompanied the draft. The proceeds of the copies benefited the Soldier's Home and the Sanitary Commission.[66]

By the President of the United States of America:
A Proclamation.

Whereas, on the twentysecond day of September, in the year of our Lord one thousand eight hundred and sixtytwo, a proclamation was issued by the President of the United States, containing, among other things, the following, towit:

"That on the first day of January, in the year of our Lord one thousand eight hundred and sixty-three, all persons held as slaves within any State or designated part of a State, the people whereof shall then be in rebellion against the United States, shall be then, thenceforward, and forever free; and the Executive Government of the United States, including the military and naval authority thereof, will recognize and maintain the freedom of such persons, and will do no act or acts to repress such persons, or any of them, in any efforts they may make for their actual freedom.

"That the Executive will, on the first day of January aforesaid, by proclamation, designate the States and parts of States, if any, in which the people thereof, respectively, shall then be in rebellion against the United States; and the fact that any State, or the people thereof, shall on that day be, in good faith, represented in the Congress of the United States by members chosen thereto at elections wherein a majority of the qualified voters of such State shall have participated, shall, in the absence of strong countervailing testimony, be deemed conclusive evidence that such State, and the people thereof, are not then in rebellion against the United States."

Now, therefore I, Abraham Lincoln, President of the United States, by virtue of the power in me vested as Commander-in-Chief, of the Army and Navy of the United States in time of actual armed rebellion against authority and government of the United States, and as a fit and necessary war measure for suppressing said rebellion, do, on this first day of January, in the year of our Lord one thousand eight hundred and sixtythree, and in accordance with my purpose so to do, publicly proclaimed for the full period of one hundred days, from the day first above mentioned, order and designate

20820

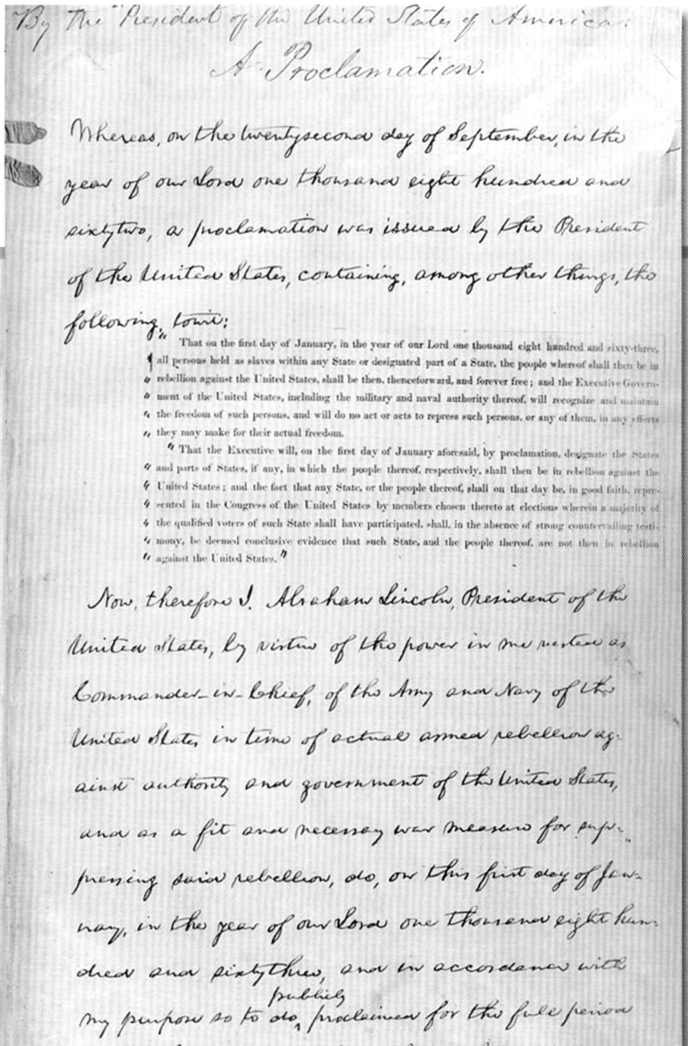

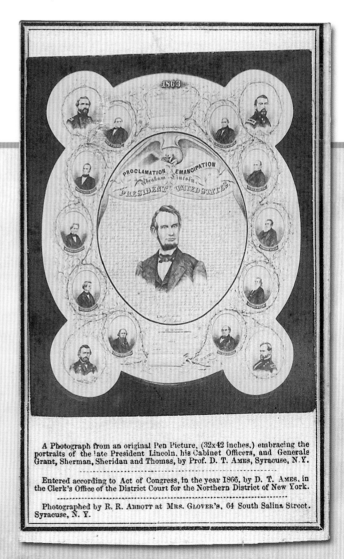

Fig. 1.118. The final copy of the Emancipation Proclamation that the president sent to the printer; it includes Lincoln's printed, preliminary draft and handwritten additions. This historic document is in the Library of Congress.

Fig. 1.119. A *CDV* from an original 32 x 42–inch pen-and-ink picture of Lincoln, his cabinet, and generals Grant, Sherman, Sheridan, and Thomas. The artist, D.T. Ames, was a business-school proprietor in Syracuse and a teacher of penmanship. Ames also did a similar pen-and-ink drawing, reproduced as *CDVs*, of George Washington.

The original Emancipation Proclamation was destroyed by the great Chicago fire of 1871.[67] The Library of Congress owns the photographic copy (fig. 1.118) from which the document was set in type and printed. It includes superscriptions by a clerk, Lincoln's handwritten text, and the printed insertion from the preliminary proclamation he had issued in September. Illustrated lithographs and engravings of the Emancipation Proclamation were also prepared by other printers, including R.A. Dimmick in New York, Chas. Shober and A. Kidder in Chicago, B.B. Russell in Boston, and Chas. Moss in Jersey City. More inventive than these typescript representations were the calligraphic presentations of the proclamation by G.R. Russell and Professor D.T. Ames. Ames was a professor of penmanship and proprietor of Ames Business College in Syracuse, New York, which he'd founded in the early 1860s. His inventiveness produced a pen picture of the Emancipation Proclamation (32 inches by 42 inches), which also includes pen portraits of Lincoln, his cabinet officers, and generals Grant, Sherman, Sheridan, and Thomas. To replicate his masterpiece, Ames had the picture photographed and reproduced as *CDVs* (fig. 1.119).

1863 November 8. Lincoln visits Alexander Gardner's Washington studio in the company of his private secretary, John G. Nicolay; they are joined by another of Lincoln's private secretaries, John Hay. Gardner takes a great many poses, including Lincoln with his secretaries. The president's generally unruly hair is coifed, his beard trimmed, and his suit pressed as he sits erect in the "Brady" posing chair. The most memorable image of that session is the so-called "Gettysburg Lincoln photo" (fig. 1.121), showing Lincoln full-faced, his lazy, wandering left eye very apparent. Lincoln photo historian Lloyd Ostendorf comments: "The dramatic power of this camera study is enhanced by its intimacy. The firm but irregular set of the lips and the cavernous depth of the eye-sockets with the upward roll of the left eye add to its impact."[68] This is acclaimed by many as Lincoln's finest photograph. Unfortunately, it has never been used on federal paper money.

1863 November 19. On Thursday afternoon Lincoln speaks at the dedication of the Soldier's National Cemetery in Gettysburg, Pennsylvania, although he is not the principal speaker (an honor intended for fiery New Englander Edward Everett). Lincoln's "few appropriate remarks" compass but 271 immortal words and two minutes on the podium. This is Lincoln's finest speech.

Edward Everett, particularly engaged by Lincoln's remarks, wrote Lincoln on November 20 to express his appreciation. "I should be glad if I could flatter myself that I came as near to the central idea of the occasion, in two hours, as you did in two minutes," Everett wrote.[69] Later he and Mrs. Hamilton Fish asked Lincoln for a copy of the Gettysburg Address for sale to benefit the New York Sanitary Fair. Lincoln complied with the request, and sent Everett a revised manuscript. According to Lincoln authority Gabor Boritt, "Though it was advertised, no evidence appears to exist that the item sold, though much later a $1,000 price surfaced."[70] The American public heard about the event in the pages of the press. The Cemetery Monument Fund published several pamphlets of Lincoln's and Everett's speeches, together with a history and map of plans for the cemetery, which it sold for the benefit of improvements there.

1863 November 26. Mrs. D.P. Livermore and Mrs. A.H. Hoge, on behalf of the Northwestern Sanitary Fair, send Lincoln a watch in appreciation of his donation of the Emancipation Proclamation to assist the fair.[71]

1863 December 2. Crawford's statue *Freedom* is mounted atop the U.S. Capitol dome. The dedication is marked by a gun salute that traveled around the nation's capital. The bronze statue, standing 19 feet, 6 inches tall and weighing approximately 15,000 pounds, appears on $5 Demand Notes and Legal Tender Notes.

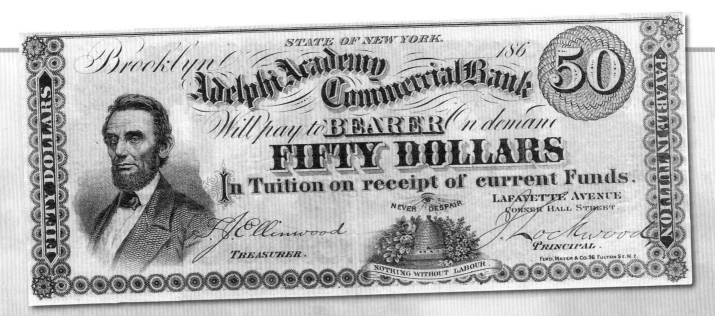

Fig. 1.120. Adelphi Academy in Brooklyn was a business school established in 1863. In its practical curriculum it employed various school notes, printed in New York City by Ferd. Mayer. These notes' patriotic motifs included Crawford's *Freedom* and portraits of Washington, Grant, and Lincoln. The Lincoln portrait on the $50 Adelphi note (Schingoethe-NY450/50) is a mirror image of the $10 greenback portrait.

Fig. 1.121. The so-called "Gettysburg Lincoln" (Ostendorf-77), considered by most viewers the greatest photo of Lincoln. This intimate image reveals the president's lazy left eye.

1863 DECEMBER 15. Former New Orleans Mint official John Leonard Riddell writes Abraham Lincoln informing him of affairs in New Orleans.[72]

1863 DECEMBER 18. Abraham Lincoln approves Congressional Joint Resolution to present General U.S. Grant a gold medal.

1864. With the president's first term winding down, and the war dragging on, Lincoln's critics are out in full force. Particularly pointed are the attacks on "Black Republicanism," which label Lincoln "Abraham Africanus I." One of the anti-Lincoln pamphleteers is New Yorker J.F. Feeks, who depicts Lincoln's head with a crown on it and the title "Abraham Africanus I" under it. Another Feeks booklet is titled *The Lincoln Catechism, wherein The Eccentricities and Beauties of Despotism are full set forth,* which he issued as a guide to the presidential election of 1864.

1864 JANUARY 12. President Lincoln purchases $8,000 in $5 to $20 Treasury Notes.[73]

1864 JANUARY 30. Lincoln receives a request from photographers Bell & Bros., 480 Pennsylvania Avenue, to make and sell his photograph to aid the Sanitary Fair. The Great Central Fair of the U.S. Sanitary Commission opened in Philadelphia June 7, 1864. Lincoln was unable to accept an invitation to dedicate the event. Small medalets in silver and bronze commemorating the event, with a pro-file bust of George Washington prepared by Mint chief engraver James Longacre, were struck at the fair on a U.S. Mint press supplied for the purpose. Twenty copies of Lincoln's Emancipation Proclamation were printed on parchment and signed by Lincoln for sale to raise funds for the Sanitary Commission.

1864 FEBRUARY 1. Lincoln calls for 500,000 more troops for three-year enlistments, effective March 10.

1864 FEBRUARY–AUGUST. Portrait painter Francis Bicknell Carpenter arrives at the White House on February 6 and remains there through August, commemorating Lincoln's Emancipation Proclamation on a large canvas. Carpenter was given unprecedented access to the chief executive. "The central thought of the picture once decided upon and embodied, the rest naturally followed; one after another the seven figures surrounding the President dropped into their places. Those supposed to have held the purpose of the Proclamation as their conviction, were placed prominently in the foreground in attitudes which indicated their support of their measure; the others were represented in varying moods of discussion or silent deliberation," Carpenter wrote. Once completed, the painting went on display in the White House East Room, then in the Rotunda of the U.S. Capitol, followed by a national tour. The work achieved acclaim, but for partisan reasons some viewers found fault with the effort.

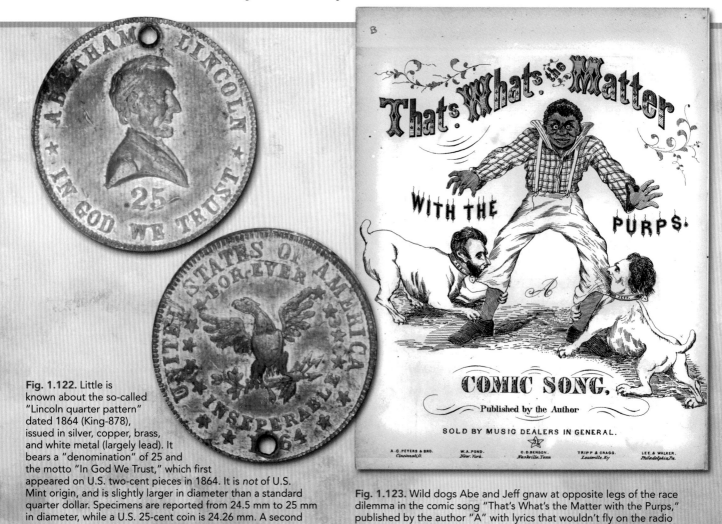

Fig. 1.122. Little is known about the so-called "Lincoln quarter pattern" dated 1864 (King-878), issued in silver, copper, brass, and white metal (largely lead). It bears a "denomination" of 25 and the motto "In God We Trust," which first appeared on U.S. two-cent pieces in 1864. It is *not* of U.S. Mint origin, and is slightly larger in diameter than a standard quarter dollar. Specimens are reported from 24.5 mm to 25 mm in diameter, while a U.S. 25-cent coin is 24.26 mm. A second variety, King-870, is a Lincoln assassination commemorative.

Fig. 1.123. Wild dogs Abe and Jeff gnaw at opposite legs of the race dilemma in the comic song "That's What's the Matter with the Purps," published by the author "A" with lyrics that wouldn't fly on the radio today. During the Civil War, "purps" applied to fighting dogs.

1864 FEBRUARY 5. Under the Act of March 3, 1863, $20 five-percent, one-year Interest-Bearing Treasury Notes are issued with the NBNCo Lincoln portrait and bank-note company imprint. Additionally, plates for the note faces in possession of the new Treasury Printing Bureau bore the legend "Engraved and Printed at the Treasury Department." Since it was vital that the date these notes were issued be recorded, notes were overprinted in a pigeon's-blood-red ink. Observed note dates range from February 5, 1864, to May 25, 1864. On February 5, Treasury Department engraver James Duthie placed "secret marks" in the gown of Liberty and in Lincoln's coat, and he'd recorded a memorandum on official Treasury Department, National Currency Bureau, First Division letterhead. It states: "This is to certify that I have this day placed upon the face plate of the $20 one year 5 per cent Treasury Note which has the imprint of the Treasury Department and marked from As to Ds the following private marks [Duthie marks clipped vignettes affixed to the memorandum]. I further certify that it is within my personal knowledge that no impressions have been printed from the plate up to the time at which I engraved the private marks on them. [signed] James Duthie." In total, 822,000 notes were issued. These notes bear two shields on face with mottos "God And Our Right" and "In God Is Our Trust."

1864 FEBRUARY 9. Lincoln makes an afternoon sojourn to Brady's Washington studio to visit photographer Anthony Berger. This event is three days before Lincoln's 55th birthday. Lincoln takes his son Tad, and is accompanied by artist Francis Carpenter. Several photographs are taken (fig. 1.126), including those adapted for the cent profile and the old-style (before 1999) $5 pose. The photographic image on our new $5 bills (which has also appeared on $500 Gold Certificates) was also photographed by Berger that day, the most numismatically significant day of Lincoln's life.

A great deal was on Lincoln's mind at the time. In addition to the chronic, twin problems with obtaining men and money, dissent within his Republican ranks was boiling. Early that month Kansas senator Samuel C. Pomeroy had sent letters detailing the shortcomings of the Lincoln administration and seeking support for his friend Salmon P. Chase as candidate for the upcoming presidential election. Chase was brilliant and egotistical. He considered himself superior to Lincoln in every way. Cartoonists emphasized both traits by giving Lincoln's Treasury secretary a bulbous, big head. The dissention spilled over when the Lincoln-Chase rivalry leaked to the press on about February 20. Chase offered his resignation; Lincoln declined to accept it.

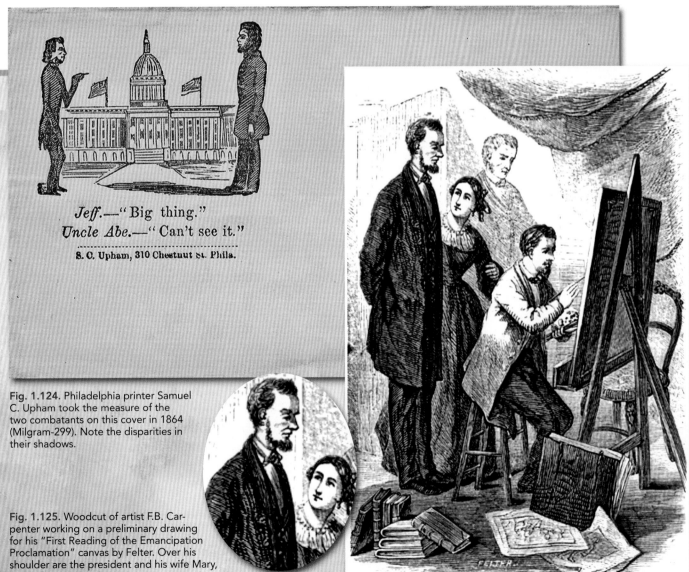

Jeff.—"Big thing."
Uncle Abe.—"Can't see it."

S. C. Upham, 310 Chestnut St. Phila.

Fig. 1.124. Philadelphia printer Samuel C. Upham took the measure of the two combatants on this cover in 1864 (Milgram-299). Note the disparities in their shadows.

Fig. 1.125. Woodcut of artist F.B. Carpenter working on a preliminary drawing for his "First Reading of the Emancipation Proclamation" canvas by Felter. Over his shoulder are the president and his wife Mary, and William Seward.

Fig. 1.126. Photographer Anthony Berger took a half dozen images of Lincoln when the president visited Brady's Washington gallery on February 9, 1864. Three of the photographs were to become the basis for enduring portraits on U.S. coins and paper money. Pictured are *(a)* O-88 from an anonymous *CDV*; and *(b)* O-92 from a cabinet card with Brady imprint; *(c)* Ostendorf-91 from a C.M. Bell, Washington, D.C., jumbo cabinet card.

Fig. 1.127. The February 9, 1864, Lincoln photo by Anthony Berger (Ostendorf-92) became a popular small "gem" tintype, often suspended from patriotic ribbons as on this ferrotype badge.

1864 FEBRUARY 22. Tromp l'oeil painter H.J. Kellogg, Rochester, New York, offers Lincoln a painting of a U.S. Treasury Note if Lincoln will tell him how to ship it or receive him for presentation of it.[74]

1864 FEBRUARY 27. "I wish I was in Dixie," a cartoon published in *Southern Illustrated News* in late February, lampoons the Union Army's ineffectiveness in the South (fig. 1.128). The cartoon was based on an 1863 *CDV* published by Charles Wheeler in New York City. *CDV* variants adapting the Southern newspaper cartoon also appeared in the North. Ironically, "Dixie Land" was Lincoln's favorite tune.

1864 MARCH. Counterfeits of Lincoln Legal Tender Notes multiply (fig. 1.129), and one Thomas Kerr is sentenced to imprisonment at hard labor for four years and a fine of one dollar, upon pleading guilty "for making and passing a counterfeit ten-dollar legal tender note."[75]

Kerr was one of the unlucky ones. The ten-spot was the most widely counterfeited note; the potential payday was great, and the potential risk for the counterfeiters of federal Legal Tender Notes was light. (The present author has written extensively on this subject in the numismatic trade press; these articles are listed in About the Author.) Two dozen different $10 Legal Tender Note counterfeits have been identified thus far. In an attempt to warn bankers and the public, counterfeit detectors illustrating genuine notes were published by many sources, the chief of whom was Laban Heath, who obtained government permission to print illustrations from genuine currency plates—without serial numbers or Treasury seal—in his detectors. The Treasury also issued a new series of notes bearing the authorization date of March 3, 1863 (Friedberg-95). When these, too, fell prey to the koniackers, the feds changed the green ink to a chromium ink patented by A.K. Eaton in 1863, and later added a second serial number printed in red on a fine line guilloche (patented

Fig. 1.128. As the war dragged on, Lincoln found it hard to get respect from a large portion of the press and public, which lampooned his appearance, character, and methods. *(a)* This cartoon, "I wish I was in Dixie," appeared in the February 27, 1864, issue of the *Southern Illustrated News.* "Dixie" was Lincoln's favorite air. The cartoon lampoons the rag-tag minstrel and his inability to win the war. *(b)* A virtually identical image appeared on an anonymous *CDV,* except that the Amnesty Proclamation in Lincoln's coat pocket has been replaced by "Proclamation 1863," the Emancipation Proclamation. *(c)* A more refined but quite similar design was circulated as a *CDV* by Charles Wheeler of New York City.

Fig. 1.129. Counterfeits and the efforts to defeat them: (a) Reed AL-CF93-14, which was taken out of circulation when a money handler scribbled "Counterfeit" across its face in red ink. (b) An example of a Treasury Note printed from an original bank-note plate in Laban Heath's counterfeit detector. (c) The Treasury also issued a new series of notes bearing the authorization date of March 3, 1863, Friedberg-95, and recalled the notes dated 1862.

Fig. 1.130. Counterfeiters were attracted to items besides the federal greenbacks. This is an unlisted photographic counterfeit of the 1862 Lincoln Bank $1 (type of Haxby-NY655C2a). The original was engraved and printed by NBNCo.

by George W. Casilear in 1868). In 1869, when fakes continued to pour from the sub-rosa presses, the Treasury cried "uncle" and issued new notes with different designs, while retiring the much-counterfeited Civil War–era greenbacks.

1864 MARCH 10. Lincoln bestows a commission as lieutenant general on Grant, and on March 12, appoints him to general in chief of all U.S. armies.

1864 MARCH 24. Painter Francis B. Carpenter accompanies Lincoln to the Treasury Department, where a temporary studio has been set up for sculptor William Marshall Swayne, who is making a bust of Lincoln.[76]

1864 APRIL 11. New York publisher James C. Derby writes John G. Nicolay requesting that Nicolay speak to Carpenter, who is working on the painting at the White House: "Will you ask [Carpenter] for me, if he has made any arrangements for the publication of it on steel. If not will he negotiate with me for publishing it." [77]

1864 APRIL 20. Lincoln visits Brady's D.C. studio again at the behest of artist F.B. Carpenter, so that cameraman Anthony Berger can capture an image of the president's head canted slightly to the left (fig. 1.131) in the attitude that Carpenter wishes to depict in his painting. This photo (or, in the opinion of Lincoln photo historian Lloyd Ostendorf, the engraving by Frederick Halpin based on the photo) serves as model for Charles Burt's engraving used on the Fourth Series 50¢ Fractional Currency. Halpin's portrait measures 12 inches by 10.5 inches, but is printed on a much larger sheet (17 inches by 13 inches). Included is the statement "Engraved by F. Halpin, after a painting from life by F.B. Carpenter." The Halpin print cost original purchasers $15, a high price for the time. It was acclaimed as one of the finest Lincoln engraved images.

1864 APRIL 26. Berger packs up his equipment (no mean feat in the era of 8-by-12, wooden-and-brass view cameras and large glass negatives) and comes to the White House, once again at Carpenter's request. This time Berger sets up in the Cabinet room.

Carpenter recorded the event succinctly: "Today, Mr. Berger took several pictures for me of Mr. Lincoln in the Cabinet room. Succeeded very well!" Carpenter had Lincoln adopt a seated pose at the end of the conference table, while private secretary John G. Nicolay took the position of William Seward (seated facing Lincoln), and Carpenter himself sat behind the president in Edwin Stanton's position. Carpenter

Fig. 1.131. One of the photos of Lincoln taken at the request of artist F.B. Carpenter for his Emancipation canvas is this portrait (Ostendorf-97), taken by cameraman Anthony Berger at Brady's Washington, D.C., gallery on April 20, 1864.

continues: "The legs in the white trousers are those of Mr. Nicolay the private secretary. The legs at Mr. Lincoln's right are my own. October 26, 1898." Another holographic note of the same date says: "This photograph was taken under my direction in 1864 at the White House in Mr. Lincoln's office. Mr. Lincoln unfortunately moved his head which blurred his features, as represented, but it gives a faithful representation of his arm chair, desk, carpet, mantel, and dark wall paper etc. The end of the table on which his hand and book rests is the historic table of this famous room from the time of Polk to Lin-

coln, around which the cabinet ministers sat and where the Proclamation of Emancipation was signed. F.B. Carpenter Oct. 26, 1898."

1864. Editorial cartoonist, abolitionist, and political satirist Henry Louis Stephens lambasts Lincoln in a series of searing cartoons for trampling the Constitution under guise of "military necessity," suppression of liberties, and suspension of habeas corpus and freedom of the press. One of Stephens's most cloying cartoons, "Love me little, love me long," shows Lincoln bending low to tell a Black child he is

Fig. 1.132. During 1864, sharp political pencils habitually treated Lincoln as the buffoon in criticizing his policies. These illustrations are typical. *(a)* Joseph Baker posed a disheveled, disinterested (inebriated?) Lincoln as waxing stupidly over matters of life and death in "Columbia Demands Her Children!" *(b)* Currier & Ives posited a similar Lincoln figure, although this time dapper and jocular, at a cabinet meeting as Treasury Secretary William Pitt Fessenden cranks the greenback mill around the clock.

free. "You's werry long, dat so massa Lincum, and de people want you longer yet," the child says.

1864 MAY 6. Lincoln receives New York engraver George E. Perine's request for a favorite photograph to be rendered as a steel engraving. Perine wrote: "His Excellency President Lincoln. Dear Sir. I desire engraving in the best style and large size Your Portrait on Steel, and wishing a reliable Photograph to copy from—I have taken the liberty to address you for the purpose of obtaining one pleasing to yourself & family. Will you please favor me with the same, together with your autograph to engrave on the plate by mail or otherwise."[78] Perine engraved several likenesses of Lincoln.

1864 MAY 14. Missouri congressman J.W. McClurg intercedes with Lincoln on behalf of H.T. Blow and L.J. Cist on a request for an autographed photo to be auctioned off at the Mississippi Valley Sanitary Fair. Lincoln acceded to the request on May 16. He wrote Cist: "I am glad to give it, in the hope that it may contribute, in some small degree at least, to the relief and comfort of our brave soldiers."[79]

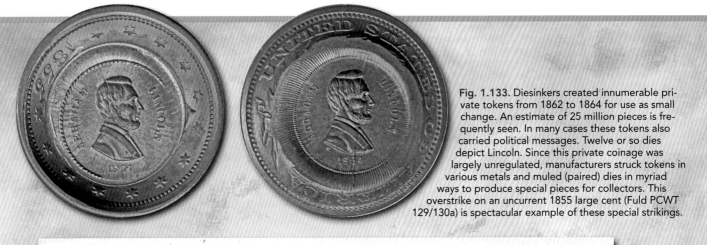

Fig. 1.133. Diesinkers created innumerable private tokens from 1862 to 1864 for use as small change. An estimate of 25 million pieces is frequently seen. In many cases these tokens also carried political messages. Twelve or so dies depict Lincoln. Since this private coinage was largely unregulated, manufacturers struck tokens in various metals and muled (paired) dies in myriad ways to produce special pieces for collectors. This overstrike on an uncurrent 1855 large cent (Fuld PCWT 129/130a) is spectacular example of these special strikings.

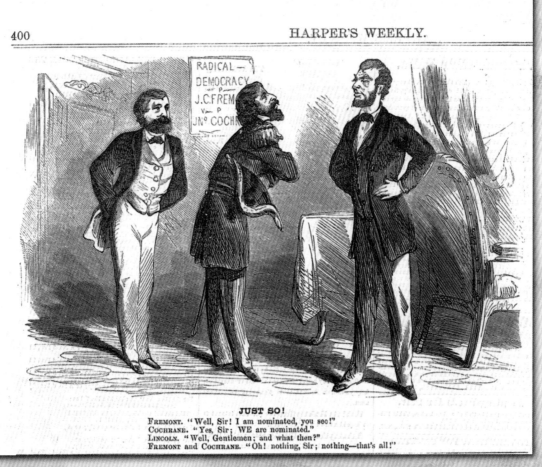

Fig. 1.134. The Fremont-Cochrane candidacy (discussed in main text) didn't amount to much, and fearing that their presence on the ballot would lead to a Democratic victory, they withdrew from the canvas in September. The bust was predicted in this June 18, 1864, *Harper's Weekly* cartoon "Just So."

1864 MAY 24. Register of the Treasury Lucius Chittenden advises President Lincoln that he is about to resign.[80] The register of the Treasury is one of the two government officials whose engraved facsimile signatures appeared on large-size government Treasury Notes of the period.

1864 MAY 31. Disaffected Republicans gather in Cleveland, Ohio, for a rump convention, and nominate John C. Fremont for president and John Cochrane for vice president (fig. 1.134). Fremont says he will withdraw if the Baltimore convention nominates anybody but Lincoln.

1864 MAY 31. In New York City, U.S. marshal for the southern district of New York Robert Murray writes Abraham Lincoln regarding the case of Winthrop Hilton.[81] Murray tells Lincoln that John H. White, Esquire, a New York attorney in good standing, is interested in procuring the release of Hilton, having concluded that Hilton is entirely innocent. Murray says he arrested Hilton believing him guilty, but now is convinced that "he is a victim of a conspiracy set on foot by Rebel Agt's to procure his arrest, as he was certainly inflicting great damage upon their cause." Murray tells Lincoln that discharging or paroling Hilton will be "of great value to the Government."

Winthrop Hilton had been arrested five months earlier on charges of abetting the rebels by printing their treasury notes. In reality, he was printing facsimiles, which he advertised widely at deep discounts in thinly veiled ads as souvenirs. Hilton had been engaged in this business for more than a year. In the October 4, 1862, issue of *Harper's Weekly*, Hilton advertised as follows: "Confederate (Rebel) Money. Perfect Fac-similes [*sic*] of Confederate Treasury Notes for sale at $4 per 1000. Specimens of all kinds sent by mail for 50 cents, by W.E. Hilton, 11 Spruce Street, New York." Three months later, his ad was more to the point: "Confederate (Rebel) Money.—Facsimile Treasury Notes, so exactly like the genuine that where one will pass current the other will go equally as well. $500 in Confederate Notes of all denominations, sent by mail, postage paid, on the receipt of $5."[82] Similar advertising appeared through April.

Hilton was engaged in the same trade as Philadelphian Samuel C. Upham. However, on December 31, 1863, U.S. Marshal Murray telegraphed the secretary of war that he had arrested Hilton, the counterfeiter, for printing Confederate treasury notes and bonds.[83] The message was transmitted under cover of cipher. "I have arrested Hilton and his partner [Haney] and foreman, and secured the plates for the rebel bonds, also 5's, 10's, 20's and 50's, Confederate Notes," Murray reported. "I have arrested the lithographer and printer and taken possession of Hilton's premises, and the lithographer's, and placed a guard over them until the morning, and I have no doubt I shall get the machinery also."[84] The *New York Times* reported Hilton's arrest on January 4, 1864. According to this account, the government raid seized about $6 million in Confederate bonds and a million dollars in Confederate treasury notes, as well as dies, presses, lathes, and other material.[85] The *New York World* reported the arrest on January 10. On January 21 Confederate treasury secretary C.G. Memminger denied that Winthrop E. Hilton was working for the Confederacy.[86]

1864 JUNE 6. John H. White writes a long letter to Abraham Lincoln regarding the case of Winthrop Hilton.[87] "When I saw you in Washington on Thursday last, you told me you would give Hilton's Case further consideration," White says, "and if I would send you a 'brief & points,' you would give them a careful perusal." However, upon returning to New York, White found that Hilton had already been paroled by General John A. Dix. "Through what instrumentality this was accomplished I am not advised, only it was by reason of the fact that General Dix had become fully convinced of his entire innocence," White continued.

He apprised Lincoln that his own interest in the case was on Lincoln's behalf after he'd discovered two weeks earlier that "a movement was in progress, which was beginning to assume a gran[d] importance; having its object, the calling of a public meeting at Cooper Institute to explain & denounce what was being regarded as a high-handed outrage, in keeping in confinement a man who only asked permission to be allowed to substantiate his innocence." It seemed the stink over Hilton's incarceration was about to boil over. Hilton was a prominent Mason, White explained, and "he was being looked upon as 'a brother in distress' by his lodge brothers who intended to make the case a special cause at their upcoming state convention." At that point, White had said he would approach Charles A. Dana and the president on the matter because he feared the Hilton case would add fuel to the fire with regard to the rump candidacy of John C. Fremont in Lincoln's own party. Tongue in cheek, White cautioned the president that "those Holy Patriots, who recently assembled at Cleveland want just such ammunition as this, to fire their 'Noble hearts.' It is true these people are wiser and better than any class of being now living, and would find fault with the decrees of Providence, did they not suppose they had a hand in framing them." He urged Lincoln to set Hilton free "unconditionally, for that act will make all things right, so far as you are concerned." In a footnote to the main letter, White hastily added: "since the above was written, word has come to me, that Gen'l Dix has not yet paroled Hilton, but thinks he ought to be paroled, and will telegraph the Secy of War, for permission to do so. In my judgment, it will be a terrible mistake, if Hilton is detained in custody inasmuch as Briggs; who caused Hilton's arrest has been set at liberty."

1864 JUNE 7–8. The National Union Convention, held in Baltimore, nominates Lincoln. Tennessee war Democrat Andrew Johnson, whom Lincoln tapped to be military governor there in 1862, is chosen as his running mate. Lincoln responds to his re-nomination: "I am reminded," he says, "of a story of an old Dutch farmer, who remarked to a companion once that 'it was not best to swap horses when crossing streams.'" His platform calls for a constitutional amendment to abolish slavery.

1864 JUNE 9. Some (the quantity is unknown) $20 six-percent, three-year Compound Interest Notes with the NBNCo Lincoln portrait are issued under the Act of March 3, 1863 (Friedberg-192).[88] According to U.S. Treasurer Gilfillan, issue commenced on June 9, 1864 (FinRept-1881).[89] According to numismatic historian Q. David Bowers, interest on these notes ceased to accrue on June 10, 1867.

1864 June 11. Lincoln instructs his secretary of the Treasury to "fix up" (reinvest at best rates) $54,515.07 in U.S. Treasury Notes, certificates of deposit, two uncashed pay warrants, and some greenbacks (fig. 1.138). Secretary Chase invests the securities and cash in Treasury Notes of 1881.[90]

1864 June 16. Former Pennsylvania governor James Pollock, the U.S. Mint director, presents Abraham Lincoln a silver medal on behalf of the Ladies of the Great Central Fair for his support of its objectives.

1864 June 18. Ten days after Lincoln's re-nomination, New York City entrepreneur John Gault writes Lincoln "to get a perfect photograph to copy from," as Gault intends "circulating three or four million medals or metallic cases containing likenesses of yourself and Andrew Johnson for President and Vice President." Gault produced ferrotypes encased in brass holders, in similar style but different design to his Encased Postage stamps of two years earlier (Sullivan AL 1864–94). Gault duplicated a recent photo of Lincoln taken by Mathew Brady in Washington, D.C., on January 8, 1864 (fig. 1.140). In the Gault

Fig. 1.135. Covers poking fun at the Union and Confederate presidents abound. *(a)* Philadelphian Sam Upham, printer, author, and the principal Confederate-note facsimilist, claimed to have been instrumental in wrecking the Confederate economy with his myriad fake Confederate notes. He also created numerous covers. His 1861 "Star of the North, or the Comet of 1861" was issued in two styles: Lincoln ascending (Milgram AL-145) and Lincoln descending (Milgram AL-144). Judging by available specimens known, the cover showing Lincoln crashing was far the more popular with his customers. *(b)* Philadelphian J. Magee's cover (Milgram AL-302) pokes childish fun at the combatants. *(c)* New York Envelope Co. produced this cover (Milgram AL-320) showing Lincoln kicking Davis in the tail.

ferrotype, the Lincoln image on the obverse is flopped (fig. 1.141), and flanked by patriotic symbols. The reverse has a ferrotype of Andrew Johnson. Gault also produced similar pieces for George McClellan and running mate George Pendleton (Sullivan GMcC 1864–49) and for the abortive campaign of John C. Fremont and John Cochrane (Sullivan JF 1864–7/8). These campaign medals carried Gault's encased-stamp patent date of August 12, 1862.

Gault rushed the Lincoln and other campaign medals into production. Less than a month after he wrote Lincoln, he was advertising them for sale. In early July his ad read, "Photographic Medallions, Or Campaign Medals, with accurate likenesses of candidates on metal, and enclosed in neat metallic cases, sent by mail, 15 cents each, or $1.50 per dozen. Liberal discount to the trade. Manufactured and sold wholesale and retail by John Gault, No. 1 Park Place, New York."[91] In late September the ad read, "Photographic Medallions. Campaign Medals. Best Style for 1864. For sale by John Gault, No. 1 Park Place,

New York."[92] Although these brass ferros really were an artistic success for Gault, his sales must have disappointed him. Judging by the frequency with which Gault's political medals are encountered today in the marketplace, his sales were not nearly so brisk as he'd hoped. The marketplace was full that campaign season, and he was up against larger competitors B.T. Hayward, E.N. Foote, and John W. Everett.

1864 JUNE 20. G.H. Briggs, who according to attorney John H. White was responsible for W.E. Hilton's arrest on charges of abetting the enemy by printing its treasury notes and bonds, writes Abraham Lincoln confessing that W.E. Hilton had been arrested on false charges of printing notes and bonds for the C.S.A.[93]

1864 JUNE 24. Lincoln's secretary writes Edwin M. Stanton, referring G.H. Briggs's June 20 letter to Lincoln in which he confessed that Winthrop E. Hilton was imprisoned on false charges.[94]

Fig. 1.136. Philadelphia engraver William H. Key produced this excellent likeness of Lincoln in 1864 for the campaign, with applied suspension (Sullivan AL 1864-5).

Fig. 1.37. With lots of alternative Lincoln images available, the official $10 (and now $20) portrait remained popular in 1864. (a) J.C. Spooner published this jumbo cabinet card, while (b) Currier & Ives employed the image on its "Grand, National Union Banner for 1864," shown opposite, depicting Lincoln and his running mate, Tennessee Democrat Andrew Johnson.

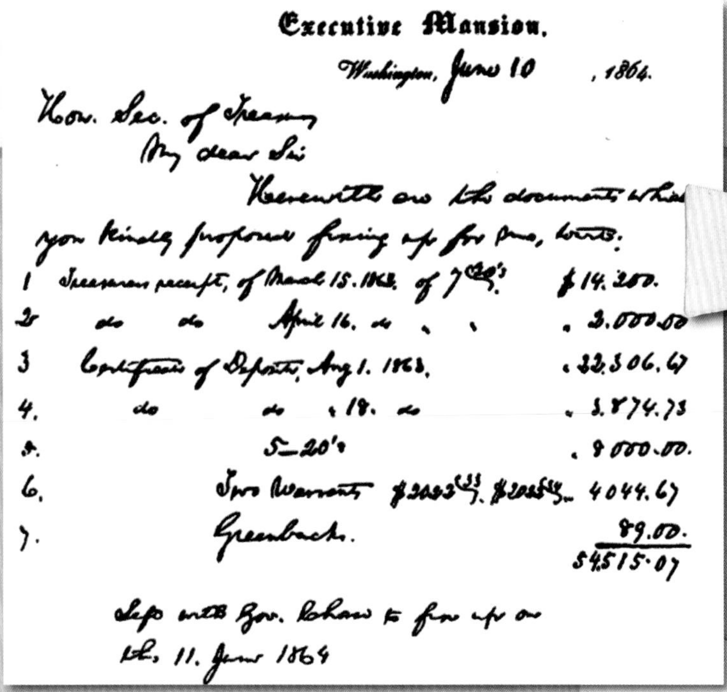

Executive Mansion.

Washington, June 10 , 1864.

[Handwritten memorandum by Abraham Lincoln listing personal financial documents and amounts, totaling 54,515.07]

Fig. 1.138. At Treasury Secretary Chase's request, Lincoln wrote a memorandum on June 10, 1864, of his personal finances so Chase could reinvest the money at best available rates.

Fig. 1.139. A former curator at the Smithsonian Institution described this cigar band as an 1864 Lincoln campaign item, but it appears much later.

Fig. 1.140. John Gault's 1864 campaign ferrotype badges for all three nominees, like this one for Lincoln-Johnson (Sullivan AL 1864-94), are very attractive and often holed for suspension.

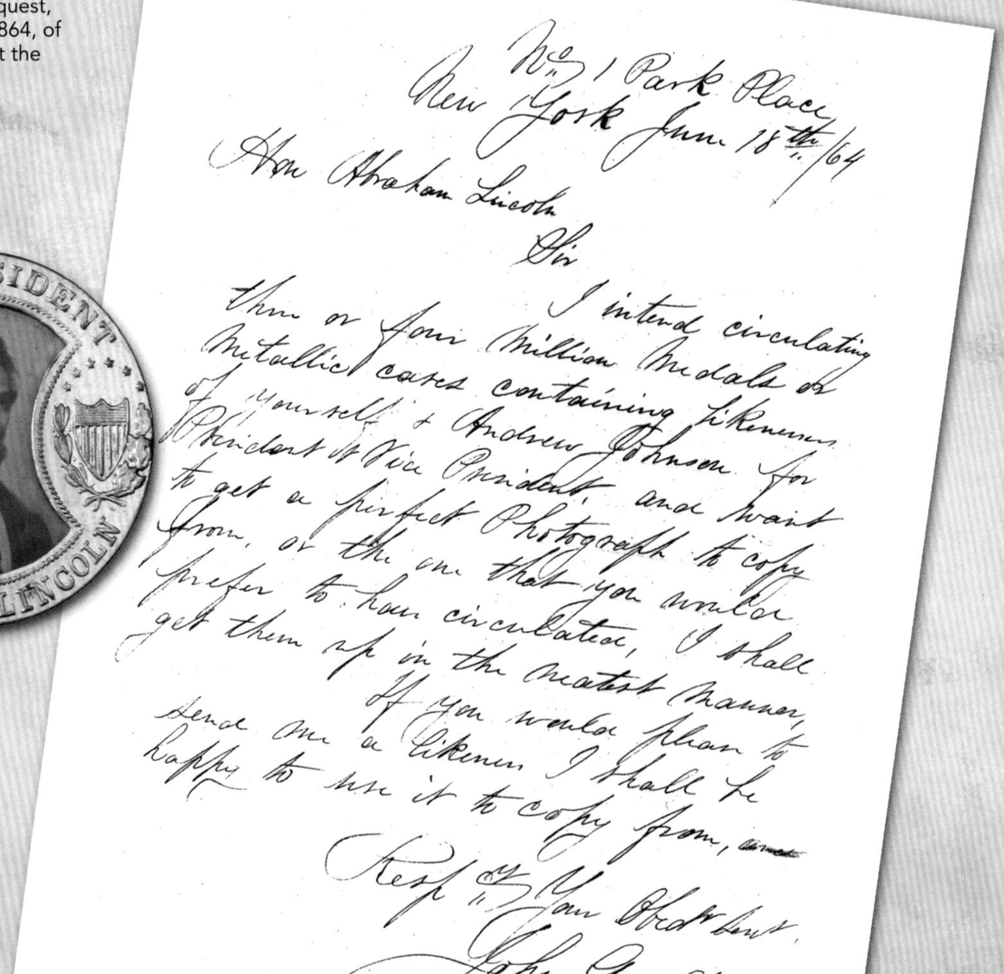

[Ferrotype badge: FOR PRESIDENT ABRAHAM LINCOLN]

[Ferrotype badge: FOR VICE PRESIDENT ANDREW JOHNSON]

Fig. 1.141. In 1864 New York entrepreneur John Gault requested *(a)* a photograph of Lincoln's choosing to duplicate on campaign ferrotypes. It is unclear whether Lincoln responded to the request, but Gault circulated elegant badges using a January 8, 1864, photograph *(b, facing page)* of Lincoln by Mathew Brady (Ostendorf-86).

[Handwritten letter from John Gault to Abraham Lincoln, dated New York June 18th/64, beginning "No. 1 Park Place"]

33822

1864 JUNE 24. Cincinnati publisher William H. Moore sends Lincoln two copies of Joseph H. Barrett's updated campaign biography of Lincoln, which has a frontispiece of a Brady photo engraved by Alexander Hay Ritchie. More wrote, "I hope Mr. Carpenter will not feel jealous of his friend Mr. Ritchie, when he sees how very successful Ritchie has been in engraving your portrait from Brady's photography! Your friends here—the few who have seen it,—pronounce it much the best likeness that has ever been published. I trust you will be pleased with it."

1864 JUNE 28. Lincoln accepts Treasury Secretary Chase's fourth offer of resignation (fig. 1.143).

1864 JUNE 29. Republican newspaperman Amor J. Williamson, editor and proprietor of the *New York Dispatch,* writes Lincoln in the cause of Winthrop Hilton, vouching for Hilton's loyalty to the Union and his innocence. "His friends (who are numerous, and among our most loyal citizens) claim that they can show that he is not guilty of the crime with which he is charged," Williamson writes. The writer tells the president that Hilton's friends demand an opportunity to clear his name, but have been rebuffed by government officials. "I cannot believe such a fact," Williamson continues, "as I feel sure that you would not sanction any outrage on the personal rights of your fellow citizens . . . it is one which should receive immediate attention in order to avoid injury to our cause in the coming political camps."[95] (For additional information about the Hilton case, see George Tremmel, *A Guide Book of Counterfeit Confederate Currency,* 2007.)

1864 JULY 4. Lincoln writes Edwin M. Stanton, referring petition of Horace Greeley and others for trial or release of Winthrop E. Hilton.[96]

1864 JULY 15. Twenty-dollar, six-percent, three-year Compound Interest Notes with the NBNCo Lincoln portrait, issued under the Act of June 30, 1864, are released to the public. Since it was important to record when these notes were issued, they were overprinted in pigeon's-blood-red ink. Observed note dates range from July 15, 1864 to September 15, 1865; some 390,000 of the $20 notes were issued. These notes have the Treasury Department imprint. According to Treasurer Gilfillan, issue of these Compound Interest Treas-

Fig. 1.42. The King of 1864 Lincoln-Johnson jugate campaign pins (Sullivan AL 1864-84): *(a)* When E.N. Foote advertised the pin in the October 15, 1864, issue of *Harper's Weekly,* he called it the "newest and best thing out." It is unpriced in his ad, but respondents could get 18 samples of his wares for $2. *(b)* When the example shown sold at public auction in 2007, it brought $47,800.

MR. LINCOLN. "MIKE, remove the SALMON and bring me a TOD."
MIKE. "The TOD's out; but can't I fetch something else, Sir?"

Fig. 1.143. Lincoln's Treasury secretary, Salmon P. Chase, was a pain in the president's side. During conflicts, he repeatedly challenged the president with brinksmanship by offering his resignation while believing he was irreplaceable. Lincoln declined Chase's proffers until June 1864. This Frank Bellew cartoon in *Harper's Weekly,* July 16, 1864, reinforces the point: Lincoln has filleted Chase. "Bring me a Tod" refers to Lincoln's choice for Chase's replacement, Ohio governor David Tod, who declined the post.

ury Notes ceased July 24, 1866.[97] In *100 Greatest American Currency Notes,* Q. David Bowers and David M. Sundman point out that interest ceased to accrue May 16, 1868, "although any bill issued after May 16, 1865, would still have some time to run."

1864. According to newspaper correspondent George Alfred ("Gath") Townsend, photographer Mathew Brady tells him: "Mr. Seward got the gallery for the Treasury to do the bank-note plates by conference with me." (It is conceivable this could have occurred in 1869.)

1864. In New York, T.R. Dawley, "publisher for the millions," issues *The President Lincoln Campaign Songster.* In Cincinnati, J.R. Hawley circulated *The Republican Songster for the Campaign of 1864.*

1864. The thirst for Lincoln images remains unsated, and print-makers tout "new" and "latest" images, including photographs, engravings, and photographs of engravings. Sometimes these images were not all they purported to be. In trying to meet the demand for Lincoln imagery and make a buck to boot, printmakers rushed out composed images, often placing Lincoln's head on some other indi-vidual's body. To multiply their wares and meet the demand, engravers sometimes took old prints and morphed Lincoln's head onto the existing bodies, like those of John C. Calhoun, Martin Van Buren, or Francis P. Blair (fig. 1.145c.). Most times, artistic sleight of hand was disguised. But for some artists, as in the case of the great engraver John Sartain, this composite depiction was owned up to, and in fact celebrated. On a circa-1864 engraving of a seated Lin-coln the inscription below the picture explains the source of image: "The head after a photograph from life, the picture by Boyle." In other words, as explained by a print historian, "Boyle composed the body and the background, and Sartain based the portrait likeness from a photograph." "Boyle" may have been Ferdinand Thomas Lee Boyle, who painted a portrait of Lincoln. In addition to appearing in prints this pseudo-Lincoln figure proliferated on *CDVs.*

1864. Campaign biographies are issued once again, but of course this time around Lincoln is no longer largely unknown. New York editor Henry J. Raymond publishes several different biographies and histories to improve Lincoln's chances.

Fig. 1.144. Campaign covers adjunct to the 1864 presidential canvas: *(a)* an elegant cover for the "Union Standard Bearers" (Milgram-157), produced by Gates & Gamble of Cincinnati; *(b)* an attractive cover with excellent portrai-ture (Milgram-155) published by Boston lithographer Louis Prang.

Fig. 1.145. The photograph on which this *CDV (a)* is based (Ostendorf-79) was taken November 8, 1863, by Alexander Gardner. Lincoln images were in such demand with the public that this *CDV* duplicates an engraving. *(b)* A similar engraving, but *not* the engraving which the *CDV* replicates, was engraved by George E. Perine for the *Eclectic Magazine of Foreign Literature, Science and Art,* published in New York by Leavitt and Trow. *(c)* The last *CDV* is a strange mule. The Lincoln portrait (head) was photographed by Mathew Brady in Washington, D.C., on January 8, 1864, but the body is not Lincoln's. The *CDV* reproduced John Sartain's mezzotint on which he had engraved Lincoln's head on the body of Congressman Francis P. Blair Jr., a much smaller man, whose "paunch is inappropriate, and his fine hands never split rails," according to Lincoln image historians Harold Holzer, Gabor Boritt, and Mark Neely.

1864. Edward Dalton Marchant creates a painting of the president from sittings at the White House. Like Francis B. Carpenter, Marchant had a studio in the White House for nearly four months while he drew the president in a variety of poses and settings. Marchant called Lincoln a most difficult subject. Lincoln is depicted seated beside a cloth-covered table, his arm resting on a document representing the Emancipation Proclamation. To the rear, broken shackles hang from a statue of Liberty.[98] Marchant's painting was acquired by the Union League in Philadelphia. In 1864 a superb mezzotint, engraved by John Sartain after the portrait from life by Marchant and with Lincoln's facsimile signature, was published by Bradley & Co., Philadelphia.

1864. The "Lincoln Gun," a 15-inch Rodman Columbiad, is shown at Fortress Monroe, Hampton, Virginia. Thomas Jackson Rodman was an ordnance officer who developed a method to cool large, cast gun barrels and increase the pop of black gunpowder. This smoothbore coast artillery was bottle-shaped, and 15 feet, 10 inches long. The barrel weight was 49,000 pounds, so it was only practical as a fixed-position munition. However, as can be seen in figure 1.147,

this enormous artillery piece was mounted on a rail to absorb recoil, and pivoted on a track so it could fire across a panorama guarding the approaches to the fort from the sea. The gun fired two types of projectile, a 450-pound solid shot, and a 330-pound explosive shell, with a maximum range of about 2.6 miles. During the Civil War, the federal government purchased about 130 of these large guns and several hundred smaller versions. After the Civil War, Confederate president Jefferson Davis was incarcerated for two years in a bleak cell at Fortress Monroe before release on bail.

1864. The president's humor is a source of constant public scrutiny, and acquaintances are generous in passing along his stories. In serious conversations, Lincoln often interjected humorous asides, disgruntling his listeners. A species of literature called "jokesters" presented Old Abe's humor to a wide audience. One of the best was compiled by Park Row, New York, publisher T.R. Dawley, in 1864. It was titled *Old Abe's Jokes, Fresh from Abraham's Bosom, containing all his issues, excepting the "Greenbacks," To call in some of which, this work is issued.* Following Lincoln's death, Dawley repackaged the material as *Honest Abe's Jokes; Being authentic Jokes and Squibs of Abraham Lincoln.*[99]

Fig. 1.146. One of the most attractive of the 1864 Lincoln-Johnson campaign medals is this jugate by Philadelphia medalist William H. Key (Sullivan AL 1864-1).

Fig. 1.147. The "Lincoln Gun," a 15-inch Rodman Columbiad at Fortress Monroe with a 15-foot, 10-inch barrel. A coast artillery weapon, perfected by artillerist Thomas Jackson Rodman, the gun had a range of up to 2.6 miles.

Fig. 1.148. Howe's Business College, Worcester, Massachusetts, employed this instructional note in 1864. Styled Merchant's Bank $1, it bears printed signatures of A. Lincoln as cashier and A. Jackson as president (Schingoethe MA-550-1 [unlisted]).

1864. A most interesting, and somewhat scarce, sepia *CDV* depicts Lincoln with bits of Second Issue Fractional Currency (fig. 1.149). Titled "Uncle Abes [*sic*] Last Joke. 'A Big Thing on Currency. For Further particulars see small Bills,'" it bears a legend beneath the collage—a bit of doggerel with several puns:

> "Handsome is that handsome does" Let Uncle Abe rejoice,
> There's comfort for that lengthy man our President by choice,
> But when he issues little jokes, Oh may he tender be,
> Never again upon the land, Inflict such currency.

The card also bears the copyright notice "Entered according to Act of Congress in the year 1864 by G.D. Brewerton in the Clerks Office of the District Court for the southern District of New York," indicating it was produced at or near New York City during the middle of the Civil War.

George Douglas Brewerton was a "popular" writer of the post–Civil War era. Several of his compositions ("Catching a Man-Eater," "How the Bear Hunted Me," and "My Room-Mates in Texas") are indexed for a 19th-century publication called *Our Young Folks.* Before taking up the pen and the brush (he was also a landscape artist),

Fig. 1.149. Reproductions of the "Speed photo": *(a)* This wonderful 1864 numismatic composite *CDV,* "Uncle Abes Last Joke," refers to the Fractional Currency authorized by Congress to fill the small-change void when silver coins were hoarded during the Civil War. Bits and pieces of second-issue 5-, 10-, 25-, and 50-cent notes are shown. The doggerel poem was written by G.D. Brewerton, a popular writer of the day. *(b)* The "Speed photo" likewise was incorporated into A. Kidder's 1864 Emancipation Proclamation calligraphy.

Brewerton served in the U.S. Army in California and the Southwest (including campaigning with Kit Carson) during the Gold Rush era. (Brewerton's father was superintendent of West Point.) Resigning from active duty, Brewerton contributed to such periodicals as *Harper's Monthly.* He also published a great many poems and articles, edited a short-lived magazine, penned the lyrics to a Civil War tune, and wrote at least four books. Brewerton died in 1901.

1864 August 23. Lincoln tells his cabinet he does not expect to be reelected. He pens a memo (fig. 1.151): "This morning, as for some days past, it seems exceedingly probably [*sic*] that this Administration will not be re-elected. Then it will be my duty to cooperate with the [strikes out "Government"] President elect, as to save the Union between the Election and the inauguration; as he will have secured his Election on such ground that he cannot possibly save it afterwards."

Currier & Ives published a print titled "Abraham's Dream" (fig. 1.152), in which Lincoln sees Columbia waving a skull overhead and giving him the boot back to Illinois, while General McClellan nonchalantly enters the wide-open door to the White House. "This don't remind me of any joke," Abe bellows.

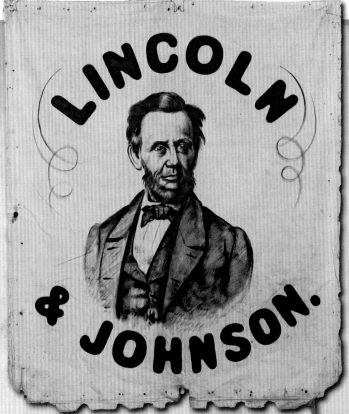

Fig. 1.150. 1864 Lincoln-Johnson campaign banner.

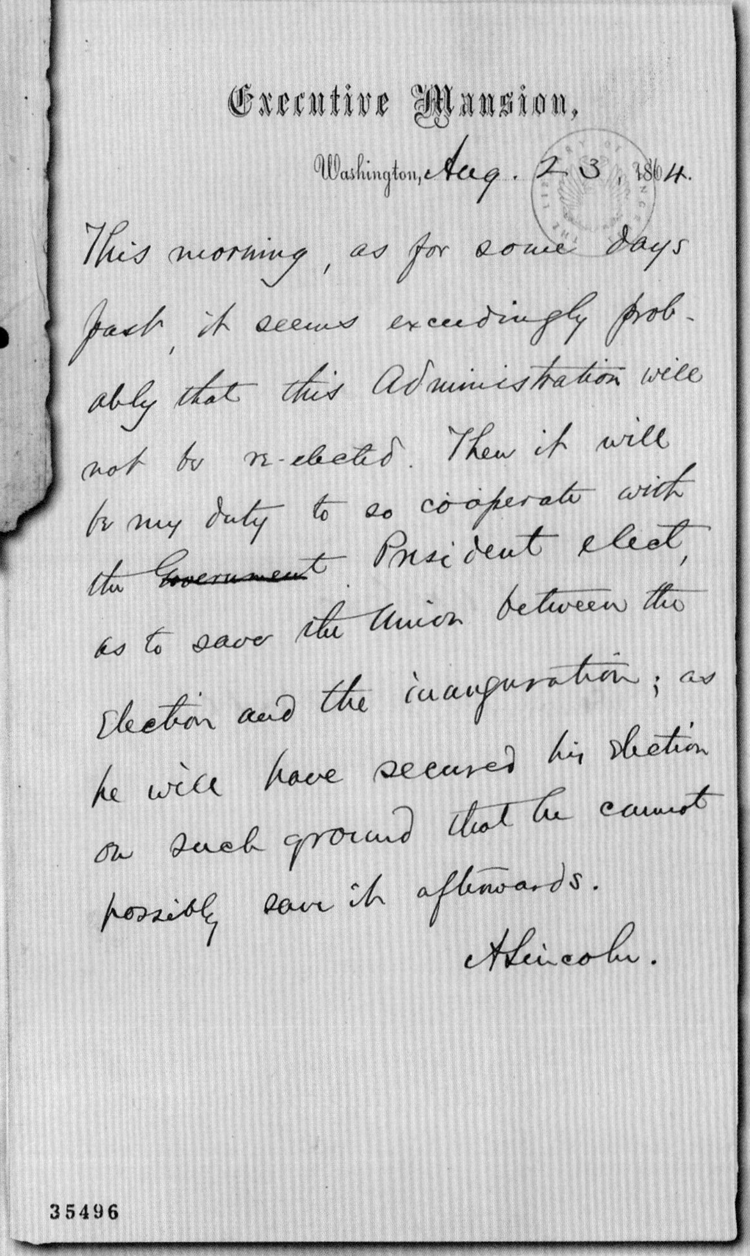
Executive Mansion,

Washington, Aug. 23, 1864.

This morning, as for some days past, it seems exceedingly probably that this Administration will not be re-elected. Then it will be my duty to so co-operate with the ~~Government~~ President elect, as to save the Union between the Election and the inauguration; as he will have secured his election on such ground that he cannot possibly save it afterwards.

A. Lincoln.

35496

Fig. 1.151. Lincoln expressed his doubts about his chances for reelection in this August 23, 1864, missive to cabinet members. "This morning, as for some days past" the president wrote, "it seems exceedingly probably [*sic*] that this Administration will not be re-elected."

1864 AUGUST 31. Democrats nominate General George B. McClellan for president.

1864. In New York a series of illustrated *CDVs* depicts the Lincoln-McClellan canvass as gamesmanship. In photographer J. Gurney & Son's view, "Check-Mated," drawn by C.C. Wood, the general checkmates Lincoln. Columbia points Lincoln out, and readies to hand the garland to a self-satisfied McClellan (see fig. 1.153a). In J.E. Holley's "The Winning Hand," also published by Gurney, a smug McClellan tips his winning cards ready to claim Washington represented by the Capitol on the card table between him and a distraught incumbent Lincoln (see fig. 1.153b). Similar pro-McClellan views are expressed in Currier & Ives's "The True Issue or 'Thats Whats the Matter'" (fig. 1.154a). The litho shows McClellan attempting to mediate the conflict between Lincoln and Jefferson Davis, who are tearing the Union asunder. "No peace without Abolition!" Lincoln vows. "No peace without separation!!" Davis rejoins twice as emphatically. While caught in the middle, McClellan pleads, "The Union must be pre-served at all hazards!" Even more biting pro-McClellan satire is expressed in "The Commander-in-Chief conciliating the Soldier's Votes on the Battle Field" (see fig. 1.154b). On a field strewn with Union casualties, Little Mac weeps and attempts to restrain his commander's boorish jest, "Now Marshal, sing us 'Picayune Butler,' or something else that's funny." Still more pointed is artist Howard's take on Shakespeare's *Hamlet,* wherein regal Chicago nominee McClellan lifts Lincoln's (Yorick's) skull and intones, "I knew him Horatio, a fellow of infinite jest . . . where be your jibes now?" while the gravedigger smirks with anticipation (see fig. 1.155a). Compare that to the rather mild, but pro-Lincoln *Harper's Weekly* cartoon published September, 17, 1864, in which Abe holds Little Mac in the palm of his hand, and cracks "This reminds me of a little joke" (fig. 1.155b).

1864 AUGUST 27. Philadelphia engraver Anthony Paquet has a private Lincoln medalet struck at the U.S. Mint in both silver and gold (fig. 1.156). It reads, "Abraham Lincoln—An Honest Man; The Crisis Demands His Re-Election, 1864." It would, of course, be impossible

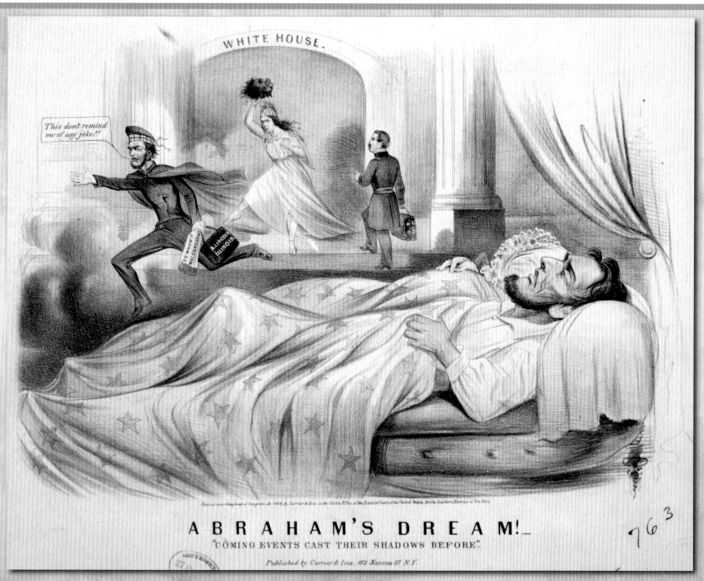

Fig. 1.152. Currier & Ives's 1864 print "Abraham's Dream!" dramatized Lincoln's foreboding premonition that he would lose his reelection bid. The artwork shows Columbia kicking Lincoln out the door as Gentleman George McClellan enters the White House. Lincoln is wearing the Scots disguise that he'd allegedly donned to sneak into Washington in the first place.

today that such a partisan medalet would be struck at the U.S. Mint. "This is one of the few purely political medals struck at the Philadelphia Mint," researcher Bob Julian observed. He found that medals were struck from August up to the eve of the election, and that an additional order for this medal was placed the day before Lincoln's assassination.

1864 September 12. From his studio in New York City, artist Francis B. Carpenter writes Lincoln's personal secretary Nicolay requesting "an autograph letter from the President expressing in brief his opinion of my picture. In publishing the picture we of course expect to get many subscribers among those who are not familiar with the faces of the illustrious originals and if the President will say as much upon

"CHECK-MATED."

Entered according to the Act of Congress, in the year 1864, by J. GURNEY & SON, in the Clerk's Office of the District Court of the United States, for the Southern District of New York.
Gurney & Son   Photo NY

Fig. 1.153. Similar cartoon *CDVs* published by Jeremiah Gurney & Son during the 1864 Lincoln-McClellan campaign: *(a)* "Check-Mated," drawn by C.C. Wood, and *(b)* "The Winning Hand," by J.E. Holley.

"THE WINNING HAND."

Entered according to the Act of C   ess, in the year 1864, by J. E. HOLLEY, in the Clerk's Office   e District Court of the United States, for the Southern District of N   York.
Gurney & Son   Photo NY

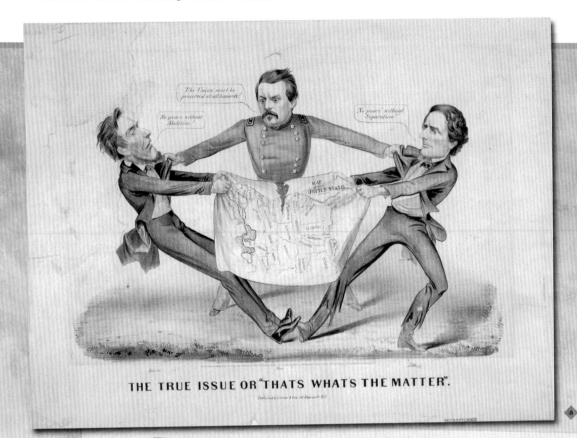

Fig. 1.154. Two examples of pro-McClellan political graphics: *(a)* a Currier & Ives depiction of Little Mac as the conciliator between the belligerents' irreparable positions which tear the country apart; and *(b)* Lincoln playing the fool while McClellan (back to viewer) weeps over battlefield casualties and motions with his hand for Lincoln to back off.

paper, as he frequently said to me personally, in regard to my success in representing the scene, and the men, I shall prize it very highly, not only as a testimonial to exhibit to my friends, but as an heirloom for my children!"[100] It is reported that Lincoln felt the painting was successful. "In my judgment," Lincoln said, "it is as good a piece of work as the subject will admit of . . . and I am right glad you have done it."[101]

1864 SEPTEMBER 21. After nomination by the radical wing of the Republican Party, Gen. John C. Fremont withdraws from the 1864 election, citing the importance of unity in the Republican Party for the future of the country, even though he says he considers "[Lincoln's] Administration has been politically, militarily and financially, a failure, and that its necessary continuance is a cause of regret for the country."[102]

1864 SEPTEMBER. The U.S. Mint strikes Anthony Paquet's Lincoln-Washington medalets. Researcher Bob Julian says these were private medalets stuck for individuals associated with the Mint.[103]

Fig. 1.155. The contrast between these two cartoons could not be more pointed: (a) Howard's "I knew him, Horatio"; and (b) the *Harper's Weekly* cartoon of September 17, 1864, "This Reminds Me of a Little Joke."

1864 OCTOBER. Samuel R. Wells, of Fowler & Wells, and editor of the *American Phrenological Journal and Life Illustrated,* publishes a front-page assessment of candidate Lincoln from his publication's viewpoint (fig. 1.160). The article also has an illustration of Lincoln based on an Anthony Berger photo from the February 9 photo shoot earlier in the year. Wells claims to be unbiased in his approach, claiming a higher calling of phrenological principles and loyalty to the Union.

According to Wells's reading of Lincoln's cranial features, Lincoln's large head is a fine one "most fully developed in the superior portions. . . . The reader will observe," he continues, "how high, long,

Fig. 1.156. Philadelphia diesinkers were active producing Lincoln exonumia. (a) William H. Key produced this commemorative for the National Union League (Sullivan AL 1864-32; also Fuld PCWT 131-479b). (b) Anthony C. Paquet's "The Crisis Demands His Re-Election" (Julian PR-35) is one of the few private, political medals actually struck at the U.S. Mint. This gold example is one of 29 struck at the Mint, which also struck 700 pieces in silver.

Fig. 1.157. Two fine medals contributed by New York diesinkers to Lincoln's 1864 bid for reelection: (a) George H. Lovett's "Honest Old Abe" medal (Sullivan AL 1864-4), and (b) Frederick B. Smith's "Slavery Must be Abolished" medal (Sullivan AL 1864-3).

and broad the top-head is, and how honest, truthful, and decided the accompanying expression of countenance is." Wells says Lincoln is not given to flights of fancy: "His whole make up denotes a matter-of-fact mind." Although Lincoln's features are not classical, he definitely does not present "the repulsive face his prejudiced opponents or enemies would make it out to be. On the contrary, it will pass, in all coming time, for the face of a well-meaning man." If the voters will only choose their officers on phrenological principles, "then we may hope to have, not a set of noisy, drunken rowdies to fill important posts—but capable and honest men. THEN [emphasis in the original] we shall have in each department 'The Right Man In The Right Place,'" a pretty ringing endorsement of Lincoln, after all.

1864 OCTOBER 6. Lucius Chittenden forwards a clipping of a letter he wrote refuting the charge published in the pro-Democrat press that Lincoln demanded his own pay in specie or Gold Certificates while requiring soldiers to accept greenbacks.[104]

1864 OCTOBER 13. Treasurer Spinner also counters claims in the Democrat

press that the president demands that he be paid in "gold or Gold Certificates" while soldiers are being paid in 50-percent greenbacks.[105]

1864 OCTOBER 15. William Seymour Alden sends Lincoln 25¢ "for your autographic *CDV*."[106]

1864 NOVEMBER 5. Lincoln sends autographed photo to Charlotte B. (Mrs. Henry A.) Wise of Boston for use at the National Sailors' Fair. She had written: "I am getting up a Navy Photograph Book for our Sailors' Fair, which opens on the 9th. I want your likeness to begin the book, as head of the Navy. Will you write your name on your Photographic Cards & sent [*sic*] it to me?" To which Lincoln replied most courteously, "It gives me pleasure to comply with your request." On November 8, however, Lincoln declined Alexander H. Rice's request that Lincoln make an appearance at the occasion, but did donate the "mammoth ox, General Grant," for their benefit.[107]

1864 NOVEMBER 8. With 55 percent of the popular vote but 90 percent of the electoral vote, Abraham Lincoln is reelected president of the United States. His second term began the following March.

Fig. 1.159. This rather free interpretation of Lincoln's profile adorns several very rare Civil War–era tokens and storecards, muled with brass button dies. Although it is known to collectors as the "Lincoln Redeemed" die (Fuld PCWT 134) and fetches very fancy prices, the owner of this piece and the present author (among others) doubt that it was intended to show Lincoln.

Fig. 1.158. Lincoln 1864 campaign ferrotypes: (a) Sullivan AL 1864-96, suspended from a ribbon; and (b) AL 1864-103, manufactured under Humphrey Copeley's April 3, 1861, patent.

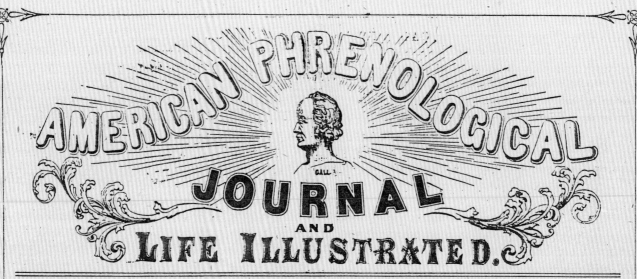

AMERICAN PHRENOLOGICAL JOURNAL AND LIFE ILLUSTRATED.

SAMUEL R. WELLS, Editor.   NEW YORK, OCTOBER, 1864.   [Vol. 40.—No. 4. Whole No. 310.

Published on the First of each Month, at $3 00 a year, by FOWLER AND WELLS, 389 Broadway, New York.

Contents.

	PAGE		PAGE
Abraham Lincoln, Portrait, Character, and Biography...	97	Jennings Demorest, Portrait, Character, and Biography....	113
Debate in Crania...............	99	The African...............	114
Marriage in Oudh...........	102	Marriage in Lapland...........	114
Married Belles...............	103	The Gulf Stream.............	115
Our Teeth and Jaws.........	104	Language...............	116
Stammering—Causes and Cure.	107	Something in Dreams.........	116
Immortality Again...........	109	Benefits of Phrenology.......	117
Wounds of the Brain........	109	Plants Without Seed.........	118
Small-est Human Brain.......	109	First Principles of Phrenology.	119
In Prison...............	110	Railroad Men...............	119
Bible Contradictions.........	110	The New Bishops.............	120
Perils of Cities.............	110	Good Grapes...............	121
Christ's Preaching...........	111	Literary Notices	121
Hymn for America.........	111	To Correspondents...........	122
Mortality—Prayer...........	111	General Items...............	124
A Jewish Wedding	111	Advertisements...........	125
Wm. Pitt Fessenden, Portrait, Character, and Biography...	112	Lobsters and their Habits......	125
		A Pleasant Courtship.........	125

The Journal.

Man, know thyself. All wisdom centers there;
To none man seems ignoble, but to man.—*Young.*

ABRAHAM LINCOLN.

PORTRAIT, CHARACTER, AND BIOGRAPHY.

PRESIDENTIAL CANDIDATES.—It is our intention to publish from time to time, portraits and descriptions of the several candidates nominated by the different conventions. We disclaim any mere party bias, but profess loyalty to the Government, and to look on from a higher stand-point. We may therefore take an impartial view of the different would-be "public servants," and describe them accordingly. When the time comes for the people to choose their officers of trust on phrenological principles, we shall feel a deeper interest. Then we may hope to have, not a set of noisy, drunken rowdies to fill important posts—but capable and honest men. *Then* we shall have in each department "THE RIGHT MAN IN THE RIGHT PLACE."

PHRENOLOGICAL CHARACTER.

OUR portrait of Mr. Lincoln is from a recent photograph by Brady, and was engraved for our use. If not perfect, it is at least one of the best yet produced.

Mr. Lincoln has a tall, spare, large-boned frame, with which his thin, prominent features perfectly correspond, and a head above the average size, and most fully developed in the su-

PORTRAIT OF PRESIDENT LINCOLN.

perior portions. The reader will observe how high, long, and broad the top-head is, and how honest, truthful, and decided the accompanying expression of countenance....

Mr. Lincoln has not a poetical or a sentimental organization, nor has his training been such as to foster romance or fancy. His whole make-up denotes a matter-of-fact mind...

Taken separately, his features are by no means classical, but in combination, they assume a very decided and strongly marked expression of character. Nor is this the repulsive face his prejudiced opponents or enemies would make it out to be. On the contrary, it will pass, in all coming time, for the face of a well-meaning man. Let us look again at this not unattractive face which has

Fig. 1.160. According to the October 1864 issue of *American Phrenological Journal and Life Illustrated,* Lincoln was intelligent, practical, and soulful. The illustration by R.S. Bross was based on Anthony Berger's February 9, 1864, image (Ostendorf-91). "If not perfect," editor Samuel R. Wells wrote, "it is at least one of the best yet produced."

Long ABRAHAM LINCOLN a Little Longer.

1864 NOVEMBER 8. Dennis H. Mahan writes Lincoln that a Honeypod tree at West Point, New York, has been dedicated in his honor as "President Lincoln's tree."[108]

1864 NOVEMBER. Following Lincoln's election, artist Frank Bellew draws one of the classic icon Lincoln images, titled "Long Abraham Lincoln a Little Longer," for *Harper's Weekly* (fig. 1.161a). Bellew stresses both the stature and the second-term aspect of the Lincoln-Johnson victory.

1864. As may be imagined, not everyone is overjoyed by the prospects of another four years of Lincoln's administration. Race-baiting of the type circulated in New York City by L. Seaman, LLD, predicted miscegenation as the fruits of the reelection with a lurid picture of a Black man kissing a white woman.

THE FEDERAL PHŒNIX.

Fig. 1.161. Two of the iconic images of Lincoln's resurgent 1864 election victory: (a) Frank Bellew's "Long Abraham Lincoln a Little Longer," published in the November 26, 1864, issue of *Harper's Weekly,* visually analogizes Lincoln's tall frame with his extended claim on the executive mansion. (b) For John Tenniel in the December 3, 1864, issue of *Punch,* which had despised Lincoln for four years and expected him to be buried, Lincoln's victory achieved mythic proportions. Arising from the burning embers of incinerated commerce, credit, free press, states rights, habeas corpus, and the Constitution, Lincoln's unrepentant visage glares aloof and skyward.

1864 NOVEMBER 16. Eight days after Lincoln's reelection, John Wilkes Booth opens an account at Jay Cooke & Co. Bank with a $1,500 deposit. It is believed that through the funds in this account, Booth would implement his developing plan to do harm to President Abraham Lincoln.

1864 NOVEMBER 21. Attorney General Edward Bates advises President Lincoln that Lincoln has no authority to remit a judgment against a Pennsylvania man in a case involving the counterfeiting of $10 greenbacks, which ironically bear Lincoln's image. The counterfeiting of the federal currency was rife. Prosecutions were hard to come by, and Lincoln's extreme leniency toward those caught up in the crime is a rough patch in his presidential resumé. Fifty-seven times, President Lincoln parted prison gates for convicts charged and convicted in federal courts of counterfeit offenses of federal coins and currency. In terms of historical precedent, Lincoln's executive clemency rate was over the top. Sometimes his moves were strategic. Lincoln pardoned soldiers to improve morale, and granted amnesty to belligerents to tie up the nation's wounds. Many people forget that Lincoln was an experienced courtroom attorney, having served as a licensed, practicing lawyer in Illinois for more than 25 years. During that time, he was involved in more than 5,000 cases, mostly civil litigation, but occasionally criminal trials, including nine counterfeiting cases. Although these counterfeiting cases were not the celebrated cases from Lincoln's professional practice, they do shed light on his actions as president. Case details are given in *The Law Practice of Abraham Lincoln,* second edition. What we find is that Lincoln had been involved as an advocate for the defense several times. His clients had generally been found not guilty or escaped punishment by the quashing of indictments on several occasions. In another case, Lincoln had served as intermediary in the release of a convicted counterfeiter. When he was on the bench as judge, all defendants had been acquitted or been released. In two cases, Lincoln's client had been convicted, but in one of the cases the governor had pardoned the convict. The only case in Lincoln's personal professional experience where a conviction for counterfeiting stuck arose in Federal District Court, where the defendant Swerenger was charged and convicted on multiple offenses of counterfeiting the coin of the realm. In this case, the felon received a tepid fine of $50 and a modest three years' imprisonment. Thus, Lincoln's client was treated very leniently. He could have garnered 3 to 10 years at hard labor or been given up to five years and a fine up to $5,000 for *each* offense.[109]

Under Article II, Section 2 of the U.S. Constitution, presidents have the power to "grant reprieves and pardons for offenses against the United States, except in cases of impeachment." President Lincoln, known for his generous mercy, frequently sprung convicted counterfeiters from their cells. It appears that Lincoln's later use of executive clemency in federal counterfeiting cases is not linked to his handling of pardons in cases relative to desertion, malfeasance, treason, mutiny, conspiracy, and rebellion, where a reasonable motive of strategic interests can be proffered. In contrast, in matters of counterfeiting, his actions imply his rather cavalier consideration of the crime of counterfeiting itself, which may well have been borne out of his experience in Illinois courtrooms. The present author has examined a number of these executive pardons in a series on counterfeiting published in the numismatic trade press. Once in the White

House, Lincoln can be seen engaged in politicking by handing out several of his clemency warrants as political favors. In other cases he exudes almost a "no harm, no foul," laissez-faire approach. Pardons for counterfeiting offenses constituted the single most prevalent crime category for which Lincoln showed clemency. In one egregious case, Lincoln pardoned a notorious counterfeiter, Frederick Biebusch, out of the Missouri State Prison, and on the very next day Biebusch engaged an engraver to prepare fake $10 greenback plates—ones, ironically, with Lincoln's image on them.[110] In another instance Lincoln pardoned counterfeiter John Lawson, alias John Lassano, who had been sentenced to seven years' imprisonment at hard labor.[111] Political Science professor P.S. Ruckman Jr. has nominated Lincoln's pardon of Lawson as the number-four, all-time most egregious "Stink-Bomb [controversial] Pardon" in the centuries of executive clemency in these United States.[112] Absent any consideration of the facts of this case, Lincoln's arbitrary directive might even be said to have been positively *lawsonic!* In Richmond, by contrast, counterfeiting of the Rebel currency brought outrage and capital deterrence up to and including execution for convicted counterfeiters. The culprits were hanged. It is no mystery why fake greenbacks proliferated. While rebels ranted and raved, enacted strict legislation, and prosecuted vigorously, their Northern cousins sat on their hands and effectively yawned. The irony is that, to combat counterfeiting and enforce revenue laws, the Secret Service was created during Lincoln's last cabinet meeting on the day he was assassinated, April 14, 1865, on recommendation of new Treasury secretary Hugh McCulloch.

1864 DECEMBER 6. President Lincoln's annual message to Congress reports organization of 584 national banks by November 25 instant.

1864 DECEMBER 6. Abraham Lincoln names ex–Treasury secretary Salmon P. Chase chief justice of the U.S. Supreme Court because, he said later, Chase on the court would uphold the coming challenges to the legality of the Legal Tender Act and the Emancipation Proclamation. On the court, Chase twice ruled against the Legal Tender Act. He delivered the court's 4 to 3 majority opinion February 7, 1870, in *Hepburn v. Griswold,* declaring the Legal Tender acts unconstitutional. He also delivered a dissent May 1, 1871, in the court's 5 to 4 ruling reversing itself, after President Grant had packed the court for that purpose.

1864 DECEMBER 6. Lincoln's message to Congress recommends restricting currency circulation to national banking institutions alone.

1864 DECEMBER 15. Lincoln pays his special income tax, in the amount of $1,279.13, to defray expenditures for war bounties.

1864 DECEMBER 24. On Christmas Eve, Boston lithographer Louis Prang presents an album of lithographs to Abraham Lincoln.

1864 DECEMBER 30. Middleton & Strobridge publishes a chromolithograph of Lincoln in fall 1864, and evidently sends Lincoln a copy of the print. Lincoln wrote Elijah C. Middleton, the principle of the Cincinnati firm, "Your picture by Mr. Lutz is, in the main, very good. From a line across immediately above the eye-brows, downward it appears to me perfect. Above such line I think it is not so good,— that is, while it gives perhaps a better fore-head, it is not quite true."[113]

1864. Lincoln calls Thomas Nast "our best recruiting sergeant," adding that "his emblematic cartoons have never failed to arouse enthusiasm and patriotism, and have always seemed to come when these articles are getting scarce."[114]

1865 JANUARY 13. The San Francisco Board of Education names a new, public boys' school after President Abraham Lincoln. Lincoln Grammar School in San Francisco was dedicated six months later, in July 1865, in historic downtown San Francisco on the east side of Fifth Street near Market. A brick building was constructed there in 1865. In the interim, of course, Lincoln had been assassinated. Pietro Mezzara's standing sculpture of Lincoln was placed there in 1866. By 1870 Lincoln Grammar School had 960 stu-

dents and about 20 teachers. In 1940 Abraham Lincoln High School was founded in the city. The school was dedicated September 22, 1940.

1865 FEBRUARY 2. President Lincoln requests $5,000 from U.S. House of Representatives "to provide for the usual distribution of medals to the Indians." According to Bob Julian, no Lincoln Indian Peace medals were struck for presentation after April 1863.

1865 FEBRUARY 11. "Sixty days before Lincoln was shot," according to Lincoln's secretary, John Hay, a second life mask is taken (fig. 1.166). According to a Smithsonian Institution researcher, sculptor Clark Mills cast Lincoln's bearded face on February 11, 1865, at the White House: "On February 11, 1865, Abraham Lincoln consented to having another life mask made of him by the sculptor Clark Mills.

FRANK LESLIE'S BUDGET OF FUN.

THE GIANT MAJORITY CARRYING ABE LINCOLN SAFELY THROUGH TROUBLED WATERS TO THE WHITE HOUSE.

Fig. 1.162. Artist Frank Bellew dramatizes Lincoln's 1864 reelection victory in "The Giant Majority Carrying Abe Lincoln Safely Through Troubled Waters to the White House," which appeared in the December 1, 1864, issue of *Frank Leslie's Budget of Fun.* Lincoln is high and dry and all smiles. His opponent is left in the giant's wake, up to his knees in the wash and carrying the demonized minority on *his* back. The importance of the military vote is highlighted by the army club and navy belt-fob.

Fig. 1.163. This muling commemorating the December 1864 Springfield, Massachusetts, Soldiers' Fair combines Joseph Merriam's 1860 Lincoln obverse (Merriam 210a) with John Adams Bolen's Soldiers' Fair reverse (Bolen 123). Note that Merriam's die had been so often used that this example shows a die break across the entire die face from 12 o'clock to 5 o'clock.

The process began with an application of oil over Lincoln's face, followed by the application of a thin coat of wet plaster paste that dried quickly. After fifteen minutes, Mills asked Lincoln to twitch his face, and the plaster loosened, falling off in large pieces into a cloth. The pieces were then reassembled to form the finished mask."[115] Comparison of this mask with the one done five years earlier by Leonard Volk shows a Lincoln looking emaciated and weary from toil. A friend said Lincoln "looked badly and felt badly." Said famous American sculptor Augustus Saint-Gaudens, who used the mask in part in sculpting his great paeans to Lincoln: "So sad. A look as of one on whom sorrow and care had done their worst without victory is on all the features." Mills is perhaps most famous for his equestrian statue of Washington.

1865 MARCH 2. Mathew Brady writes Lincoln: "I have repeated calls every hour in the day for your photograph and would regard it as a great favor if you could give me a sitting to day so that I may be able to exhibit a large picture on the 4th" (inauguration day). "If you cannot call today, please call at your earliest convenience."

1865 MARCH 3. Lincoln signs into law an act to incorporate the Freedman's Savings and Trust Co., commonly known as the Freedman's Bank. The Freedman's Bank opened 37 offices in 17 states, mostly in the South and the District of Columbia. The bank's purpose was to provide a safe place for the savings of African-American veterans, freed ex-slaves, and their families. Most accounts were small.

Fig. 1.164. Lincoln's domestic life was of great public interest: (a) Anthony Berger's intimate February 9, 1864, photograph (Ostendorf-93) of Lincoln and his young son Thaddeus examining a photograph album, reproduced by Boston lithographer Louis Prang; (b) an image of Lincoln and Tad (Ostendorf-114) taken by Alexander Gardner on February 5, 1865, showing the youngster in his custom-made military uniform.

Fig. 1.165. Actor George A. Billings reposed before the fire as Lincoln in *The Dramatic Life of Abraham Lincoln.*

Fig. 1.166. In February 1865 Lincoln posed for Washington, D.C., photographer Lewis Emory Walker, a government cameraman in the employ of the architect of the U.S. Capitol. Lincoln's hair was closely cropped, as in this stereoview (image *a*; Ostendorf-103). His hair stuck out all over the place "like an oven broom," an observer com- mented. The reason for Lincoln's shearing, photo historian Lloyd Ostendorf speculates, is that he was to sit for a second life mask and had experienced difficulty with his hair sticking to the plaster previously. *(b, c)* Sculptor Clark Mills cast Lincoln's face at the White House on February 11, 1865, with this excellent result.

Nearly a half million depositors trusted the institution with $3.7 million. At first, bank assets could be invested only in government securities, but speculation was later permitted. The bank operated until 1874, when an economic downturn coupled with mismanagement and fraud caused it to fail. Frederick Douglass was the bank's last president. Congress permitted the trustees to close the bank, which was formally done June 29, 1874. After its failure, the institution was placed in receivership, and small "dividend checks," with a portrait of Abraham Lincoln, were issued by the U.S. Treasury for several years. Most depositors lost their funds.

1865 MARCH 4. At his second inaugural (fig. 1.168), Lincoln charitably urges "With Malice Toward None." This wonderful and brief speech was lithographed in colors immediately following the event by James B. Rodgers of Philadelphia, on a letter sheet measuring 4.5 inches by 11 inches.[116]

1865 MARCH 6. The last photographs of Lincoln are taken by Henry F. Warren of Waltham, Massachusetts, on the balcony of the White House. It is said that Lincoln was perturbed by the interruption, accounting for his rather stern visage.

1865 MARCH 6. Lincoln appoints Comptroller of the Currency Hugh McCulloch to be secretary of the Treasury.

1865 MARCH 6. In early March 1865, the *New York Times* Chicago correspondent announces plans for the upcoming sanitary fair to benefit Union soldiers. "We have just received assurances that President Lincoln will be present and deliver an opening address at the great fair. Nothing but pressing public duties will prevent." This would have been a triumphant return for Lincoln following the conclusion of hostilities. The Northwestern Sanitary Fair opened in Chicago May 30 and continued to June 21. Of course Lincoln did not attend, but a beautiful bronze memorial medal (fig. 1.170) by German-American engraver and diesinker Anthony C. Paquet and

struck by the U.S. Mint was issued for the occasion. These medals were struck at the U.S. Mint in June, and delivered to the commission's representative on June 20.[117]

1865 MARCH 7. President Abraham Lincoln forwards to Lt. Gen. U.S. Grant his Congressional gold medal, approved by Congress December 17, 1863.

1865 MARCH 18. John Wilkes Booth withdraws the final $25 from his account at Jay Cooke & Co. It is four weeks before he will assassinate the president.

1865 APRIL 3. Richmond falls to federal forces.

1865 APRIL 4. Lincoln enters Richmond in the company of his young son Tad. He walks around the city and is joyfully received as a savior by its African-American population (fig. 1.171).

1865 APRIL 9. Gen. Robert E. Lee surrenders to Gen. U.S. Grant at Appomattox Court House.

1865 APRIL 13. U.S. Mint receives an order for additional Lincoln "The crisis demands his re-election" medals for sale to collectors on the day prior to his assassination.

1865 APRIL 14. In one of his last acts on the day he is assassinated, President Lincoln endorses a check in amount of $500 payable to him for deposit in his bank account[118]; on the same day Lincoln also approves the Treasury plan to create a Secret Service to combat counterfeiting of federal paper money.

1865 APRIL 14. On Good Friday, Lincoln, his wife, and guests attend Ford's Theatre (fig. 1.173) to view *Our American Cousin*. Among items in Lincoln's billfold is a Confederate $5 bill (fig. 1.174). John Wilkes Booth carries out his infernal plan.

Fig. 1.167. A "dividend" check of the Freedman's Savings & Trust Co. These checks were engraved and printed at the BEP with the then-current official Lincoln currency portrait by Charles Burt. Freedman's Savings and Trust Co. passbooks bore the statement: "Abraham Lincoln's Gift to the Colored People. . . . He gave Emancipation, and then this Savings Bank."

2ND. INAUGURATION, MARCH 4, 1865

Fig. 1.168. Lincoln's second inauguration took place on March 4, 1865: (a) a photograph of the event at the U.S. Capitol (Ostendorf-108), taken by an unknown photographer; (b) the handbill for a lottery conducted by J.B. Westbrook, New York City (Vlack-2880), imprinted "Inauguration // Washington March 4, 1865 // Inauguration," with Lincoln currency portrait mimicked to create "value" for the ad note (this is the Vlack plate specimen); (c) inaugural medal (King-866) created by John Adams Bolen.

Fig. 1.169. Keepsakes of the 1865 inaugural celebration: *(a)* a woven silk Stevensgraph ribbon (Sullivan-Fischer AL-14), containing part of Lincoln's inaugural address, made by B.B. Tilt & Son, New York and Patterson, New Jersey; and *(b)* an invitation to the inaugural ball, engraved by Dempsey & O'Toole.

Fig. 1.170. Anthony C. Paquet's excellent medal for the June 1865 North-western Sanitary Fair (Julian CM-45).

Fig. 1.171. The Confederate capital at Richmond fell to Federal forces on April 3, 1865. The very next day Lincoln, accompanied by Tad and officials, toured the city, welcomed by jubilant freed slaves, according to this drawing by L. Hollis, engraved by J.C. Buttre.

Fig. 1.172. This Lincoln portrait (Ostendorf-118) was taken by Alexander Gardner on February 5, 1865, the same day as the photo of Lincoln with Tad in his military uniform. It is often billed as the "last" photograph of Lincoln from life, which it is *not*. Interestingly, the glass negative cracked and the resulting prints show this fault, which has been imaginatively credited as a forewarning of John Wilkes Booth's deadly shot to Lincoln's head.

Fig. 1.173. Following the assassination at Ford's Theatre: *(a)* the building draped in mourning ribbon; *(b)* the presidential box, decorated to honor the fallen president.

Fig. 1.174. In 1976, during the observance of the U.S. Bicentennial, it was unexpectedly revealed that President Abraham Lincoln had been carrying a Confederate $5 bill when he was fatally shot and killed by an assassin. Other items included a pocket knife, two pairs of glasses, a handkerchief, newspaper clippings, and incidentals (re-creation).

Fig. 1.175. An anonymous ribbon with small ferrotypes of Abraham and Mary Todd Lincoln, issued circa 1865.

1865 APRIL 15. Abraham Lincoln dies at 7:22 a.m., across the street from the theater in a boarding-house room. Secretary of War Edwin M. Stanton advises Maj. Gen. John A. Dix of the fact succinctly. By tradition, Stanton also uttered, "Now he belongs to the ages," by which Lincoln has become immortal. For many years, illustrations of clocks in advertisements showed 7:22 in Lincoln's honor. On news of the president's death, the greenback dollar fell from 68¢ versus specie to 60¢.[119]

1865 APRIL 15. Navy Department issues General Order 51 in which the secretary of the Navy announces the death of the president and orders the officers of the Navy and Marine Corps to wear mourning for six months. The following day, the Army's adjutant general issues General Order 66 and subsequent directives specifying the Army's response.

1865 APRIL 15. Philadelphia coin dealer Edward Cogan, the "granddaddy of the American coin trade," postpones the J.N.T. Levick sale of this date due to the Lincoln's assassination. The sale was held two weeks later at Bangs & Co.

Fig. 1.176. Wistful portrayals of the martyred president: (a) George A. Billings in *The Dramatic Life of Abraham Lincoln;* (b) Walter Huston in *Abraham Lincoln;* and (c) Joseph Henabery in *The Birth of a Nation.*

THE ASSASSINATION OF PRESIDENT LINCOLN AT FORD'S THEATRE ON THE NIGHT OF APRIL 14, 1865.

THE ASSASSINATION OF PRESIDENT LINCOLN AT FORD'S THEATRE—AFTER THE ACT.

Chapter 2

Lincoln the Ideal

1865–1909

Fig. 2.1. Lincoln mourning ribbons: *(a)* "In Memoriam, The Nation Mourns" (Sullivan-Fischer AL-M34); *(b)* an unlisted mourning ribbon, "The Martyr President."

The first image the country had of the heinous and cowardly act at Ford's Theatre on the evening of Good Friday, April 14, 1865, was through the illustrated weeklies. Artist Thomas Nast's impression of that fatal scene (facing page) appeared in *Harper's Weekly* on April 19. The tragedy transformed Lincoln from man to martyr. Almost immediately the country's grief translated the mortal Lincoln into the idealized Lincoln. Honest Old Abe the Rail-Splitter, who cracked vulgar jokes and trampled civil liberties, became Father Abraham, The Great Emancipator and Savior of our Nation. Washington may have still been first in the hearts of his countrymen, but Lincoln quickly became a close second. Printmakers equated the two national heroes as father and savior. With the successful end of the war, political antagonisms melted away. The hatchet was buried. Critics in the press repented of their previous harsh views toward the now-deceased martyr. From pulpits across the nation, beginning that Black Easter Sunday and continuing for months, clerics attempted to assuage national grief. On April 19, the day of the Lincoln obsequies in Washington, Treasury Department employees wore black mourning badges with the Lincoln money portrait engraved thereon. Politicians strove to get right with Lincoln and the tenor of public opinion. Merchants fed the national mania with badges, buttons, ribbons, song sheets, and prints expressing a communal empathy. Medalists commemorated the tragic event. Over time, monuments to Lincoln sprang up in Springfield, Illinois, and Washington, D.C.; in New York, Philadelphia, Boston, San Francisco, Chicago, and elsewhere. Repeated efforts were made to name a territory in his honor, so that it would eventually become the State of Lincoln. His sympathizers, such as authors William H. Herndon, Ida Tarbell, John Nicolay, and John Hay, created a Lincoln canon promoting a positive image of the late president.

Ten months after Lincoln's death, Congress held a special ceremony on February 12, 1866, marking what would have been Lincoln's 57th birthday. On the publication of the memorial address, the official Lincoln currency portrait appears as the centerpiece of an elaborate memorial cartouche. In 1867 the Treasury Department used this engraved portrait in an official capacity once again. The occasion was the creation of the National Lincoln Monument Association, incorporated by Act of Congress, March 30, 1867. The association, headquartered in Washington, D.C., solicited funds from individuals to erect a suitable memorial. In 1866 the government decided to put out a black Lincoln memorial stamp. The Springfield

The Lincoln assassination as depicted in *Harper's Weekly*, April 19, 1865 (facing page).

photo, which had been so successful on the government securities and Treasury Notes, was modeled this time by Joseph Ourdan of National Bank Note Co. for this stamp and a second one in 1869.

That year, however, a changing of the guard occurred. Burt's presidential Lincoln portrait was overturned in favor of two new Lincoln images that the talented engraver produced for U.S. securities. The first was used for the 50-cent fractional note based on a photo taken for F.B. Carpenter. Burt's portrait is an exquisite, if ephemeral, design. The notes were quickly counterfeited and replaced. His second new Lincoln portrait was used on the $100 Legal Tender Note

in 1869. The following year it also served on the $500 Gold Certificate. In 1882, yet a fourth Burt engraving was employed on the new series of $500 Gold Certificates. It is reported that the engraver was paid $600 for each. The second $500 Gold Certificate portrait lasted into the Roaring Twenties. It was the Burt engraving that was first used on the $100 Legal Tender Note, however, that was destined to become the most enduring portrait of Lincoln, appearing through the early 20th century, when it was translated for use on the $5 bill, and continued down until recent years. Like their predecessors on government paper money, the new Burt images spawned imitators.

Unheralded in Lincoln literature until now, Charles Burt is truly *the* engraver most responsible for creating the public Lincoln persona through his four Lincoln currency engravings.

1865 APRIL 15. The news of Lincoln's demise travels like a lightning bolt; Rhode Island governor James Y. Smith issues a

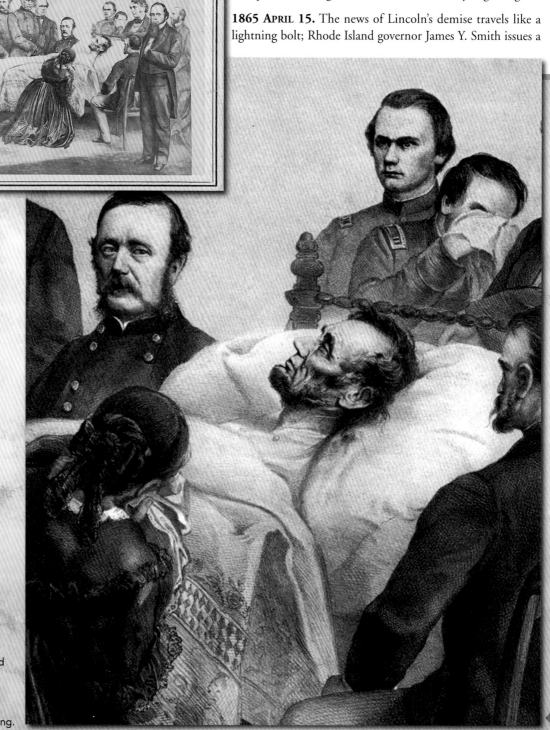

Fig. 2.2. This Lincoln death bed *CDV (a)* was taken from an engraving by N.P. Beers. The close-up *(b)* showing Lincoln being mourned by his wife is from the Beers original engraving.

proclamation to residents of his state requesting the clergy to assemble their congregations the next day "to offer up prayers to Almighty God." In Philadelphia, the city's Select Council meets immediately on Saturday and passes resolutions regarding Lincoln's death. On the 20th, the Philadelphia Common Council did the same. The following day the city's Select Council issued a circular inviting citizens to attend obsequies in the city, according to Boyd. Portsmouth, New Hampshire, and many other cities followed suit.

1865 APRIL 16. "Lincoln as Martyr" is a common theme in many sermons. On Black Easter Sunday, April 16, 1865, "Lincoln the Martyr of Liberty, the Second Christ" was preached from pulpits throughout the North. Thousands of such sermons were preached that day and over the coming weeks. Hundreds of them were printed in pamphlet form in editions of hundreds and thousands. The First Presbyterian Church in Detroit heard their pastor Duffield offer up

"The Nation's Wail." Pastor Richard Eddy called Lincoln the "martyr to Liberty" at the First Universalist Church in Philadelphia. These sentiments were echoed at congregations in Connecticut, Pennsylvania, and Washington, D.C. In Castine, Maine, Rev. Alfred E. Ives preached from II Samuel 19:2 on "victory . . . turned into mourning."

1865 APRIL 16. Lincoln is also deified as a savior. Cincinnati pastor the Reverend M.P. Gaddis of the Sixth Street Methodist-Presbyterian Church delivers a sermon titled "Washington the Father & Lincoln the Savior of Our Country" at Pike's Opera House so a larger audience can attend. His text is II Samuel 3:38: "And the king said unto his servants, Know ye not that there is a prince and a great man fallen this day in Israel." Gaddis's sentiment was on the lips of many of his colleagues and in the hearts of many Christian believers that Easter morning. The local newspaper printer released 3,000 copies. In New Bedford, Massachusetts, Alonzo H. Quint, pastor of the

Fig. 2.3. Two large Lincoln mourning cards: (a) "Memento Mori"; (b) Charles Magnus's "The Martyr of Freedom."

North Congregational Church, also saw Lincoln as the savior of his country. His message, arising from Deuteronomy and Isaiah, was, "National Sin Must Be Expiated by National Calamity: What President Lincoln Did for His Country."

Ironically, Lincoln's consecration as the "savior of our country" was presaged by a political opponent—a Democrat senator from Lincoln's birth state of Kentucky, John J. Crittenden—three years before fate declared it so. In a speech on the Senate floor April 24, 1862, against the Second Confiscation Bill (which would have stripped rebels of land, property, and slaves), Crittenden passionately urged Lincoln to back off the subject of slavery. "There is a niche in the Temple of Fame," Crittenden said, "a niche near to Washington, which should be occupied by the statue of him who shall save his country. Mr. Lincoln has a mighty destiny." Lincoln's ally Owen Lovejoy responded just as vigorously the next day. "I too have a niche for Abraham Lincoln; but it is in Freedom's holy Fane [Temple], and not in the blood-besmirched temple of human bondage. . . . Let Abraham Lincoln make himself, as I trust he will, the emancipator, the liberator, as he has the opportunity of doing, and his name shall not only be enrolled in this earthly temple, but it will be traced on the living stones of that temple which rears itself amid the throne and hierarchies of heaven."

1865 April 17. On Monday, all ministers of all denominations in the District of Columbia meet jointly at the First Baptist Church to express their "sore bereavement which the country has suffered in the sudden decease of our beloved Chief Magistrate." Ministers didn't wait for the coming Sunday to preach sermons at events throughout the following week.

1865 April 17. The assistant secretary of state orders the wearing of mourning for a period of six months to those subject to State Department orders, including consuls and ministers abroad. The Treasury Department does the same. On April 18, the secretary of the interior did likewise. Other cabinet members followed suit.

1865 April 19. Wednesday is the appointed day for funeral obsequies (orations) of the late president. Ceremonies in Washington, D.C., include funeral services at the White House. According to Boyd, admission was by special ticket only. A funeral procession (fig. 2.6) conveyed Lincoln's body to the U.S. Capitol, where he lay in state in the rotunda.

Around the country, clergy members spoke to their flocks. Scores of these sermons were later printed for distribution: 1,000 copies of the sermon by Reverend Morgan Dix of Saint Paul's Chapel in New York City; 500 copies of the remarks by Reverend Richard Duane to his flock at Saint John's Church, Providence, Rhode Island; 600

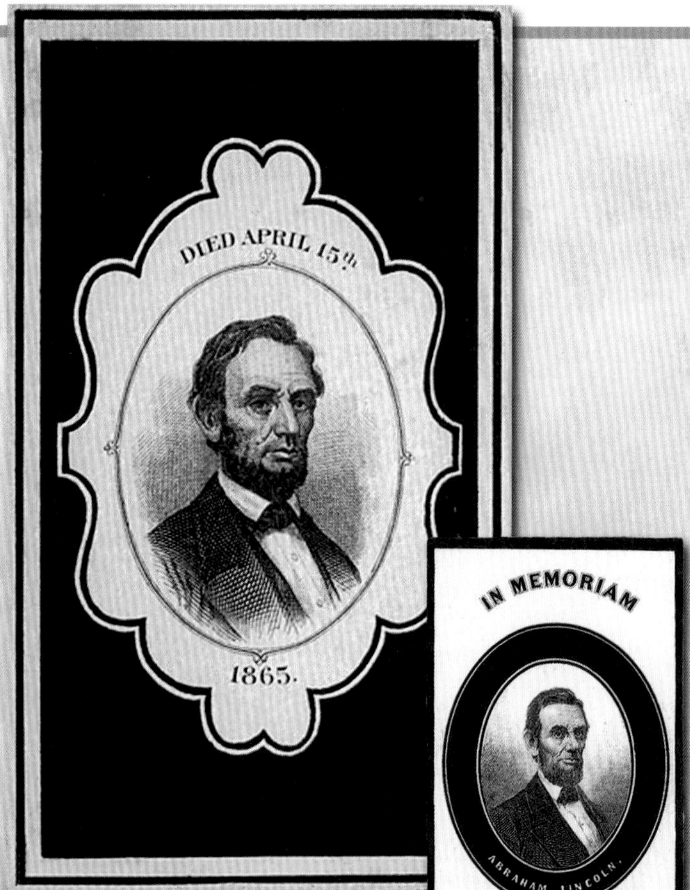

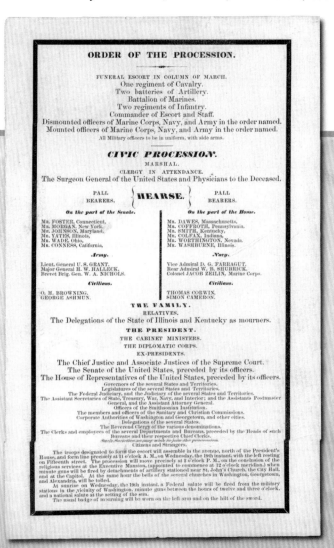

Fig. 2.4. A pair of mourning *CDVs*, the second showing the Lincoln of the $10 bill.

ORDER OF THE PROCESSION.

FUNERAL ESCORT IN COLUMN OF MARCH.
One regiment of Cavalry.
Two batteries of Artillery.
Battalion of Marines.
Two regiments of Infantry.
Commander of Escort and Staff.
Dismounted officers of Marine Corps, Navy, and Army in the order named.
Mounted officers of Marine Corps, Navy, and Army in the order named.
All Military officers to be in uniform, with side arms.

CIVIC PROCESSION.
MARSHAL.
CLERGY IN ATTENDANCE.
The Surgeon General of the United States and Physicians to the Deceased.

PALL BEARERS. { HEARSE. } PALL BEARERS.

On the part of the Senate.
Mr. FOSTER, Connecticut,
Mr. MORGAN, New York,
Mr. JOHNSON, Maryland,
Mr. YATES, Illinois,
Mr. WADE, Ohio,
Mr. CONNESS, California,

On the part of the House.
Mr. DAWES, Massachusetts,
Mr. COFFROTH, Pennsylvania,
Mr. SMITH, Kentucky,
Mr. COLFAX, Indiana,
Mr. WORTHINGTON, Nevada,
Mr. WASHBURNE, Illinois.

Army.
Lieut. General U. S. GRANT,
Major General H. W. HALLECK,
Brevet Brig. Gen. W. A. NICHOLS.

Navy.
Vice Admiral D. G. FARRAGUT,
Rear Admiral W. B. SHUBRICK,
Colonel JACOB ZEILIN, Marine Corps.

Civilians.
O. H. BROWNING,
GEORGE ASHMUN.

Civilians.
THOMAS CORWIN,
SIMON CAMERON.

THE FAMILY.
RELATIVES.
The Delegations of the State of Illinois and Kentucky as mourners.
THE PRESIDENT.
THE CABINET MINISTERS.
THE DIPLOMATIC CORPS.
EX-PRESIDENTS.
The Chief Justice and Associate Justices of the Supreme Court.
The Senate of the United States, preceded by its officers.
The House of Representatives of the United States, preceded by its officers.
Governors of the several States and Territories.
Legislatures of the several States and Territories.
The Federal Judiciary, and the Judiciary of the several States and Territories.
The Assistant Secretaries of State, Treasury, War, Navy, and Interior; and the Assistants Postmaster General, and the Assistant Attorney General.
Officers of the Smithsonian Institution.
The members and officers of the Sanitary and Christian Commissions.
Corporate Authorities of Washington and Georgetown, and other cities.
Delegations of the several States.
The Reverend Clergy of the various denominations.
The Clerks and employees of the several Departments and Bureaus, preceded by the Heads of such Bureaus and their respective Chief Clerks.
[illegible]
Citizens and Strangers.

The troops designated to form the escort will assemble in the avenue, north of the President's House, and form line precisely at 11 o'clock A. M., on Wednesday, the 19th instant, with the left resting on Fifteenth street. The procession will move precisely at 2 o'clock P. M., on the conclusion of the religious services at the Executive Mansion, (appointed to commence at 12 o'clock meridian,) when minute guns will be fired by detachments of artillery stationed near St. John's Church, the City Hall, and at the Capitol. At the same hour the bells of the several churches in Washington, Georgetown, and Alexandria, will be tolled.

At sunrise on Wednesday, the 19th instant, a Federal salute will be fired from the military stations in the vicinity of Washington, minute guns between the hours of twelve and three o'clock, and a national salute at the setting of the sun.

The usual badge of mourning will be worn on the left arm and on the hilt of the sword.

Fig. 2.5. Lincoln's funeral arrangements were very carefully controlled. Here is the "Order of the Procession" for the official observance on Wednesday, April 19, 1865. Military units formed at 11 a.m. Following "religious services at the Executive Mansion" at noon, the public procession started "precisely at 2 o'clock p.m."

copies of David Dyer's sermon to the inmates of Albany Penitentiary, a U.S. military prison. In Hudson, Ohio, Henry L. Hitchcock's theme was "God acknowledged in the Nation's bereavement." His text from Job 1:21 stressed that "the Lord gave, and the Lord hath taken away; blessed be the name of the Lord," and was printed to the extent of 1,000 copies. Spiritual messages that day were not confined to Christian clerics. In Baltimore, Rabbi H. Hochheimer's message stressed Leviticus 10:6, bewailing "the burning which the Lord hath kindled." His remarks were also reprinted, in an edition of 350. At the Synagogue of Mikvé Israel in Philadelphia, Rabbi S. Morais spoke on Joel 2:17 about the lamentation of the priests, "Spare thy people, O Lord." His remarks are reprinted in an edition of 500.

Secular voices were also heard that day: firebrand abolitionist Wendell Phillips, who had opposed Lincoln's reelection in 1864, spoke glowingly of him at Tremont Temple in Boston; 2,000 copies of his remarks were printed. In Syracuse, New York, former congressman Charles B. Sedgwick's address was reprinted in an edition of 1,000 copies. J.G. Holland, a member of the Massachusetts Historical Society, delivered a eulogy on Lincoln at City Hall in Springfield, Massachusetts; it was printed in a large edition of 5,000 copies. The following year, Holland released his monumental *Life of Abraham Lincoln,* which became a runaway best-seller (80,000 copies in print by January 1867).

1865 APRIL 20. Lincoln's body lies in state in Washington, D.C. Thursday, April 20, is set aside by New York's Governor Fenton as a day of mourning. Reverend Dr. Eugene Augs. Hoffman, rector of Grace Church, Brooklyn Heights, preached a sermon on "the Martyr President" that day, and printed 500 copies for distribution. On April 20 both the secretary of the navy and the secretary of war directed officers to accompany the president's remains to Springfield.

1865 APRIL 20. Grand Council U.S.A. of the Union League adopts resolutions relating to the death of President Lincoln. Henry Ward Beecher lamented, "Dead, dead, dead, he yet speaketh!"—a reference to Hebrews 11:4.

1865 APRIL 21. Lincoln's remains and those of his son Willie (who had died in Washington in 1862) are placed aboard a railroad car for transportation back to Springfield, Illinois. The special train wound nearly 1,700 miles, stopped at 12 major cities, and arrived home—after a 15-day trip—on May 3. The various railroad lines printed up

Fig. 2.6. This stereoview shows Lincoln's funeral procession in Washington, D.C.

Fig. 2.7. Mourning mementoes: *(a)* a Lincoln plaster plaque by J. Powell, *(b)* a "Sacred to the Memory" *CDV,* and *(c)* a Lincoln mourning crepe badge.

SACRED TO THE MEMORY OF

ABRAHAM LINCOLN

16ᵗʰ PRESIDENT OF THE UNITED STATES

DIED APRIL 15ᵗʰ 1865

WE MOURN OUR COUNTRY'S LOSS

special schedules, often trimmed in black. "Lincoln's funeral tour was the most prolonged, most elaborate, and most repeated ceremony in American history," said Dr. Thomas F. Schwartz, then–interim executive director of the Abraham Lincoln Presidential Library and Museum. He estimated that nearly a million people witnessed Lincoln's funeral tour. That same day, the funeral organizing committee in Springfield issued a black-bordered invitation to attend the ceremony.

1865 April 22. *Harper's Weekly,* which consistently praised Lincoln in life, calls him "Second only, if it be second, to Washington himself."[1]

1865 April 22. The Union League Club of New York publishes a circular for its members instructing them to take part in the funeral services scheduled to be held in the city two days hence. Perhaps the first glimmer of a national healing is the largest mass meeting in the

history of Savannah, Georgia. According to Boyd, between 8,000 and 10,000 turned out on this day to attend a tribute to the late President Lincoln.

1865 April 23. People continue to look to spiritual leaders to help them understand the seemingly senseless slaughter of the nation's lamb. Lincoln sermons continue the following Sunday. In Washington, D.C., for example, Dr. A.D. Gillette, pastor of the First Baptist Church, saw God "above all national calamities" in the events of the day. His message was based on Isaiah 6:1—"In the year that King Uzziah died, I saw the Lord seated on a throne, high and exalted, and the train of his robe filled the temple." Some 2,500 copies of his message were distributed as pamphlets. Later, at an evening service in Washington, D.C., R.J. Keeling, rector of Trinity P.E. Church, likened Lincoln's demise to the death of Moses. As Keeling preached from Deuteronomy 34:7–8 about the children of Israel weeping for

Fig. 2.8. Ceremonies were held along the route of the Lincoln funeral train, seen in the background. In Chicago, the Lincoln funeral hearse was accompanied by members of the Chicago Light Guard. George W. Gage, co-owner of Tremont House, is the prominent officer standing slightly apart from the crowd on the sidewalk.

Moses in the plains of Moab, his audience was large and "tumultuous with excitement," according to an eyewitness.

1865 APRIL 24. The Historical Society of Pennsylvania passes a resolution on the death of Lincoln. The same day, New York photographer Jeremiah Gurney sneaked into New York City Hall where Lincoln was lying in state and took a photo of the open coffin (see litho, fig. 2.11). The military sequestered Gurney's photo. Jeremiah was the "J." of J. Gurney & Sons, who had issued the pro-McClellan *CDVs* the previous fall and who would receive a silver medal for best "colored photographs" at the American Institute Fair several months later.[2]

1865 APRIL 25. Historian George Bancroft delivers funeral obsequies for Abraham Lincoln in New York City at a special ceremony held at Union Square. In Columbus, Ohio, civic leaders meet at City Hall to consider a statue to Mr. Lincoln and a monument to deceased Ohio soldiers.

1865 APRIL 26. Lincoln's assassin, John Wilkes Booth, is captured and killed at Garrett's farm in Virginia.

1865 APRIL 27. The American Numismatic and Archaeological Society in New York City resolves to strike a medal to honor Abraham Lincoln.

1865 APRIL. William Cullen Bryant's ode "Death of Lincoln" laments:

> In sorrow by thy bier we stand,
> Amid the awe that hushes all,
> And speak the anguish of a land
> That shook with horror at thy fall. . . .

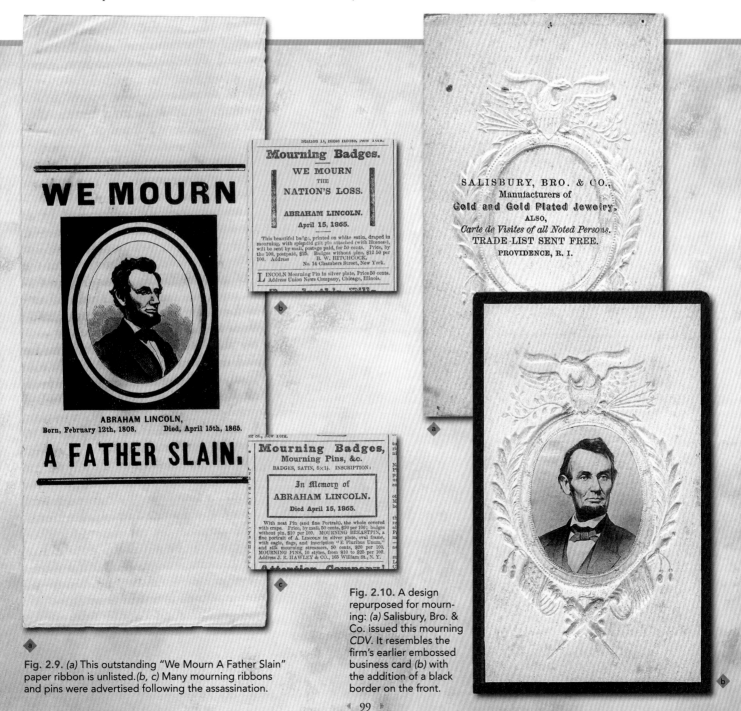

Fig. 2.9. *(a)* This outstanding "We Mourn A Father Slain" paper ribbon is unlisted. *(b, c)* Many mourning ribbons and pins were advertised following the assassination.

Fig. 2.10. A design repurposed for mourning: *(a)* Salisbury, Bro. & Co. issued this mourning *CDV*. It resembles the firm's earlier embossed business card *(b)* with the addition of a black border on the front.

THE BODY OF THE MARTYR PRESIDENT, ABRAHAM LINCOLN.
LYING IN STATE AT THE CITY HALL, N.Y. APRIL 24TH & 25TH 1865.

Pure was thy life; its bloody close
Hath placed thee with the sons of light,
Among the noble host of those
Who perished in the cause of Right.

1865. Following the assassination, Isaac Arnold says, "No pen will ever be able to do justice to the memory of Abraham Lincoln." That didn't keep our best writers from trying. Emerson wrote prophetically: "Heaven . . . shall make him serve his country even more by his death than by his life."

1865. Eulogies like "A shrine which before all good men bow" appear in *Leslie's Illustrated.* Schuyler Colfax delivers an oration on the "Life and Principles of Abraham Lincoln"

Fig. 2.11. New York City photographer Jeremiah Gurney took surreptitious photos of Lincoln's body lying in state at New York City Hall during the transfer of his remains from Washington, D.C., to Springfield, Illinois, for burial. Secretary of War Stanton destroyed the originals, but that didn't stop Currier & Ives from showing Lincoln lying in state on this *CDV* of a lithograph (facing page).

Fig. 2.12. Two interesting *CDV*s attempted to show the spiritual side of the assassination: *(a)* Satan breathes his villainy into John Wilkes Booth; *(b)* Booth is haunted by ethereal visions of Lincoln as the assassin attempts to flee the nation's capital after doing his evil deed.

Entered according to act of Congress, in the year 1865, by Francis Hacker, in the Clerk's Office of the District Court of Rhode Island.

THE ASSASSIN'S VISION

in the Court House Square at South Bend, Indiana. In Chicago he later delivered another, in which he said: "[Lincoln] bore the nation's perils, trials, and sorrows, ever on his mind. . . . I feel a presentiment that I shall not outlast the rebellion. When it is over, my work will be done."[3] Congressman George S. Boutwell delivered a eulogy on Lincoln's death at Huntington Hall before the citizens and city council of Lowell, Massachusetts. One of the largest such gatherings heard Miss Emma Hardinge's "Great Funeral Oration on Abraham Lincoln" at New York City's Cooper Institute. The audience consisted of 3,000 persons; 2,000 copies of her address were printed.

1865 MAY 1. The British House of Commons holds a memorial tribute service for Lincoln. Benjamin Disraeli said Lincoln's death "touches the heart of nations, and appeals to the domestic sentiments of mankind." In the House of Lords, Lord John Russell praised Lincoln's "character of so much integrity, sincerity and straightforwardness, and at the same time of so much kindness."

1865 MAY 2. President Andrew Johnson issues a proclamation offering rewards for Confederate president Jefferson Davis and others for complicity in the murder of Abraham Lincoln. The proclamation

Fig. 2.13. Pictures of a nation grieving: *(a)* Lincoln the martyr stereoview; *(b)* "The Nation Mourns" cover (Milgram-371 variant); and *(c)* "Columbia weeping at Lincoln's casket" by Thomas Nast, *Harper's Weekly*, April 29, 1865.

Fig. 2.14. New York manufacturing jeweler B.T. Hayward advertised the first memorial badge in *Harper's Weekly* April 29, 1865. This is believed to be King-258, produced by George H. Lovett.

charged that "it appears, from evidence in the Bureau of Military Justice, that the atrocious murder of the late President Abraham Lincoln, and the attempted assassination of the Honorable William H. Seward, secretary of state, were incited, concerted, and procured by and between Jefferson Davis, late of Richmond, Virginia, and Jacob Thompson, Clement C. Clay, Beverly Tucker, George N. Saunders, William C. Cleary, and other rebels and traitors against the government of the United States, harbored in Canada," and offered rewards.

1865 MAY 2. Memorial obsequies are not restricted to U.S. houses of worship: on May 2 Dr. Henry P. Tappan preaches on the death of Lincoln in the Dorothean Church in Berlin, Germany. Over the

course of the next month, Rev. James Wayman (Newington Chapel, Liverpool, Great Britain) spoke on the passing of human greatness and the death of Lincoln; Rev. Newman Hall (Surrey Chapel, London) preached a sermon on the Lincoln assassination; Rev. A.G. Simonton (Rio de Janeiro) preached a Lincoln-themed message at a special Divine Service; Right Rev. Dr. Wm. Ingraham Kip preached at Frankfort-am-Main, Germany. Foreign civil services were also conducted, such as the April 19 ceremony for Lincoln conducted by Kingston, Canada, mayor, John Creighton. In Vienna, Austria, a play was staged entitled *Four Years of Civil War in America; or the death of Abraham Lincoln.*[4] The Manchester (Great Britain) Union and Emancipation Society also held a special ceremony.

Fig. 2.15. Handmade engraved mementoes of the martyr president are especially prized: *(a)* the engraved silver dollar, redated 1865, praised Lincoln's "emancipation of the oppressed;" *(b)* the splendid engraved likeness is the familiar $10 pose. The legend states this medal was presented by General Lafayette C. Baker, who commanded the national detective police that tracked down presidential assassin John Wilkes Booth, to Captain G. Cottingham. Baker and his soldiers split the $100,000 reward for apprehension of Booth. Cottingham received $1,000 of that sum.

Fig. 2.16. Due to the sudden calamity of Lincoln's assassination, medalists reworked dies in their inventory to prepare memorial pieces. Both of these are dual 1865/1864-dated pieces: *(a)* an 1864 campaign medalet with a commemorative inscription dated 1865 on reverse (King-278), and *(b)* a tiny brass amulet (King-125).

1865 MAY 4. Lincoln is buried in Springfield, Illinois, at the Oak Ridge Cemetery. Poet Walt Whitman memorializes the sad day of Lincoln's burial with the verse "Hush'd Be the Camps To-Day," which calls for singing "of the love we bore him." Whitman's poem was imprinted on silk mourning ribbons with Lincoln's picture based on the $10 Legal Tender Note model, and with the words "God Save the Union and Our Martyr." Interestingly, the date of Lincoln's death was incorrectly listed as April 16! Whitman had witnessed Lincoln's second inauguration in March.

1865 MAY. *Frank Leslie's Illustrated Newspaper* publishes a special memorial edition, in paper covers, of its several papers covering the assassination and funeral ceremonies in Washington, Philadelphia, New York City, Albany, Buffalo, and Springfield.

1865. For the rest of the year, the daily newspapers weave a lot of ink, and the weeklies—mostly the illustrated weeklies—embroider word and picture stories describing the aftermath of the Lincoln assassination. This nation had never experienced a similar tragedy. The country was on an unfamiliar path toward an uncertain future. Each observer seem-

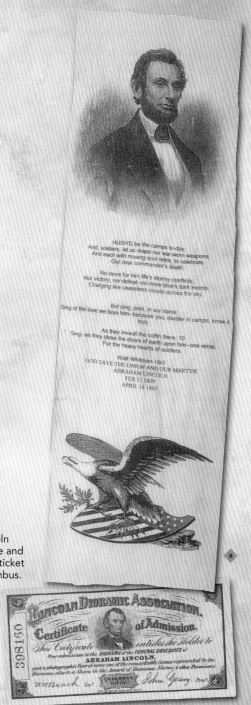

Fig. 2.17. "In Memory of Abraham Lincoln, the Reward of the Just," by William Smith, Philadelphia, shows the martyr Lincoln robed in white (purity) and purple (royalty) ascending the celestial light into the heavens accompanied by angelic beings. Below on earth Lincoln is both venerated by the people and the state, and mourned by people, Liberty, and America. The print is a copy of an earlier engraving "Apotheosis of George Washington," with the substitution of Lincoln's face for Washington's.

Fig. 2.18. (a) Walt Whitman's paean to Lincoln appeared on a moving ribbon. (b) Strobridge and Co., Cincinnati, lithographed this admission ticket to the Lincoln Dioramic Association in Columbus. It also represents itself as a "share." Although the Lincoln funeral train passed through Columbus, and his remains laid in state at the state capitol, the impossibly large numbers on these "tickets," their flimsy but generally pristine condition, and the lottery aspect of the undertaking cast doubts on the motives of the promoters, causing one contemporary cataloger to remark: "no doubt another 19th-century way to milk the public for their grief and make a buck!"

ingly grasped at something familiar in the chaos. The monthlies had to wait until their May issues: *Sailor's Magazine and Seaman's Friend* celebrated Lincoln as "the Commander-in-chief of the Army and Navy, a Christian."[5] *Hunt's Merchants' Magazine* had a fine engraving of the president by W.G. Jackman. Fowler and Wells, the New York proprietors of the *Phrenological Journal,* also reported on the death, as if their readers had been caught short, but slanted it to their particular niche; editor S.R. Wells trimmed the story in black. In 1866 Wells's *Illustrated Annual of Phrenology and Physiognomy* carried another illustrated paean to the "Martyr President."

1865. Scores of memorial engravings and lithographs pour off the presses in a dozen cities following the calamity of Good Friday. The first response, naturally, was sorrow, or as one printmaker observed, "His life the brightest page of our Nation's glory; his death the saddest of our Nation's sorrows." In New York, Currier & Ives issued a mourning lithograph in three sizes, one for every pocketbook. Kimmel and Forster, Bufford, and Prang also issued new or revised lithographs. All of the engravers who chronicled Lincoln's rise to fame now contributed to his immortal presence, including J.C. Buttre (see fig. 2.19a), John C. McRae, John and Samuel Sartain, H.B. Hall, and George E. Perine.

Fig. 2.19. New York engraver John Chester Buttre created this wonderful mourning item *(a)*. The cartouche surrounding the engraving of Lincoln photo Ostendorf-92 depicts the slaying of the dragon of rebellion and the restoration of peace. Also shown *(b)* is an Ostendorf-92 ABRHAM [*sic*] LINCOLN cabinet card by Mason, New York.

1865. Mourning songs, mourning covers, and mourning cards trimmed with black borders proliferate. Philadelphia publishers J. Magee and Sam Upham, and New York publisher Charles Magnus, all of whom had celebrated Lincoln's rise and trials with printed notices, covers, and so on, were quick to supply mourning sheet-music, too. Both Magnus and Upham published Upham's wife Louise's funeral ode, "The Nation is Weeping." Lincoln funeral marches (see fig. 2.20) included a funeral march by F. Hoffmann published in German in Leipzig.[6]

1865. "Apotheosis" (from the Greek "apotheoun," *to deify*)—in other words, Washington and the angels crowning Lincoln in the clouds—becomes a theme for coping with the national sadness (see

fig. 2.21). John Sartain's engraving of "The Martyr, Victorious" was full of the heavenly host playing harps, the crowning of Lincoln with a wreath, the paternal welcoming home of the martyr by the father of our country (see fig. 2.22). Lincoln's translation into the heavens was a popular theme. H.H. Lloyd's large (36-by-27-inch) print was titled "Abraham Lincoln . . . Ours the Cross, his the crown," featuring as a border to the portrait incidents from Lincoln's life. Another, smaller Lloyd print showed Columbia weeping and depositing evergreens on a monument to the slain leader. The message embroidered on Bostonian Louis Prang's color lithograph was, "He left it [Springfield] in peace, to preside over a Nation then in bondage. He now reposes under its soil, a martyr to the Freedom he won."[7]

Fig. 2.20. New York City lithographer Charles Magnus issued (a) the colorful lettersheet "The 25th of April 1865 in New York," and (b) the songsheet "The Nation is Weeping" with Louise S. Upham's poem and somewhat similar design; (c) Magnus's "The Nation Mourns" songsheet bears his version of the ubiquitous $10 bill Lincoln portrait.

1865. Washington-and-Lincoln-themed prints of all kinds appear. James F. Bodker, of Madison, Wisconsin, publishes a composite photograph employing the Lincoln head on John C. Calhoun's body, and sells the image as a jumbo cabinet card (about 8.5 inches by 11 inches; see fig. 2.23). Kimmel & Forster in New York City publish the lithograph "Columbia's Noblest Sons," which also achieves wide distribution on *CDVs*. In this illustration, Columbia crowns father Washington and savior Lincoln with wreaths, her foot staunchly upon the neck of a crouched lion (see fig. 2.24a). Currier & Ives show the two pillars of American history, Washington and Lincoln, shaking hands at the altar of liberty (see fig. 2.24b).

1865 MAY 6. A less garish, more domestic scene becomes popular, Lincoln and his son in repose. A very large woodcut of a photograph of Lincoln and Tad dominates the front page of *Harper's Weekly*, accompanying an article by Lincoln intimate, correspondent Noah Brooks (fig. 2.25).

1865 MAY 6. Vilification to veneration: *London Punch* editor Tom Taylor (Mark Lemon) writes a lengthy lament in the May 6, 1865, issue of his magazine, which had been so critical of Lincoln's motives for four years. The elegy is also reprinted as a quarto sheet with illustrator John Tenniel's *Britannia Sympathizes with Columbia* (see fig. 2.26). In the poem, Taylor takes himself to task savagely "for his mocking pencil . . . [and] self-complacent British sneer." The editor apologizes for making fun of Lincoln's appearance and lack of debonair ways. He says Lincoln's martyrdom shames him, lames his pencil, and confutes his pen. He calls Lincoln "this rail-splitter, a true-born king of men." The

WASHINGTON & LINCOLN, (APOTHEOSIS.)

Fig. 2.21. S.J. Ferris's poignant "Washington & Lincoln (Apotheosis)" was published as a *CDV* by Philadelphia Photo Co., showing Washington crowning Lincoln with the laurel of deification.

Fig. 2.22. Detail of "Abraham Lincoln, The Martyr Victorious," engraved by John Sartain and published by W.H. Hermans, Penn Yann, New York.

editor has come to rue, Taylor confides, his own shallow judgments of Lincoln. Several stanzas will show its tenor:

> He went about his work—such work as few
> Ever had laid on head, and heart and hand—
> As one who knows where there's a task to do;
> Man's honest will must Heaven's good grace command; . . .
>
> So he grew up, a destined work to do,
> And lived to do it: four long-suffering years
> Ill-fate, ill-feeling, ill-report, lived through,
> And then he heard the hisses change to cheers,
>
> The taunts to tribute, the abuse to praise,
> And took both with the same unwavering mood;

> Till, as he came on light, from darkling days,
> And seemed to touch the goal from where he stood,
>
> A felon hand, between the goal and him,
> Reached from behind his back, a trigger prest—
> And those perplexed and patient eyes were dim,
> Those gaunt, long-laboring limbs were laid to rest!

1865. Remorse over critics' treatment of Lincoln is more general than exceptional. Even the vitriolic Baltimore illustrator Adalbert Volck, who had been a savage critic of Lincoln while he lived, found room for generosity.

1865 MAY 11. Almost immediately—in fact, only a week after Lincoln's internment—plans are laid for a permanent monument. Arti-

Fig. 2.23. "The Father, and the Savior of Our Country" links Washington and Lincoln in important ways. Washington has his hand on the Constitution; Lincoln's hand is near the quill, representing the Emancipation Proclamation. This image was extremely popular as *CDVs*, cabinet cards, and prints. This example was published by Jas. F. Bodtker, Madison, Wisconsin. Purchasers didn't know and wouldn't have cared to know that the Lincoln figure is actually Lincoln's head on an earlier engraving of John C. Calhoun.

Fig. 2.24. In death, Lincoln was immediately linked to Washington: *(a)* in "Columbia's Noblest Sons," by Kimmel & Forster, the goddess Liberty crowns them with laurels; *(b)* in Currier & Ives's "Washington and Lincoln, the Father and the Saviour of Our Country," Washington welcomes Lincoln at the altar of Liberty.

cles of association and by-laws, rules, and regulations of the National Lincoln Monument Association were adopted at Springfield, Illinois, May 11, 1865. This was followed quickly by publication of circulars on the proposed Lincoln monument by the State Superintendent of Public Instruction. In June 1865, the association sent out additional circulars on their project to the public, requesting support for the venture, and the following month a similar appeal was addressed to soldiers and sailors. On January 24, 1868, the organization issued another circular to the public. Four days later the association called for "Artists of the United States" to supply ornamentation for the memorial. It was, art historians have pointed out, "the only open competition for a monument to Lincoln held in the 19th century."[8] The competition was won by American sculptor Larkin G. Mead. In 1869

the association issued a certificate of subscription, including a view of the proposed monument "to be erected at a cost of $200,000."

1865 MAY 15. Auguste Laugel's tribute "Le President Lincoln" in *Revue de Deux Mondes* is published in Paris.[9] Among other incidents, Laugel praises Lincoln's sympathy for a destitute army wife, his patience with his son's interruptions, and his devotion to Shakespearean drama. "It matters not to me," Laugel quotes Lincoln as saying, "whether Shakespeare be well or ill acted; with him, the thought suffices."[10]

1865 MAY 16. Following closely on the heels of the Springfield memorial is the Colored People's Educational Monument Association to the Memory of Abraham Lincoln, organized May 16, 1865, at Washington, D.C. (see fig. 2.30). "By the Act of Emancipation, Mr. Lincoln built for himself forever the first place in the affections of the African race in this country. The love and reverence manifested

Fig. 2.25. After publishing salacious and gory images of the Lincoln assassination in its issues immediately following the tragic events, *Harper's Weekly* turned to a quiet domestic scene for the cover of its May 6, 1865, issue. This woodcut (shown top right), based on a photograph, accompanies a story by Lincoln intimate Noah Brooks. The photograph became particularly popular after Lincoln's death, but the president autographed at least one example (shown top left) which fetched nearly $125,000 in a 2004 Mastro Auctions sale.

Fig. 2.26. The same day as the Lincoln and Tad image appeared in *Harper's Weekly,* across the pond the London *Punch,* which had been super critical of Lincoln in his lifetime, published this moving tribute by John Tenniel, "Britannia Sympathises with Columbia."

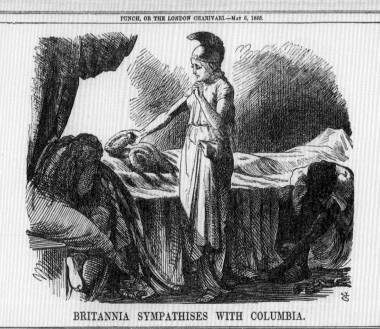

PUNCH, OR THE LONDON CHARIVARI.—MAY 6, 1865.

BRITANNIA SYMPATHISES WITH COLUMBIA.

for him by many of these poor, ignorant people has, on some occasions, almost reached adoration."[11]

1865 MAY 18. George Alfred Townsend, special correspondent for several New York newspapers under the pseudonym "GATH," publishes *The Life, Crime and Capture of John Wilkes Booth . . . and the Pursuit, Trial and Execution of his Accomplices,* Dick & Fitzgerald, 64 pages, in an edition of 40,000 copies!

1865 MAY 31. The Abraham Lincoln five-cent oblate Internal Revenue stamp design is approved (see fig. 2.50).

1865 JUNE 1. Many churches and synagogues in the North observe a national Day of Prayer, Fasting, and Humiliation called for by President Andrew Johnson in light of the events of Lincoln's assassination. Many of these observances were joint services that bring communities together, such as the united service of the Congregational and Methodist Churches in Springfield, Massachusetts. Others included Professor H. Harbaugh's lecture on "Treason and Law" at Clearspring, Maryland. Baltimore rabbi H. Hochheimer's enlisted Deuteronomy for his message on the burning justice of the Lord. Philadelphia rabbi S. Morais spoke on "The Treacherous Deal Very Treacherously," citing Isaiah 24:16, "Woe unto me!" as his text. Rev-

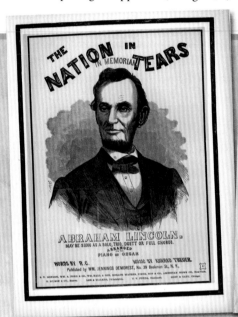

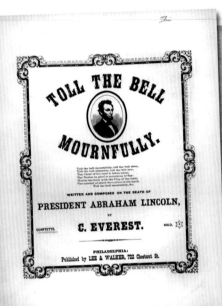

Fig. 2.27. Musical compositions played an important role in public and private remembrances. "The Nation in Tears" was published by Wm. Jennings Demorest, and "In Memory of Abraham Lincoln" was published by Beer & Schirmer, both in New York. "Toll the Bell Mournfully" was published Lee & Walker, Philadelphia.

Fig. 2.28. The memory of Lincoln the great statesman and beloved president "is enshrined in every loyal heart," according to this small medal by Miller, New York (King-284).

Fig. 2.29. This mourning *CDV,* published by W.I. Pooley, New York, sold for 25 cents. It shows the familiar image of Lincoln and Tad perusing a photo album at Brady's Washington, D.C., studio. Published quickly after Lincoln's assassination, it was captioned, more in spirit than in truth, "President Lincoln reading the Bible to his son Tad." The disingenuous Pooley ads are from an anonymous newspaper (left) and *Harper's Weekly,* May 13, 1865 (right).

erend T.R. Howlett, from Washington's Calvary Baptist Church, talked about God's dealings with our nation. Reverend E.S. Johnston, of the Second English Evangelical Lutheran Church of Harrisburg, Pennsylvania, used Daniel 4:25, preaching on God's teaching mankind that "the most High ruleth in the kingdom of men, and giveth it to whomsoever He will."

1865 JUNE 1. In Massachusetts, Governor John A. Andrew also issues a proclamation calling for a special day of prayer in the commonwealth in recognition of the bereavement by the president's death. Charles Sumner delivers a Lincoln eulogy before the municipal authorities of Boston. Ticknor & Fields published 3,000 copies of

his address. Rhode Island governor James Y. Smith issued a similar proclamation, which was printed as a large poster for distribution.

1865. Books lamenting the sordid tragedy and extolling Lincoln's virtues pour off the presses. Some of the most well circulated were authored by Mrs. P.A. Hanaford, who in 1865 published *Our Martyred President,* in an edition of 2,000 copies, and "Abraham Lincoln, his Life and Public Services," in an edition of 20,000. Her book was immediately translated by W. Würzburger, and 5,000 German-language copies were printed. Books honoring the fallen leader were published in Berlin, Paris, and Athens in 1865, and in Florence and Utrecht in 1866. In 1865 Thayer's "Pioneer Boy" juvenile biography

Fig. 2.30. Constitution of the (Colored People's) Educational Monument Association to the Memory of Abraham Lincoln, organized May 16, 1865.

CONSTITUTION

OF THE

Educational Monument Association

TO THE

MEMORY OF ABRAHAM LINCOLN.

ORGANIZED MAY 16, 1865.

WASHINGTON, D.C.:
McGILL & WITHEROW, PRINTERS.
1865.

Fig. 2.31. Used mourning covers such as this May 29 (1865) posting from South Weymouth, Massachusetts, to a soldier still stationed in Washington, D.C. (Milgram-370), are prized by collectors.

Fig. 2.32. Lincoln's image appeared on various revenue strips (stamps), including: (a) 1865 100 cigars revenue stamp (Springer TC26/27); (b) 1870 4 oz. tobacco revenue stamp (Springer TG16B); and (c) 1870s 16 oz. tobacco revenue stamp (Springer-TG49A, BEP die no. MISC1449).

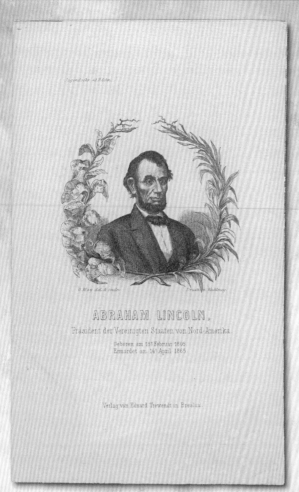

Fig. 2.33. The tragedy of Lincoln's death transcended national borders. This memorial engraving by O. May was published in Breslau, Germany, by Druck & Kuhlmey.

Fig. 2.34. Medals were popular items by which to remember the fallen president: *(a)* Swiss medalist Hugues Bovy created this memorable memorial medal (King-230) in Geneva, especially desirable in silver. *(b)* Bovy also created the small amulet (King-280) with a loop for suspension (reverse shows actual size).

Fig. 2.35. This cased tintype of Lincoln (Ostendorf-92) is likely a memorial item manufactured in 1865.

Fig. 2.36. This small evocative mourning medal (King-266) employs an urn under a weeping willow tree, and the verse "A Sigh, the Absent Claim, the Dead, a Tear," a sentiment of British philosopher Edmund Burke that was frequently duplicated on colonial samplers.

was translated into Greek. Engravings commemorating Lincoln were published in London by Alexander Strahan.

1865 JUNE. Artist Francis B. Carpenter publishes a tribute "In Memoriam" in *Hours at Home* magazine. One of the odder tributes to Lincoln was artist Carpenter's publication of President Lincoln's favorite poem entitled "Oh! Why Should the Spirit of Mortal be Proud?" Carpenter said he copied down the poem "while our lamented Chief was reciting it," in March 1864.[12] In 1865 Derby and Miller, New York published Henry J. Raymond's *The life and public services of Abraham Lincoln . . . together with his state papers, including his speeches, addresses, messages, letters, and proclamations, and the closing scenes connected with his life and death . . . To which are added anecdotes and personal reminiscences of President Lincoln, by Frank (Francis) B. Carpenter.* Carpenter's contribution was a long, rambling narrative, mostly from secondhand accounts. Among his insightful remarks: "It has been the business of my life to study the human face, and I have said repeatedly to friends that Mr. Lincoln had the saddest face I ever attempted to paint."[13]

1865 JUNE 2. New York sculptor Adolph Leconte files for a patent for an Abraham Lincoln medallion.

1865 JUNE 20. Anthony Paquet's North Western Sanitary Fair medal "Memoria in Aeterna" (In Eternal Memory) is delayed. Due to a snafu at the U.S. Mint (the Mint's medal press was broken when the medal was ordered) delivery of these medals to the sponsoring organization was delayed until June 20. Since the Fair closed June 21, it is improbable that many, if any, of these delightful medals actually were sold at the Fair. According to U.S. Mint medal historian Bob Julian, the representative of the organization Sanitary Commission, a Mr. Bryan, received 1,000 of these medals on June 20, but the original order had been for 3,000.[14] Perhaps delay in the striking of this medal accounted for the scaled-down production.

1865 JUNE 27. Washington, D.C., sculptor Franklin Simmons files for a patent for an Abraham Lincoln medallion design.

1865 CIRCA. The so-called Lincoln "quarter" (see page 54, fig. 1.122) is struck or restruck. Note King-878 is dated 1864, but a second variety, listed King-870, also has his date of assassination.

1865 JULY 4. After nearly three months of national mourning, the country is ready for respite. The annual Fourth of July celebration of 1865 proves an elixir. Washington/Lincoln ribbons proliferate at celebrations across the Northern states (see fig. 2.38). The Colored People's Educational Monument Association stages a celebration in memory of Abraham Lincoln on the Presidential Grounds in Washington, D.C. (see fig. 2.39). At Gettysburg, Pennsylvania, Major General O.O. Howard dedicates the laying of the corner stone of the monument in the Soldier's National Cemetery there.

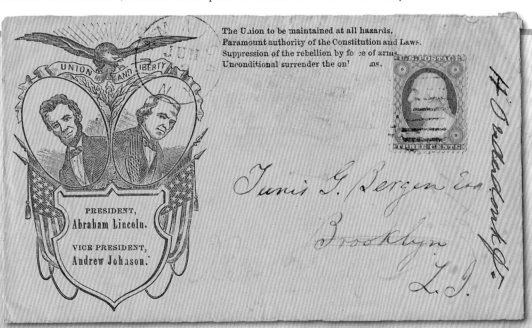

Fig. 2.37. This enigmatic Lincoln-Johnson campaign cover (Milgram-153) was manufactured by S. Raynor, New York. It was originally sent to Bay Ridge (Brooklyn). The address was effaced and stamp removed, and then posted in June (1865) at Jamaica, New York, to another addressee in Brooklyn with an uncurrent, demonetized postage stamp.

Fig. 2.38. After nearly three months of national wailing and gnashing of teeth, the Fourth of July celebration in 1865 gave America a chance to blow off steam. The Colored People's Educational Monument Association in Memory of Abraham Lincoln staged its celebration on the Presidential Grounds. It is suspected that this Washington-Lincoln ribbon was distributed at that event.

1865 JULY 4. Surprisingly, Lincoln was honored on Mexican national/state bonds issued-dated July 4, 1865, printed by United States Bank Note Co. in New York City. These 1,000-peso bonds of los Estados Unidos de Mexico y los Estados de Tamanlipas y San Luis Potosi were payable 20 years from September 1, 1865. A portrait vignette of Washington also appeared on these large, very ornate bonds (fig. 2.40).

1865 JULY 17. James Russell Lowell recites his ode "The First American" at a ceremony honoring Harvard graduates who gave their lives during the Civil War, calling Lincoln "our Martyr-Chief."

1865 JULY 18. Maine sculptor Franklin Simmons receives a design patent for a medallion of Abraham Lincoln. This medallion has a profile brass bust, 15.5 inches by 10 inches by 3 inches deep, affixed to wooden panel 22 inches by 17.25 inches, and weighs 25 pounds. It was manufactured by Wm. Miller & Co. Metallists of Providence, Rhode Island.

1865 JULY 19. Within 100 days of Lincoln's assassination, a provincial town named Lincoln is initiated near Buenos Aires, Argentina, in honor of the martyred American president, through a decree of the Chamber of Deputies of the province (see fig. 2.41). The Brazilian Senate sanctioned the project on June 13th, and the Executive okayed the plan three days later. Through a series of additional enactments, surveys were undertaken, land allotments were granted, and the town limits were established. By February 23, 1875, the city was officially organized. Initially municipal officials were appointed until constitutional provisions provided for elections. In 2001, Lincoln, Argentina, had about 27,000 residents.

1865. Domingo Faustino Sarmiento, Argentina's minister to the U.S., writes *Vida de Abrám Lincoln Decimo-sesto Presidente de los Esta-*

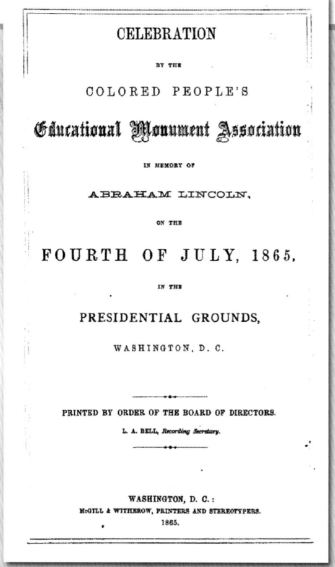

Fig. 2.39. The July 4, 1865, celebration of the Colored People's Educational Monument Association in Memory of Abraham Lincoln was supported by Frederick Douglass, Massachusetts governor John Andrew, General John C. Fremont, Chief Justice Salmon P. Chase, and Charles Sumner, and featured speeches by Wm. Howard Day and Senator Henry Wilson, and the poetry of John Pierpont. Thousands gathered, including government officials, in day-long festivities to celebrate "a nation redeemed by the commingled blood of the Anglo-Saxon and Anglo-African races" and the memory of Abraham Lincoln.

Fig. 2.40. July 4, 1865, was also the issue date of this magnificent 1,000 pesos United States of Mexico bond, States of Tamanlipas and San Luis Potosi (only half of which is shown to emphasis the Lincoln portrait), printed by United States Bank Note Co., New York City. In a similar position on the right side is a vignette of George Washington.

dos Unidos, supposedly the first Spanish-language Lincoln biography, to be published by D. Appleton & Co. (1866, 306 pages). Two years later Sarmiento became Argentina's president.

1865. Shortly after Lincoln's assassination, Chicago renames Lake Park, converted from an old cemetery the previous year on the city's north side, to Lincoln Park in the president's honor. The city allocates $10,000 for improvements. Today the park occupies 1,208 acres, Chicago's largest, and includes the city's zoo, Chicago History Museum (formerly Historical Society), and Chicago Academy of Sciences.

1865 AUGUST 10. The first statue in honor of Abraham Lincoln erected in the United States following his assassination is unveiled at the San Francisco Mechanics Institute Fair in Union Square. The plaster cast of a standing Lincoln with his arm outstretched and crushing the serpent of rebellion was accomplished by Pietro Mezzara, a San Francisco sculptor and cameo cutter. According to a con-

temporary newspaper account: "[Mezzara's Abraham Lincoln is] standing beside the tree of liberty, with his right foot firmly planted on the reptile of Secession that issues from the roots. The left arm being stretched out at full length with the hand grasping the scroll of the Emancipation Proclamation. His right hand with open palm spread out as a protection to the Constitution and the emblem of Union, that rest upon the trunk of the tree of liberty." The statue was on display in the square for 26 days. Mezzara offered the figure to the San Francisco school board, but the Board of Education had no funds available for that purpose, so a group of civic-minded citizens raised the money and purchased the statue from the sculptor. At the sculptor's request, the re-unveiling of the statue in place outside the Lincoln Grammar School was held on the anniversary of Lincoln's assassination, April 14, 1866. The heroic-sized figure stood 9 feet tall on a pedestal of 10 feet in height (fig. 2.43). After standing tall for 23 years, Lincoln's outstretched left arm fell off. Answering an

Fig. 2.41. Within a hundred days of Lincoln's assassination, a provincial town in Argentina was named in his honor.

Fig. 2.42. This hand-colored memorial lithograph by Kimmel & Forster, New York, was one of the author's first purchases of Lincolniana.

ABRAHAM LINCOLN,
SIXTEENTH PRESIDENT OF THE UNITED STATES.
Born Feb. 12th 1809. Died April 15th 1865.

Published by Christiansen & Forster 254 & 256 Canal St. N.Y.

appeal from the school board, an anonymous donor came forward to have the entire statue cast in bronze. On January 25, 1889, the new bronze casting of Mezzara's Lincoln statue was placed on its original pedestal, where Lincoln cast out the demons of rebellion and slavery for another 18 years. On April 18, 1906, the city of San Francisco succumbed to the violent demons of fire, set loose by a great earthquake which leveled much of the city's downtown. The flames set off by the shockwaves burned for up to three days. Mezzara's bronze Lincoln was one of its casualties. It melted in the conflagration, and only a single finger from its right hand was found.

1865 FALL. U.S. Mint strikes Paquet assassination medals, including a small copy of William Key's Broken Column medal (see fig. 2.45).

1865 FALL. Whitman's elegy "When Lilacs Last in the Dooryard Bloom'd," written in the weeks following Lincoln's death, first appears in *Sequel to Drum-Taps,* published by Gibson Brothers.

1865 SEPTEMBER 21. The American Numismatic and Archaeological Society Lincoln medal committee exhibits a "rough cast from the obverse die, which gives great promise," according to a report in the September 24 *New York Times.* The artist, Emil Sigel, "expects to have the first installment of medals ready by the middle of October." At the meeting, the Society also reviewed a communication from "Mr. Barber, a distinguished member of the Royal Academy, and now of Providence, concerning a large bronze medallion of Lincoln, executed under his superintendence."

1865 OCTOBER. The October 1865 issue of *Atlantic Monthly* publishes a 13-page poetic tribute to Lincoln by Henry Howard

Fig. 2.43. The first monumental statue raised to the memory of Lincoln was by sculptor Pietro Mezzara, originally for the Mechanics Institute Fair in San Francisco in August 1865. Thereafter it was placed in front of Lincoln School House, Fifth Street, San Francisco. Unfortunately it did not survive the inferno touched off by the Great San Francisco Earthquake of 1906.

Fig. 2.44. One of the first uses of Continental Bank Note Co.'s die no. 1, its version of the $10 bill Lincoln portrait, was on this Soldiers Monument Association certificate from Galena, Illinois, dated August 28, 1865.

Fig. 2.45. The broken-column symbol: *(a)* The reverse of this small U.S. Mint medal, Julian PR-38, depicts a "Broken Column," emblematic of Lincoln's life having been cut short. Dies were originally made by Anthony C. Paquet in fall 1865, but new dies were cut four years later by William Barber to meet demand for the popular memento. *(b)* Paquet's small "Broken Column" medal was a cheap knock-off of fellow Philadelphia engraver William H. Key's magnificent two-inch "He is in glory and the Nation in tears" / "Broken Column" medal. This rich, chocolate bronze example is one of the originals, with the engraver's initials still prominent.

Brownell. "We looked on a cold, still brow, but Lincoln could yet survive; He never was more alive, Never nearer than now."

1865 OCTOBER. In October 1865, the government introduces a 25-cent revenue stamp for newspapers and periodicals. This large-sized imprint featured an odd profile of Lincoln. The stamp measured nearly four inches tall by slightly over two inches wide. The stamps were engraved and printed by the National Bank Note Co., and issued in carmine, orange, and gold, although trial printings were done in other colors, such as blue-black (fig. 2.49). Like many of the government currency and revenue imprints of the time, counterfeiters quickly duplicated this issue, too.

1865 NOVEMBER 4. *New York Saturday Press* publishes poet Walt Whitman's melancholy lament "O Captain! My Captain!" It is an immediate success, is widely reprinted, and solidifies Whitman's reputation. "O Captain! . . . the prize we sought is won . . . But O heart! . . . You've fallen cold and dead." Whitman revised the poem in 1871.

1866 JANUARY 18. Painter Francis B. Carpenter records in his diary that the American Bank Note Co. surprised him with an offer of $1,000 for the right to use the Halpin-Lincoln portrait on the $3 bill.[15] Many hobbyists know that the $3 denomination was normal for paper money of that era. In fact, the U.S. government minted a $3 gold coin. The original designs for the $1 and $2 Legal Tender notes, issued-dated August 1, 1862, anticipated the issuance of a companion $3 bill, since they bore medallion counters with all three denominations shown. The U.S. Treasury, however, never authorized the $3 notes, and it wasn't until 1869 that Charles Burt's engraving based on the Halpin-Lincoln model was finally used on U.S. currency, but on a 50-cent note.

Fig. 2.47. The stylized Lincoln monument in the upper right of this 1865 California Lincoln Testimonial donation receipt shows a block "L" crowned by a laurel wreath on a pediment.

Fig. 2.48. This cover (cropped at right), "The Nation Mourns // Its Chief Has Fallen," Milgram-372, uses a similar likeness of Lincoln as the donation receipt in figure 2.47, a recent photograph by Alexander Garner, Ostendor-116, taken February 9, 1865.

Fig. 2.46. Anthony Berger's photo of Lincoln taken February 9, 1864 (Ostendorf-92) became increasingly popular. Here it is represented by *(a)* a hand-colored engraving by W.G. Jackman, and *(b)* an 1865 *CDV* of a similar engraving by J.C. Buttre.

Fig. 2.49. National Bank Note Co. printed this 25-cents newspaper/periodical revenue stamp, Springer PR3, used for prepayment of postage on bulk shipments of publications in 1865. Some believe this to be the first U.S. stamp portraying Lincoln (BEP die no. P0129).

Fig. 2.50. An 1865 revenue imprint (Turner Type P, RN-P6) from a stock certificate scrip for the Panama Rail Road Co., New York, dated October 25, 1865. The design had been approved May 31, 1865.

1866. In the aftermath of Lincoln's assassination, all is not sorrow and melancholy; anger is also rife. Sherman & Co., in Philadelphia publishes a screed (harangue), "Jefferson Davis and his complicity in the Assassination of Abraham Lincoln . . . and where the traitor shall be tried for treason" in 1866. In 1868 poet J. Dunbar Hylton coined the term "Praesidicide" to apply to John Wilkes Booth's act.

1866 FEBRUARY 11. Dr. George H. Perrine of the American Numismatic and Archaeological Society delivers bronze examples of the ANAS "Salvator Patriae" Lincoln medal by Emil Sigel to President Johnson and George Bancroft in the name of the society (see fig. 2.54). "It was intended to deliver these medals in due form tomorrow, as part of the proceedings at the Capitol, but this could not be done without a disturbance of the previously prepared programme. Both the President and Mr. Bancroft expressed themselves delighted with the medals, and the remarkable accuracy of the likeness."[16]

1866 FEBRUARY 12. On the anniversary of what would have been Lincoln's 57th birthday, Congress holds a special ceremony in his honor. Printed invitations were sent out by L.F.S. Foster, president of the Senate, and Schuyler Colfax, Speaker of the House, dated February 5, 1866. Admittance was by special ticket only. In attendance were both houses of Congress, President Andrew Johnson, the Cabinet, General Grant, Chief Justice Salmon Chase, foreign ministers, and other dignitaries, to hear a memorial oration by historian George Bancroft. A severe Lincoln critic during the war, Bancroft professed a largely altered view of Lincoln's significance. "Lincoln is the genuine fruit of institutions where the laboring man shares and assists to form the great ideas and designs of his country," the historian told the solons. The Government Printing Office printed and distributed 10,100 copies of the speech . The volume had a memorial frontispiece engraved and printed at the Treasury Department (see fig. 2.55). The NBNCo Lincoln portrait die appears as the centerpiece of an elaborate memorial cartouche of weeping angels surmounted by an eagle with a facsimile "A. Lincoln" autograph below. These items are highly prized by collectors as forerunners of the souvenir card series.

1866 APRIL 6. The Grand Army of the Republic is founded at Decatur, Illinois, by Benjamin F. Stephenson as a political and fra-

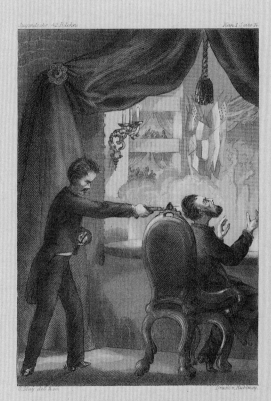

Lincoln's Ermordung.

Verlag von Eduard Trewendt in Breslau

Fig. 2.52. Crosby Opera House in Chicago was billed as the finest theatrical venue west of the Atlantic coast. Performances included Shakespearean plays, and popular crooners. This $5 certificate "entitles the bearer to one fine steel engraving" as a premium. It also carries a 5-cent Lincoln revenue imprint, Turner Type P, RN-P5.

Fig. 2.53. This very rare, circa 1866 $50 remainder note with Lincoln's image was necessitated by the delayed receipt of national currency for the First National Bank of Idaho, Boise City, Idaho Territory. These notes were essentially circulating drafts to be drawn on the bank account of B.M. DuRell & Co., Silver City (Owyhee), Idaho Territory, at the First National Bank. Notes do not bear an imprint, but do have the unmistakable Lincoln $10/$20 note portrait type. Another, less rare but still scarce variety of this scrip, presumably issued subsequently, has the location as Idaho City in upper left on face, and right end on back.

Fig. 2.51. German engraver O. (probably Otto) May interpreted Lincoln's assassination in this grizzly manner in "Lincoln's Ermordung," for Druck & Kuhlmey and published circa 1866 by Eduard Trewendt in Breslau, Germany.

ternal organization for honorably discharged veterans of Union war service between April 12, 1861, and April 9, 1865. Local groups were organized as posts, and posts generally worked within states as departments. On the national level was the commander in chief. Members were elected by casting black and white balls. Members met annually in encampments, which were held over several days, essentially as conventions with speeches, banquets, and fraternizing. In 1868 GAR commander-in-chief General John A. Logan instituted the first Memorial Day for remembering the sacrifices of fallen comrades and decorating their graves. The GAR was active in relief work, backed pension legislation, and founded soldiers' homes for the care of its members. In post–Civil War America, the GAR was also very powerful and mostly Republican in politics. Five of its members were elected presidents of the United States: U.S. Grant, Rutherford B. Hayes, James A. Garfield, Benjamin Harrison, and William McKinley. "For a time it was impossible to be nominated on the Republican ticket without the endorsement of the GAR voting bloc," according to an historian of the organization. Membership in 1890 (including the group Sons of Union Veterans of the Civil War) was still more than 400,000 veterans.

1866 April 14. A year after Lincoln's assassination, former Union major general, the Honorable Congressman James A.

Garfield of Ohio, delivers an address in memory of Abraham Lincoln in the U.S. House of Representatives. Fifteen years later, as president, Garfield too would be the victim of an assassin's bullet, forever linking their memories.

1866 April 15. One year after Lincoln's death, the United States issues a 15-cent memorial stamp (Scott 77). Although trials appear in several other colors (e.g., blue), the stamp is issued in black as a formal death tribute to the slain leader (see fig. 2.56). This denomination was deliberately chosen to export veneration of our slain leader across the seas, since 15 cents was the normal rate for international mail to England and France, among other places. The earliest known usage on cover was August 14, 1866. Approximately 2,139,300 of these stamps were issued.

1866 May. New copper-nickel five-cent coins, called "nickels," are authorized by the Act of May 16, 1866. Previously the five-cent coin had been exclusively a silver half dime. The U.S. Mint experimented with portrait designs of both George Washington and Abraham

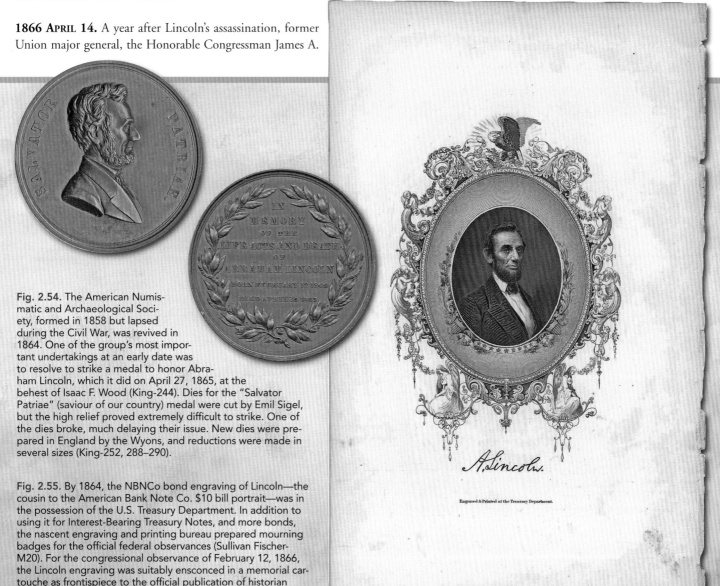

Fig. 2.54. The American Numismatic and Archaeological Society, formed in 1858 but lapsed during the Civil War, was revived in 1864. One of the group's most important undertakings at an early date was to resolve to strike a medal to honor Abraham Lincoln, which it did on April 27, 1865, at the behest of Isaac F. Wood (King-244). Dies for the "Salvator Patriae" (saviour of our country) medal were cut by Emil Sigel, but the high relief proved extremely difficult to strike. One of the dies broke, much delaying their issue. New dies were prepared in England by the Wyons, and reductions were made in several sizes (King-252, 288–290).

Fig. 2.55. By 1864, the NBNCo bond engraving of Lincoln—the cousin to the American Bank Note Co. $10 bill portrait—was in the possession of the U.S. Treasury Department. In addition to using it for Interest-Bearing Treasury Notes, and more bonds, the nascent engraving and printing bureau prepared mourning badges for the official federal observances (Sullivan Fischer-M20). For the congressional observance of February 12, 1866, the Lincoln engraving was suitably ensconced in a memorial cartouche as frontispiece to the official publication of historian George Bancroft's memorial address on what would have been Lincoln's 57th birthday.

Lincoln, striking patterns in the adopted 75 percent copper, 25 percent nickel composition and other metals. Washington had previously been considered for bronze two-cent coins two years earlier. In this instance, as previously, the presidential portraits were scrapped in favor of patriotic mottos and shields. If either the Lincoln or Washington nickels had been issued, it would have been the first circulating U.S. coin with a real portrait of an individual. Columbus and Isabella would appear on U.S. commemorative coins in 1892–1893 and Washington and Lafayette in 1900, but it would be 1909 before Lincoln would appear on a coin of the realm.

1866. Artist Francis Bicknell Carpenter publishes his book *Six Months at the White House with Abraham Lincoln.*

1866 MAY 1. Carpenter's painting is a huge success, and as early as May 1, 1866, Alexander Hay Ritchie's engraving of Carpenter's "First Reading of the Emancipation Proclamation" is published (see fig. 2.59). The following year *New York Galaxy* editor Fred. B. Perkins published a history of the work. His title was as long as it is descriptive: *The Picture and The Men: Being Biographical Sketches of President Lincoln and his Cabinet; together with an account of the Life of the celebrated Artist, F. B. Carpenter, Author of the Great National Painting. The first reading of the emancipation Proclamation before the Cabinet by President Lincoln; including also an account of the Picture; An Account of the crisis which produced it; And an Appendix containing the great Proclamation and the Supplementary Proclamation of January 1, 1863; together with a Portrait of the Artist, and a Key to the Picture.* Perkins's book was published in New York by A.J. Johnson, and also in Cleveland and Chicago, 190 pages. Other publishers engaged engravers such as Serz and Herline to do their own renditions of the presentation of the historic document to the cabinet.

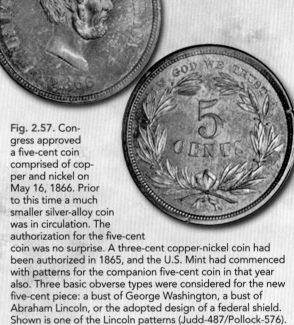

Fig. 2.57. Congress approved a five-cent coin comprised of copper and nickel on May 16, 1866. Prior to this time a much smaller silver-alloy coin was in circulation. The authorization for the five-cent coin was no surprise. A three-cent copper-nickel coin had been authorized in 1865, and the U.S. Mint had commenced with patterns for the companion five-cent coin in that year also. Three basic obverse types were considered for the new five-cent piece: a bust of George Washington, a bust of Abraham Lincoln, or the adopted design of a federal shield. Shown is one of the Lincoln patterns (Judd-487/Pollock-576).

Fig. 2.56. Officially, when the government issued a memorial postage stamp in Lincoln's honor (Scott 77) on the anniversary of his death April 15, 1866, it returned to the $10/$20 bill model. A small portrait of the same style was engraved by Joseph Ourdan, BEP die no. P0110, and the 15-cent stamps were printed in black by NBNCo. A proof block is shown.

Fig. 2.58. Presidents of the United States *CDV*, Washington to Andrew Johnson, circa 1866.

1866 MAY 25. Harrison Brothers & Co. files a design patent for the Lincoln Pure White Lead label, which pictures Lincoln and the slogan "In Memoriam. By its purity & excellent qualities, this lead deserves the name bestowed upon it." (See fig. 2.60.)

1866 JULY 28. Congress awards 18-year-old sculptor Vinnie Ream a commission for a Lincoln statue to be placed in the U.S. Capitol, by H.R. Joint Resolution 197 (fig. 2.62).

1866. John Sartain publishes his masterpiece *Abraham Lincoln, the Martyr Victorious,* depicting George Washington and a heavenly host escorting the martyr into the heavens (refer back to fig. 2.22).

1866. The Lincoln Institute is founded in Jefferson City, Missouri, by veterans of the 62nd and 65th United States Colored Infantry. The institution's program combined education and labor for freedmen. The school was redesignated as Lincoln University of Missouri in 1921, but remained segregated until 1954. Today it provides both undergraduate and graduate degree programs.

Fig. 2.59. Francis B. Carpenter's painting "First Reading of the Emancipation Proclamation" was displayed to great acclaim, and engraved by Alexander Hay Ritchie to achieve commercial success. However, the perfectionist in Carpenter caused him to overpaint his canvas, particularly the Lincoln portrait, several times before *(a)* the historical canvas was acquired by the United States by gift. *(b)* Ritchie's engraving was eventually published by Derby & Miller. *(c)* Ritchie's Lincoln is shown in close up.

Fig. 2.60. Commercialization of the Lincoln image may have arisen during his lifetime, but certainly by May 25, 1866, when Harrison Brothers & Co. filed its Lincoln Pure White Lead paint label design with the U.S. Patent and Copyright Office.

Fig. 2.61. *(a)* At the White House in the first half of 1864, artist F.B. Carpenter painted a portrait of Lincoln from life as part of a study for his large canvas "First Reading of the Emancipation Proclamation." *(b)* Later New York engraver Frederick Halpin translated the painting into a print for public sale. Halpin, an itinerant English printer, had just recently returned from the South and a stint in the firm of Archer & Daly, producing Confederate treasury notes and stamps.

1866 OCTOBER. William Edgar Marshall's engraving of Lincoln is published by Ticknor & Fields (see fig. 2.65). This large stipple-and-line engraving measures 21 inches by 16 inches. The publisher also issues a 13-page pamphlet on the engraving. From the first, Marshall's Lincoln was acknowledged as one of the best Lincoln images. Proof prints cost $20.[17]

1866 OCTOBER 13. Author Victor Hugo writes a letter to Lincoln's widow Mary Todd Lincoln to accompany presentation of a gold memorial medal from the eminent citizens of France. Translated, it read: "MADAM: On behalf of more than forty thousand French citizens, anxious to manifest their sympathies for the American Union, in the person of one of its most illustrious and purest representatives, we are instructed to offer you the medal which has been coined in honor of the great and good man whose name you bear. If France had the freedom enjoyed by republican America,

not thousands, but millions among us would have been counted as admirers of LINCOLN, and believers in the opinions for which he devoted his life, and which his death has consecrated. Deign to accept, madam, the homage of our profound respect." The letter was signed by Victor Hugo and 19 other eminent Frenchmen. The medal, executed by Franky Magniadas, is a striking production, with a superb left-facing Lincoln profile on obverse, the hair, brows, and beard detail, even the veins in his temple, rendered with absolute precision. The bust is surrounded by French text meaning "Dedicated by the French democracy to LINCOLN, twice elected President of the United States." The reverse, also by Magniadas, is of a monument surmounted by a federal eagle and a glory of stars, at which Columbia with a wreath and two freed slaves with a palm branch worship (see fig. 2.66). The legend translates as "LINCOLN, an honest man; abolished slavery, saved the republic, and was assassinated the 14th of April, 1865." "LIBERTY!

Fig. 2.62. In 1866 the U.S. Congress awarded teenage sculptor Vinnie Ream a commission for a Lincoln statue for the U.S. Capitol. She is shown circa 1870, at about age 22, with a study for that statue.

Fig. 2.63. Counterfeiting of the federal greenbacks was so prevalent that the Treasury went to extreme measures in attempting to stem the fakes. On July 19, 1866, Derby, Connecticut, entrepreneur Robert C. Naramore patented small-size photographs of genuine notes mounted on a poster or on *CDV*-sized cards as a counterfeit detector. He then submitted his idea to the Treasury for approval. Treasury Secretary Hugh McCulloch granted him permission on July 30, 1866, so long as the images were only one-fourth actual size. McCulloch then instructed the bank-note companies to comply, and wished Naramore well in his venture. Images of the notes on the Naramore cards show legal tender and national currency in all denominations from $1–$1,000, without seals and serial numbers.

Fig. 2.64. Business colleges were widespread in 19th-century America, teaching thousands of young men and women practical penmanship, accounting, and business practices. Most utilized custom notes designed to look like contemporary bank notes in their practical exercises: (a) the $3 note of Bryant and Stratton, New York City and elsewhere, Schingoethe NY-1020-3A/B, and (b) the $2 of Burnham's Business College, Springfield, Massachusetts (Schingoethe MA-400-2B variant), were lithographed by Hatch & Co., New York. Each employs that firm's likeness of the Lincoln $10/$20 greenback portrait to make these notes more realistic.

EQUALITY! FRATERNITY!" A reported 40,000 Frenchmen contributed to the project to strike this special gold medal for Mrs. Lincoln. However, Napoleon III prohibited its production in France, so the committee had it struck in Geneva. The original gold medal weighs nearly 17 troy ounces, and is 3.25 inches in diameter and half an inch thick.[18]

1866 NOVEMBER 24. *Leslie's Illustrated* publishes a front-page illustration of the proposed Lincoln monument in Springfield by Larkin G. Mead (see fig. 2.67).

1866 DECEMBER 4. John Bigelow, American consul in Paris, accepts the gold memorial medal from the citizens of France on behalf of presidential widow Mary Todd Lincoln. A Committee of "distinguished republicans" delivered the French people's gift to Bigelow to be forwarded to America and presented to Mrs. Lincoln.[19]

1866 DECEMBER 7. U.S. ambassador John Bigelow sends widow Mary Todd Lincoln the gold memorial medal from the French Republicans.[20]

1867 JANUARY 3. The president's widow, Mary Todd Lincoln, acknowledges receipt of the gold medal from the citizens of France. She writes in response, "So grand a testimonial to the memory of my husband, given in honor of his services in the cause of liberty, by those who labor in the same great cause in another land, is deeply affecting." Privately, the president's widow had been anxious about receiving the medal. "She had expressed concern that the French medal would never find its way into her hands," historian Jennifer Bach has written.[21] In 1866 she had asked Alexander Williamson "to inquire about the medal's status, fearing that William Seward, or President Lincoln's former secretaries John Hay and John Nicolay, 'could stop its reaching me. . . . They are a great set of scamps.'"[22]

Fig. 2.65. William Edgar Marshall painted and then engraved a portrait based on his painting, which was published in Boston by Ticknor & Fields. Marshall's Lincoln achieved critical and commercial success.

Fig. 2.67. Larkin Mead's original proposed design for a Lincoln Monument to be constructed at Springfield, Illinois, as published in the November 24, 1866, issue of *Leslie's Illustrated*. Note this was the monument proposed to be built by the National Lincoln Monument Association, which had been formed in Springfield on May 11, 1865.

Fig. 2.66. The most celebrated of the Lincoln memorial medals is the solid gold medal (King-245) presented on behalf of the people of France to Lincoln's widow Mary Todd Lincoln. The medal was underwritten by subscription of 40,000 French citizens. Dies were executed by Franky Magniadas. When Emperor Napoleon III would not permit the medal to be struck in France, it was accomplished in Switzerland. The letter of transmittal to Mrs. Lincoln was written by Victor Hugo. Mrs. Lincoln's letter of acknowledgment and thanksgiving was written January 3, 1867. Examples were also struck in bronze for presentation to dignitaries and for sale.

Fig. 2.68. Fantasy $3 gold "patterns," sometimes attributed to Boston medalist Joseph Merriam, bear the dates 1866 or 1868, the legend GOD AND OUR COUNTRY and the Roman numeral III. In addition to gold, examples are known in silver, copper, nickel, and lead. Shown is Pollock-5080 in gold.

1867 FEBRUARY 5. Secretary of State William Seward transmits correspondence to Congress from the Brazilian ambassador representing that country's condolences on the death of Abraham Lincoln. On February 28 the Senate considered a resolution S. Res. 183, Thanking the Chambers of Senators and Deputies of Brazil for their Resolutions of Sorrow and Sympathy on the Death of President Lincoln. It passed on March 2 and requested concurrence of the House, but apparently in the crush of business at the end of that session of Congress, no action was taken on the matter.

1867 FEBRUARY 12. Celebrations of Lincoln's birthday include the presentation of a portrait of Abraham Lincoln at the New Jersey Assembly, Trenton, New Jersey. In Louisville, Kentucky, Lincoln intimate James Speed gives the dedicatory address at the unveiling of a bust of Lincoln there.

1867 FEBRUARY 12. Eight Jersey City civic leaders meet at Zachau's Union House, 146 Newark Ave., to celebrate Lincoln's birthday. On May 3, 1867, they formed the Abraham Lincoln Association of Jersey City. This organization has since remembered Lincoln annually on February 12 with banquets and public celebrations at the city's Lincoln Monument by James Earle Fraser, located at the entrance to Lincoln Park on Kennedy Boulevard and Belmont Ave.

1867 MARCH 2. The Senate and House pass a joint resolution authorizing the printing of papers relating to foreign affairs expressing sympathy or condolence that had been inspired by the Lincoln assassination and the attempted assassination of Secretary of State William H. Seward on the same evening (see fig. 2.73). Accordingly, the State Department published *The Tributes of the Nations to Abraham Lincoln,* a compilation of nearly 1,000 pages, on fine paper with gilt morocco bindings, printed by the Government Printing Office (see fig. 2.74). John H. Haswell of the U.S. State Department edited and arranged the volume. Messages from all over the world appeared. Official and personal condolences and editorials from the press were received from the Argentine Republic, Austria, Bavaria, Belgium, Brunswick, the Duchy of Baden, Brazil, Bolivia, Chili, China, Costa Rica, Denmark, Ecuador, Egypt, France, Great Britain and her Dependencies, Greece, Guatemala, the Hanseatic Republics, the Duchy of Hesse-Darmstadt, Hayti, the Hawaiian Islands, Honduras, Italy, Japan, Liberia, Mexico, Morocco, The Netherlands, Nicaragua, Peru, Prussia, Portugal, Russia, Rome, Spain, Sweden and Norway, Saxe-Meiningen, Switzerland, Salvador, Turkey, Tunis, the United States of Colombia, Uruguay, Venezuela, and Württemburg, as well as from all parts of the United States.

These missives are very revealing about how Lincoln's memory was viewed overseas. In Argentina, all flags were ordered to be flown at half staff. "The Argentine government laments with the most profound sorrow the irreparable loss that deprives the United States of their noble President, Abraham Lincoln, whose persevering efforts were just being crowned by victory in favor of the cause of Union," its minister of foreign affairs wrote. The government of China was amazed at the peaceful transition of power. "That on the same day the Vice-President succeeded to the position without any disturbance, and the assassin had been arrested, so that the affairs of government

were going on quietly as usual," the Chinese secretary of state for foreign affairs in Peking said with admiration. In Great Britain, a "Mauritian [native to Mauritius] colored gentlemen resident in London" said the events "horrified the civilized world." They felt disgust on hearing of Lincoln's assassination. The assassination had "not only deprived the United States of one of its noblest citizens, of one of its most virtuous patriots, but also the suffering and enslaved colored race living in abjectness in your country of their kind and stanch protector." In Switzerland, Alex Schoni, from Bienne, wrote on behalf of 800 of his fellow countrymen "to express their approbation of the address of sympathy and condolence of the inhabitants of little Switzerland to the great sister republic of the United States. What man, what true Swiss, did not feel the warm blood run swifter in his veins and his heart pulsate audibly at the news of the great events in America, the perpetual abolition of slavery!" In London, the German national Verein chairman Gottfried Kinkel expressed "horror of the crime perpetrated upon the life of your noble President, whose fidelity to the cause of humanity we admired, long before his kindness to the conquered and his glorious martyrdom reconciled to him even those who had so long been his antagonists."

Nearly 50 messages were received from individuals and organizations in Paris alone. Pierre Napoleon Bonaparte expressed his country's cordial fraternity with the United States, and the very painful duty in expressing his countrymen's sympathy. "This regret shall be shared by all noble hearts in all countries," he predicted, "and the glorious name of Lincoln, standing by the side of Washington's, shall be the everlasting honor of your great republic." In the press, the *Liverpool Daily Post* lamented, "The world will echo with loud and bitter detestation the hellish act by which Abraham Lincoln was sacrificed; while those who have watched with sympathy the conduct of the departed President will rejoice that he lived just long enough to be consoled by appreciation and success." This compendium had a voluminous circulation. Sufficient copies were printed and bound for each member of Congress, each foreign government, and each "corporation, association, or public body whose expressions of condolence or sympathy [were] published in said volume," in an edition of 3,000 copies at an expense of $18,179.54, according to Boyd. It was also printed for public distribution. Charles Henry Hart reported that 21,000 copies were printed.[23] The work was also reprinted in Brussels, Belgium.

1867 MARCH 19. Senator John Sherman acknowledges receipt of a copy of the gold medal the French people presented to the widow of Abraham Lincoln.

1867 MARCH 25. S. 112, a bill to incorporate the Lincoln Monument Association, is introduced (fig. 2.76).

1867 MARCH 25. Representative William Lawrence introduces H.R. 86, a bill to "provide a temporary government for the Territory of Lincoln" (see fig. 2.77). The proposed territory was to be bounded by Kansas on the north, by New Mexico Territory and Texas on the west, by Texas on the south, and Missouri and Arkansas on the east. Of course, we know this land area today as the state of Oklahoma. The bill preserved the rights of Native Americans already living in the

ABRAHAM LINCOLN.

Born, Feb. 12th 1809.   Died, April 15th 1865.

Fig. 2.69. A memorial Lincoln *CDV* with photograph Ostendorf-91 surrounded by a black, engraved cartouche.

Fig. 2.70. This game counter, "Prasident Lincoln // Compositions Spiel Marke" (King-861), was struck by Lauer in Nüremberg, Germany.

Fig. 2.71. Rare green fifty-cent (Turner Type V, RN-V1) and five-cent (Type P, RN-P unlisted) Lincoln revenue imprints on $1,000 bond of the Dubuque and Sioux City Railroad Company.

Fig. 2.72. Boston expatriate sculptor Thomas Ball, then living in Florence, Italy, proposed this monument to honor Lincoln. The sculpture shows Lincoln and a freedman in a liberty cap. Inscribed at the base is: "And upon this act I invoke the considerate judgment of mankind and the gracious favor of Almighty God," from his Emancipation Proclamation. Eventually, Ball's design was substantially adopted for the Lincoln Freedom Monument in Washington, D.C., because of the excessive expense of competing designs. The stereoview is copyrighted by A.A. Childs & Co., Boston, 1867.

district, and significantly called for both the governor and secretary to "be an American of African descent." It also specified a legislature, a territorial attorney, and a judiciary all comprised of "American citizens of African descent."

1867 MARCH 30. Congress incorporates the National Lincoln Monument Association, under S. 112 (see fig. 2.76). This should not be confused with the similarly named organization organized in Illinois

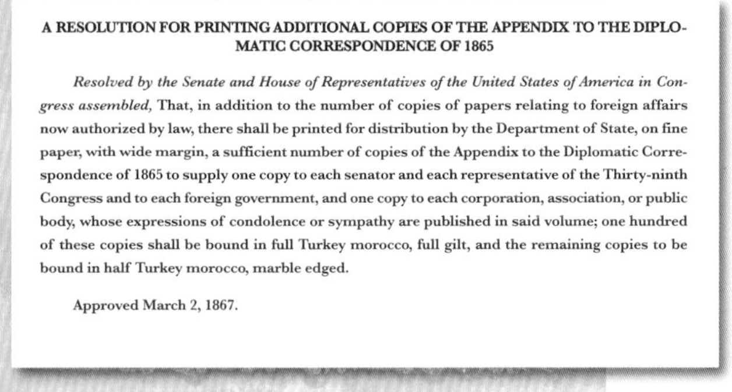

A RESOLUTION FOR PRINTING ADDITIONAL COPIES OF THE APPENDIX TO THE DIPLO-
MATIC CORRESPONDENCE OF 1865

Resolved by the Senate and House of Representatives of the United States of America in Congress assembled, That, in addition to the number of copies of papers relating to foreign affairs now authorized by law, there shall be printed for distribution by the Department of State, on fine paper, with wide margin, a sufficient number of copies of the Appendix to the Diplomatic Correspondence of 1865 to supply one copy to each senator and each representative of the Thirty-ninth Congress and to each foreign government, and one copy to each corporation, association, or public body, whose expressions of condolence or sympathy are published in said volume; one hundred of these copies shall be bound in full Turkey morocco, full gilt, and the remaining copies to be bound in half Turkey morocco, marble edged.

Approved March 2, 1867.

Fig. 2.73. This March 2, 1867, joint resolution of Congress provided for printing *Tributes of the Nations to Abraham Lincoln,* comprising official and personal messages of condolence and sympathy from around the world on the death of Lincoln.

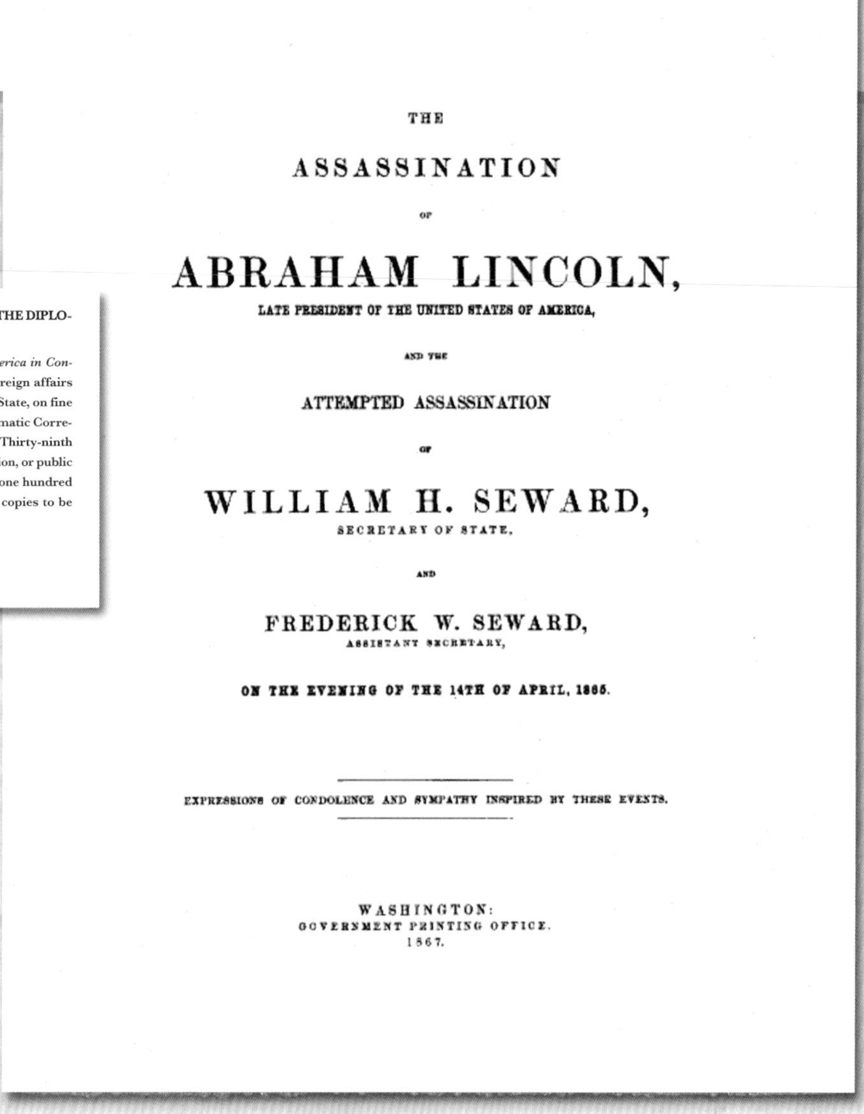

THE

ASSASSINATION

OF

ABRAHAM LINCOLN,

LATE PRESIDENT OF THE UNITED STATES OF AMERICA,

AND THE

ATTEMPTED ASSASSINATION

OF

WILLIAM H. SEWARD,

SECRETARY OF STATE,

AND

FREDERICK W. SEWARD,

ASSISTANT SECRETARY,

ON THE EVENING OF THE 14TH OF APRIL, 1865.

EXPRESSIONS OF CONDOLENCE AND SYMPATHY INSPIRED BY THESE EVENTS.

WASHINGTON:
GOVERNMENT PRINTING OFFICE.
1867.

Fig. 2.74. Title page of the *Tributes of the Nations to Abraham Lincoln.*

Fig. 2.75. This imitation $50 Treasury Note looks the part right down to its mimic Lincoln greenback portrait. Issued in St. Louis for agent J.C. Brooks's New York Jewelry Co., this note is not listed in Vlack's advertising currency book.

in 1865 to erect a suitable memorial at Lincoln's tomb in Springfield, Illinois. The National Lincoln Monument Association in Washington, D.C., solicited funds from individuals to erect a suitable memorial there. U.S. Treasurer F.E. Spinner was treasurer of the association and suitable donation receipts were engraved and printed at the Treasury Department and signed in his famous Spenserian script (see fig. 2.78). These are exquisite items bearing the NBNCo's full original Lincoln portrait vignette without the 13-star border, but with the symbolic flags, Capitol, and "Constitution and Law" images that were employed on the third and fourth series Five-Twenty bonds from the June 30, 1864, issue. This time, however, it was not necessary to reverse the Lincoln portrait so he was depicted in his "normal" manner facing the observer's right. An additional vignette depicts the Union offering sacrifices on the Altar of Freedom. The fund-raising activity was not very successful. Surviving pieces of this rare certificate are dated 1868.

1867 May 15. General O.O. Howard of the Freedmen's Bureau suggests a Lincoln Temperance Society be formed to discourage intemperance among the freedmen. "There is a great appropriateness in the name, from the well-known character of Mr. Lincoln, and from the love the colored people bear him," Howard affirms (see fig. 2.79).

1867. Congress designates Lincoln Square a mile east of the U.S. Capitol in Lincoln's honor, the first federal site to bear his name. This square, which had been in L'Entant's original master plan for Washington as the point from which all distances on the continent would be measured, had previously been the location of Lincoln Hospital (also named in his honor) as a soldier's hospital during the Civil War. This was one of the places served by Walt Whitman as a male nurse during the war.

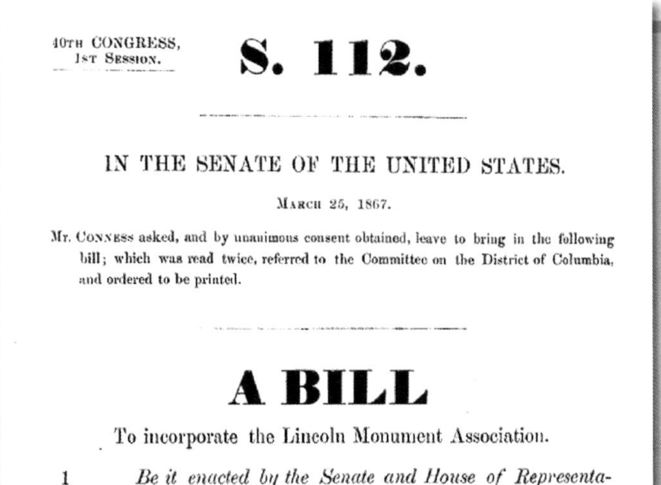

40TH CONGRESS,
1ST SESSION.

S. 112.

IN THE SENATE OF THE UNITED STATES.

MARCH 25, 1867.

Mr. CONNESS asked, and by unanimous consent obtained, leave to bring in the following bill; which was read twice, referred to the Committee on the District of Columbia, and ordered to be printed.

A BILL

To incorporate the Lincoln Monument Association.

1   Be it enacted by the Senate and House of Representa-
2 tives of the United States of America in Congress assembled,
3 That Alexander W. Randall, James Harlan, Alexander Ram-
4 sey, Nathaniel P. Banks, Sidney Perham, John Conness, John
5 T. Wilson, Godlove S. Orth, Delos R. Ashley, Halbert E. Paine,
6 Charles O'Neill, Burt Van Horn, John F. Driggs, Frederick
7 E. Woodbridge, Jacob Benton, John Hill, Shelby M. Cullom,
8 Thomas A. Jenckes, Orin S. Ferry, N. B. Smithers, Francis
9 Thomas, Samuel McKee, Horace Maynard, John F. Benja-
10 min, Rufus Mallory, Sidney Clarke, Daniel Polsley, Walter
11 A. Burleigh, John Taffe, and their successors, are constituted
12 a body corporate in the District of Columbia, by the name of
13 the Lincoln Monument Association, for the purpose of erect-
14 ing a monument in the city of Washington, commemorative
15 of the great charter of emancipation and universal liberty in
16 America.

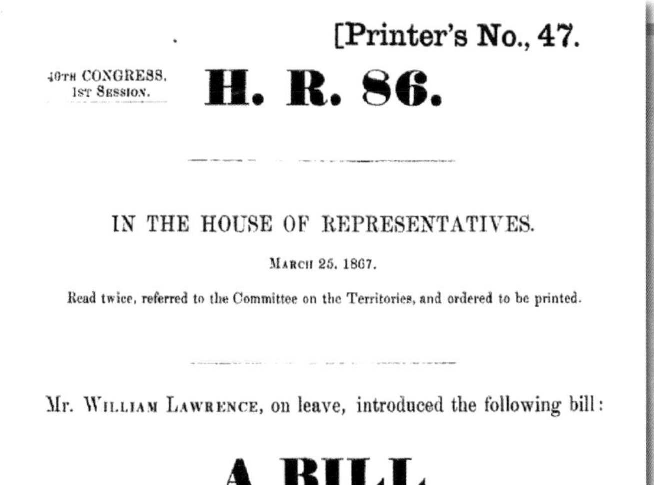

[Printer's No., 47.

40TH CONGRESS.
1ST SESSION.

H. R. 86.

IN THE HOUSE OF REPRESENTATIVES.

MARCH 25, 1867.

Read twice, referred to the Committee on the Territories, and ordered to be printed.

Mr. WILLIAM LAWRENCE, on leave, introduced the following bill:

A BILL

To provide a temporary government for the Territory of Lincoln.

1   Be it enacted by the Senate and House of Representa-
2 tives of the United States of America in Congress assembled,
3 That there be, and is hereby, created and established within
4 the territory of the United States, bounded as follows, to wit:
5 on the north by the southern boundary of the State of
6 Kansas, on the west by the eastern boundary of the Terri-
7 tory of New Mexico and the State of Texas, on the south
8 by the northern boundary of the State of Texas, and on the
9 east by the western boundary of the States of Arkansas and
10 Missouri, a temporary government by the name of the Ter-
11 ritory of Lincoln: *Provided*, That nothing in this act con-
12 tained shall be construed to impair the rights of person or
13 property now pertaining to the Indians in said Territory, so

Fig. 2.76. A bill to incorporate the Lincoln Monument Association, S. 112, March 25, 1867. This group was organized to erect a memorial in Washington D.C. to Lincoln's "great charter of emancipation and universal liberty." Incorporators included Iowa Senator James Harlan, General Nathaniel P. Banks, and Vermont congressman Frederick Enoch Woodbridge.

Fig. 2.77. Several attempts were made to establish a Lincoln territory in the West. This bill to provide for a temporary government for the Territory of Lincoln (H.R. 86, March 25, 1867) would have created Lincoln Territory in the area of present-day Oklahoma. This measure failed to become law, but a Lincoln County was carved out of the central part of Oklahoma Territory later.

1868 JANUARY 1. A design by American sculptor Harriet Hosmer for a large and complex monument for the congressionally chartered Freedmen's Memorial to Lincoln (originally the Educational Lincoln Monument Association) in Washington, D.C., appears in the January 1, 1868, issue of *Art Journal* in London (see fig. 2.82a).[24] A contemporary American description of what Ms. Hosmer had planned for the monument was supplied by Lincoln enthusiast Andrew Boyd:

> The Freedman's Monument to Abraham Lincoln now being executed by Miss Hosmer, and about to be erected in the grounds of the Capitol at Washington, is described as follows: The total height is sixty feet; the sides of the base are filled with bas-reliefs, illustrating the life of the president: the first symbolizes his birth and his various occupations as a builder of log cabins, flat boatman and farmer; the second illustrates his career as a lawyer, and his installation as president of the United States; the third contains four memorable events of the late war; while the fourth shows the closing scenes of his life, the assas-

sination in the theatre, the funeral procession, and his burial at Springfield. The four tablets above these contain respectively the following inscriptions: Abraham Lincoln, Martyr—President of the United States—Preserver of the American Union—Emancipator of Four Millions of men. The circular bas-reliefs higher up show thirty-six female figures, symbolizing the union of the same number of states; each of these figures represents the peculiarity of that state whose shield occupies the medallion beneath. The four colossal statues placed at the outer angles, display the progressive stages of liberation during Lincoln's administration."[25]

Boyd provided details of Ms. Hosmer's vision:

> The negro appears, first, exposed for sale; second, laboring in a plantation; third, guiding and assisting the loyal troops; and, fourth serving as a soldier of the union. In the pillared "temple" surmounting the whole, is a colossal statue of Lincoln, holding in one hand the Proclamation of Emancipation, and in the other the broken chain of Slav-

Fig. 2.78. The National Lincoln Monument Association was chartered by Congress to erect a Lincoln monument in the city of Washington, D.C. Since U.S. Treasurer Francis E. Spinner was also treasurer of the association, donation receipts were engraved and printed at the U.S. Treasury Department. The authoritative bond/currency Lincoln portrait, originally engraved by the NBNCo and virtually identical to the ABNCo $10 portrait, was used on the association's impressive donor receipts.

Fig. 2.79. After NBNCo surrendered its Lincoln bond portrait die, the firm executed a very similar Lincoln image based on the same C.S. German photographic model. This time, it had secured the copyright to its work. In 1867 this new Lincoln portrait, which mirrors Lincoln's currency image, was used on the Lincoln Temperance Association pledge (membership) card.

Fig. 2.80. CBNCo's die no. 1 Lincoln portrait, which mirrored the Treasury Note and bond portraits, appeared on the $100 Union Military Scrip, Topeka, issue-dated June 1, 1867, Whitfield-426. Highest number seen is 905.

Fig. 2.81. John Sherman, General William Tecumseh Sherman's younger brother, was a U.S. senator, congressman, secretary of the Treasury, and secretary of state. This check on his account at the First National Bank of Mansfield, Ohio, October 26, 1867, was printed by Sage, Sons & Co., Buffalo, New York.

ery. The four female figures, also of colossal size, represent Liberty bearing their crowns to the freedman. On the architecture of the temple are inscribed the concluding words of the Proclamation of Emancipation; "And upon this, sincerely believed to be an act of justice, I invoke the considerate judgment of mankind, and the gracious favor of Almighty God."

The architectural portions were to be constructed of granite, and the figures and bas-reliefs cast in bronze. The cost was estimated at $250,000.[26]

1868. Sculptor John Rogers creates a small figural sculpture, *The Council of War,* which portrays a seated Lincoln holding a map, flanked by General U.S. Grant and Secretary of War

Edwin Stanton (see fig. 2.83). Stanton's hands are raised at the back of Lincoln's head, which creates an uproar among partisans who link Stanton with the assassination. Rogers remedies this statue brouhaha by lowering Stanton's hands on later editions. "J. Rogers, Sculptor" advertises his business with a cabinet-sized trade card having an engraving of Lincoln and a facsimile of Lincoln's autograph.

1868 APRIL 15. Lieutenant Lot Flannery's Lincoln statue in Washington, D.C. (see fig. 2.84), is dedicated on the third anniversary of Lincoln's death. The monument consists of a Tuscan pillar 35 feet high, surmounted by a colossal statue of Lincoln all of white marble. The statue is erected in front of the D.C. City Hall. Managers of the

Fig. 2.82. *(a)* Harriet Hosmer planned an elaborate memorial to Lincoln and emancipation in Washington, D.C. The architectural rendering was done by Bullard & Bullard. When funds were not forthcoming for Hosmer's national emancipation monument, Thomas Ball's Emancipation figures of a standing Lincoln and a kneeling freedman were substituted in its stead. This cabinet card dates circa late 1860s. *(b)* Noted illustrator C.S. Reinhart had a much simpler vision for a suitable memorial.

Fig. 2.83. Sculptor John Rogers was the people's sculptor, producing plaster groups for the Victorian-era parlor. One of the favorites, shown on this advertising stereoview, was "The Council of War." It depicts General U.S. Grant, Secretary of War Stanton, and a seated Lincoln perusing a battle map. A silly controversy over the positioning of Stanton's hands at the rear of Lincoln's head resulted in slight modifications to the design.

Lincoln Monument Association were Richard Wallach, Noble D. Larner, and Asbury Lloyd. The dedication address was delivered by Benjamin B. French.

1868 MAY 25. H.R. 1831, a bill to place damaged and captured ordnance at disposal of National Lincoln Monument Association, Springfield, passes in Senate. It provided for the "casting of some 15 figures to be placed on a granite shaft 60 feet high. He [Mr. Harlan, president of the association told Congress] that the Secretary of the Treasury, who is the Treasurer of the association, is daily receiving contributions from all parts of the country, and that these bronze and brass cannon are not to be placed at the disposal of the association until $100,000 has been raised." The *State Gazette* at Springfield had printed a 15-page pamphlet, "A Memorial in regard to the Lincoln Monument to be erected at Springfield, Ill.," in 1867 soliciting these funds.

1868 MAY 29. The goal of establishing a Territory of Lincoln does not pass away meekly. The *New York Times* reports on another such district, this time to be carved out of four existing territories, Utah, Idaho, Colorado, and Dakota, with principle settlements at Cheyenne and Fort Bridger. A California newspaper said it wasn't necessary to gild Lincoln's reputation in this way. This area eventually became Wyoming.[27]

1868 CIRCA. Memorializing Lincoln isn't the only way his presence remains with his countrymen following his abrupt departure. Pitchmen, who had capitalized on his person and image in life, quickly realize that his persona is no less powerful a magnet in death. "Honest Abe" was reputed for honesty. Manufacturers are quick to translate that to honest product value. By the late 1860s, Lincoln's image had been appropriated for writing instruments, tobacco, clothing labels, and other products. Boyd listed an 1869 "A. Lincoln" used on a segar [*sic*] box label by F. Heppenheimer, New York.

By 1869 another brand, Old Abe cigars, were already a well-known product (fig. 2.87). This brand lasted for three-quarters of a century at least, and a great many labels, boxes, cigarette packs, and other ephemera still exist. Less well known, and believed even earlier, is the ultra-rare Honest Old Abe brand listed by Boyd and illustrated on the rare tobacco label here (fig. 2.88). Also from the 1860s are A. Summerville and Co.'s Abraham Lincoln pen nibs (fig. 2.89), not to be confused with R. Estabrook and Co.'s Lin-

Fig. 2.84. Lieutenant Lot Flannery's Lincoln statue was dedicated in Washington, D.C., on the third anniversary of Lincoln's death, Wednesday, April 15, 1868, the first public monument to Lincoln in the city. The monument originally consisted of a Tuscan pillar thirty-five feet high, surmounted by a colossal statue of Lincoln all of white marble. Lincoln's left hand rests on a fasces, the symbol of authority. The statue was erected in front of City Hall. In 1920 when the city hall was undergoing renovation, the statue was kept in storage for two years until replaced on a pedestal about 12 feet high.

coln pen. In Holyoke, Massachusetts, the Lincoln Paper Company was established. A Philadelphia undertaker plastered Lincoln's portrait on its trade cards, and Lincoln portraits appeared on several business college bank bills about that time (fig. 2.90). Lincoln's image graced ad bills of J.B. Westbrook & Co. of New York. In New York City, capitalists established the Lincoln Fund Insurance Co.

1868. Flush from the success of his engraving of Carpenter's *First Reading of the Emancipation Proclamation,* Alexander H. Ritchie publishes a companion deathbed scene in 1868, styled as *Ritchie's Historical Picture, Death of President Lincoln.* The engraving was large in size, 32.5 inches by 21.5 inches. Artist's proofs sold for $30, and included an engraved key to the large crowd assembled in the small room in which Lincoln died.[28] Ritchie copyrighted a second print of the same title in 1875.[29]

1868 SEPTEMBER 12. *Harper's Weekly* publishes a large front-page illustration of the Lincoln tomb (see fig. 2.93).

1868 NOVEMBER 13. Due to collector demand for the small Lincoln-Washington medalets, William Barber prepares a new Lincoln die and additional medals are stuck and sold commencing November 13. The following year Barber prepared a new die to restrike the Broken Column medalets (refer back to fig. 2.45) for sale to collectors too.

1869 MARCH 3. Congress appropriates $3,000 for the purchase of a portrait of Abraham Lincoln. Two Chicago artists compete for the prize. One, William Cogswell, paints a full length portrait of Lincoln, while G.P.A. Healy paints a seated figure. On June 25 President U.S. Grant declared Cogswell the winner and directed that the portrait be placed in the Executive Mansion. "Healy presented a very good picture of Mr. Lincoln," the *New York Times* correspondent opined, "in a favorite sitting position, which struck many as very natural and lifelike." Cogswell's full length portrait, however, "was so

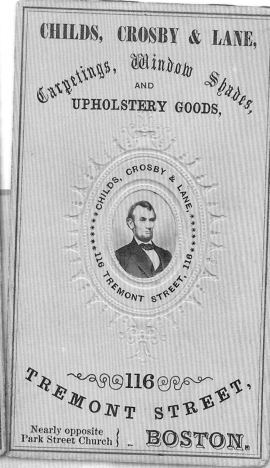

Fig. 2.85. Lincoln's popularity could always be counted on to sell products: *(a)* In the late 1860s Providence, Rhode Island, druggist Edward Sutton issued an embossed Bicknell's Syrup advertising card with an inset paper photograph of Lincoln. *(b)* About the same time Boston dry-goods vendor Childs, Crosby & Lane did the same.

Fig. 2.86. The green ink on notes was changed to a different chromium compound, patented by A.K. Eaton, to foil counterfeiters. This Friedberg-95b has Eaton's patent date of April 28, 1863. It didn't work. Before the feds gave up in 1869 and changed currency designs altogether, more than 11.8 Lincoln $10 Legal Tender Notes reinforced public consciousness of Lincoln, originally created by his identical portrait on two million $10 Demand Notes early in the war. The Lincoln on the money was the Lincoln the man on the street knew.

much the superior in the facial lines and in the expression most always worn by the late President that it easily carried off the prize."

1869 April 7. In the president's honor, Lincoln, Nebraska, is incorporated as a town, and then as a second-class city March 18, 1871.

1869 April 19. First issue of United States Notes (Series 1862–1863) ceases, according to U.S. Treasurer Jas. Gilfillan.[30]

1869 May 10. After experimenting with Lincoln's portrait on a several stamp essays, the Post Office Department issues a carmine and

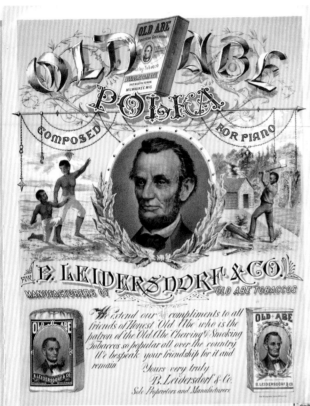

Fig. 2.87. "Old Abe": (a) In the late 1860s, according to the Library of Congress, B. Leidersdorf & Co. of Milwaukee popularized its Old Abe smoking tobacco with an "Old Abe Polka" composed for the piano. (b) In 1883, the firm also marketed one- and two-ounce packages in a proprietary Old Abe tin label.

Fig. 2.88. Believed to be the oldest type of Lincoln tobacco label, this Havana Honest Old Abe cigar label dates from the 1860s. Some contend it could in fact date to the early 1860s, since it features the beardless Lincoln of the "Cooper Union" photo.

Fig. 2.89. Pens may have been the most appropriate (or perhaps the least inappropriate) products to carry Lincoln's name: (a) Sommerville & Co. sold the Abraham Lincoln pen. (b) Pen points were embossed with the Lincoln brand.

black 90-cent postage stamp with Lincoln's image in May 1869 (see fig. 2.96). With this stamp, Lincoln replaces Washington on the highest value in the series. The bi-color stamp (Scott 122) was issued in spring (earliest date used May 10, 1869, off cover). According to

experts "There is only one cover known with the 90¢ 1869 stamp, the famous 'Icehouse cover,' with a penciled-in date on the front of August 8, 1873."[31] About 55,500 were issued.

Fig. 2.90. Evergreen City Business College in Bloomington, Illinois, used this $10 note in its practical classes during the 1870s (Schingoethe IL-225 unlisted). Indicative of the changeover in Lincoln currency portraiture, the Milwaukee Lithographic and Engraving Co. vignette on the note is the then-current $100/$500 image to make the practice note more realistic.

Fig. 2.91. Little is known about this small GOP medal (King-882), enlarged to show detail.

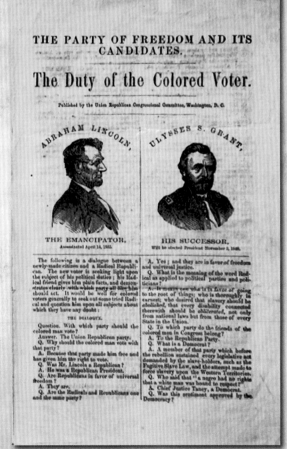

Fig. 2.92. "The Duty of the Colored Voter," published in 1868 by the Union Republican Congressional Committee, Washington, D.C., outlines the benefits bestowed by the emancipator and how African-American voters should respond in the upcoming general election by sending U.S. Grant to the White House.

Fig. 2.93. The tomb of Abraham Lincoln at Oak Ridge Cemetery in Springfield, sketched by F.D. Skiff, Harper's Weekly, September 12, 1868.

1869 JUNE 15. The son of noted sculptor Clark Mills, Fisk Mills receives a patent for the "Postal-Currency Envelope," which may be used as currency and for prepayment of three-cent postage (see fig. 2.98). The design is a vignette of Abraham Lincoln (Patent 91473). "I make my said postal-envelope currency or envelope postage-stamp, in size large enough to admit to being folded so as to form the envelope of any desirable or any suitable size or style for use in the reception of printed or written letters for transportation through the mails," the patent specification says. Mills assigned the patent to himself, Marcus P. Norton of Troy, New York, and George H. Penfield of Hartford, Connecticut. According to Mills, there were many benefits of his new invention. Marking an address on the envelope would serve as cancellation of its use as currency, thus preventing fraud. Businessmen could buy stocks of the envelopes and pay them out in change, he reasoned. Postmasters could do the same, which would increase use of the mails and postal revenue, the inventor contended.

Furthermore, envelopes could be sized to any size required by the postmaster general. The Post Office did not adopt Mill's proposal.

1869 AUGUST 3. Counterfeit ten-spots with Lincoln's image continue to pour off midnight presses. Finally, pushed by the intractable problem with counterfeit bills, Treasury Secretary George S. Boutwell shifts from a defensive strategy of trying to suppress the bogus notes, and goes on the offensive. The *New York Times* reports this new tactic in its issue of August 3, 1869.

"In consequence of the spurious issue of the $10 greenbacks, or Legal Tender Notes," the *Times* reported, "Secretary Boutwell has concluded to have a new issue of all denominations of greenbacks, from $1 to the $1,000 note." Plates for these new notes were then being engraved at the Bureau of Engraving and Printing, the account continued. "The designs are entirely new. No likeness of any living man will be placed on any note. None of the former or present

Fig. 2.94. Master engraver John Chester Buttre created this plate with portraits of Washington, Lincoln, Jackson, and Andrew Johnson for Abbott's *Lives of the Presidents.*

Fig. 2.95. Lincoln beardless revenue stamp essay portrait, originally engraved by CBNCo (ABNCo vignette V47371).

Fig. 2.96. In 1869 the U.S. issued a new series of postage stamps. Once again Joseph Ourdan's Lincoln portrait, which mirrored the currency pose, was used. Originally, Lincoln was considered for the 10-cent denomination, but later it was decided to put him on the 90-cent value (Scott 122, BEP die no. P0326). These are the first bicolor U.S. postage stamps. They were printed by the NBNCo. Shown is (a) a 10-cent essay (Scott 116-E), (b) a proof of the issued 10-cent design (Scott 116P), (c) a 90-cent essay (Scott 122-E4A2), and (d) a proof of the issued 90-cent stamp (Scott 122P).

greenbacks were engraved or printed at the Treasury Department. The engraving, however, of the new issue, and the printing of the faces and the seals of all denominations, will be performed in the Printing and Engraving Bureau, while the backs will be printed in New-York. There will be every possible caution to prevent frauds, including the taking of lead impressions for electrotype plates," the *Times* concluded.

1869 JULY–AUGUST. Charles Burt engraves an additional Lincoln portrait for use on 50-cent Fractional Currency based on a photographic session of Lincoln undertaken by Anthony Berger at Brady's Washington, D.C., gallery on April 20, 1864. It is believed that Burt executed this die on/about July 14, 1869. However, issue of the new notes was delayed for two months. This issue was printed in sheets of three across and four down, with a large red Treasury seal and fibers embedded in the paper as a counterfeit deterrent. For added secu-

rity, the faces were printed by the American Bank Note Co. and the backs by the National Bank Note Co. on watermarked paper.[32] Unfortunately, when they were finally issued, counterfeits (see fig. 2.101) rapidly appeared, leading to abandonment of this note. Henry Russell Drowne, an early collector and historian of this series, said that this Charles Burt engraving "is generally regarded as the finest example of portraiture in the entire line, and in fact it has been referred to as one of the finest engraved portraits of Lincoln." Burt's portrait speaks for itself. Drowne is incorrect, however, when he further stated, "Two portraits were engraved for this note; the first was without the beard and much better looking, but was condemned and preference given to the later picture, which was considered more accurate." According to the BEP, no clean-shaven engraving of Lincoln for currency use was ever undertaken.[33] The BEP issued 19,152,000 new Lincoln notes. Though Friedberg's *Paper Money of the United States* has long listed an un-watermarked variety of this

Fig. 2.97. A very rare 1869 essay for a 3¢ Emancipation Proclamation commemorative stamp made by the CBNCo. When the new 1870 series of stamps was issued by NBNCo, however, the stamps were portraits (Scott 147-E1a variety).

Fig. 2.98. The son of noted sculptor Clark Mills, who had cast the second life mask of Lincoln, Fisk Mills patented his postal-currency envelope June 15, 1869.

Fig. 2.99. St. Louis residents did not enjoy the benefits of a free Public School Library in 1869. It was a subscription service, and the society's $1 receipt for a three-month membership bore St. Louis lithographer R.P. Studley's Lincoln portrait, once again patterned after the familiar currency portrait.

note (Friedberg-1375), most experts believed all notes known are of the watermarked variety. However, acknowledged authority Len Glazer cataloged just such a piece. A unique sheet of 50-cent Lincolns brought $44,850 in Stack's John J. Ford Sale of May 12, 2004.

1869 SEPTEMBER. The U.S. Mint offers small medalets of Lincoln and Grant to collectors.

1869 SEPTEMBER 3. According to the *Brooklyn Daily Eagle,* the Treasury Department printing division sends the first $30,000 of new Abraham Lincoln 50-cent Fractional Currency to the U.S. treasurer.[34] The newspaper's Washington correspondent reported, under the headline "The Supply of Currency," "Yesterday the printing division at the Treasury Department sent to the Treasurer, among other currency, $30,000 of the new fifty cent notes, the first issued, and on Wednesday a lot of the new twenty-five cent notes. The first was sent to the Treasurer for

issue. Thirty presses are now at work on the ten and fifteen cent notes, and the remainder on the twenty-five and fifty cent notes."

1869 SEPTEMBER 7. Part of the delay in issuing the new Lincoln Fractional Currency is caused by a strike by printers at the National Bank Note Co. wanting a 10-cent/hundred increase in pay for all kinds of currency. This strike is called off on September 7, when the NBNCo agrees to increase payments to its printers according to the following schedule: five cents/hundred for 10-, 25-, and 50-cent fractional currency, and 10 cents/hundred on 15-cent currency. The raise, according to officers of NBNCo was conditioned "on their making an extra number of issues daily from the presses on a trial period." ABNCo printers did not go on strike but supported their brethren financially. When it heard of the settlement, ABNCo voluntarily matched the increases for its employees.[35] The strike lasted at least two weeks. During the strike, NBNCo lost 19 of its plate printers, who accepted work elsewhere.

Fig. 2.101. The new Lincoln 50-cent fractional currency (Friedberg-1374) was a miserable failure. As the highest denomination of the so-called Fourth Issue notes, the Lincoln came under immediate attack by currency counterfeiters. Shown is a comparison of a genuine note (a) and a counterfeit example (b), which ironically is slightly shorter than the original. Circles correspond to similar areas of engraving, while arrows indicate the colored fibers in the genuine note, and the ink marks on the fake placed there to simulate the fibers. New 50-cent notes with a portrait of the late Edwin M. Stanton made their appearance in March 1870. They were also widely counterfeited and replaced with yet another new note depicting Samuel Dexter.

Fig. 2.102. Small presidential medals were a staple of Mint offerings. During 1864 and thereafter a popular design was a cent-sized medal with Washington on one side and Lincoln on the other (Julian PR-30/31). In September 1869, the Mint added this medal depicting Lincoln with U.S. Grant (Julian PR-39).

Fig. 2.100. Charles Burt, who had engraved the Lincoln portrait used on the $10 bills for the ABNCo, was engaged by the Treasury Department to engrave a new Lincoln portrait for use on currency. The model selected was the Halpin engraving after F.B. Carpenter's portrait of Lincoln. Burt's new elegant Lincoln engraving was used on the 50-cent fractional notes, Friedberg-1374, first issued in fall 1869. Shown are (a) a special printing of the face design (Milton 4S50F.ia); (b) the issued note Friedberg-1374; and (c) the enigmatic un-watermarked Friedberg-1375, which has been observed by fractional-currency expert Len Glazer.

1869 October 21. Henry Kirke Brown's Lincoln statue in Prospect Park, Brooklyn, is dedicated (see fig. 2.105). According to Andrew Boyd "On Thursday, October 21, 1869, this statue was unveiled by its sculptor, Mr. H.K. Brown. It is of bronze, about nine feet high, and represents the figure of the late president standing, with the folds of a cloak draped about him; his left hand is extended and holds a manuscript. The head is uncovered. The figure stands upon a base of Scotch granite and faces to the west. On the sides of the base are various emblems and inscriptions. On the east and west, wreaths enclose the letters 'U. S. A.' and 'U. S. N. Y.'; on the south an eagle holds a shield, in the center of which is a female holding an axe, and supported by a bundle of reeds, with the motto, 'Een draght maakt maght'; on the north is an eagle with a broken shackle in his talons."[36]

1869 December 4. The proliferation of $10 counterfeits of the government's Legal Tender Note causes Treasury Secretary Boutwell to call for a new series of notes with heightened security features. These notes are termed "Rainbow Notes" because of their Technicolor blue, green, and red colors. On the new series, Lincoln is replaced on the $10 note by a stern visage of Daniel Webster. The martyred president is instead elevated to the $100 bill. The Series of

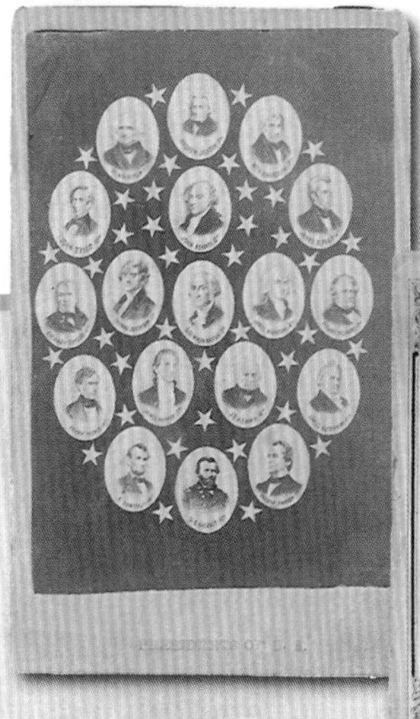

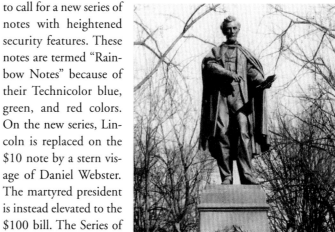

Fig. 2.103. Grant's election also brought about updating of the popular *CDVs* depicting the U.S. presidents.

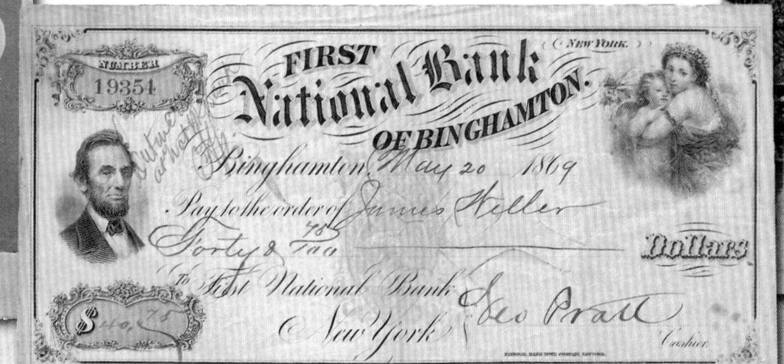

Fig. 2.104. NBNCo's new 1867 Lincoln portrait, based on the same model as its bond portrait die which it surrendered to the U.S. Treasury in 1864, adorns this First National Bank of Binghamton draft issued in 1869.

Fig. 2.105. Henry Kirke Brown's homage to Lincoln the Emancipator was dedicated in a commanding position in Prospect Park, Brooklyn, on October 21, 1869. The bronze is nine feet tall on a granite base. The significance of the event was accorded the front page of the November 13, 1869, issue of *Harper's Weekly*. The paper reported: "It is creditable to the patriotism of the citizens of Brooklyn that the first monument erected in their Park is one dedicated to the memory of the Saviour of his Country."

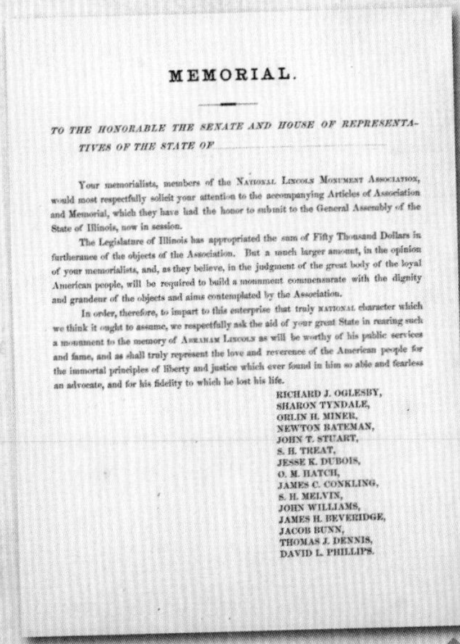

MEMORIAL.

TO THE HONORABLE THE SENATE AND HOUSE OF REPRESENTATIVES OF THE STATE OF ______

Your memorialists, members of the National Lincoln Monument Association, would most respectfully solicit your attention to the accompanying Articles of Association and Memorial, which they have had the honor to submit to the General Assembly of the State of Illinois, now in session.

The Legislature of Illinois has appropriated the sum of Fifty Thousand Dollars in furtherance of the objects of the Association. But a much larger amount, in the opinion of your memorialists, and, as they believe, in the judgment of the great body of the loyal American people, will be required to build a monument commensurate with the dignity and grandeur of the objects and aims contemplated by the Association.

In order, therefore, to impart to this enterprise that truly national character which we think it ought to assume, we respectfully ask the aid of your great State in rearing such a monument to the memory of Abraham Lincoln as will be worthy of his public services and fame, and as shall truly represent the love and reverence of the American people for the immortal principles of liberty and justice which ever found in him so able and fearless an advocate, and for his fidelity to which he lost his life.

RICHARD J. OGLESBY,
SHARON TYNDALE,
ORLIN H. MINER,
NEWTON BATEMAN,
JOHN T. STUART,
S. H. TREAT,
JESSE K. DUBOIS,
O. M. HATCH,
JAMES C. CONKLING,
S. H. MELVIN,
JOHN WILLIAMS,
JAMES H. BEVERIDGE,
JACOB BUNN,
THOMAS J. DENNIS,
DAVID L. PHILLIPS.

a

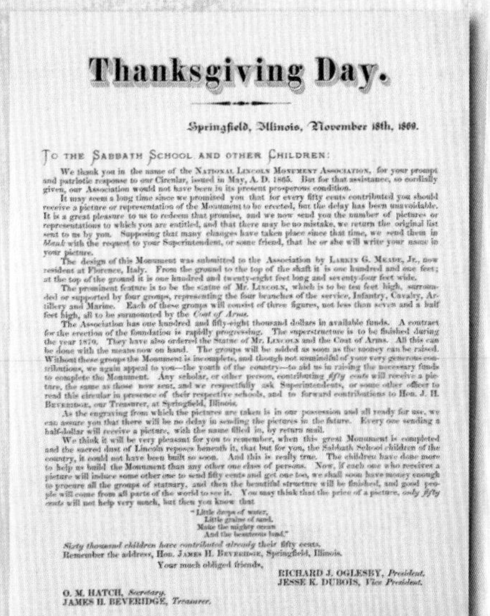

Thanksgiving Day.

Springfield, Illinois, November 18th, 1869.

To the Sabbath School and other Children:

We thank you in the name of the National Lincoln Monument Association, for your prompt and patriotic response to our Circular, issued in May, A. D. 1865. But for that assistance, so cordially given, our Association would not have been in its present prosperous condition.

It may seem a long time since we promised you that for every fifty cents contributed you should receive a picture or representation of the Monument to be erected, but the delay has been unavoidable. It is a great pleasure to us to redeem that promise, and we now send you the number of pictures or representations to which you are entitled, and that there may be no mistake, we return the original list sent to us by you. Supposing that many changes have taken place since that time, we send them in *blank* with the request to your Superintendent, or some friend, that he or she will write your name in your picture.

The design of this Monument was submitted to the Association by Larkin G. Meade, Jr., now resident at Florence, Italy. From the ground to the top of the shaft it is one hundred and one feet; at the top of the ground it is one hundred and twenty-eight feet long and seventy-four feet wide.

The prominent feature is to be the statue of Mr. Lincoln, which is to be ten feet high, surrounded or supported by four groups, representing the four branches of the service, Infantry, Cavalry, Artillery and Marine. Each of these groups will consist of three figures, not less than seven and a half feet high, all to be surmounted by the *Coat of Arms*.

The Association has one hundred and fifty-eight thousand dollars in available funds. A contract for the erection of the foundation is rapidly progressing. The superstructure is to be finished during the year 1870. They have also ordered the Statue of Mr. Lincoln and the Coat of Arms. All this can be done with the means now on hand. The groups will be added as soon as the money can be raised. Without these groups the Monument is incomplete, and though not unmindful of your very generous contributions, we again appeal to you—the youth of the country—to aid us in raising the necessary funds to complete the Monument. Any scholar, or other person, contributing *fifty cents* will receive a picture, the same as those now sent, and we respectfully ask Superintendents, or some other officer to read this circular in presence of their respective schools, and to forward contributions to Hon. J. H. Beveridge, our Treasurer, at Springfield, Illinois.

As the engraving from which the pictures are taken is in our possession and all ready for use, we can assure you that there will be no delay in sending the pictures in the future. Every one sending a half-dollar will receive a picture, with the name filled in, by return mail.

We think it will be very pleasant for you to remember, when this great Monument is completed and the sacred dust of Lincoln reposes beneath it, that but for you, the Sabbath School children of the country, it could not have been built so soon. And this is really true. The children have done more to help us build the Monument than any other one class of persons. Now, if each one who receives a picture will induce some other one to send fifty cents and get one too, we shall soon have money enough to procure all the groups of statuary, and then the beautiful structure will be finished, and good people will come from all parts of the world to see it. You may think that the price of a picture, *only fifty cents* will not help very much, but then you know that

"Little drops of water,
Little grains of sand,
Make the mighty ocean
And the beauteous land."

Sixty thousand children have contributed already their fifty cents.
Remember the address, Hon. James H. Beveridge, Springfield, Illinois.

Your much obliged friends,

RICHARD J. OGLESBY, *President*,
JESSE K. DUBOIS, *Vice President*.

O. M. HATCH, *Secretary*.
JAMES H. BEVERIDGE, *Treasurer*.

b

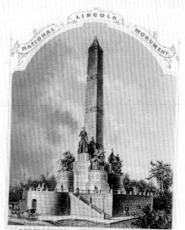

Fig. 2.106. This National Lincoln Monument Association is the one based in Springfield to erect a monument there in Lincoln's memory, not the similarly named organization that was seeking to raise a monument to Lincoln in Washington, D.C. *(a)* The Springfield group sent the memorial to state legislatures seeking their assistance. *(b)* The Springfield organization sent a form letter to school children thanking them for their support which had helped the association to its "present prosperous condition." Donors received *(c)* this fine certificate engraved and printed by Western Bank Note & Engraving Co., and featuring Larkin Mead's design for the monument.

Fig. 2.108. Destined to become *the* iconic Lincoln image for more than a century, Charles Burt's third engraved Lincoln portrait was also completed in 1869 for the U.S. Treasury. Burt based his engraving on Anthony Berger's February 9, 1864, Lincoln photograph (Ostendorf-92). Again the official U.S. currency portrait became *the* public perception of the nation's martyred 16th president, appearing on billions and billions of notes over the next 130 years, and spawning a host of look-alikes in advertising, prints, and other secondary media. From the late 19th century on, this was *the* iconic Lincoln on public and private view.

Fig. 2.107. "In consequence of the spurious issue of the $10 greenbacks, or legal tender notes," the *New York Times* reported, "Secretary (George S.) Boutwell has concluded to have a new issue of all denominations of greenbacks, from $1 to the $1000 note." These new Series 1869 notes carried a stern warning to potential fakers.

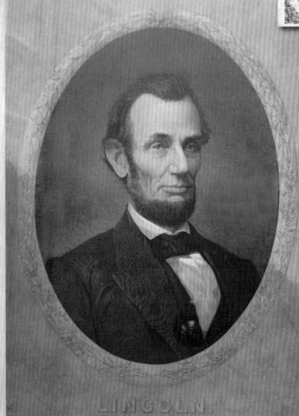

Fig. 2.110. On the new Series 1869 Legal Tender Notes, Charles Burt's new Lincoln portrait (BEP die no. MISC1029) appeared on the $100 denomination (BEP die no. MISC1039). These notes are called "Rainbow Notes" due to the localized blue stain and bright red overprinting of seals and serial numbers. The $100 Lincoln note debuted December 4, 1869. Robert Todd Lincoln pronounced this the "most satisfactory likeness" of his father. Burt's original die was on display at the Smithsonian Institution for many years.

Fig. 2.111. Sculptor Henry Kirke Brown's bronze statue "The Orator," based on Lincoln's Second Inaugural, was dedicated at the north end of the busy Union Square, New York City, on September 16, 1870.

Fig. 2.109. In 1869 Henry Gugler engraved John H. Littlefield's painting of Lincoln in an elaborate and expensive manner, achieving both financial and critical success in the process.

1869 $100 Rainbow Note (Friedberg-168) showing Lincoln is released to circulation December 4, 1869 (see fig. 2.110). This was another vignette engraved by Charles Burt, and also another likeness based on a single photo shoot of the president by Anthony Berger, February 9, 1864. Burt's portrait was popular. Most readers are familiar with it through its use on the old-style $5 small-sized currency that was issued for most of the 20th century. *Heath's Counterfeit Detector, at Sight* called the vignette "the best likeness extant of the lamented Abraham Lincoln."[37] Burt was paid $600 for this engraving, the standard fee for this work. This has to rate as one of the best expenditures ever by the federal government. This regal Lincoln portrait graced the $100 greenbacks for 42 years, until 1912. During this time it appeared on more than 1.5 billion notes. Additional engraved portraits of Lincoln based on Burt's original also appeared on $500 Gold Certificates for Series 1870 through 1875, printed from circa 1870 until 1876. When new notes were called for following the passage of the Federal Reserve Act on December 23, 1913, slightly cropped versions of the Burt engraving appeared on more than a billion large-sized $5 Federal Reserve Notes and $5 Federal Reserve Bank Notes. In 1923 it appeared on the famous $5 Silver Certificate "Porthole Notes," so called because the legend THE UNITED STATES OF AMERICA rings the Lincoln portrait like a ship's porthole. When the United States converted to small-sized currency in 1928, another cropping of Burt's Lincoln portrait was retained on the $5 denomination, and until 1999 was used on all classes of currency of that denomination, some tens of billions of notes, all told. A similar portrait was even used on $5 Food Stamps in 1970 because the portrait was already familiar to the recipients.

1869 CIRCA. John Sartain, "the father of mezzotint engraving in the United States," produces a masterful Lincoln portrait based on the same model as the $100 Legal Tender Note portrait by Charles Burt.

1869. Henry Gugler engraves Littlefield's Lincoln portrait (see fig. 2.109). Considered one of the best images of Lincoln, the Littlefield portrait served as the basis for a U.S. four-cent stamp.

1869 DECEMBER 4. Hundred-dollar U.S. notes bearing Lincoln's image are released to circulation (fig. 2.110). These were the first to employ an image of Lincoln based on the photo widely known as the "Universal Lincoln" (Ostendorf-92), due to its prevalence on U.S. paper money of the 20th century.

1870. Henry Kirke Brown's statue "The Orator" is dedicated in Union Square, New York City (see fig. 2.111). According to Andrew Boyd, writing before the ceremony, "This statue is intended to be placed in Union Square, New York. Mr. Lincoln is represented with his right arm thrown across his breast and the left hand holding the Emancipation Proclamation. The statue is of bronze, is nearly 11 feet high, weighs about 2,600 pounds, and entirely cost about $22,000. The design is by H.K. Brown, and the casting by Robert Wood & Co., Philadelphia."[38]

1870. Postwar scrip in the South demonstrates the effects of carpetbagger influence. Witness issues from Tennessee, Mississippi, and South Carolina on pages 141, 144, and 148. In Woodrow Wilson's *History of the American People* he labeled these Northern carpetbaggers "adventurers [who] swarmed out of the North, as much enemies of the one race as of the other, to cozen, beguile, and use the negroes."

1870 FEBRUARY 28. The *New York Times* reports on the progress in replacing the Lincoln 50-cent notes in its issue of February 28, 1870. Under the headline "New Fractional Currency," the *Times* states: "Models for the new fifty cent notes have been completed. The size is the same as the old ones. A vignette of the late [he died December 24, 1869] Hon. E.M. Stanton, pronounced a most excellent likeness, and executed by one of the best engravers in the United States,

Fig. 2.112. Organizations such as the Lincoln Brotherhood and the Lincoln Union were established after the Civil War to promote Black Americans' interests and enforce civil rights protections. This large (actual size is 4.25 x 6.75 inches) ceremonial "Ladies Ticket" was issued January 5, 1870. Although the location of this club in not known, the message of photographic reproduction of Ritchie's engraving after Carpenter's painting "First Reading of the Emancipation Proclamation" is loud and clear.

Fig. 2.113. U.S. Grant inherited the good will of his predecessors George Washington and Abraham Lincoln. Although his administration was rocked by political corruption, his popularity with the generation that had fought the Civil War continued throughout the 19th century. This medallion, "Defender, Martyr, Father," was engraved by Henry A. Thomas in 1870, and published by Chas. H. Crosby & Co., Boston.

will ornament the left end of the note." This Stanton portrait was engraved by none other than Charles Burt, who had also engraved the Lincoln image. Once again, the engraver was paid $600 for the Stanton likeness. To increase security for the new note, an open space of about an inch on the right end of the note was purposely left blank to show the localized jute fibers introduced into the paper as a counterfeit deterrent. Once again, the bogus-money mills duplicated the real Stanton 50-cent bills. Another new replacement was called for, this time depicting Samuel Dexter—another engraving by Burt, and another $600 pay check.

1870 MARCH. Carmine Lincoln six-cent stamps (Scott 137 with grill and Scott 148 without grill) were printed by NBNCo. The earliest known usage was on April 11, 1870, for Scott 137 and March 28, 1870, for Scott 148; 27.5 million were issued (fig. 2.114a).

1870 MARCH 29. *Brooklyn Daily Eagle* Washington correspondent "Peconic" reports that Lincoln 50-cent Fractional Currency will be replaced because the bills are easily counterfeited.

1870 APRIL 12. New 50-cent Stanton notes are issued to replace the counterfeited Lincoln notes. According to the April 11, 1870, issue of the *Brooklyn Daily Eagle,* "the new fifty cent notes will be issued to-morrow—not a day too soon, as the last batch put in circulation [the notes with Lincoln's portrait] are universally pronounced a wretched failure. Considering what the recent specimens of currency are, it is not wonderful that $576,800 worth of notes was destroyed by the Treasury Department last week."

1870s. Almost from the first, authors translate the Lincoln success story into juvenile literature. In 1863 Massachusetts author William M. Thayer wrote *The Pioneer Boy, and how he became President.* The

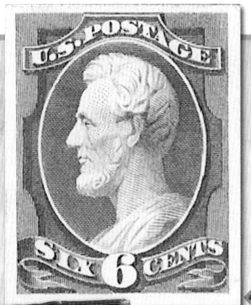

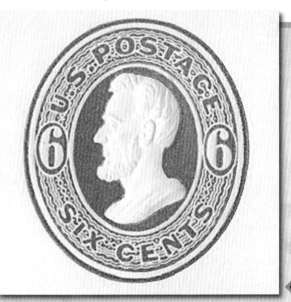

Fig. 2.114. The six-cent Lincoln profile stamp by NBNCo was issued April 11, 1870; a proof (a) is shown (Scott 137P). The vignette is by Joseph P. Ourdan (BEP die no. P0139). In 1873 CBNCo produced official stamps for the various executive departments of similar style. Shown are (b) the six-cent stamps for the Department of the Interior (Scott O18, BEP die no. P0192); and (c) Treasury Department (Scott O75, BEP die no. P0152). (d) In 1870/1871 contractor George H. Reay, Brooklyn, produced embossed envelopes for public use. A similar image of Lincoln appeared on the six-cent covers (Scott U85). All these designs are understood to be based on a white marble bust of Lincoln by Sarah Fisher Clampitt Ames, that had been purchased for the U.S. Capitol for $2,000 in 1868.

Fig. 2.115. The state of Ohio issued this Civil War infantry medal to veterans following the war.

Fig. 2.116. (a) Johnson's free post-office box label Var. 1, Philadelphia, 1865. (b) S. Allan Taylor Lincoln subscription label 10 (cents), circa 1870; other denominations are known.

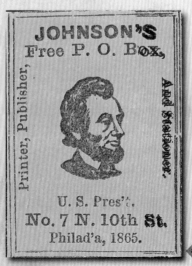

following year Thayer wrote *The Life and Character of Abraham Lincoln.* Thayer's books were translated and spread to foreign countries. In the 1870s these juvenile tales also became a part of curricula for instructing youth. The account of the self-made man appealed to American self-reliance and initiative. A tale of Lincoln's life in terms not dissimilar to the story of the ugly duckling that became a swan appealed to the country's sense of fair play and support for the underdog. Poet Bayard Taylor contributed a piece of juvenile fiction in 1870, *The Ballad of Abraham Lincoln,* which was printed with illustrations by Sol. Eytinge Jr.

1870 APRIL. Lincolnphile Andrew Boyd publishes *A memorial Lincoln bibliography: being an account of books, eulogies, sermons, portraits, engravings, medals, etc., published upon Abraham Lincoln, sixteenth president of the United States, assassinated Good Friday, April 14, 1865,* which has been cited throughout this book for its excellent reportage.

"This Bibliography may fairly be said to be a catalogue of a collection of Lincoln matter at present in my possession," Boyd wrote, "as I have everything mentioned, except a very few pamphlets, two of the engravings, and a few of the medals. It is, without doubt, the largest Lincoln collection extant," he claimed in the foreword (which he labeled "Preliminary Egotism") to his Lincoln bibliographia. Boyd had started his collection a year and a half after Lincoln's death, and spent the next four years passionately pursuing Lincolniana. He wrote more than 2,000 letters and "ransacked . . . every book and print store that seemed at all likely to contain matter relating thereto." The Lincoln fanatic also possessed many Lincoln letters and personal items, photographs, and curiosities which did not fall within the compass of his volume and were not listed. A biographical essay and a list of the print runs of the various publications were also supplied by fellow Lincoln collector Charles Henry Hart, historiographer of the Numismatic and Antiquarian Society of Philadelphia.

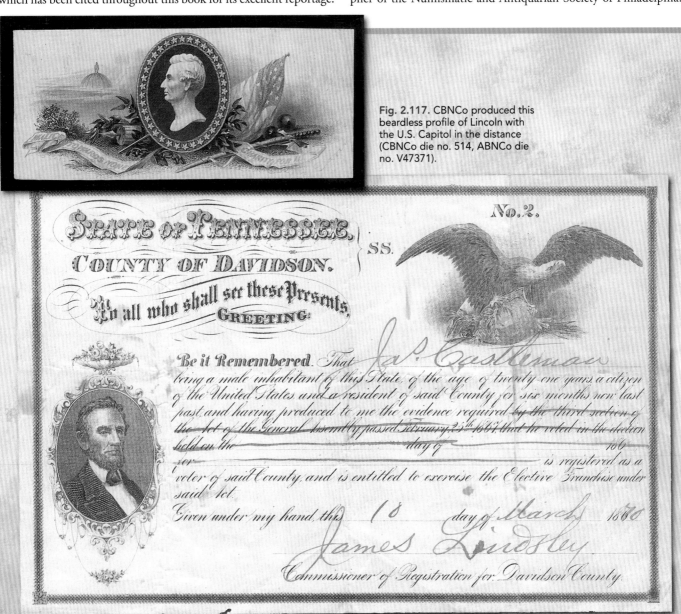

Fig. 2.117. CBNCo produced this beardless profile of Lincoln with the U.S. Capitol in the distance (CBNCo die no. 514, ABNCo die no. V47371).

Fig. 2.118. President Lincoln had tapped Andrew Johnson, a war Democrat, to be military governor of occupied Tennessee, and thereafter his running mate in the 1864 presidential election. This Tennessee voter's registration for Davidson County (Nashville), issued March 10, 1870, reflects the political tenor of the times. It also shows a lithographed copy of the Lincoln $10 bill portrait which looked official and would have been familiar to voters of all political stripes.

Fig. 2.119. Vinnie Ream's white marble statue of Abraham Lincoln was dedicated in the U.S. Capitol Rotunda, January 25, 1871.

Fig. 2.120. Randolph Rogers commemorated Lincoln the emancipator. His bronze Lincoln statue was dedicated at Fairmount Park in Philadelphia on September 22, 1871.

Fig. 2.121. This Series 1871 one-sixth barrel, 16-2/3 cents beer revenue stamp (Scott REA21) includes a small Lincoln portrait of the newly popular style by an unknown engraver at the Bureau of Engraving and Printing (BEP die no. MISC1315).

The frontispiece was a laid-in copyright photograph of Marshall's Lincoln portrait. He also included laid-in photographs of a plaster cast of Lincoln's right hand, which he owned, and of the "original Emancipation Proclamation" that had been sent to the government printer, including pasted in insertions from the printed preliminary proclamation. The book cataloged hundreds of printed eulogies, sermons, and orations delivered at the time of Lincoln's demise, hundreds of additional publications on Lincoln during his lifetime and up to the time of publication, additional prints and engravings, medals and medalets, and mourning cards and badges. It is a striking work and a must-have for the collector of Lincolniana.

1870 APRIL 11. The Post Office issues a six-cent, pale carmine postage stamp as part of a new series produced by the National Bank Note Co. (see fig. 2.114).

1870. Series of 1870 $500 Gold Certificates utilize the same Burt engraving that appears on the $100 Rainbow Notes.

1870. Jules Verne publishes his classic *20,000 Leagues Under the Sea*. The story's action takes place aboard the sailing frigate *Abraham Lincoln*.

1870 DECEMBER 23. The Illinois Watch Company, manufacturer of the "A. Lincoln" pocket watch, is founded by Lincoln's former banker John W. Bunn and several of Lincoln's influential former neighbors in Springfield, Illinois, including Lincoln's former law partner John T. Stuart.

1871 JANUARY 25. A marble statue of Lincoln by 23-year-old Vinnie Ream is unveiled in the Capitol Rotunda (fig. 2.119).

1871. Randolph Roger's Lincoln statue at Fairmount Park in Philadelphia is erected (see fig. 2.120). According to Andrew Boyd, writing before the event:

This statue now being cast at Munich is intended to be erected at Philadelphia. The figure presents Mr. Lincoln seated in a chair over which is thrown a cloak. In one hand it holds an open scroll representing the emancipation, and in the other a pen. The upper side panels of the pedestal will be decorated with the arms of the United States on one side, and those of the city of Philadelphia on the other, in bronze the corners being supported with Roman fasces, also in bronze. On the lower corners of the pedestal are four American eagles, supporting festoons of laurel, all in bronze. Appropriate inscriptions will be placed in the several unoccupied panels of the pedestal. The monument will be of bronze and granite, its total height being 23 feet. The granite work will be done in this country, and the bronze work at the Royal Foundry, Munich. The design is by Randolph Rogers.[39]

1871 MARCH 1. A Congressional Joint Resolution awards George Robinson a gold medal and $5,000 "for his heroic conduct on the 14th of April 1865 in saving the life of the Hon. William H. Seward, then Secretary of State of the United States." The obverse depicts Robinson in profile; the reverse shows Private Robinson's struggle to deter a Booth confederate, would-be assassin Lewis Payne. In the attack, both Seward and Robinson were injured. After his trial, Payne was hung. Dies were engraved by Anthony C. Paquet, and the medal was struck in October 1873.

1871. A gold medal bearing Lincoln's portrait, this by Mint engraver Charles E. Barber, is presented to Mexican War, Seminole War, and Civil War veteran, Maj. Gen. John Cleveland Robinson (see fig. 2.122). This medal was a token of affection from the officers and men of the 114th Pennsylvania Volunteers. Robinson was recipient of the Medal of Honor for valor near Spotsylvania Courthouse, Virginia, in 1864. After the war, he entered politics, rising to lieutenant governor of New York, and acted as head of the Grand Army of the Republic. A bronze statue of Robinson was erected at Gettysburg National Military Park.

Fig. 2.122. This very medal in gold was struck at the U.S. Mint circa 1871 or 1872, and presented to Major General John Robinson (Julian PE-28). Robinson was a veteran of the Mexican and Civil wars. The engraver was Charles Barber. King reported an example in bronze (King-522), but Julian could find no Mint records, nor a specimen to illustrate in his tome. Doubtless in gold, this is unique.

Fig. 2.123. This Series of 1871 forty-pound, $12.80 tobacco revenue stamp (Springer-TF59) is from an engraving by Joseph P. Ourdan (BEP die no. MISC633).

1871 OCTOBER 6. Lincoln Chapter No. 147 RAM is chartered at Lincoln, Illinois, according to a Masonic chapter penny for the organization.

1871 OCTOBER 26. Treasury agents arrest three in Brooklyn with a large quantity of counterfeit $10 greenbacks and plates for the Lincoln 50-cent Fractional Currency.[40]

1872 NOVEMBER 19. Fort McKeen, opposite Bismarck, Dakota Territory, is renamed Fort Abraham Lincoln. In 1876 post commander Lt. Col. George Armstrong Custer and his Seventh Cavalry departed Fort Abraham Lincoln, North Dakota, on an ill-fated expedition against the Sioux, which culminated in their defeat at the Little Big Horn.

1871 DECEMBER. The U.S. Mint strikes William Barber's Lincoln Emancipation medal (see fig. 2.124). A gold specimen of the "Eman-cipation Proclaimed" medal is given to the Pennsylvania National Guard, according to medal author Bob Julian.[41]

1873. A student of Chicago artist Leonard Volk, New York sculptor Byron Pickett executes a very large bronze plaque featuring Lincoln's profile (see fig. 2.127), "which has often been called the finest profile in metal of Abraham Lincoln," scholar Dr. Louis A. Warren wrote. Warren traced the model to a bearded profile photograph of Lincoln taken in Springfield a couple days before Lincoln left for his inauguration, and also saw the influence of Volk's bust (see figure 1.34) in Pickett's work.[42] Quite frankly, though, the hairline alone should rule out the photographic model cited. The execution is superb, whatever the source. Pickett's Lincoln bust is 12 inches by 18 inches; the overall dimensions of the elliptical bronze plaque measure 19 inches by 24 inches. The original bronze came into the hands of L.G. Muller, who copyrighted the design in 1908, and issued

Fig. 2.124. In 1871 U.S. Mint engraver William Barber executed this fine medal to commemorate the Emancipation Proclamation (Julian CM-16).

Fig. 2.125. Carpetbaggers from the North took prominent positions in the post-war South. This Adams County, Mississippi, warrant, lithographed by R.P. Studley of St. Louis, sports a Lincoln portrait modeled after the familiar official Lincoln $10 image.

Fig. 2.126. A fine example of NBNCo's new Lincoln portrait die, after the same model as its earlier $10 note, is shown on this draft drawn by Ferdinand Schumacher, December 10, 1872.

Fig. 2.127. New York sculptor Byron Pickett executed a very large and fine bronze profile plaque of Lincoln in 1873. The bust measures 12 by 18 inches, and the overall dimensions of the elliptical bronze plaque are 19 by 24 inches. Pickett's profile would be an enduring one, serving as the model for a postal card and frequently replicated for the next 70 years.

metal replicas. The Pickett profile was used as the basis of the U.S. postal card issued in 1911.

1873. Collector Andrew Zabriskie authors *A Descriptive Catalogue of the Political and Memorial Medals struck in Honor of Abraham Lincoln, Sixteenth President of the United States.* Zabriskie later became president of the American Numismatic Society. His Lincoln medal catalog lists 187 medals (note that his preface states 189). "No President or public man in this country—Washington excepted—has been honored with an equal number of medallic memorials," Zabriskie wrote in the preface to his work. Following the war a great many of the war-era medalets, tokens, and store cards depicting Lincoln were restruck for sale to collectors in a variety of exotic metals and mulings (mixing of dies from differing pieces to create new varieties). Many of these pieces were restruck so often that the dies actually broke, as evidenced by die cracks in some struck pieces, but the man-

ufacturers kept the presses running to meet the demand. Zabriskie took offense at the practice of muling dies to multiply varieties. "I believe very few pieces have escaped my observation, and they are probably those known as 'mules,'" he wrote. "The infamous practice of muling, at one time carried to a great extent . . . can be looked upon only with contempt by any true student of Numismatics," he charged. According to Jay Monaghan, Zabriskie's privately printed catalog was limited to 75 copies.[43] It is decidedly uncommon today.

1873 DECEMBER 18. House of Representatives refers to its Committee on the Judiciary "The memorial of Julius Francis, and other citizens of Buffalo, New York, that the twelfth day of February, being the birthday of Abraham Lincoln, be declared a national holiday."

1874 FEBRUARY 12. Lincoln Memorial Club of Cincinnati presents a petition signed by nine of its members to the Senate and House of

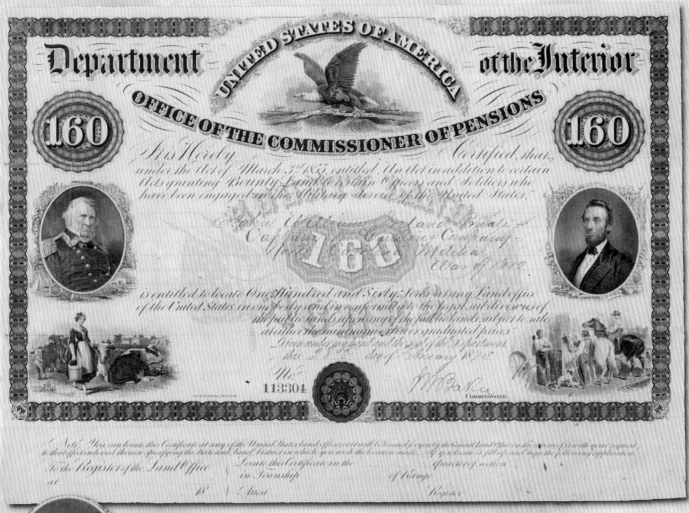

Fig. 2.128. This spectacular land-grant certificate, dated February 28, 1873, was issued by the Office of the Commissioner of Pensions to a veteran for 160 acres. The recipient was John William Ireland for service in a North Carolina Militia Company during the War of 1812. In addition to the official government portrait of Lincoln, and a vignette of General Winfield Scott, it bears the imprint "Geo. D. Baldwin, New-York." Baldwin was an engraver and plate printer from the 1840s and a principal in several engraving firms in the decade prior to the formation of the "association," the ABNCo, in 1858. From then until his death in 1872, Baldwin worked independently. Author Gene Hessler credits him for several vignettes appearing on U.S. currency. The BEP itself credits "Baldwin Bank Note Co." with the Lincoln portrait on the Series 1864 five-percent, $10,000, registered ten-forty bond; the Series 1862 and 1864 six-percent, $500, five-twenty coupon bond; and the Interior Department Bounty Land Warrant. All of this seems sufficient evidence that George D. Baldwin was the engraver of the iconic Lincoln bond portrait for NBNCo, which was later used on the $20 Interest-Bearing Treasury Notes.

Representatives asking that "the anniversary of Abraham Lincoln's birthday be declared a legal holiday."

1874 FEBRUARY 21. In the House, Mr. Banning, by unanimous consent, presents the petition of N.C. Liverpool, Peter H. Clark, and other citizens of Cincinnati, Ohio, asking that the anniversary of Lincoln's birthday be declared to be a legal holiday; which was again referred to the Committee on the Judiciary.

1874 FEBRUARY 24. Agitation to establish Lincoln's birthday as a national holiday continues. In the U.S. Senate, John Sherman (brother of Civil War general William Tecumseh Sherman) "presented a petition of citizens of Ohio, praying that the birthday of Abraham Lincoln be declared a legal holiday." The petition was ordered to be laid on the table.

1874 MAY 27. In the House of Representatives, on motion of Mr. Potter, the Judiciary committee discharges from further consideration the memorial of citizens of Buffalo, New York, praying that the birthday of Lincoln may be made a national holiday. The same was

ordered to be laid upon the table. The petition from the Buffalo citizens, endorsed "by representatives and alternates from each state" was resubmitted to the Senate and House in 1875, 1877, and 1879.

1870s. In the 1870s prints and lithographs memorializing Lincoln and his sacrifice for his country continue to be popular. A certain detachment was possible with the passage of time. H.H. Lloyd & Company's Lincoln memorial print was titled "The Martyr Dies, But Freedom Lives."

1874 OCTOBER 14. President U.S. Grant and the National Lincoln Monument Association dedicate the partially completed Lincoln Tomb, memorialized by scrip issue. According to Andrew Boyd:

> The National Lincoln Monument. This monument is intended to be placed over the remains of Mr. Lincoln at Oak Ridge Cemetery, in Springfield, Illinois. It was designed by the American sculptor, Larkin G. Meade [*sic*], and is described as follows: The total height will be 100 feet. The foundation and the sub-base are of granite, the architectural work of Raverceoni marble, and the statue of bronze. The obelisk is surmounted by the eagle and globe. At the base a pedestal

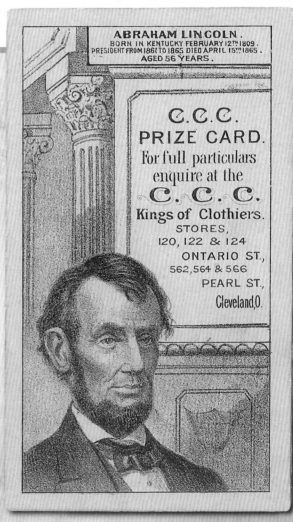

Fig. 2.129. This Society of California Volunteers membership certificate issued to J.W. Sim, First Lieut. Cal. Hundred, June 21, 1873, was engraved by Nahl Brothers, San Francisco, and printed by L. Naugel. Admiral David Farragut and General U.S. Grant join Lincoln, and army and navy vignettes.

Fig. 2.130. A stock advertising card. Notice the Lincoln portrait is the new $100 Lincoln image. This Cleveland prize card was a trade card from C.C.C. Clothiers, printed by Bufford, Boston & New York. The author has observed other companies using this stock design.

ABRAHAM LINCOLN.
BORN IN KENTUCKY, FEBRUARY 12th 1809.
PRESIDENT FROM 1861 TO 1865. DIED APRIL 15th 1865.
AGED 56 YEARS.

PRESENTED with the Compliments of
DAMBMANN BROS. & CO.
BALTIMORE, MD.

a

A. Lincoln
J.D.Larkin & Co.
BUFFALO, N.Y.
"SWEET HOME" SOAP

b

Fig. 2.131. The Lincoln $10 currency image remained popular in the 1870s as a model for commercial printing. Here are two trade cards with interpretations of the image: (a) for Dambmann Bros. of Baltimore, and (b) for Larkin's "Sweet Home" soap. The former was a stock card, and the author has observed several other businesses advertised thereon.

Fig. 2.132. ABNCo still owned Charles Burt's Lincoln-portrait die, originally created in 1861 for the U.S. Demand Notes, having successfully thwarted Treasury Department attempts to obtain it from them. The company was free to use it for commercial work, and during the last half of the 19th century was very active in soliciting paper-money contracts abroad. During the 1870s, ABNCo created this splendid sample of its workmanship utilizing Lincoln-portrait die number 141, and vignettes of Russian Alexander II, U.S. Grant, Benjamin Franklin, and George Washington, printed on the card.

is projected in front, on which is a colossal statue of Lincoln. On a plane below, at the four cardinal points, are four pedestals, on which are groups representing the infantry, cavalry, artillery and marine arms of the service. Encircling these pedestals are tablets on which are written the names of all the states. These tablets are linked together. On the four sides of the base are tablets for inscriptions. That in front and under the statue bears the name in full, Abraham Lincoln. The sub-base is reached by stairs from the corners of the base, and under the base is the crypt for the remains. The door of the crypt is also the entrance to the passage and stairway, which ascends the monument's inside. It will cost $200,000.[44]

1875. Series 1875 $500 Gold Certificates continue the use of Burt's Lincoln portrait from the earlier Series 1870 (see fig. 2.134), which they also share with the $100 Legal Tender Notes.

1875. The Treasury abandons its vaunted Rainbow Notes with a new Series 1875 $100 Legal Tender Notes, because the expensive security features of the prior series proved expensive, and no effective deterrent to counterfeiting.

1876 MARCH 2. A newspaper reports on "The Lincoln Tower in London" at the New Christ Church, in Westminster, London. The report says the church "is especially interesting on account of the tower built by subscription as a memorial to Abraham Lincoln."[45]

1876 APRIL 14. On the 11th anniversary of Lincoln's assassination, Thomas Ball's Freedmen's Memorial Monument to Abraham Lincoln (also known as the Emancipation Memorial, or Freedom Memorial) is dedicated in Lincoln Park, a mile east of the U.S. Capitol in Washington, D.C., with President U.S. Grant in attendance.

Fig. 2.134. The Treasury also quickly utilized Charles Burt's new $100 Legal Tender Note portrait on Series 1870 Gold Certificates in the $500 denomination (Friedberg-1166i). This design was carried over to $500 Gold Certificates of the Series of 1875 (Friedberg-1166n).

Fig. 2.133. Circa 1874 the City of Lincoln, Nebraska, attempted to issue municipal scrip to fund public improvements. The notes were ordered from CBNCo in New York City. (a) The back of the $1 note bears a Lincoln portrait from CNBCo die number 1, which the company patterned after the other bank-note companies' currency/bond engravings. (b) The face of the $2 note has a small Lincoln profile. Before notes could be put into circulation, city fathers were dissuaded, and the notes were stored in city hall. At a later time, parties "liberated" the cache of notes, signed them, and attempted to make them look circulated in an attempt to pass them off on unwitting recipients.

Fig. 2.135. Lincoln's image on this extremely rare Oxford, Lafayette County, Mississippi, scrip note was another political message toward the South after the war. This is another lithograph of R.P. Studley, St. Louis, featuring his version of the Lincoln $10 portrait on the greenbacks.

Fig. 2.136. South Carolina Rail Road, Charleston, attempted to issue scrip during the early 1870s. This style was printed by ABNCo, but it is unclear whether any of this type were ever actually issued. Notes were printed in sheets of $1, $1 (different designs), $2, and $3. Remainders are plentiful and bear 5-cent Lincoln revenue imprints (Turner Type P, RN-P5). Shown is Shull-662.

Fig. 2.137. This unlisted company-store scrip from the 1870s was issued for Brownsport Furnace Store, payable for $3 in merchandise except liquor. An iron smelter, Brownsport Furnace operated in Decaturville, Tennessee, northeast of Memphis, from 1848 through the end of the century. There's no imprint, but once again the note has a fair representation of the official Lincoln currency portrait.

Principle speaker for the event is Frederick Douglass. This is the first federal memorial in the district to honor Lincoln. Ball was an important figure in post-war art circles, became rich, expatriated to Italy, and his home became an academy for young artists. Ball's statue depicts Lincoln holding his Emancipation Proclamation standing over the bowed figure of Archer Alexander, who is breaking the chains of slavery. Alexander was the last slave captured under the Fugitive Slave Act in Missouri. The sculptor was living in Italy and worked from a photograph of Archer supplied by William Greenleaf Eliot. The statue was financed by donations through the efforts of an African-American woman named Charlotte Scott of Virginia, which commenced shortly after the assassination. She contributed her first five dollars earned as a free woman "as a way of paying homage to the President who had issued the Emancipation Proclamation that liberated the slaves in the Confederate States," according to the bronze plaque on the memorial (see fig. 2.141). The sponsoring organization

was the Western Sanitary Commission, based in St. Louis. Ball had the figures cast at von Müller's Royal Foundry in Munich in 1875 at a cost of $17,000. Congress accepted the memorial from the "colored citizens of the United States," and appropriated $3,000 for the pedestal on which it stands. In 1877 a copy was erected in Ball's hometown of Boston. Ball's Emancipation Group was praised in a poem by John Greenleaf Whittier, a portion of which reads:

> Take the worn frame, that rested not
> Save in a martyr's grave;
> The care-lined face, that none forgot,
> Bent to the kneeling slave.
> Let man be free! The mighty word
> He spake was not his own;
> An impulse from the Highest stirred
> These chiselled lips alone.

Fig. 2.138. B.F. Corlies and Macy, New York, printed this certificate of deposit for the First National Bank, New York City, during the 1870s. It bears a five-cent Lincoln internal revenue imprint (Turner Type P, RN-P5).

Fig. 2.140. Another commercial use by ABNCo of its Lincoln-portrait die number 141 in association with portraits of the other presidents was this ornate Dwight Company centennial label, 1876. ABNCo produced similar imprints for at least two other companies.

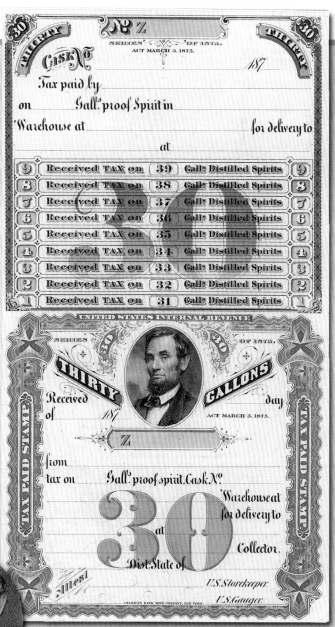

Fig. 2.139. Distilled spirits were taxed, too. This is a Series 1875 Thirty Gallons Tax Paid Stamp, by ABNCo, proof on card. Similar stamps were issued in 10-gallon increments from 10 to 130 gallons (BEP die no. MISC3040).

1876 OCTOBER 26. Lincoln Park Chapter No. 177 RAM is chartered at Chicago, according to a Masonic chapter penny for the organization issued circa 1890.

1876 NOVEMBER 7. A gang of Chicago counterfeiters attempts to steal Lincoln's body to hold it for ransom.

1878 FEBRUARY 1. Congress by joint resolution accepts Francis Bicknell Carpenter's *First Reading of the Emancipation Proclamation,* a gift of Elizabeth Thompson of New York City, who had purchased the painting from Carpenter for $25,000.

1878 FEBRUARY 12. On what would have been Lincoln's 69th birthday, Congress assembles in joint session to formally receive Carpenter's painting *First Reading of the Emancipation Proclamation.* Unfortunately, this was not the work that Lincoln had seen, and had

been viewed at the U.S. Capitol, and elsewhere before the end of the war. It was altered over the years. Following its national tour the *First Reading* had remained in the artist's possession, during which time he painted "improvements" to it. These changes are noticeable by comparing the painting to Ritchie's engraving based on it. Unfortunately in the process, Carpenter fogged Lincoln's head, arguably the most important single element of the work. In the words of a U.S. Senate historian, "During this time, he made so many revisions to heads and to details that the painting finally looked very different from the engraving that had popularized it. Carpenter's much-revised Lincoln became a weaker portrait than he had originally achieved."[46] On that day, however, Carpenter, who attended the ceremony, heard nothing but praise for his efforts from such widely disparate parties as Congressman James A. Garfield, who had been a Union general in the war, and Congressman Alexander H. Stephens, who had been the vice president of the Confederate States of America. After several

Fig. 2.141. American expatriate and sculptor Thomas Ball's Emancipation group was dedicated on the 11th anniversary of Lincoln's assassination, April 14, 1876, in Lincoln Park, a mile east of the U.S. Capitol in Washington, D.C. The statue shows Lincoln imparting freedom to a former slave. President Grant attended the dedication. Pictured are (a) the entablature on the face of the pedestal and (b) the statue itself.

Fig. 2.142. The Lincoln Park Chapter Royal Arch Masons' lodge number 177 was founded in Chicago in 1876, according to the reverse of this medal. The medal is of a later date (King-432).

restorations, the painting now hangs in the Capitol over the west staircase in the U.S. Senate Wing.

1878 MARCH 25. The goal of Republicans to create a Territory of Lincoln dies hard. The *New York Times* Washington correspondent called a new proposal to carve a Territory of Lincoln out of the Black Hills centered on Deadwood, a "pocket borough," "contrived for the convenience of a few individuals who desire to combine office-holding with speculation." It was likened to Nevada, which the *Times* considered a fiefdom of rich Californians. South Dakota was the result.

1879 APRIL 14. Poet Walt Whitman first delivers his celebrated lecture "Death of Lincoln," at Steck Hall in New York City. His tribute is on the 14th anniversary of Lincoln's assassination. This performance had been planned the previous year, but Whitman was ill. This time, the performance finally came off. The following April,

he gave the lecture in Philadelphia, and the year after that in Boston. In 1886 Whitman undertook a "Death of Lincoln" tour, speaking in Elkton, Maryland; Camden and Haddonfield, New Jersey; and Philadelphia.

1879 SEPTEMBER 25. National Republican Club organizes in New York City. This group incorporated in 1886 as the Republican Club of the City of New York. It held the first of its annual dinners on Lincoln's birthday in 1887.

1880 FEBRUARY 23. Lincoln Cork-Faced horse collars are patented by the Cork-Faced Collar Co., Lincoln, Illinois. The company registered its trademark in 1892.

1881. George B. Ayers, who had purchased Alexander Hessler's Chicago photo studio shortly after the Civil War, reprints Hessler's

Fig. 2.143. Under the Act of June 6, 1872, the BEP engraved and printed tobacco revenue stamps. The 5- and 40-pound stamps have a profile of Lincoln. Shown is an example used in 1876, First Series (Springer TF83B).

Fig. 2.144. Counterfeiting of internal revenue stamps was a big problem for the revenue agents. NBNCo printed a series of experimental essays in the mid-1870s with improved counterfeit deterrence. This lovely rose and gray-blue example (Turner Essay 21) employs NBNCo's patented cycloidal lathework and surface printing in a fugitive rose-colored ink.

Fig. 2.145. "Lincoln hirelings" was a disparaging nickname for Union soldiers during the Civil War, but evidently an endearing term after the war. This silk ribbon from an 1880 reunion was found tucked into a family Bible.

beardless photos of Lincoln. He also makes a duplicate set of the negatives (later acquired by the Chicago Historical Society).

1881 JUNE 16. Isaac N. Arnold reads his paper on Abraham Lincoln before the Royal Historical Society, London, which is then printed by Fergus Printing Co., Chicago. A revised edition was published in 1883 with "a note from Robert T. Lincoln" added.

1881 JULY 2. Destiny links Abraham Lincoln and James A. Garfield. Garfield's brief presidency is terminated when Garfield is shot by Charles Julius Guiteau. Lincoln's eldest son and surviving heir, Robert Todd Lincoln, was Garfield's secretary of war. Secretary Lincoln was in the presidential party at the Sixth Street train station in Washington and was an eyewitness to the sad affair.

1881. Immediately following President James A. Garfield's death on September 19, 1881, the U.S. Mint strikes Lincoln-Garfield medalets engraved by William Barber in two sizes (fig. 2.147).

1881 NOVEMBER 12. Lincoln National Bank of the City of New York is organized.

1881 DECEMBER. Sculptor Leonard Volk's account of how his Lincoln life mask was made in 1860 is published in *Century* magazine.

1882. Another likeness of Abraham Lincoln, also engraved by Charles Burt and also based on an Anthony Berger photograph taken February 9, 1864, appears on the Series 1882 $500 Gold Certificates (see fig. 2.148). This engraving could have been done in 1869, but BEP records indicate nothing earlier than an 1882 hardening date. Burt's likeness of Lincoln had already appeared on the $500 Gold

LINCOLN. GARFIELD.

Soldiers' Nat'l Monument,

Fig. 2.146. This cabinet card commemorates the "two Martyrs of Liberty and Union," Lincoln and Garfield, and the Soldier's National Monument at Gettysburg. The card was copyrighted in 1881 by Rev. A.E. Tortat "for the benefit of the Soldiers' Memorial Church of the 'Prince of Peace,'" Gettysburg. The card reverse includes Lincoln's Gettysburg Address, and Garfield's address on the death of Lincoln. Garfield was a major general during the war.

Certificate (an image it shared with the $100 Legal Tender Notes and the more modern, familiar pose of the 20th-century $5 bills). These high-valued Gold Certificates were not currency per se, but rather portable receipts for gold deposits. They were issued as needed through 1927. Although 356,000 of these $500 Gold Certificates were issued, fewer than 200 are believed extant today. The first-issue $500 Gold Certificate (Friedberg-1215a) was unknown until a Memphis 2000 auction. Prior to that, the earliest known in collector's hands were Friedberg-1216 examples which bore Lyons-Roberts signatures, issued circa 1898 to 1905. The Federal Reserve Bank at San Francisco also owns two of the earliest issues in its paper-money collection.

1882 JULY 16. Mary Todd Lincoln dies.

1883. Horatio Alger Jr., author of the *Boyhood and Manhood Series of Illustrious Americans* which emphasized personal success sto-ries, publishes *Abraham Lincoln, the Backwoods boy; or, How a young rail-splitter became President.*

1883 NOVEMBER. Osborn Hamiline Oldroyd turns Lincoln's Springfield home at 10th and Jackson into the Lincoln Museum, charging visitors to view the Oldroyd Lincoln Memorial Collection.

1880s. In the 1880s tobacco companies such as Allen & Ginter and Goodwin & Co. begin inserting small collector's cards as a premium in cigarette, loose tobacco, and chewing-tobacco packages to boost sales. These were the forerunners of modern baseball and other trading cards. The original tobacco cards portrayed baseball players, thespians, military figures, world leaders, and even presidents of the United States such as Abraham Lincoln and U.S. Grant. Lincoln's "rookie card," his first trading card, is considered to be the "Honest Long Cut Chewing and Smoking" tobacco card produced by

Fig. 2.147. Destiny linked James A. Garfield with Abraham Lincoln when Garfield died September 19, 1881, from fatal gunshot wounds inflicted July 2. (*a, facing page*) The U.S. Mint struck its small Lincoln medalets with a Garfield reverse (reverse shows actual size; Julian PR-41), and another slightly larger version (Julian PR-40). (*b, facing page*) This elegant glass platter was embossed with busts of Lincoln, Washington, and Garfield. (*c*) Littleton View Co. published the stereoview "The Martyrs—Lincoln & Garfield" in 1884; it was sold by Underwood and Underwood.

Fig. 2.150. This Citizens Bank, Dysart, Iowa, check with Lincoln vignette was lithographed by Henry Gugler & Son, Milwaukee, dated July 7, 1882.

Fig. 2.148. A fourth Lincoln currency portrait by Charles Burt entered circulation on the $500 Series 1882 Gold Certificate, Friedberg-1215a, and remained on the denomination through the Great Depression. Shown is Friedberg-1216b, Department Series, with facsimile signatures of Houston B. Teehee and John Burke (BEP die number MISC2844). Burt's Lincoln engraving was modeled on a photograph taken February 9, 1864, by Anthony Berger.

Fig. 2.149. The Series 1869 "Rainbow Notes" were not immune to counterfeiting, and the Treasury Department introduced new series repeatedly with what it hoped was additional security. Its $100 Series 1880 note with Lincoln's portrait also fell prey to forgery. Master faker Emanuel Ninger drew this pen-and-ink counterfeit entirely by hand. It was seized by the Secret Service and presently resides in the National Numismatic Collection, Smithsonian Institution.

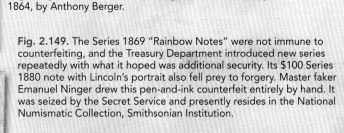

W. Duke, Sons & Co. N.Y. (see fig. 2.152). This card has a real photographic image of Lincoln, similar to the engraved image on the $100 bill of the time. Another early Lincoln tobacco card was a lithographed portrait issued for Yum Yum smoking and chewing tobacco by August Beck & Co., Chicago, which reproduces Marshall's famous Lincoln portrait (see fig. 2.153). This Yum Yum card was not only a premium but could be redeemed for prizes from the company. For 100 such cards, a gentleman could obtain a briar pipe, a dozen corn cob pipes, a pocket knife, or other items.

1886. *Century Magazine* commences publishing excerpts from the biography written by Lincoln's personal secretaries John Nicolay and John Hay. Over the next four years, this magazine published 40 of these excerpts to whet the appetites for the company's publication of Nicolay and Hay's multivolume Lincoln history.

1886 FALL. George Morgan's three-inch Lincoln presidential medal (fig. 2.155) is struck at the U.S. Mint. Mint-medal authority Bob Julian called Morgan's obverse "one of the finest artistic efforts ever struck at the U.S. Mint."[47]

1886. Augustus Saint-Gaudens casts a bronze copy of Volk's life mask, which he presents to the Smithsonian Institution. This bronze bust became the model for additional copies.

1886. William Herndon manages the Lincoln Memorial Collection's Lincolniana exhibition in Chicago, displayed by Munson and Keyes.

1887 FEBRUARY 12. The Lincoln Birthday Association of Buffalo, New York, stages an exhibition of Civil War relics and autographs at the Buffalo Historical Society.

UNION COMMANDERS.
THE NOTMAN PHOTO. CO., Limited, 3 PARK ST., BOSTON.

Fig. 2.151. In 1884 Notman Photo Co., Boston, published a composite cabinet card named "Union Commanders," which featured a seated Lincoln in the "Brady" pose with his principal military and naval officers. These cabinet cards were distributed compliments of the Travelers Insurance Co. Notman also issued a larger lithograph of the same style.

Fig. 2.152. This tobacco card with a photo of Ostendorf-92, the model for the Lincoln $100 bill portrait, is considered Lincoln's "rookie card" by specialists. It is larger than a *CDV*, and was issued by W. Duke & Sons, New York, for its Abe Lincoln Honest Long Cut chewing and smoking tobacco. Specialists date this card to the late 1870s or early 1880s.

Fig. 2.153. A rare 1890s Yum Yum Tobacco card, with an image based on the Marshall engraving.

1887 APRIL 14. Poet Walt Whitman delivers his memorial "Death of Lincoln" lecture at Madison Square Theatre on the 22nd anniversary of Lincoln's assassination (see fig. 2.156). Reserved seats are $1.50; general admission, a dollar. Whitman netted $600. Following the festivities a reception was held at Westminster Hotel. Whitman took Lincoln's death personally and was much aggrieved, publishing a series of reminiscences and verses including his classics "When Lilacs Last in the Door-Yard Bloom'd" and "O Captain! My Captain!" Whitman also lectured frequently on Lincoln. The February 12, 1888, issue of the *New York Herald* published his poem "Abraham Lincoln (Born February 12, 1809)." Whitman wrote: "To-day from each and all, a breath of prayer, a pulse of thought, To memory of Him—to birth of Him."

1887. Robert Todd Lincoln presents his parents' former Springfield home to the State of Illinois.

1887 OCTOBER 22. Augustus Saint-Gaudens's majestic standing Lincoln statue (fig. 2.157) is dedicated in Lincoln Park, Chicago. The main speaker for the event is Leonard Swett. This large public monument was financed from a bequest from Chicago businessman Eli Bates. Bates, who rose from humble beginnings, admired Lincoln's similar achievement. The monument committee invited Saint-Gaudens to participate in a design contest. Despite a personal interest in Lincoln, the sculptor declined to compete. The committee awarded him the contract anyway. Saint-Gaudens was proud that he'd personally witnessed Lincoln as president-elect, and knew this commission was a great opportunity for his career. He based his larger-than-life, iconic image in part on the Volk mask.

Fig. 2.154. Lincoln tobacco labels were numerous and very attractive in the 1880s and 1890s. Shown are inside cigar box embossed labels: *(a)* "Lincoln Bouquet," trademarked by B. Newmark & Co., and *(b)* "Los Inmortales" which means just what it sounds like and includes Lincoln, Washington, and Grant. "Los Inmortales" was registered by Grommes and Ullrich. The label was printed by Louis C. Wagner & Co., New York.

Fig. 2.155. In autumn 1886 Mint engraver George T. Morgan completed his Lincoln presidential medal (Julian PR-12). Mint-medal historian R.W. Julian calls Morgan's Lincoln obverse one of the best efforts ever done at the U.S. Mint. This is *not* faint praise; the details of Morgan's efforts are apparent to all.

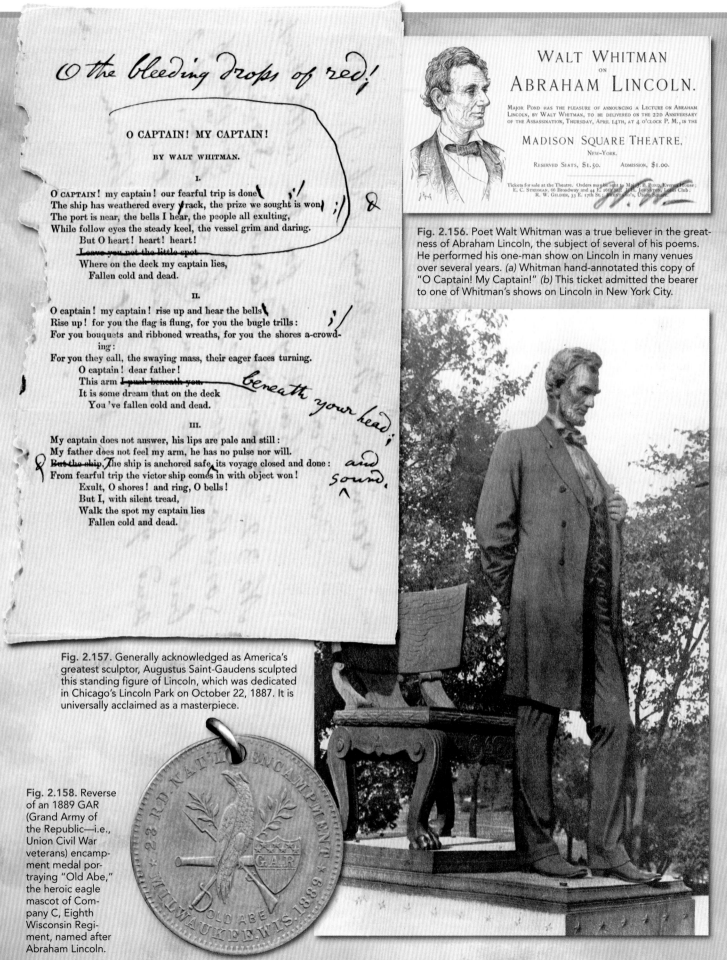

O the bleeding drops of red!

O CAPTAIN! MY CAPTAIN!

BY WALT WHITMAN.

I.

O CAPTAIN! my captain! our fearful trip is done
The ship has weathered every wrack, the prize we sought is won,
The port is near, the bells I hear, the people all exulting,
While follow eyes the steady keel, the vessel grim and daring.

　　But O heart! heart! heart!
　　Leave you not the little spot
　　Where on the deck my captain lies,
　　　　Fallen cold and dead.

II.

O captain! my captain! rise up and hear the bells
Rise up! for you the flag is flung, for you the bugle trills:
For you bouquets and ribboned wreaths, for you the shores a-crowd-
　　ing:
For you they call, the swaying mass, their eager faces turning.
　　O captain! dear father!
　　This arm I push beneath you, *beneath your head;*
　　It is some dream that on the deck
　　　　You 've fallen cold and dead.

III.

My captain does not answer, his lips are pale and still:
My father does not feel my arm, he has no pulse nor will.
But the ship, The ship is anchored safe, its voyage closed and done: *and*
From fearful trip the victor ship comes in with object won! *sound.*
　　Exult, O shores! and ring, O bells!
　　But I, with silent tread,
　　Walk the spot my captain lies
　　　　Fallen cold and dead.

WALT WHITMAN
ON
ABRAHAM LINCOLN.

MAJOR POND HAS THE PLEASURE OF ANNOUNCING A LECTURE ON ABRAHAM
LINCOLN, BY WALT WHITMAN, TO BE DELIVERED ON THE 22D ANNIVERSARY
OF THE ASSASSINATION, THURSDAY, APRIL 14th, AT 4 O'CLOCK P. M., IN THE

MADISON SQUARE THEATRE,
NEW-YORK.

RESERVED SEATS, $1.50.　　ADMISSION, $1.00.

Tickets for sale at the Theatre. Orders may be sent to Major B. Pond, Everett House;
E. C. Stedman, 66 Broadway and 44 E. 26th St.; J. H. Johnston, Lotos Club;
R. W. Gilder, 33 E. 17th St.; Brentano's, Union Square.

Fig. 2.156. Poet Walt Whitman was a true believer in the greatness of Abraham Lincoln, the subject of several of his poems.
He performed his one-man show on Lincoln in many venues
over several years. *(a)* Whitman hand-annotated this copy of
"O Captain! My Captain!" *(b)* This ticket admitted the bearer
to one of Whitman's shows on Lincoln in New York City.

Fig. 2.157. Generally acknowledged as America's
greatest sculptor, Augustus Saint-Gaudens sculpted
this standing figure of Lincoln, which was dedicated
in Chicago's Lincoln Park on October 22, 1887. It is
universally acclaimed as a masterpiece.

Fig. 2.158. Reverse
of an 1889 GAR
(Grand Army of
the Republic—i.e.,
Union Civil War
veterans) encamp-
ment medal por-
traying "Old Abe,"
the heroic eagle
mascot of Com-
pany C, Eighth
Wisconsin Regi-
ment, named after
Abraham Lincoln.

Saint-Gaudens portrayed Lincoln in a contemplative mood, as if he'd just risen from his chair. The figure was installed at the top of a rise of stairs forming an amphitheater.

1887. Log Cabin syrup is introduced by Minnesota grocer Patrick J. Towle in honor of his childhood hero Abe Lincoln. For decades, Towle marketed his syrup in tins made to look like log cabins with the spout formed by the chimney in the roof.

1888. The Society for Promoting Christian Knowledge in London, England, publishes *Abraham Lincoln: Farmer's Boy and President.* Also in 1888, Noah Brooks publishes *Abraham Lincoln: A Biography for Young People.* A Civil War correspondent and intimate of Lincoln's, Brooks's purpose was "to give the new generation a picture of Lincoln as he appeared to one who knew him."

1889. Lincoln's former law partner, William H. Herndon, and Jesse W. Weik publish *Herndon's Lincoln: The True Story of a Great Life.* This volume, present-day scholars feel, is of inestimable importance in understanding the public's perception of Lincoln. "Without any doubt, no single presidential biography—perhaps no American biography, period—has had as much influence in shaping both popular and scholarly conceptions of its subject," claims historian Kenneth J. Winkle. Herndon's book has been much discussed (and cussed) since, but it represents "a Lincoln as perceived by the man who seems to have been closer to him for a longer time than any other," according

to Lincoln scholar Douglas L. Wilson, coauthor of a new edition of the volume with Rodney O. Davis.

1880s. Lincoln clubs and associations are formed in all the principal cities and many of the smaller ones, as well. The Lincoln Club of Cincinnati, the New York Republican Club, and the Abraham Lincoln Association of Jersey City are among the most prominent. Each threw annual bashes in February in connection with a patriotic observance of Lincoln's birthday. These groups, Lincoln's surviving son, Robert Todd Lincoln—who served as Garfield's and Arthur's secretary of war, and Benjamin Harrison's ambassador to the United Kingdom—and other Lincoln intimates became the keepers of the Lincoln legacy, cultivating the image of Robert's father.

1890 APRIL. Poet Walt Whitman delivers his "Death of Lincoln" lecture for the final time in Philadelphia.

1890 JUNE 2. A dark brown Lincoln four-cent stamp (Scott 222), based on a portrait by Henry Gugler after an engraving by Littlefield, is released as part of the first Bureau Issue (engraved and printed at the Bureau of Engraving and Printing), which debuted on Washington's birthday, February 22, 1890 (see fig. 2.160).[48] A total of 66,759,574 were released. Four cents was the double letter rate (two ounces) for domestic mail. Additional varieties were subsequently created by the addition of small triangles at the upper corners.

Fig. 2.159. Cincinnati was a hotbed of Republicanism, as indicated by (a) this badge of the Lincoln Club of Cincinnati, established 1879, and (b) this chromolithograph on canvas by Middleton-Strobridge Lithographic Co.

Fig. 2.160. A new Lincoln four-cent stamp was issued June 2, 1890 (Scott 222), as part of a series honoring presidents and other important figures. Shown is an ABNCo proof. The Lincoln vignette was engraved by Alfred Jones after the John H. Littlefield painting, which had been commercially engraved by Henry Gugler. Littlefield's inspiration was the same photographic model as the $100 bill portrait (Ostendorf-92), so the stamp bears a striking similarity to the then-current currency portrait. In 1894 the BEP took over printing the stamps and altered the dies slightly; the new Lincoln four-cent stamp (Scott 254) was issued beginning September 11 (BEP die number P071, altered from die number P037).

1890. Richard Lovett authors a penny biography in London for the Religious Tract Society entitled *Abraham Lincoln* for distribution to English youths. "The career of Lincoln," the pamphlet observes, "affords a most striking illustration of the possibilities of life in the United States."

1891. M.P. Rice publishes and copyrights the "Gettysburg Lincoln" photo, which becomes very popular as a cabinet card (see fig. 2.162a), and is reproduced in many prints and engravings. This image had a profound effect on the types of images selected for book covers and frontispieces. A study by the present author that appeared in the winter 2007 issue of the *Lincoln Herald* shows that, after the publication of the M.P. Rice Gettysburg Lincoln photo, this image became a preferred likeness of Lincoln as book ornamentation; prior

to that time, there was little to no interest in the Gettysburg Lincoln image for such uses. This image has been perennially popular since Rice's time, and in fact is the most popular Lincoln image with authors, editors, and publishers for book illustrations.

1891 APRIL 7. Lincoln leather postcards are issued under Philipp Hake's "illuminated embossed paper" patent (number 449,675). Hake filed his patent application on May 28, 1890.

1891 OCTOBER 18. *New York Times* praises John G. Nicolay and John Hay's 10-volume, 4,750-page biography, *Abraham Lincoln: A History,* published by the Century Co.

Fig. 2.161. *(a)* Homer Lee Bank Note Co., New York, had its own version of the Lincoln $100 currency portrait. It appeared on this 1890 Republican National Committee $10 contributor receipt. Similar certificates for other years in various colors have been noted. *(b)* The 1892 Republican National Committee $10 donor receipt was printed by ABNCo., with its famous $10 greenback Lincoln portrait in tow.

Fig. 2.162. M.P. Rice acquired the original negative created by Alexander Gardner, November 8, 1863, for the so-called "Gettysburg Lincoln" photograph (Ostendorf-77). This is acclaimed by many, including the present author, as the finest photograph of Lincoln. In 1891 Rice copyrighted this image and sold cabinet cards with a commemorative inscription to great fanfare. "Rice's" photo was duplicated in numerous etchings, engravings, and lithographs, and became a dominant Lincoln likeness for book and periodical illustration. It was also engraved for security uses by master engraver Lorenzo Hatch before 1902. Shown are *(a)* Rice's cabinet card and *(b)* an artists' second proof by Hatch.

1891 NOVEMBER 5. An exhibition of medals of famous men, including Washington, Lincoln, and Franklin, highlights a meeting of the American Numismatic and Archaeological Society.

1891 DECEMBER 17. Andrew C. Zabriskie displays his collection of medals honoring Abraham Lincoln to invited guests at his home. This collection included a copy of the French medal presented to Mrs. Lincoln.

1892 APRIL 27. A U.S. Grant birthday medal (fig. 2.166a) depicts Grant with his predecessors Washington and Lincoln as "Father, Saviour, Defender."

1892. The Chicago World's Fair, the World's Columbian Exposition, offers visitors to the Lincoln Museum a view of the president "from the cradle to the grave" (fig. 2.167). Displays include the Lincoln funeral car and a replica of Lincoln's "old log cabin." Lincoln is depicted on souvenir tickets for the second year of the fair (fig. 2.166b) as well as on several medals (see fig. 2.168).

1893. A Lincoln statue by George Edwin Bissell is erected in Edinburgh, Scotland, as a memorial in the Old Carlton Hill Burial Ground to Scottish-American soldiers in Civil War (see fig. 2.169). It was the first bronze statue of Lincoln erected in Europe. In an impressive ceremony the provost of Edinburgh and the American consul dedicated the ground as a burial place for five Scottish soldiers who died fighting for the Northern cause.

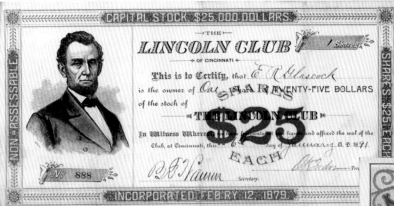

Fig. 2.163. The Lincoln Club of Cincinnati, incorporated February 12, 1879, sold shares for an unknown purpose. The 888th share was sold to E.R. Glascock on January 6, 1891, evidently bringing proceeds to nearly 90 percent of the group's goal.

Fig. 2.164. Circa-1890s Lincoln tobacco labels include (a) "National Stars," lithographed by American Lithographic Co., New York, which groups Lincoln with Washington and Jefferson. (b) The "Great Liberator" label, with scenes from Lincoln's life, was lithographed by Krueger & Braun, New York.

Fig. 2.165. Colorful lithographs also appeared on tobacco cards of the period. This 1888 W. Duke Great Americans card (N412) featured Lincoln, Grant, and Garfield.

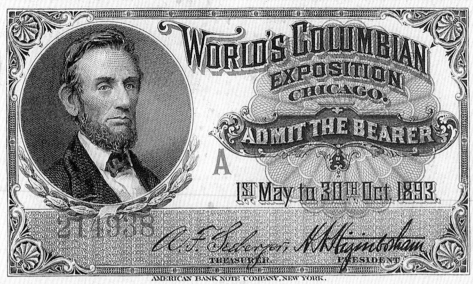

Fig. 2.166. The World's Columbian Exposition, the Chicago World's Fair was held in Abraham Lincoln's back yard, and Lincoln commemoration was all over the lot. *(a)* This small Columbian Expo medal linked another Illinoisan, U.S. Grant, with Lincoln and Washington, and *(b)* this commemorative admission ticket was specially printed by ABNCo with their Lincoln $10 portrait die.

Fig. 2.167. The 1892 Chicago World's Fair was famous for its Ferris Wheel. Nestled at its base was the Lincoln Museum, covering the Great Emancipator "from the cradle to the grave." Featured exhibits included "Abraham Lincoln's old log cabin" and the Lincoln funeral car.

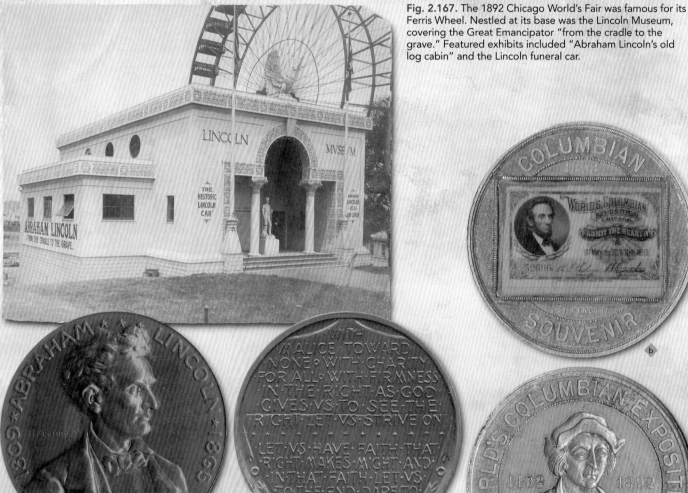

Fig. 2.168. Exonumia from the World's Columbian Expo include *(a)* Henry Zearing's medal with beardless portrait and excerpts from Lincoln's second inaugural and Cooper Union addresses (King-504). *(b)* A medallic pass to the fair encased a small photograph of the commemorative ticket shown at figure 2.166 under a sheet of mica.

1893. After the Springfield Lincoln home is donated to the State of Illinois, Osborn H. Oldroyd moves his family and Lincoln collection to Washington, D.C., to the Petersen House, where Lincoln had died. With the permission of the government, Oldroyd and his family lived rent-free and charged the public 25 cents to view his Lincoln memorabilia (see fig. 2.170).

1893. A photograph of a painting, *Lincoln and Sojourner Truth,* is popularized. In it, Lincoln is showing Sojourner Truth a Bible given him by the Black residents of Baltimore at the Executive Mansion, October 29, 1864.

1894. SEPTEMBER 11. A Lincoln four-cent stamp, part of the second BEP-produced series of U.S. postage stamps, is placed on sale.

1895 FEBRUARY 12. An act of Congress is passed providing for a Lincoln Gettysburg Address memorial at the Gettysburg Battlefield.

1895. *McClure's* magazine begins a serialization of Ida M. Tarbell's Lincoln biography (see fig. 2.173). S.S. McClure, a graduate of Knox College in Galesburg, Illinois (the site of the fifth Lincoln-Douglas debate), had long been interested in Lincoln. He turned the magazine's offices into a "Lincoln Bureau" for propagation of the Lincoln message, and assigned Tarbell to the task. Her two-volume Lincoln biography was published in 1900.

1895. The Lincoln National Monument Association transfers the title of the Lincoln monument in Springfield to the State of Illinois.

1896. Lincoln is listed among those 23 noble individuals included on the "History Instructing Youth" faces of the Series 1896 $1 Silver Certificates (see fig. 2.174), part of what is known to modern collectors as the Educational Series. This series of paper money, and this note in particular, is widely acclaimed as the most beautiful of all federal paper money. The face was based on a painting, *History Instructing Youth* by artist Will H. Low, that hung in the Bureau of Engraving and Printing. Thomas F. Morris adapted the image for currency

Fig. 2.169. The first Lincoln statue erected in a foreign country was George E. Bissell's bronze statue in Edinburgh, Scotland, erected on the Old Carlton Burial Ground to commemorate soldiers of Scots descent who died in the U.S. Civil War. It was dedicated August 21, 1893.

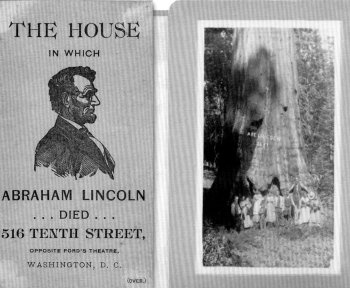

Fig. 2.170. O.H. Oldroyd had a private museum in the Petersen House where Lincoln had died. This trade card advertises his museum.

Fig. 2.171. Several giant redwoods are named for Abe Lincoln. This cabinet card, circa 1890s, claims this Abe Lincoln tree is 326 feet tall.

Fig. 2.172. Labor-exchange scrip was a barter system that spread across the country in the 1890s. Much of the scrip was rather drab, but the $1 note for the Cincinnati Labor Exchange was far from it. Notes were prepared by the local Strobridge Lithographic Co., and included the Lincoln money image in the design.

usage. The engraving was done by Charles Schlecht. Nearly 58 million of these notes were printed through 1898. It was believed that the elaborate designs would not only beautify U.S. paper money, but be difficult for counterfeiters to copy. Alas, the very ornateness of the design only made it difficult for the man on the street to spot a phony, and the Educational Notes were rapidly abandoned.

1896 NOVEMBER 10. The U.S. government takes possession of Peterson House, across from Ford's Theatre, where Lincoln died.[49]

1897 FEBRUARY 12. Lincoln Memorial University is chartered by the state of Tennessee for "educating young Lincolns." The school is still unabashedly pro-Lincoln. "Lincoln Memorial University grew out of love and respect for Abraham Lincoln," the school's Web site affirms. The school was founded by former Civil War general O.O. Howard, who according to legend was asked by President Lincoln to organize a great university for the loyal people of Eastern Tennessee after the war. Howard and a group of financial backers purchased a resort hotel in Harrogate to set up a school. Through the years, in addition to its educational mission, the school has fostered Lincoln research and scholarship. Today it continues to honor Lincoln's "name, values, and spirit." Lincoln Memorial University is a private, coeducational institution nestled in the Appalachian Mountains near the Cumberland Gap, where Kentucky, Virginia, and Tennessee come together. The campus in Harrogate is gorgeous, pristine, and idyllic. The Abraham Lincoln Library and Museum on the campus houses one of the most diverse collections of Lincolniana in the country, including many rare items and approximately 30,000 books, manuscripts, and other items related to Lincoln and his times. The *Lincoln Herald* is published by Lincoln Memorial University Press.

1898 FEBRUARY 12. Attendees at the Lincoln birthday celebration of the Republican Club of the City of New York receive silver medals as souvenirs of the occasion.[50]

1898 FEBRUARY 15. Proof sheets of the Educational Notes series with the Bruce-Roberts signatures are approved by BEP director Claude Johnson (see fig. 2.174).

1898. Sculptor and medalist Charles Calverley copyrights an Abraham Lincoln medallion, later issued in 1909 as a plaque and medals. Calverley's Lincoln portrait proved very popular for reissuing, according to medallic historian Dick Johnson. It was also "one of the few bas-reliefs issued cast, galvano and die struck [as both a shell and solid medal]." After its use on Lincoln centennial items, medals with Calverley's Lincoln portrait were issued in 1934, 1959, 1960, 1965, 1971, and 1972, by Johnson's reckoning.[51]

1899. A miniature Lincoln portrait appears on $1 Silver Certificates, Series of 1899 (see fig. 2.177). BEP chief engraver G.F.C. Smillie based his engraving of Lincoln on the same portrait model as the $100 note engraving by Charles Burt 30 years earlier. The Lincoln die was completed by February 3, 1899, because on that date BEP director Claude Johnson forwarded a proof impression of the die to Assistant Secretary of the Treasury William B. Howell (the original correspondence is in the author's possession). On the note, Lincoln is paired with U.S. Grant and a dramatic War Eagle vignette titled "Eagle of the Capitol," a nod to the Spanish-American War. Smillie, the highest-paid engraver in the United States at the time, was at the top of his craft. All the vignettes on the note face were his work, although Marcus Baldwin engraved the wreaths around the portraits at the bottom. This note is very popular with collectors, who refer to it as the Black Eagle note. Total issue of this style of note from 1899 through 1928 was 3.75 billion.

1899 APRIL 8–22. Engraved Lincoln currency and other portraits are exhibited at New York's Grolier Club. In addition to club members, Lincoln collectors Maj. W.H. Lambert and W.C. Crane contributed items

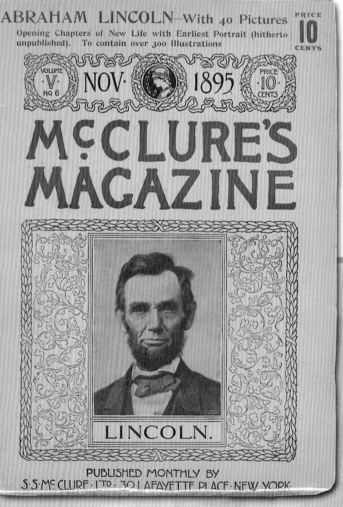

Fig. 2.173. *McClure's Magazine* printed Ida Tarbell's popularized Lincoln biography at the end of the 19th century, and published many previously obscure images. Shown is the November 1895 cover.

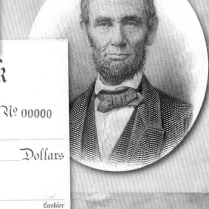

Fig. 2.174. A $1 Series 1896 Silver Certificate (Friedberg-224/225), one of the so-called "Educational Notes," lists Lincoln as one of 23 eminent Americans about whom History should instruct Youth.

Fig. 2.175. ABNCo created a wonderful check for the Lincoln National Bank of Rochester, New York, with an engraving based on the Gettysburg Lincoln photograph.

Fig. 2.176. Robert Jackson's "Will You Ever Give the Colored Race a Show," copyrighted August 8, 1898, made the point that Black soldiers were good enough to fight in the Spanish-American War but were being left out of the prosperity that followed.

Fig. 2.177. George F.C. Smillie's small Lincoln portrait on the Series 1899 one-dollar Silver Certificate is based on the same photographic model as the $100 bill portrait then in favor, and in circulation for a generation. Lincoln is paired with U.S. Grant (BEP die number MISC4485). The importance of Smillie's Lincoln portrait on the dollar bill in shaping the Lincoln image in the public mind should not be underestimated. For another generation, nearly four billion of these notes passed repeatedly from hand to hand, establishing this view of Lincoln as the predominant one not only on money, but in secondary media such as advertising, books, and periodicals.

to the exhibition. The 156 items on display included Carpenter's portrait of Lincoln from life.

1900. Minnesota judge and major Lincolniana collector Daniel Fish publishes *Lincoln Literature: A Bibliographical Account of Books and Pamphlets Relating to Abraham Lincoln.* Following that, William Henry Lambert and Judd Stewart, two other "Big Five" Lincoln collectors of the period, gave Fish additional titles from their collections, and in 1906 Fish published a revised listing. The so-called "Big Five" collectors of Lincolniana at the turn of the last century were Daniel Fish, William Henry Lambert, Judd Stewart, Joseph Benjamin Oakleaf, and Charles W. McLellan.

1900 CIRCA. Composer Paul Dresser publishes "Give Us Just Another Lincoln" (see fig. 2.180b) as both a march and a two-step. His lyrics cry out "Give us just another Lincoln. . . . To guide the Ship of State aright."

1900. The United States House of Representatives considers "A Bill to Authorize the Erection of a Statue of the Late President A. Lincoln at Gettysburg, PA."

1900. Lincoln and 28 others are elected to the Hall of Fame for Great Americans at New York University, the first "Hall of Fame" in this country. A "national shrine" is erected on the grounds of the school (now Bronx Community College of the City University of New York). The Hall of Fame was dedicated on May 30, 1901. Joining Lincoln among that first induction class were George Washington, Daniel Webster, Benjamin Franklin, U.S. Grant, John Marshall, Thomas Jefferson, Robert Fulton, Samuel F.B. Morse, preacher Jonathan Edwards, Ralph Waldo Emerson, Henry Wadsworth Longfellow,

Fig. 2.178. In 1899 and again in 1903, the Post Office issued (a) four-cent envelopes (Scott U372) and (b) five-cent envelopes (Scott U393).

Fig. 2.179. A 1900 GAR Encampment badge.

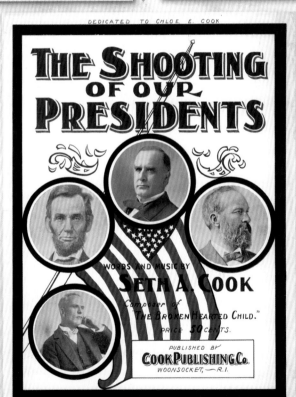

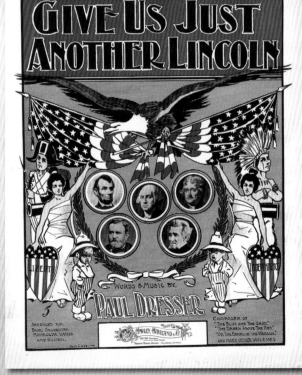

Fig. 2.180. If popular music at the time is any indication, the American psyche was aching in 1901 following the assassination of William McKinley. (a) Seth Cook's "The Shooting of Our Presidents" laments the recurrence of national calamity. (b) Paul Dresser's "Give Us Just Another Lincoln" yearns wistfully for the great national leadership.

and Washington Irving. Each was commemorated by a bronze tablet. Later busts were added along a 500-foot colonnade.

1901 SEPTEMBER 14. Just as it had 20 years earlier with the assassination of James Garfield, the murder of President William McKinley in 1901 kicks off another round of national mourning. Naturally, a multitude of commemoratives linked the three slain national leaders, Lincoln and Garfield and McKinley (see fig. 2.182).

1901. BEP chief engraver G.F.C. Smillie engraves a wonderful die of the *First Reading of Emancipation Proclamation,* after Ritchie's engraving and Carpenter's painting (see fig. 2.183). A black-and-white, somewhat faded to sepia, cabinet-sized photograph of the painting that Smillie used as a model was passed down in his family, along

with several proofs of the engraving at various stages. On one he has written, "After painting by Carpenter." However, this remarkable miniature also owes a great deal to the Ritchie engraving, as can be seen by comparison to figure 2.59b, especially in its depiction of the seated Lincoln. Unfortunately, Smillie's die was not used to prepare plates for U.S. currency. It is believed that it was created for use on the back of a note in anticipation of a new series of large-sized Legal Tender Notes issued that year. However, only the $10 denomination of the Series of 1901 Legal Tender Notes was issued. Smillie's design could have been used on the new $1,000 Series 1914 Federal Reserve Notes with ease, since it fit the style and filled the bill of the historical engravings which appear on the high-value notes (all except the $1,000, which was barren save for a federal eagle grasping flags and arrows). Alas, this wonderful design went unused once again, although it was tested as a small-note design sometime after 1928.

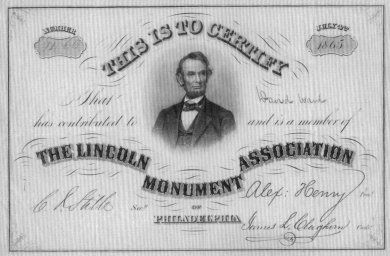

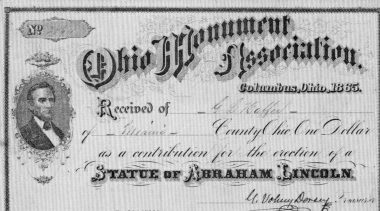

Fig. 2.182. Lincoln's assassination was once again brought back to public remembrance by the slaying of President William McKinley in 1901. *(a)* The button "Our Country's Martyr's [*sic*]" and *(b)* this stereoview depict the three slain presidents: Lincoln, Garfield, and McKinley.

Fig. 2.181. In the aftermath of the Lincoln assassination, groups sprang up throughout the country to memorialize him in some way, principally with statues. Shown are 1865 certificates for *(a)* the Lincoln Monument Association of Philadelphia and *(b)* the Ohio Monument Association in Columbus, Ohio. The latter, lithographed by Ehrgott, Forbriger and Co. of Cincinnati, uses its version of the $10 bill Lincoln portrait. The CNBCo Lincoln portrait was used on Jo Daviess Soldiers' Monument Association, Galena, Illinois, membership certificates.

Fig. 2.183. BEP chief picture engraver G.F.C. Smillie engraved a wonderful die of the "First Reading of Emancipation Proclamation" after Ritchie's engraving and Carpenter's painting in 1901. Unfortunately, Smillie's die was not used on U.S. currency, although it was tested as a small-note essay design sometime after 1928.

1901 SEPTEMBER 26. Lincoln's remains are interred a final time in the refurbished Springfield monument.

1902 JANUARY 4. The *Harper's Weekly* cover features Ida Tarbell's photograph of a Black youth genuflecting in adoration of a Lincoln family picture set on a chair that is remarkably akin to an altar (fig. 2.184).

1902. Ida M. Tarbell's *The Life of Abraham Lincoln,* volume 1, is republished by the Lincoln History Society.

1903. The Lincoln Legion is founded under the auspices of the Anti-Saloon League. To broaden the appeal of the temperance group, the organization is subsequently renamed Lincoln-Lee Legion to capture Southerners' infatuation with Robert E. Lee (see fig. 2.185a).

1903. The Library of Congress publishes *A List of Lincolniana in the Library of Congress,* edited by George Thomas Ritchie.

1903 JANUARY 20. A Lincoln five-cent stamp (Scott 304) is issued (fig. 2.186; earliest known usage is February 9, 1903), as part of a Great Americans stamp series of 1902. Marcus W. Baldwin engraved the Lincoln portrait, Lyman F. Ellis engraved the letters and numerals, and Robert Ponickau engraved the frame; 550 million were issued. In the first Bureau Issues of 1890, Lincoln had been on the

Fig. 2.184. Ida Tarbell staged the cloying cover photo for the January 4, 1902, issue of *Harper's Weekly*. It showed a young African American boy virtually genuflecting at a Lincoln family altar.

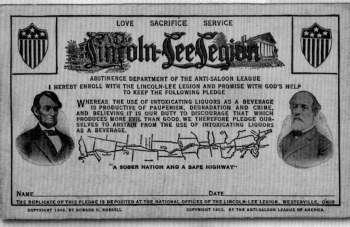

Fig. 2.185. (a) The Lincoln-Lee Legion was a cold-water abstinence league. The pledge card was copyrighted in 1903 by Howard H. Russell and Anti-Saloon League of America. Interestingly a route not dissimilar to the eventual Lincoln Highway route is illustrated at center, above the motto "A sober nation and a safe highway." Eventually Lincoln was everything to everybody. Everyone claimed his blessings. (b) In 1897 Pabst Malt Extract, "the best tonic" around, issued an advertising trade card showing Lincoln holding Old Glory under a headline "Perfection in brewing is reached in America."

four-cent and Grant on the five-cent. They were swapped for the Series of 1902. Lincoln was deliberately chosen for the five-cent stamp, as five cents was the rate for foreign letters.

1904. Lincoln is in attendance at the 1904 St. Louis World's Fair, but not nearly so prodigiously as at the Chicago World's Fair the previous decade. Tributes to the Great Emancipator from the Missouri exposition include the farm display "Lincoln in Seeds" (fig. 2.187) and the Weller ceramic portrait plaque (fig. 2.188).

1904. The Grand Old Party celebrates its 50th anniversary in 1904 with Theodore Roosevelt in the White House (see fig. 2.189). Roosevelt adored Lincoln. He had a portrait of him right in front of his desk (fig. 2.190). He called Lincoln "the spirit incarnate of those who

won victory in the Civil War—[he] was the true representative of this people, not only for his own generation, but for all time, because he was a man among men. A man who embodied the qualities of his fellow-men, but who embodied them to the highest and most unusual degree of perfection, who embodied all that there was in the nation of courage, of wisdom, of gentle, patient kindliness, and of common sense." Roosevelt was responsible for the Lincoln cent in 1909.

1904. The U.S. Senate again considers a "Joint Resolution to Provide for Opening to the Public Free of Charge the Lincoln Museum in the District of Columbia." This was also considered in 1902.

1905 FEBRUARY 16. A resolution is submitted to Congress to declare a national celebration on the centennial of Lincoln's birth in 1909.

1904 JUNE CIRCA. The *Lincoln Magazine,* "the Herald of a Great Cause, a Home Journal of Social and Civic Reform" is launched by

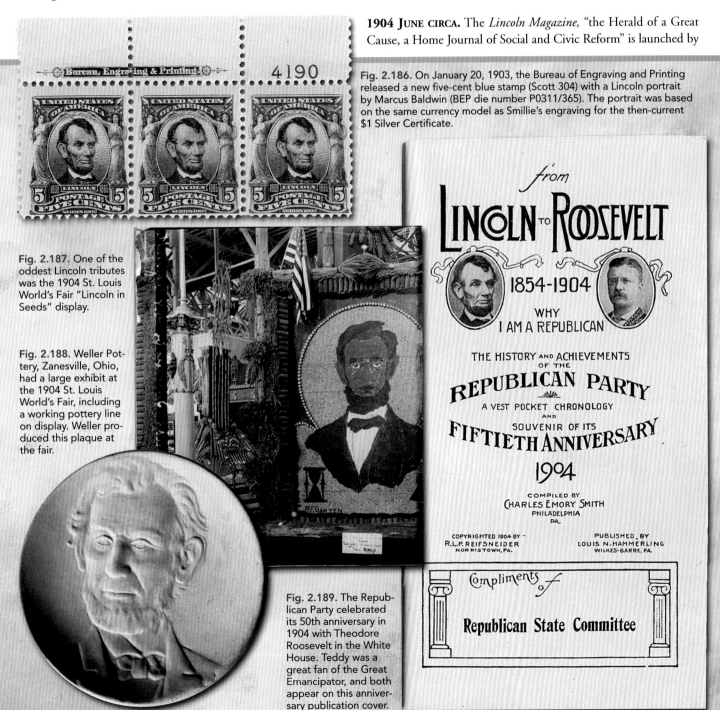

Fig. 2.186. On January 20, 1903, the Bureau of Engraving and Printing released a new five-cent blue stamp (Scott 304) with a Lincoln portrait by Marcus Baldwin (BEP die number P0311/365). The portrait was based on the same currency model as Smillie's engraving for the then-current $1 Silver Certificate.

Fig. 2.187. One of the oddest Lincoln tributes was the 1904 St. Louis World's Fair "Lincoln in Seeds" display.

Fig. 2.188. Weller Pottery, Zanesville, Ohio, had a large exhibit at the 1904 St. Louis World's Fair, including a working pottery line on display. Weller produced this plaque at the fair.

Fig. 2.189. The Republican Party celebrated its 50th anniversary in 1904 with Theodore Roosevelt in the White House. Teddy was a great fan of the Great Emancipator, and both appear on this anniversary publication cover.

the New York Anti-Saloon League. The periodical was published at least until volume 2, number 9, in February 1906.

1905 January 6. A public auction of John G. Nicolay's library is held.

1905 June 12. Lincoln National Life Insurance Co. is founded in Fort Wayne, Indiana. Arthur Hall and its other 32 founders "envisioned an insurance company rooted in dependability and honesty." To convey this spirit of integrity, they adopted the name of our 16th president to represent the ideals upon which the new company was founded. Robert Todd Lincoln, the president's only surviving son, gave the founders permission to use his father's name and likeness on August 5, 1905. Hall, a lifelong admirer of Lincoln, had written Lincoln's son "to ask for a photograph that the company might use on its letterhead." Robert replied, "I find no objection whatever to the use of a portrait of my father upon the letterhead of such a life insurance company named after him as you describe: and I take pleasure in enclosing you, for that purpose, what I regard as a very good photograph of him." The photo was Ostendorf-92.

1906 February 10. *Collier's* magazine publishes one of its many "Lincoln's Birthday Numbers." The issue promotes the Lincoln Farm Association & Birthplace Memorial (see fig. 3.19).

1906. William Randolph Hearst buys the 60 acres of the original site of New Salem, Illinois, the home of Abraham Lincoln as a young adult. Hearst conveys the property in trust to the Old Salem Chatauqua Association.

1906. The Hamburg-Amerika Line purchases an unfinished vessel from the Wilson & Furness Leyland Line, which was launched October 8, 1903, as ship number 353. The vessel is nearly 600 feet long

Fig. 2.190. Lincoln artwork decorated many Victorian parlors. *(a)* An early 1900s view inside Lincoln's Springfield home featured Marshall's engraving of Lincoln on the wall. *(b)* The parlor of Christian Science advocate Mary Baker Eddy's home in Newton, Massachusetts, displayed a Lincoln engraving prominently. *(c)* In May 1904 President Theodore Roosevelt's desk in his White House office faced a painting of Lincoln.

Fig. 2.191. Marshall's engraving of Lincoln was chosen as the illustration on this early 1900s Freedmen's Aid Society button.

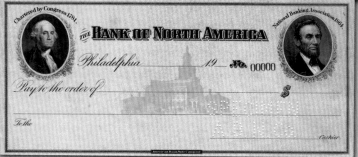

Fig. 2.192. ABNCo continued to employ the 1861 Charles Burt currency die on commercial work for clients in the early 1900s. Illustrated are *(a)* a stock certificate for the Lincoln National Bank of the City of New York and *(b)* a bank draft for the Bank of North America, the oldest banking institution in the nation.

and weighs 18,168 tons. Twin screws propel the liner at up to 14 knots. The new owners rechristened it *President Lincoln* and put the liner into North Atlantic passenger service, with ports of call at Hamburg, Boulogne, Southampton, New York City, and Plymouth, Cherbourg, and Hamburg on the return trip. Her maiden voyage was January 6, 1907. At the time of her maiden voyage, the *President Lincoln* "was both the largest freighter and the largest emigrant carrier in the world."[52] Though the ship could carry as many as 4,108 passengers, a British Admiralty court of inquiry on the *Titanic* disaster found that lifeboat capacity was a mere 1,465—had the ship sunk, only 36 percent of the passengers could have been saved.[53]

1907 JANUARY 21. A bronze Army Civil War campaign badge, 1.5 inches in diameter, is authorized for veterans of U.S. military service between April 15, 1861, and April 9, 1865 (August 20, 1866, in Texas). The medal was suspended from a red, white, and blue ribbon (in 1913, it was a navy blue and gray ribbon), and the obverse featured a portrait of Lincoln. "With Malice Toward None With Charity For All" surrounds the portrait (fig. 2.198). The reverse displays oak and olive branches, and the legend "The Civil War 1861–1865."

According to the Pentagon, the issue of campaign medals was first approved by the assistant secretary of war on January 11, 1905. The Civil War campaign badge was specifically authorized January 21, 1907, but originally only for those still on active duty. The badge was designed by artist and muralist Frank D. Millett, and approved by the army chief of staff. The army's Department of Heraldry said, "The head of Lincoln was selected because it was the only thing that could be used on the medal without offense to the sentiment then happily prevailing over the whole country in regard to the Civil War. The portrait of Lincoln must be acceptable to everybody, particularly when accompanied by the noble phrase from his second inaugural address which so tersely and accurately expresses his attitude

Fig. 2.194. The so-called Lincoln birth cabin from Hodgenville, Kentucky, was taken down and carted across the country to various fairs and displays, where it was reassembled for visitors to view. This photo, taken February 21, 1906, shows the cabin in transit.

Fig. 2.193. This National Prison Association badge was for its Lincoln, Nebraska, convention, held October 21 through 26, 1905.

Fig. 2.195. On September 8, 1906, the Bureau of Engraving and Printing issued a definitive 12-centavos postage stamp for the Philippine Islands U.S. dependency (Scott 246 and additional varieties; BEP die number MISC6584). This stamp features the Marcus Baldwin portrait of Lincoln originally used on the U.S. five-cent stamp several years earlier.

Fig. 2.196. Old Abe Strawberry Soda and Ginger Ale was founded in 1906.

during the war." Manufacture was contracted with a private firm, but then turned over to the U.S. Mint. On June 30, 1913, Army Chief of Staff M.G. Leonard Wood authorized the Mint to sell the campaign badges to those no longer serving. Originally intended as a commemorative badge, it was sanctioned as a regular military campaign service medal November 20, 1928. As such, it could be worn on Army uniforms. By an Act of Congress of August 10, 1956, the secretary of the army was directed to procure and issue without charge the Civil War Campaign Medal and other service medals to veterans or their families if the member died before it was presented to him.

1907. Sculptor Victor David Brenner copyrights his Lincoln plaque (fig. 2.199). Researcher David T. Alexander identified Brenner's 1907 Lincoln plaque cast by S.J. Klaber Co., or Brenner's 1909 Preserve, Protect, Defend medal (King-304) as inspiration for his cent portrayal of Lincoln.[54]

1907. The Illinois Watch Co. of Springfield, Illinois, which had long associated itself with Lincoln's memory, introduces its "A. Lincoln" pocket watch (see fig. 3.17). The watch proved very successful, and the company sold more than 100,000 of them in the next two decades. Possibly to minimize charges of commercially exploiting Lincoln's name, the signature was on the plate inside the watch. The company also distributed a fob and chain for the watch with Bela Lyon Pratt's 1909 Lincoln centennial portrait on obverse and the company's name on back. Illinois Watch Co. was purchased by Hamilton Watch Co. in 1928.

1907 NOVEMBER 9. Lincoln Farm Association acquires Lincoln's birthplace farm near Hodgenville, Kentucky.

1908 JANUARY 31. Senator Robert La Follette, whose grandfather lived in Kentucky on the farm next to where President Lincoln spent

Fig. 2.197. Circa 1900s Lincoln plaque made of milk-glass rails.

Fig. 2.198. This badge for Civil War veterans, authorized January 21, 1907, was designed by artist and muralist Frank D. Millett.

Fig. 2.199. Sculptor Victor David Brenner copyrighted his Lincoln profile plaque in 1907.

his boyhood, introduces a bill declaring February 12, 1909, a legal holiday in the District of Columbia.

1908. Gutzon Borglum's marble Lincoln bust is gifted to the United States by Eugene Mayer Jr. of New York City (see fig. 2.201) Placed in the U.S. Capitol building, it was originally done as a study, measuring 40 inches high and weighing 375 pounds. Borglum had studied with Rodin. His rough-hewn figure springs directly from the stone without model or plaster cast. His goal, the sculptor said, was to embody Lincoln's personality and character, rather than translate a literal portrait. Lincoln's son, Robert Todd Lincoln, was a great fan of Borglum's interpretation. "I never expected to see Father again," Lincoln commented after seeing the bust. "I think it is the most extraordinarily good portrait of my father I have ever seen," he wrote to Borglum on February 6, 1908. "It impressed me deeply as a work of art which speaks for

itself in the most wonderful manner." Emerging partially from the rock as it does, this figure presages Borglum's treatment of the Lincoln head at Mount Rushmore several decades later. Borglum designed the pedestal in 1911. For many years it occupied an honored space in the Capitol Rotunda, but since 1979 has been displayed in the Capitol Crypt, one floor down. A mold of the bust was made, and bronze casts are displayed at the White House, Chicago History Museum, College of the City of New York, University of California at Berkeley, and (of course) Lincoln's tomb in Springfield, Illinois.

1908 FEBRUARY 12. The Lincoln Fellowship of New York holds its first annual meeting.

1908. Robert Hewitt issues "The Lincoln Centennial Medal," contained in a book, published by G.P. Putnam.

LYMAN TRUMBULL.   GENL U.S. GRANT.   ABRAHAM LINCOLN.   GENL JOHN A. LOGAN.   STEPHEN A. DOUGLAS.

Fig. 2.200. Lincoln memorabilia from the early 1900s included (a) Illinois Giants tobacco brands, pins of (b) Knights of Columbus, (c) Grand Army Day, and (d) the Lincoln Club. (e) The jugate Lincoln-Douglas button celebrated the 50th anniversary of their debate at Freeport, Illinois, August 27, 1858. (f) The park scene illustrates the Lincoln Park brand of tobacco.

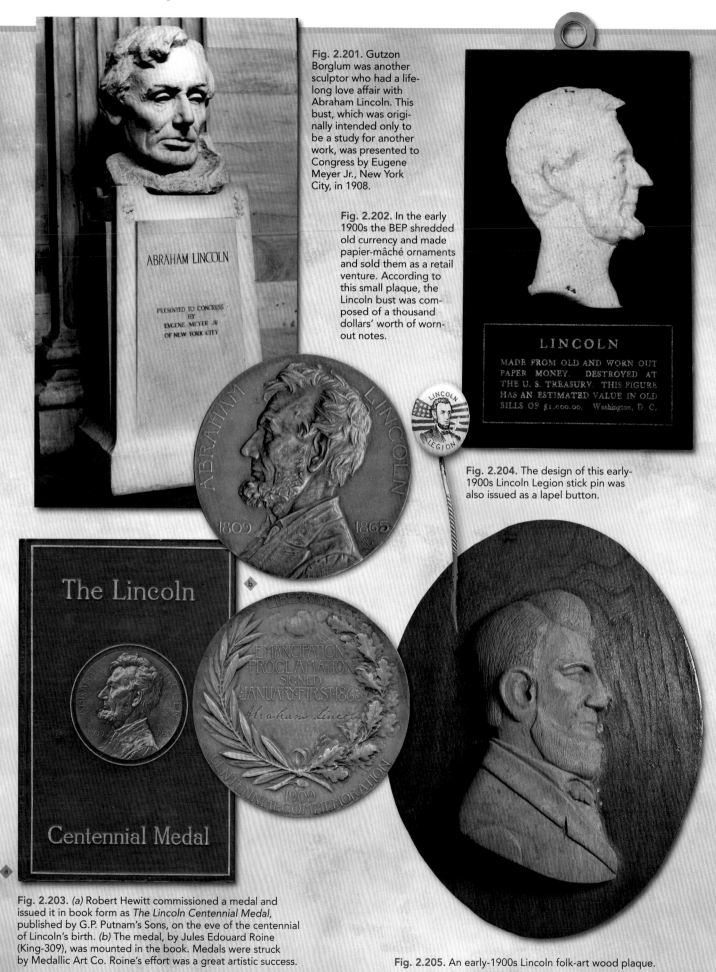

Fig. 2.201. Gutzon Borglum was another sculptor who had a life-long love affair with Abraham Lincoln. This bust, which was originally intended only to be a study for another work, was presented to Congress by Eugene Meyer Jr., New York City, in 1908.

Fig. 2.202. In the early 1900s the BEP shredded old currency and made papier-mâché ornaments and sold them as a retail venture. According to this small plaque, the Lincoln bust was composed of a thousand dollars' worth of worn-out notes.

ABRAHAM LINCOLN

PRESENTED TO CONGRESS
BY
EUGENE MEYER JR
OF NEW YORK CITY

LINCOLN

MADE FROM OLD AND WORN OUT
PAPER MONEY. DESTROYED AT
THE U. S. TREASURY. THIS FIGURE
HAS AN ESTIMATED VALUE IN OLD
BILLS OF $1,000.00. Washington, D. C.

Fig. 2.204. The design of this early-1900s Lincoln Legion stick pin was also issued as a lapel button.

Fig. 2.203. *(a)* Robert Hewitt commissioned a medal and issued it in book form as *The Lincoln Centennial Medal*, published by G.P. Putnam's Sons, on the eve of the centennial of Lincoln's birth. *(b)* The medal, by Jules Edouard Roine (King-309), was mounted in the book. Medals were struck by Medallic Art Co. Roine's effort was a great artistic success.

Fig. 2.205. An early-1900s Lincoln folk-art wood plaque.

1908. *The Perfect Tribute,* by Mary Raymond Shipman Andrews, is published by Scribners. This book is a fictional account of the Gettysburg Address. It was one of the most widely read of the Lincoln books.

1908. On the 50th anniversary of the Lincoln-Douglas debates, a committee in Alton, Illinois (site of the seventh debate) sponsors a parade and festival. A commemorative bronze plaque was dedicated at City Hall, and the area became known as Lincoln Douglas Square.

1908. L.G. Muller copyrights Byron Pickett's Lincoln portrait plaque of 1873, reissues the plaque in cast aluminum, and distributes a lithograph based on the head (figs. 2.206a, b). Prominent Lincoln collector J.B. Oakleaf writes Muller: "I have never seen anything of Lincoln which pleased me so much as your production, and you are entitled to the profound thanks and admiration of every lover of Lincoln."[55]

1908. Teddy Roosevelt's love for Lincoln is expressed in jugate badges, such as the one shown in figure 2.207b.

1908 OCTOBER 28. Possibly anticipating the Lincoln Centennial, the BEP prepares a Series 1908 $100 Gold Certificate featuring Charles Burt's Lincoln vignette from the Series 1869 $100 Legal Tender Note (see fig. 2.208). This was widely unknown until 1979, when it was reported by numismatic researcher Gene Hessler. Work on the die commenced January 31, 1908, and was completed on October 28, 1908.[56] This note was never released. In 1994, the BEP issued a souvenir card calling the design an "unfinished masterpiece."

1909. Gugler Litho Co. of Milwaukee publishes a *Portrait of Lincoln,* priced at a hefty $12.50 (Monaghan-1735).

Fig. 2.206. *(a)* In 1908 L.G. Muller copyrighted Byron Pickett's Lincoln portrait plaque of 1873, and reissued the plaque in cast aluminum. *(b)* He also distributed a lithograph based on the head. Additional plaster reproductions of the Pickett plaque were made by the Lincoln National Life Insurance Co. of Fort Wayne, Indiana, at a later date.

Fig. 2.207. Theodore Roosevelt was delighted to be paired with his hero Abraham Lincoln. They appear on *(a)* a 1904 pin-back button for the 50th anniversary of the Republican Party, and *(b)* a 1908 delegate's badge for the Iowa Republican State Convention.

Fig. 2.208. The Bureau of Engraving and Printing prepared a 1908 one-hundred-dollar Gold Certificate with the same Charles Burt Lincoln portrait that was used on the $100 Legal Tender Note, but never issued the note (BEP die number MISC7046). It is shown from a 1994 BEP souvenir card for a paper-money show in Maastricht, the Netherlands.

Fig. 2.209. Sculptor and Lincoln cent designer Victor David Brenner created this beardless Lincoln bust circa 1909. It remained in the artist's studio until Brenner's death April 5, 1924, after which it passed into the hands of the artist's brother, Samuel H. Brenner. In 1931 Clyde Curlee Trees, president of Medallic Art Co., purchased the Lincoln statuette from Samuel Brenner. On Trees's death in 1960, ownership of the Brenner statuette passed to Medallic Art Co. It was among a group of art bronzes owned by Medallic Art Co. sold at Sotheby Parke Bernet on September 29, 1997, when it was purchased by its present owner, who graciously loaned it for illustration in this book.

Chapter 3
Lincoln the Idol
1909-1959

Reverence of Lincoln, which had blossomed during the previous half century, was raised to the level of worship in the five decades that followed. Admiration and emulation turned to veneration. The civil religion of Lincoln's cult had its high priests, its liturgy, its rites, its holy sites, its feast days, its sacraments, its pilgrimages, and—of course—its venerated idol. Lincoln's image was emblazoned on our country's money, both cent and $5 bill. Every man, woman, and child carried these amulets daily. The Lincoln idol sat on his Grecian throne at the west end of the Capitol Mall flanked by the tablets of his divine revelations, his "Gettysburg Address" and "Second Inaugural Address." There the government also inscribed his mantra: "In this temple as in the hearts of the people for whom he saved the Union, the memory of Abraham Lincoln is enshrined forever." The immortal, deified Lincoln was omnipresent. He gazed protectively from the granite pantheon in the Black Hills and from monuments across the nation. Pilgrims could walk in Lincoln's earthly steps from log cabin to executive mansion to sepulcher. America's Main Street, the Lincoln Highway, spanned the country from sea to shining sea. Lincoln's words were compiled and bound as holy writ. His passion plays lit up silver screens. Enclaves of true believers celebrated his mortal rites of passage: his birth, his death, his resurrection. His birthplace was ensconced in a Greek temple. Replica cabins were constructed for the edification of tourists at the world's fair. School rooms, youth clubs, church pews, and civic groups indoctrinated novitiates in the Lincoln catechism, awarded laurels for achievement, and distributed tracts to the unwashed needing conversion. A commemorative half dollar bore his portrait. Lincoln's literature, monuments, shrines, and other trappings of divinity became the fabric of daily life. Not just here in America, mind you: missionary zeal spread his gospel increasingly abroad, too. Monuments went up in Oslo and London. Upholding the Lincoln idol image almost brought parties to blows over selection of a statue for the latter city.

One of those baptized by the Lincoln immersion was Vincente Aderente, an Italian-American muralist and illustrator as adept at creating public memorials as mass-media images. Aderente most likely painted the portrait (opposite) about the time of the centenary of Lincoln's birth. Perhaps it was originally purposed for a magazine cover, but appropriately it hung in a New Jersey attorney's office and his heirs' home for many decades before arriving at the present author's Lincoln room. Not coincidentally, Aderente modeled the portrait from the same photographs on which sculptor Victor David Brenner based his Lincoln cent portrait at about the same time. Just as in 1861, when Abraham Lincoln had become the first American president to appear on U.S. paper money, in 1909 he became the first U.S. president to appear on this nation's circulating coinage. However, there were great differences in the two commemorations, which were marked by the passage of time. During the war, the motive for Lincoln's identification with the money was a practical and patriotic one, intended to buoy confidence and bind personal interests with the public good. Lincoln could still be the most vilified president, but his image branded the paper money as legitimate. Forty-eight years later, the government's purpose was entirely celebratory. The country was readying a national festival in Lincoln's honor. Abe's Republican successor Theodore Roosevelt envisioned a souvenir within the reach of every last man, woman,

"Abraham Lincoln," by Vincente Aderente, oil on canvas, canvas size 20 inches by 24 inches, circa 1909.

and child in the nation. Five years later Charles Burt's old $100 bill Lincoln portrait was adapted for the $5 bill because it was the second most plentiful in circulation (after the dollar bill) and Lincoln was the second head of the table after Washington. Lincoln became omnipresent, familiar to all.

The years 1909 to 1959 could well be called the "Lincoln half century." During that time more than 8,500 books on Lincoln were published, including important works by Albert Beveridge, Lord Charnwood, Carl Sandburg, and Benjamin P. Thomas. Lincoln appeared as a character in more than 100 films on the silver screen, including portrayals by Walter Huston, Raymond Massey, and Henry Fonda. Lincoln the brand was appropriated for everything from cigarettes to life insurance companies to automobiles. Many numismatists started their collections as youths, as did the author, with the Lincoln cent. It was desirable to learn about the man depicted on the coin. But it was not just collectors who were pennywise; Lincoln's birthday celebrations were observed by Lincoln clubs, Lincoln associations, and Lincoln leagues. In most states, Lincoln's birthday was declared a holiday. The federal government declared it a holiday in the District of Columbia, too.

1909. The Lincoln Centennial Association is organized to properly observe the celebrations throughout the United States, and publishes *The Speeches of Abraham Lincoln*. It also issues elaborate membership certificates (fig. 3.1).

1909. *The One Hundredth Anniversary of the Birth of Abraham Lincoln, for the Schools of Illinois* is published by the State Journal Co. of Springfield. In it, editor-collector Horace White speaks on Lincolniana: "though dead, he yet speaketh to men, women and children who never saw him, and so, I think, he will continue to speak to generations yet unborn."

1909 JANUARY 9. The preface to *The Lincoln Tribute Book . . . Together with A Lincoln Centenary Medal . . . By Roiné* (fig. 3.3a) is penned by Horatio Sheafe Krans. This is the second of the two books that contain medals by Roiné (fig. 3.3b).

1909 JANUARY 18. At the request of the Grand Army of the Republic (GAR), President Theodore Roosevelt recommends that Congress "pass a law authorizing me to issue a proclamation setting apart this

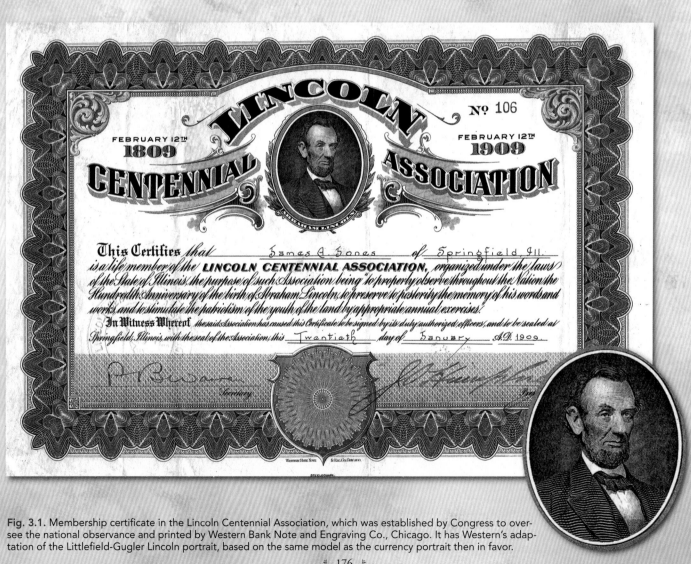

Fig. 3.1. Membership certificate in the Lincoln Centennial Association, which was established by Congress to oversee the national observance and printed by Western Bank Note and Engraving Co., Chicago. It has Western's adaptation of the Littlefield-Gugler Lincoln portrait, based on the same model as the currency portrait then in favor.

day [February 12, 1909] as a special holiday." "I regard this proposal as eminently proper," Roosevelt affirms. "It will be from every standpoint desirable to observe this hundredth anniversary of the birth of Abraham Lincoln as a special holiday." Congress acted, but not quickly. It wasn't until the eve of the event that legislation was passed permitting the president to declare a legal holiday, which he did on February 11. "It would appear that the lateness of the proclamation could have had little effect in causing the day to be observed generally," Lincoln scholar Dr. Louis A. Warren commented.

1909 FEBRUARY 12. The Lincoln two-cent centennial stamp (Scott 367–369) is issued (fig. 3.5). Marcus W. Baldwin, Edward M. Hall, and Robert Ponickau are credited as the engravers. The portrait is by Baldwin. In total, 148,387,191 stamps were issued. "This stamp marks the first time the U.S. Post Office issued a 'commemorative' stamp that did not promote a current event. . . . When the ordinary issue was changed in 1908 to designs of Washington and Franklin only, there was a public outcry about the exclusion of Lincoln, whose likeness had been on at least one denomination of each issue since 1866. Since the year 1909 marked the 100th anniversary of Lincoln's birth, a stamp commemo-

rating that event seemed a logical choice."[1] The image is based on Augustus Saint-Gaudens's standing Lincoln statue in Chicago's Lincoln Park.

1909 FEBRUARY 12. Robert Hewitt and Jules Roiné issue the Lincoln centennial medal. George N. Olcott authors *The Lincoln Centennial: The Robert Hewitt Collection of Medallic Lincolniana*, published by Columbia University, where Dr. Olcott was adjunct professor of Latin.

1909 FEBRUARY 12. The New York City celebration includes an official Lincoln birth centenary medal by Bela Lyon Pratt (fig. 3.6a). The celebration is presided over by Democratic mayor George B. McClellan Jr., son of Lincoln's antagonist and presidential rival George B. McClellan Sr. The mayor distributes the medal, which was struck by Whitehead & Hoag.

1909. The American Numismatic Society issues a centennial allegorical plaque by J.E. Roiné / MACO New York showing Liberty crowning a seated Lincoln, who is signing the Emancipation Proclamation, with a garland (fig. 3.8).

Fig. 3.2. Lincoln paper items from the centennial include (a) sheet music of the "Lincoln Centennial March" by E.T. Paull Music Co., New York, and (b) a highly decorative embossed cigar label showing Lincoln greeted by jubilant crowds in Richmond, Virginia.

Fig. 3.3. (a) Robert Hewitt and sculptor Jules Edouard Roiné published a second book, *The Lincoln Tribute Book*, with appreciations by various authors and statesmen. (b) Once again a medal by Roiné is housed in the book (King-332).

Fig. 3.4. The obverse of the medal by Jules Edouard Roiné struck for the Grand Army of the Republic by Jas. K. Davison's Sons, Philadelphia. Three obverse dies were used. Shown is the second obverse (King-300).

Fig. 3.5. The Lincoln Centennial stamp (Scott 367–369) was issued February 12, 1909. The Lincoln portrait was engraved by Marcus W. Baldwin.

Official Commemorative Medal of the Centenary
of
Abraham Lincoln
12th FEBRUARY 1909
Issued under the authority of the
LINCOLN CENTENARY COMMITTEE
of the
CITY OF NEW YORK

MAYOR.

MEDAL STRUCK BY THE WHITEHEAD & HOAG CO.

Fig. 3.6. *(a)* The official centennial medal of the New York City Centenary Committee (King-335) was engraved by Bela Lyon Pratt, and *(b)* distributed in the name of mayor George B. McClellan Jr., son of Lincoln's political rival. *(c)* Years later, circa 1948, Irving L. Hollander packaged unsold medals in his patent die cut display holder.

Fig. 3.7. U.S. Mint engraver George T. Morgan created this medal (King-311), struck at the Philadelphia Mint The reverse quote, "With Malice Toward None With Charity for All," is from Lincoln's second inaugural address.

1909 FEBRUARY 12. The National Association for the Advancement of Colored People (NAACP) holds its first meeting on Lincoln's birthday. This organization grew out of indignation over the state of race relations after a January meeting by social workers and reformers to take stock of the situation. Especially troubling had been a two-day race riot in Lincoln's home city of Springfield, Illinois, the previous summer. The NAACP started a publication the following year and has been in the forefront of the civil rights movement for a century.

1909 FEBRUARY 12. Theodore Roosevelt lays the cornerstone for the memorial building at Lincoln's birthplace and speaks on Abraham Lincoln. The address is published in *Collier's, The National Weekly* on February 13, and reprinted compliments of E.C. Patterson, manager of the *Collier's* advertising department.

1909 FEBRUARY 12. Booker Taliaferro Washington's speech "An Address on Abraham Lincoln" is delivered before the Republican Club of New York City on this night.

1909 FEBRUARY 16. Lincoln centennial speechifying includes collector Frederick Hill Meserve, who specializes in Lincoln photographs. He speaks to the Quill Club of New York at the Astor Hotel on "A Life Portrait of Abraham Lincoln."

Fig. 3.8. Fame crowns Lincoln with a laurel wreath as he writes his Emancipation Proclamation on Jules Edouard Roiné's Centennial plaque, commissioned by the American Numismatic Society (King-302).

Fig. 3.9. Large copper shell mounted on wood by sculptor Charles Calverley, approximately 11 inches in diameter, from his copyrighted 1898 design. This is acknowledged among the finest Lincoln reliefs, and was employed on later medals by Medallic Art Co.

Fig. 3.10. During the first quarter of the 20th century, many newspapers held Lincoln essay contests. This silver medal (unlisted in King) by Shreve & Co, manufacturing jewelers, was awarded in 1909 by the *San Francisco Examiner.*

Fig. 3.11. Whitehead & Hoag Co., Newark, produced a stock silvered-copper medal for Lincoln essay contests, differing only in the inscription on the reverse. This medal was awarded in 1909 by the *Cincinnati Post* (King-486).

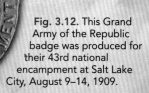

Fig. 3.12. This Grand Army of the Republic badge was produced for their 43rd national encampment at Salt Lake City, August 9–14, 1909.

1909 FEBRUARY 12. The *New York Times* institutes a Lincoln essay contest. Silver medals are struck by Tiffany, New York.

1909 FEBRUARY 12. Henry Chapman sells Henry Metzger's copy of the 1865 French medal presented to Lincoln's widow Mary from the people of France. Also circa 1909, the Paris Mint strikes a medal honoring Lincoln with a bold bust by M. Delannoy on the obverse, and the closing remarks from Lincoln's Gettysburg Address on the reverse (fig. 3.13).

1909 FEBRUARY 17. Victor David Brenner presents a revised reverse design for the proposed Lincoln cent to the Mint Bureau in Washington, D.C. (fig. 3.14). His original design, which had been patterned after the then-current two-franc coin, was rejected by Mint director Edward O. Leech. On the new reverse he models two stylized ears of durum wheat suggesting a wreath, such as formerly employed on the denomination. Leech accepts the revised designs, except that he removes Brenner's name from the obverse and substitutes his initials, "V.D.B.," on the bottom of the reverse.[2]

1909. *Abraham Lincoln and the London Punch* is published in honor of Lincoln's centenary. It chronicles the feisty oversight the English publication aimed at the U.S. president.

1909 FEBRUARY. Lincoln centennial tributes dominate the periodical press. Periodicals releasing special issues include *Hampton's Magazine, Century Illustrated, The Fra, Hints: the Entertainment Magazine,* *Leslie's Weekly, Collier's, Harper's Weekly, American Magazine, San Francisco Call Magazine, Lincoln Gedenkblatt,* and *Youth's Companion.* The *Collier's* Lincoln number, in two sections, features a 1906 painting by Charles R. Huntington on its cover, while *Hints* reproduces one of J.C. Buttre's 1864 engravings.

1909 FEBRUARY 21. Newspapers report that the Lincoln design will replace the Indian Head on the cent.

1909 MAY 12. Lincoln cent patterns without the motto "In God We Trust" are struck at the Philadelphia Mint. (See Roger Burdette, *Renaissance of American Coinage, 1909–1915,* for details.)

1909 MAY 26. President William Howard Taft approves the Lincoln cent designs by Victor David Brenner (shown in fig. 3.14).

1909 MAY 31. Adolph A. Weinman's seated Lincoln statue at Hodgenville, Kentucky (fig. 3.16), is dedicated.

1909 JUNE 10. Mintage of Lincoln cents begins.

1909 JUNE 22. Adolph A. Weinman's seated statue of Lincoln is dedicated on the campus of the University of Wisconsin.

1909 AUGUST 2. Victor David Brenner's Lincoln cent is released to the public. By summer the national zest for Abraham Lincoln and all

Fig. 3.13. French art deco sculptor M. Delannoy executed this unusual bust of Lincoln. The medal reverse contains a portion of Lincoln's Gettysburg Address. This medal was not listed in King, and the circumstances of its issue are unknown. It may be of a later date.

Fig. 3.14. *(a)* Obverse of Victor David Brenner's "Preserve Protect Defend" medal (King-304) which some scholars, including this author, believe is the actual model for Brenner's Lincoln cent design, also shown. *(b)* Copies of Brenner's original obverse and reverse designs in the National Archives illustrate a French-style reverse was anticipated. *(c)* U.S. Mint obverse galvano with LIBERTY and date in place. *(d)* One of the first Lincoln cents released, with sculptor's initials VDB, obtained by a family friend in the first days of issue.

Fig. 3.15. Lincoln appeared on numerous magazine covers, especially in February (his birthday), April (his death), and November (his Gettysburg Address). Illustrated is the February 3, 1910, issue of *Life* magazine showing Saint-Gaudens's standing bronze figure in Chicago.

Fig. 3.16. Sculptor and medalist Adolph A. Weinman's seated figure of the presidential Lincoln was dedicated in the Hodgenville, Kentucky, town square on May 31, 1909. Shown is a sculptor's model.

Fig. 3.17. *(a)* Illinois Watch Company was founded in Springfield by friends and associates of the martyred president. In his honor, the company manufactured an "A. Lincoln" pocket watch, which proved very popular in several sizes over a long period. *(b)* In order to obviate criticism of attempting to commercialize Lincoln's name, his signature was hidden inside the case.

Fig. 3.18. John A. Lowell Bank Note Co., Boston, offered a commemorative portrait patterned after the Marshall likeness during the Lincoln centennial.

HALF-TONE REDUCTION OF STEEL PLATE PORTRAIT OF

ABRAHAM LINCOLN

SIZE 15 X 18, ON HEAVY PLATE PAPER

In anticipation of the Centennial Celebration throughout the country in February, 1909, we have prepared this excellent portrait, which we offer to the public at the remarkable low price of

$1.00 PER COPY.

We believe it is the best example of the lamented Emancipator that has ever been offered within the means of the humblest admirer to possess.

Send $1.00 and a copy will be mailed securely packed to your address.

JOHN A. LOWELL BANK NOTE COMPANY, Publishers
147 Franklin Street, Boston, Mass.

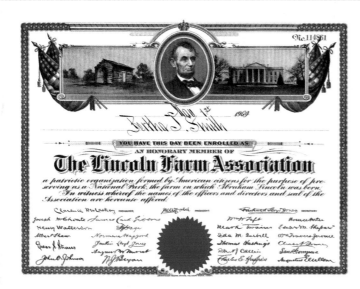

Fig. 3.19. Public subscriptions facilitated purchase of the Thomas Lincoln farm outside Hodgenville by the Lincoln Farm Association. This membership certificate was issued to Bertha J. Smith, November 1, 1909. The farm was subsequently deeded to the United States.

Fig. 3.20. Leopold Wharton starred in the 1910 silent film *Abraham Lincoln's Clemency*, dramatizing the legend of Lincoln pardoning the sleeping sentry.

he had come to represent had spilled over into the streets outside the U.S. Treasury building in Washington, where thousands thronged to obtain the first strikes of the small bronze tribute to Lincoln. Kids stood in line to resell cents at a profit. The Lincoln cent was the first regular issue U.S. portrait coin. The cent's design did not meet with universal applause, especially the stylized wheat ears.

1909 AUGUST 4. A controversy over the location and prominence of Brenner's initials develops. Treasury Secretary Franklin MacVeigh orders Lincoln cent production stopped and the V.D.B. initials removed from the dies (see fig. 3.14).

1909 AUGUST 5. Depleted supplies of new Lincoln cents at subtreasuries occasion the posting of signs reading "No More Lincoln Pennies."

1909 AUGUST 5. The *Washington Post* calls the new Lincoln cent "decidedly pretty."

1909 AUGUST 8. The *Washington Post* reports erroneously that the new Lincoln cent is too thick to be used in vending machines.

1909 AUGUST 9. The New York Sub-Treasury distributes the last of its 1909 V.D.B. Lincoln cents.

1909 AUGUST 10. Newspapers report the depletion of supplies of new Lincoln cents. The Lincoln cent shown in fig. 3.14 was forwarded on that date by attorney W.S. Burch to the son of a friend, "Master Jno. Morgan Wood," as a souvenir (letter and cent in collection of the author).

1909 AUGUST 12. Cent designer Brenner writes *The Numismatist* addressing the "fume [that] has been made about my initials." He contends, "The name of the artist on a coin is essential for the student of history."

1909 AUGUST 12. The *New York Times* prints a letter from Charles E. Schafranck stating that boys are selling the new Lincoln cents at three for five cents in the vicinity of the subtreasury in New York City.

1909 AUGUST 12. San Francisco Mint superintendent Edward Sweeny sends Mint Director Robert Preston 100 of the 1909-S V.D.B. cents. Pattern expert Andrew Pollock reports that a set of gold S-mint cents was struck: a 1908-S cent of the former Indian Head type, a 1909-S Lincoln cent with the designer's initials, V.D.B., on the reverse, and a 1909-S Lincoln cent with the designer's initials removed. Purportedly the set now belongs to a descendant of a San Francisco Mint employee.[3]

1909 AUGUST 15. Treasury Secretary MacVeagh announces the cessation of the coining of new Lincoln cents and the preparation of a new reverse die without the initials "V.D.B."

1909 AUGUST 17. The *Washington Post* erroneously reports that the new Lincoln cent is larger and heavier than the Indian Head cent it has replaced.

1909 CIRCA. Cent sculptor Victor David Brenner creates an impressive beardless bust of Lincoln (see fig. 2.209).

1909 CIRCA. The first of the great Lincoln thespians, Sam Dade Drane, takes to the stage in *Lincoln and the Soldier* (see page 194). In 1915 Drane would also portray Lincoln in the film adaptation of novelist Winston Churchill's famous book *The Crisis*.

1910 JANUARY. The Lincoln Institute (fig. 3.22) is incorporated by the trustees of Berea College as an all-Black boarding high school in Lincoln Ridge, Kentucky. It was named after Abraham Lincoln, according to the school's alumni association, who created the school when organizers realized there was no similarly named institution in

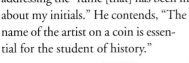

Fig. 3.21. *(a)* Colorful ribbons include this 1910 Mogul Cigarette ribbon with a likeness after the old $10 pose. The ribbon was a premium in cigarette packs; other colors have been observed. *(b)* The 1909 Lincoln centennial badge, crafted by W.F. Miller, has a representation of the Marshall engraving.

Fig. 3.22. Lincoln Institute, Lincoln Ridge, Kentucky, was incorporated in January 1910. Shown is a gold blazer button.

the state. The school closed in 1966, but the building continued to be used as a school for disadvantaged and gifted children and still later as a job corps center.

1910 FEBRUARY 12. A large medallion (fig. 3.23) is presented to guests at the 50th anniversary Lincoln dinner celebration by the Republican Club of New York. The event recalls that the club had sponsored Lincoln's 1860 Cooper Union address, propelling him to national attention.

1910 DECEMBER 10. Cincinnati civic leaders commission sculptor George Grey Barnard to create a Lincoln statue after receiving a gift for that purpose of $100,000 from Cincinnati newspaperman Charles P. Taft and his wife.

1911 JANUARY 21. The U.S. Post Office introduces a penny postal card with Lincoln's image in red (fig. 3.25). The profile is based on the Pickett bronze plaque made in 1873 (see chapter 2, fig. 2.127) and copyrighted by L.G. Muller in 1908.

1911 FEBRUARY 11. President Taft speaks at the dinner of the Lincoln Centennial Association, in Springfield, Illinois. His speech is printed by the Government Printing Office for distribution.

1911 MARCH 20–21. Stan V. Henkels sells coin dealer Charles Steigerwalt's estate collection of Lincolniana, including "An Important Collection of Eulogies on Abraham Lincoln."

1911. An "Emancipation Pageant" is held at Lyman School for Boys (fig. 3.26b), a reform school and manual labor institution established by social reformer Theodore Lyman in Westborough, Massachusetts, in 1846.

1911 MAY 20. Lincoln cents are first coined at the Denver Mint.

1911 MAY 30. Theodore Roosevelt presides over the dedication of Gutzon Borglum's seated Lincoln sculpture at the foot of the Essex County Court House steps in Newark, New Jersey (fig. 3.27). A crowd of thousands turns out for the event.

1911 JUNE 13. Sculptor James Earle Fraser writes Director of the Mint George E. Roberts about the proposed new nickel: "I think your idea of the Lincoln head is a splendid one and I shall be very glad to make you some sketches as soon as possible." Fraser produces actual-size "sketches" as electrotrial essays (fig. 3.28). He would also experiment with a Liberty head design before eventually authoring the classic Indian Head–Bison designs, which were adopted for the nickel in 1913.

Fig. 3.24. Coin dealer Tom Elder issued many small Lincoln medals. Shown is his 1910 "A Token to the Emancipator and Martyr" gold token (King-242/DeLorey-47).

Fig. 3.23. In 1860 the Republican Club of New York City had invited Abraham Lincoln to speak before them. His "Cooper Union" speech launched his successful campaign for the presidency. On Lincoln's birthday 50 years later, the New York Republicans held a grand banquet, and attendees received this yellow bronze plaque in remembrance.

Fig. 3.25. A Lincoln penny postal card was issued by the U.S. Post Office on January 21, 1911 (Scott UX23, BEP die no. MISC9084). Lincoln was engraved by Marcus W. Baldwin.

Fig. 3.26. *(a)* Thomas Ball's Emancipation group in Washington, D.C., was the inspiration for both this 1909 post card, and *(b)* this 1911 tableau by residents of Lyman School for Boys, a reform and manual labor school at Westborough, Massachusetts.

Fig. 3.27. Gutzon Borglum's viewer-friendly statue of a seated Lincoln was dedicated at Essex County Court House, Newark, New Jersey, on Memorial Day, May 30, 1911. Over the years thousands of tourists have climbed on Lincoln's bench to have their photos taken with the Great Emancipator.

Fig. 3.28. Sculptor James Earle Fraser considered a Lincoln portrait in 1911 for the obverse of the five-cent coin which two years later became the Indian Head–Bison nickel. Shown is one of Fraser's private electrotrials.

1911 NOVEMBER 8. Adolph A. Weinman's standing Lincoln is dedicated at the state capitol, Frankfort, Kentucky (fig. 3.29).

1912 MARCH 8. In a racially insensitive time, the *Greenville Daily Democrat* of Mississippi reports that Black gamblers believe Lincoln cents cause bad luck.

1912 APRIL 9. Sculptor Gutzon Borglum names his son Lincoln Borglum in honor of Abraham Lincoln, whom he so admired, and in honor of whom he would create several lasting monuments. Son Lincoln Borglum eventually finished his father Gutzon's work at Mount Rushmore, which is commemorated on U.S. coins.

1912 JANUARY. The Lincoln Gettysburg Address Memorial, designed by Louis Henrick, with a bust of Lincoln by Henry Kirke Brown (fig. 3.30), is dedicated at the Gettysburg Battlefield pursuant to an Act of Congress passed in 1895 on Lincoln's birthday, February 12.

1912 SEPTEMBER 2. Daniel Chester French's Lincoln sculpture is dedicated at Lincoln High School, Lincoln, Nebraska.

1912 LABOR DAY. Daniel Chester French's standing bronze figure "The Orator at Gettysburg" is erected at the state capitol, Lincoln, Nebraska.

1913 JANUARY 29. The Honorable Isaac R. Sherwood of Ohio champions "The Lincoln Highway to Gettysburg" from Washington, D.C., in a speech in the U.S. House of Representatives. He is seconded by the Honorable Joseph Taggart of Kansas, who calls for such a "Lincoln Memorial" in another speech to the House.

1913. The Illinois Watch Company of Springfield, Illinois, manufacturer of the "A. Lincoln" watch, introduces a chromolithograph portrait of Lincoln on canvas (fig. 3.32) as a sales promotion for its watch.

1913. Springfield poet Vachel Lindsay publishes *General William Booth Enters into Heaven and Other Poems.* His short poem "Lincoln" begins "Would I might 'rouse the Lincoln in you all! / That which is gendered in the wilderness . . . Above that breast of earth and prairie-fire— / Fire that freed the slave." The rousing first line was much later adopted by the Association of Lincoln Presenters as its slogan.

Fig. 3.29. Sculptor Adolph A. Weinman's standing Lincoln was dedicated at the state capitol, Frankfort, Kentucky, on November 8, 1911.

Fig. 3.30. The Lincoln Gettysburg Address Memorial, designed by Louis Henrick, with a bust of Lincoln by Henry Kirke Brown, was dedicated in January 1912. This photo was taken in July 1940.

1914 FEBRUARY 12. Ground is broken for the Lincoln Memorial in Washington, D.C.[4]

1914 MAY 18. Plate date engraved on $5 Federal Reserve Bank Notes with Lincoln's portrait (fig. 3.33b). Series 1914 Federal Reserve Notes with Lincoln's portrait are also issued (fig. 3.33a).

1914. The Lincoln Bank Note Co. is formed in Chicago.

1914 CIRCA. The American Peace Centenary Committee proposes to send a duplicate of Augustus Saint-Gaudens's Chicago Lincoln Park statue to London to mark the 100th anniversary of the Treaty of Ghent, which concluded the War of 1812.

1914 JULY 4. A Lincoln monument is dedicated in Frogner Park, Oslo, Norway, a gift from Norwegian descendants living in North Dakota.

1914. A "Joint Resolution for a Commemoration of the Second Inaugural of Abraham Lincoln" is introduced in the U.S. Senate. President Woodrow Wilson calls Lincoln "the supreme American of our history."

1915 FEBRUARY 12. The cornerstone for the Lincoln Memorial in Washington, D.C., is laid with a Series 1899 $1 Silver Certificate N4115830N.

1915 MARCH 3. D.W. Griffith releases *The Birth of a Nation* to critical acclaim, with Joseph Henabery (see fig. 1.14f) in the role of Abraham Lincoln (and several other bit parts).

1915 MARCH 20. The Union League of Philadelphia awards former senator Elihu Root its highest award, the Lincoln Medal, so called because Lincoln was its first recipient (see page 50).

1915. Fifty years after Lincoln's death, the Illinois legislature authorizes the State Historical Library to mark the exact route traveled by Lincoln from Kentucky through Indiana to Illinois.

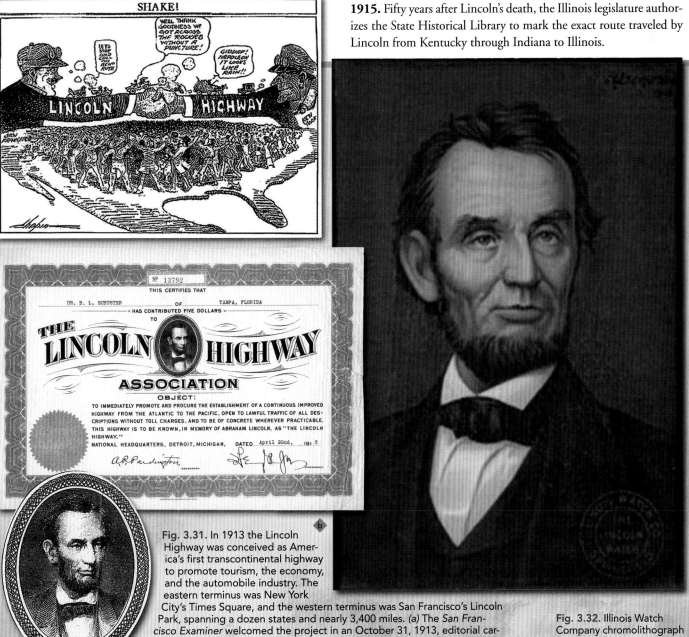

Fig. 3.31. In 1913 the Lincoln Highway was conceived as America's first transcontinental highway to promote tourism, the economy, and the automobile industry. The eastern terminus was New York City's Times Square, and the western terminus was San Francisco's Lincoln Park, spanning a dozen states and nearly 3,400 miles. (a) The *San Francisco Examiner* welcomed the project in an October 31, 1913, editorial cartoon "Shake." (b) Also shown is Lincoln Highway donor's certificate, lithographed by Hamilton Bank Note Co., dated April 22, 1916.

Fig. 3.32. Illinois Watch Company chromolithograph portrait of Lincoln.

1915 APRIL 11. For the 50th anniversary of Lincoln's death, the *New York Times* publishes a full-page illustration featuring the Saint-Gaudens standing figure, a funeral urn draped in Old Glory, the U.S. Capitol, tall cedars, and William Cullen Bryant's "Ode for the Funeral of Abraham Lincoln," which concludes: "Pure was thy life; its bloody close / Hath placed thee with the sons of light, / Among the noble host of those / Who perished in the cause of right." The paper congratulates itself for its even-handed coverage of the event as it transpired a half century earlier.

1916 FEBRUARY 10. Lincoln's birthday is celebrated at Young's Art Gallery in Chicago with a week-long exhibition of "The Portrait of Abraham Lincoln: Painted from Life" by Jesse Atwood. Atwood had traveled from Philadelphia to Springfield to paint the president-elect. Also on display were important prints, engravings and photographs, and "political cartoons and caricatures showing the intense feeling of the presidential campaign of 1864."

1916. *Abraham Lincoln,* a biography, is published in Great Britain by Lord Charnwood, emphasizing Lincoln's staunch defense of democracy. Charnwood's book would mold British public opinion toward Lincoln.

1916 SEPTEMBER 4. President Woodrow Wilson accepts the Hodgenville birthplace memorial on behalf of the people of the United States (fig. 3.34a). This shrine contains a representation of the Lincoln birthplace cabin (see fig. 1.3). Wilson speaks on "The Significance of Lincoln." At the occasion the War Department accepts a deed of gift to the Lincoln birthplace farm at Hodgenville, Kentucky, from the Lincoln Farm Association (fig. 3.34b).

1916 DECEMBER 15. The "Report of Lincoln Highway Commission" is issued by Joseph M. Cravens, the commission's chairman, and Jesse Weik, the secretary, to Indiana governor Samuel M. Ralston.

1917. World War I makes kindred spirits of Woodrow Wilson and predecessor wartime presidents Washington and Lincoln (fig. 3.35).

1917. Elbert Hubbard authors *Abraham Lincoln: Man and American,* subtitled "an intimate relation by his fellow-townsman." The book is prepared by Hubbard's Roycrofters and published by the Hartford Lunch Co. of New York. Hubbard's magazine, *The Fra,* would feature Lincoln frequently.

1917. Lincoln photo historian Frederick Hill Meserve privately publishes *Lincolniana and Historical Photographs.*

1917 FEBRUARY 12. Lincoln is claimed as the patron saint of many causes. Suffragettes demonstrate for the vote and against President Woodrow Wilson with signs bearing slogans like "Mr. President You Block the National Suffrage Amendment Today Why Are You Behind Lincoln?" and "American Women Still Ask For Freedom Will You Mr. President Still Tell Them to Wait" (fig. 3.36).

1917 MARCH 14. The United States issues a one-cent postal card with a green imprint portrait of Lincoln.

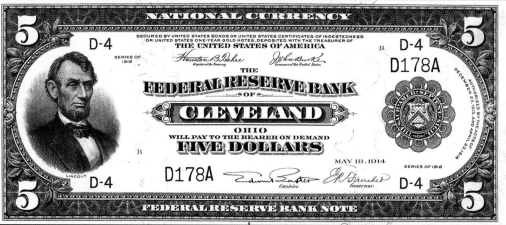

Fig. 3.33. By 1914 Lincoln had appeared on 50-cent notes, $1, $10, $20, $100, and $500 U.S. bills, but it was on the $5 note that Lincoln's most iconic image would be graven from that date down to present. Shown are (a) a Series 1914 $5 Red Seal Federal Reserve Note (Friedberg-832B, BEP die no. Friedberg-152), and (b) a Series 1918 $5 Federal Reserve Bank Note, (Friedberg-785, BEP die no. Friedberg-113).

1917 MARCH 31. Sculptor George Grey Barnard's statue of Lincoln is erected in Cincinnati, Ohio (see page 197). The dedication address is by William Howard Taft.[5] Barnard shows Lincoln as a man of the people, in a relaxed stance and coarse clothing. Although it was Barnard's masterpiece, some observers, including art critic Frederick Ruckstuhl, labeled it the "stomach ache" statue because of Lincoln's posture and facial features. It gives, wrote Ruckstuhl, the impression of a man saying "Friends, for pity's sake, relieve me of my pain—I have a colic."

1917. The sponsor of the Cincinnati Barnard Lincoln statue, Charles Taft (half brother of William Howard Taft) agrees to pay for a copy of the statue to be placed outside of Parliament in London.

1917. With World War I in full swing, a "Buy Liberty Bonds" poster is printed (fig. 3.37) with a medallion profile of Lincoln. It includes his injunction "That Government of the People, By the People, For the People Shall Not Perish From the Earth" from his Gettysburg Address. The portrait is modeled on Calverley's plaque.

Fig. 3.34. *(a)* President Woodrow Wilson accepted the Lincoln birthplace memorial on behalf of the people of the United States on September 4, 1916, and the deed to the Lincoln farm was accepted by the U.S. War Department. Shown is the crowd assembled for that historic event. *(b)* A pictorial medal (King-315) engraved by John Mobray Clark and struck by Whitehead & Hoag, Newark, honors the memorial.

Fig. 3.35. Woodrow Wilson had a penchant for Lincoln, and his identification with Lincoln and Washington as a war president was carefully cultivated.

Fig. 3.36. Early feminists took to the Washington, D.C., streets on Lincoln's birthday in 1917 to agitate for voting rights. The banner at center reads: "Lincoln stood for woman's suffrage 60 years ago. Mr. President you block the National Suffrage Amendment today. Why are you behind Lincoln?"

1917. U.S. forces overseas include the 84th Army Lincoln "Rail-splitter" Division (see page 216).

1917 APRIL. The U.S. government seizes the Hamburg-Amerika Line *President Lincoln,* which had been interned at Hoboken, New Jersey, since July 1914, after England and France had declared war on Germany. The ship (shown in fig. 3.39a as an ocean liner and in fig. 3.39b in an official military photograph) is turned over to the United States Shipping Board, overhauled, lengthened to 619 feet, and commissioned for use as a Navy troop ship on July 25, 1917, at Brooklyn, New York.

1917 JULY. The *Ladies Home Journal* publishes artist J.L.G. Ferris's stirring painting *Lincoln the Orator,* showing Lincoln silhouetted against an enormous American flag. Ferris specialized in American historical paintings, and Lincoln was a favorite. Ferris's Lincolns also illustrated the covers of the February 1919 *Ladies Home Journal* and the February 8, 1930, *Literary Digest.*

1917 OCTOBER 21. The *New York Times* exposes the "lively controversy" raging over plans to erect "the people's Lincoln," George Grey Barnard's frontiersman statue, in London, England. Critics call Barnard's figure graceless, undignified, and a travesty. Robert Todd Lincoln was a harsh critic of the statue. Others included Henry Cabot Lodge and artists Kenyon Cox and Childe Hassam. Theodore Roosevelt and William Howard Taft were among its advocates. Roosevelt, particularly, prized Barnard's rugged interpretation. "I have always wished that I might see him; now I do," he said. Lincoln's son complained bitterly to Taft: "That my father should be represented . . . by such a work . . . would be a cause of sorrow to me personally, the greatness of which I will not attempt to describe."[6]

1917 OCTOBER 26. The *New York Times* reports on the developing brouhaha over plans to erect duplicates of Barnard's pre-presidential Cincinnati Lincoln statue across the pond in London and now also in Paris. The protest comes from "33 leaders in architecture, painting, literature, the professions, and business" who contend that the

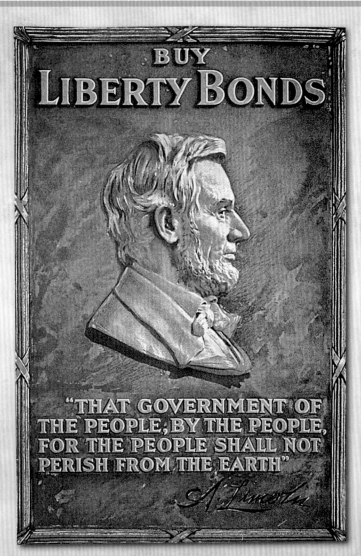

Fig. 3.37. This World War I "Buy Liberty Bonds" poster had the look of a large bronze Lincoln plaque.

Fig. 3.38. World War I poster by Chas. Gustring, Chicago, "True Sons of Freedom" honors the "Colored Men: The First Americans Who Planted Our Flag on the Firing Line," 1918.

choice of sculpture should be subject to the approval of the Commission of Fine Arts.

1917 NOVEMBER 28. A Series 1917 $1,000 First Liberty Loan bond design depicting Abraham Lincoln is approved by Bureau of Engraving and Printing (BEP) director Claude Johnson.

1917 DECEMBER 19. Perhaps with tongue in cheek, the London periodical *Punch* suggests that the Barnard statue will be erected in Parliament Square after all, "despite the protest of Lord Charnwood."

1918. Cent designer Victor David Brenner's initials are restored to the cent (fig. 3.41), below the truncation of the bust on the obverse, at the direction of Treasury Secretary William Gibbs McAdoo.

1918 SEPTEMBER 21. William Granville Hastings's bronze statue of Lincoln is dedicated at the Green County Court House in Jefferson, Iowa, on the Lincoln Highway.

1918 MAY 31. After four successful round trips ferrying nearly 23,000 American troops, the SS *President Lincoln* is sunk on her fifth transatlantic passage by a German U-boat. The vessel was hit by three torpedoes from point-blank range, and sank within 20 minutes. In addition to its crew, the *President Lincoln* carried 715 wounded and sick soldiers returning to the States. Twenty-six men were lost with the ship, and one officer was taken prisoner by the German U-boat. The rest of the ship's complement were rescued from lifeboats that night by two U.S. destroyers. The sinking sent shock waves through the press, public, and government.

1918 JUNE 1. Congress authorizes 100,000 Lincoln-Illinois commemorative half dollars (fig. 3.42a), with proceeds to finance centennial celebrations in the state. This was the first state commemorative half dollar. The beardless Lincoln profile on the obverse was sculpted by Mint engraver George Morgan, and is considered by many to be his magnum opus. Morgan based his design on a photograph of Andrew O'Connor's statue, which was dedicated that fall. The reverse was

Fig. 3.39. *(a)* The Hamburg-Amerika Line's glitzy ocean liner *President Lincoln* was confiscated during World War I by the United States and outfitted as a troop ship *(b)* the USS *President Lincoln* in 1917. It was sunk with great loss of life by a German U-boat. (U.S. Army Signal Corps photo)

Fig. 3.40. In 1916 Marcus W. Baldwin engraved the BEP large die portrait of the Great Emancipator. The following year, he engraved Lincoln's portrait after the same model as the $5 bill image for this $1,000 First Liberty Loan, 3.5 percent registered bond (BEP die no. MISC9205). Similar Lincoln images appeared on a wide variety of $1,000 U.S. bonds in war and peace from that point on.

Fig. 3.41. In 1918 designer Victor David Brenner's initials were added at the truncation of Lincoln's bust on the cent obverse.

engraved by assistant Mint engraver John Sinnock. Many of the coins were sold by the State Centennial Commission for one dollar each, but apparently a large number appear to have been spent in change.

1918 CIRCA. In a stirring painting by German illustrator Carl Rudolph Sohn, German widows weep before Lincoln for their husbands slain in the war. The painting is published with a verse by Karl Bröger (fig. 3.43).

1918 AUGUST 16. Because of wartime anti-German sentiment, the German Co-Operative Savings and Loan Assoc. of Buffalo, New York, changes its name to Lincoln Savings & Loan Assoc.

1918 OCTOBER 5. Andrew O'Connor's statue of Lincoln is dedicated on the state capitol grounds in Springfield, Illinois.

1918 DECEMBER 21. The *New York Times* reports that a decision has been made to erect the Saint-Gaudens statue in London through the auspices of the Anglo-American Society, successor to the American Peace Centenary Committee, proponent of the gift. "The Barnard work has been widely criticized in Great Britain for its uncouth characteristics," the paper said, adding, "The Barnard Statue [is] to be offered to some other prominent British city." "We perceive here [Great Britain]," wrote George Bernard Shaw, "that Lincoln was essentially a saint." The Barnard statue was erected in the "provincial"

Fig. 3.42. Andrew O'Connor's bold beardless Lincoln statue dedicated at the state capitol grounds in Springfield on October 5, 1918, served as model for Mint engraver George T. Morgan's obverse portrait (a) on the 1918 Illinois Centennial commemorative half dollar. (b) An artist's study by O'Connor is also shown.

Fig. 3.43. In German illustrator Carl Rudolph Sohn's moving depiction, German war widows entreat Lincoln's benevolence.

city of Manchester September 15, 1919. Barnard experimented a great deal with Lincoln figures, including his colossal bust (fig. 3.44) and two busts depicting Lincoln as Christ in the collection of the Kankakee County Museum of Illinois.

1919 JANUARY 30. Massachusetts governor Calvin Coolidge sets aside February 12 as "Lincoln Day" in the commonwealth; "its observance [is] recommended as befits the beneficiaries of his life and admirers of his character, in places of education and worship wherever our people meet one with another." Lincoln "overcame evil with good. His presence filled the Nation. He broke the might of oppression. He restored a race to its birthright. His mortal frame has van-

ished, but his spirit increases with the increasing years, the richest legacy of the greatest century," a solemn Coolidge explained. "Men show by what they worship what they are," he continued. "It is no accident that before the great example of American manhood our people stand with respect and reverence . . . for in him is revealed our ideal, the hope of our country fulfilled."

1919 MAY 17. Literary figure Charles Van Doren coins the phrase "The Poetical Cult of Lincoln" in *Nation* magazine.

1919. *Abraham Lincoln,* a play by Englishman John Drinkwater, makes its U.S. stage debut (fig. 3.46) after opening in England the

Fig. 3.44. American sculptor George Grey Barnard grew up in Illinois and studied at the Art Institute of Chicago and in Paris. He early on came under the influence of the French sculptor Rodin. Barnard poses with an enormous Lincoln tribute head in his New York City studio in 1917, during the controversy over installing a copy of his rough-hewn Lincoln statue in England.

Fig. 3.45. Lincoln memorabilia during the World War I era included *(a)* this Lincoln Legion pin back, *(b)* a circa 1915 Kraeuter iron plaque after the Borglum statue in Newark, *(c)* a Lincoln pin and flag badge, and *(d)* Mary Lincoln Old Fashioned Candies from Buffalo.

Fig. 3.46. Lincoln dramas were very popular between the World Wars. They included (a) John Drinkwater's 1919 play *Abraham Lincoln*, (b) Samuel D. Drane's performances in several films and plays, (c) D.W. Griffith's 1930 movie *Abraham Lincoln* with Walter Huston, and (d) Al and Ray Rockett's 1924 film *The Dramatic Life of Abraham Lincoln* with George A. Billings.

year before. Drinkwater dedicates the play to fellow Englishman Lord Charnwood, on whose Lincoln biography it is based. The play was later adapted to the silver screen.

1919. Robert Todd Lincoln deposits Abraham Lincoln's papers in the Library of Congress. On January 23, 1923, he deeds them to the library, with the stipulation that they remain sealed for 21 years following his death.

1919 NOVEMBER 20. Treasury Secretary Carter Glass reports to Congress on standardizing portraiture by denomination on "all issues of paper money," including continuing Lincoln on the $5 note.

1920. Lincoln Paint & Color Co. of Lincoln, Nebraska, trademarks its Lincoln Paints and Varnishes (fig. 3.47a).

1920. The Lincoln Record Corporation of New York is established, publishing 50¢ dance records as a division of Cameo Records; the division lasted until 1930.

1920 JULY 28. Ending all the controversy, Saint-Gaudens's Lincoln statue is dedicated at Westminster, London (fig. 3.48a).

1920 AUGUST 31. Lincoln Logs (fig. 3.49), "America's National Toy," are patented by Chicago resident John Lloyd Wright (patent number 1,351,086); application was filed January 8, 1920. The name was registered August 28, 1923. Wright was the son of eminent architect Frank Lloyd Wright. In his patent, the younger Wright claimed to "have invented certain new and useful improvements in toy-cabin construction . . . calculated to develop a child's constructive inclinations" as an educational toy.

1920. The 1920 *Boy Scouts' Year Book* carries an essay by Ida Tarbell that dramatizes various character traits of Lincoln, the "patron saint" of the Scouting movement. Entitled "Abraham Lincoln, True Scout," the essay summarizes Lincoln as "Trustworthy, Loyal, Helpful, Friendly, Courteous, Kind, Obedient, Cheerful, Thrifty, Brave, Clean, Reverent." This is just the kind of human being scouts were taught to aspire to be. Scouting literature claimed, "The courageous spirit of great Americans is the rich heritage of all Boyhood. In 1910

Fig. 3.47. Commercialism of Lincoln's name and likeness proliferated. Examples include (a) circa 1910s Lincoln Paints & Varnishes, (b) circa 1910s Jas. S. Kirk & Co. White Palace Bouquet soap, and (c) circa 1920s Lincoln Record Corporation, New York.

Fig. 3.48. (a) A copy of Augustus Saint-Gaudens's Chicago standing presidential Lincoln figure was installed in Parliament Square in London, England, on July 28, 1920. This ended the controversy that had arisen whether a copy of George Grey Barnard's standing "Lincoln the Candidate" statue at Cincinnati would be placed there. (b) The copy of Barnard's statue was relegated to Manchester, England.

on the eighth day of February, the month of Washington and Lincoln . . . the Boy Scouts came into being."

1920 December 1. The Alliance Bank of Rochester, New York, changes its name to the Lincoln-Alliance Bank.

1921 July 20. Agitation to declare Lincoln's birthday a federal holiday continues. The House Committee on the District of Columbia holds a "Lincoln's Birthday Hearing" on House Report number 2310, *A Bill to Declare Lincoln's Birthday a Legal Holiday in the District of Columbia.*

1921. Lincoln Motor Co., founded by Henry M. Leland in admiration of Abe, introduces its "L" (Luxury) model (fig. 3.50a). "The avowed purpose behind the building of the Lincoln is to make this car beyond question the finest that can be built," stated a 1924 ad.

1922. Steven A. Douglas Volk, son of Chicago sculptor Douglas Volk, who executed the Lincoln life mask in 1860 (see fig. 1.33), paints an important Lincoln portrait (fig. 3.52a). Volk's rough-hewn

work is destined to be the model for an important medal in 1924, the cover of the February 1941 issue of *The Instructor,* and a U.S. postage stamp in 1954. In 1908 (copyright 1912) the younger Volk had painted a similar Lincoln portrait, but cropped tighter, which coincidentally appeared on the *Mid-Week Pictorial* of February 9, 1922, and also the February 7, 1943, issue of *The Railroad Trainman.*

1922 May 30. The Lincoln Memorial is dedicated on Memorial Day (Decoration Day, set aside in 1868 by General John Logan, national commander of the GAR, to place flowers on the graves of Civil War veterans buried in Arlington National Cemetery). Daniel Chester French's majestic seated Lincoln is ensconced in Henry Bacon's Greek temple (fig. 3.53c). "In this temple as in the hearts of his fellow men" is inscribed above his head. The memorial's success owes a great deal to Senator Joe Cannon, who ran on Lincoln's ticket in 1860. At the request of then-president Warren G. Harding, the Military Order of the Loyal Legion of the United States (MOLLUS) was responsible for the arrangement and coordination of the dedication. MOLLUS has been responsible for the annual commemorative ceremonies ever since. At the dedication were the chief justice of the United States

Fig. 3.49. Lincoln Logs, "America's National Toy," were patented by Chicago resident John Lloyd Wright August 31, 1920. Shown is Lincoln Logs Set No. 1, circa 1923.

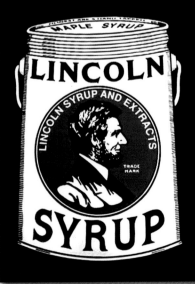

Fig. 3.51. Lincoln Syrup and Extracts porcelain sign, circa 1920s.

Fig. 3.50. (a) Henry M. Leland founded Lincoln Motor Co. due to his admiration for Old Abe. This 1924 Lincoln Motor Co. ad pays homage to Augustus Saint-Gaudens's Lincoln statue in Chicago, too. (b) Likewise, Patrick J. Towle introduced his Log Cabin Syrup in honor of his childhood hero. Shown is a Towle's Log Cabin Maple Syrup blotter, circa 1920s.

and former president William Howard Taft, who was also chairman of the Lincoln Memorial Commission. Taft presented the memorial to the current chief executive, Warren G. Harding. Surviving Lincoln heir Robert Todd Lincoln made one of his last public appearances before dying four years later. While French is rightly credited with the majestic figure in the memorial, the job of actually carving the white marble was undertaken by the Piccirilli Brothers at their studio in Mott Haven, Bronx, New York. The statue was carved in pieces and assembled on site. The Piccirillis also sculpted the twin lions that guard the entrance of the New York Public Library.

1922 JUNE 10. The *Illustrated London News* reports on the dedication of the Lincoln Memorial under the headline "A Shrine Where All Can Worship: The Saviour of the Union."

1922 JUNE 21. An Act of Congress is passed to re-erect Lot Flannery's Lincoln statue in the District of Columbia, which was re-dedicated April 15, 1923.

1922. The original Onstot cooperage from Lincoln's own time is moved back and restored to what is presumed to have been its original foundation in New Salem, Illinois. The area had been purchased by newspaperman William Randolph Hearst in 1906 and donated to the local Chatauqua Association. The reconstruction includes one original structure and various replicas to recreate the town of New Salem near Springfield, where Lincoln lived in the 1830s. Today it is administered as a state historic site.

1922 NOVEMBER 1. At the Cathedral of St. John the Divine, New York City, Bishop William T. Manning dedicates the white marble parapet (fig. 3.54), a memorial to Civil War veteran Brigadier Gen. Richard Delafield. The parapet (low wall) in front of the chancel stairs has 20 panels, "one for each of the Christian centuries."[7] The 19 figures put in place, including Lincoln for the 19th century and Washington for the 18th century, "represent the foremost workers for world uplift since Christ".[8]

Fig. 3.52. *(a)* Douglas Volk painted this vibrant likeness of Lincoln in 1922, one of several he produced. *(b)* At Volk's insistence, sculptor Charles L. Hinton was enlisted to sculpt the portrait for a Lincoln essay contest medal. The contest began in 1924, sponsored by the Illinois Watch Co. Medals were struck by Whitehead & Hoag, Newark (King-891/892).

Fig. 3.53. In 1922 the collaboration of sculptor Daniel Chester French and architect Henry Bacon on Lincoln's Memorial at the west end of the Capitol Mall in Washington, D.C., finally realized the visions of the early monument associations which had sought such a lasting tribute to Lincoln. *(a)* The 1915 Lincoln Memorial Ladies Citizens Committee badge has additional photos on the suspender under the artist's rendering of the Memorial face. *(b)* Four decades later, students on a school excursion gather at the foot of French's statue in 1955. *(c)* An uncustomary view from behind the Lincoln Memorial shows the Washington Monument and U.S. Capitol in the distance. *(d)* This Lincoln Statue Junior Founder probably dates from 1922 and the dedication of French's Lincoln Memorial figure, or perhaps from 1912 and the dedication of French's Lincoln statue at Lincoln, Nebraska.

1923 FEBRUARY 12. The post office releases the Lincoln Memorial one-dollar stamp (Scott 571); 34 million would be issued (fig. 3.56a).

1923 FEBRUARY 12. The three-cent purple bust, flat plate definitive stamp (Scott 555) by G.F.C. Smillie is also issued to mark Lincoln's birthday (fig. 3.56b). The following year, the BEP switches to rotary presses; over the next several years, it issues several additional varieties, including stamps overprinted "Kans." or "Nebr." In all, nearly 2.9 billion of these stamps were produced.

1923 MAY 22. French ambassador Jean Jules Jusserand dedicates the Abraham Lincoln bust unveiled by Mrs. Mary Lincoln Isham, granddaughter of the honoree, in the Hall of Fame for Great Americans of New York University. "Saint-Gaudens created the hall's bust of Abraham Lincoln, who was elected the first time around, in 1900; twenty years later the artist himself was elected."[9] The bust was cast posthumously.

1923. The U.S. Treasury issues the so-called Lincoln Porthole note, a $5 Silver Certificate, given the moniker because of the frame around the Lincoln vignette (fig. 3.57b). The Charles Burt $100 vignette of 1869 was employed, and 6.3 million of the notes issued.

1923 JUNE 1. Whitehead & Hoag contacts painter Douglas Volk regarding the use of his Lincoln portrait as the basis for an Illinois Watch Company essay contest medal. Walter C. Heath passes along watch company president Jacob Bunn's regards for Volk's painting: "This picture is my ideal of a Lincoln portrait. I like it better than any I have ever seen."[10]

1923 NOVEMBER 1. Frank Duffield publishes "Obsolete Notes with Portrait of Lincoln" in *The Numismatist.*

1924. The U.S. House of Representatives considers *A Bill for the Purchase of the Oldroyd Collection.* Similar measures had been considered in 1909 and 1911.

1924 JANUARY 15. ANA member Edward S. Raynor reports in *The Numismatist*—evidently for the first time in print—that "V.D.B." initials appear on the obverse of Lincoln cents back to 1918.

Fig. 3.54. On November 1, 1922, the Historical Parapet at the Cathedral of St. John the Divine, New York City, was dedicated with figures representing the 20 Christian centuries. Lincoln was selected for the 19th century and George Washington for the 18th century.

Fig. 3.55. In 1921 a small copy of Charles Burt's Lincoln portrait, BEP die no. MISC10323 by G.F.C. Smillie, was used on a $5 War Savings stamp (Scott WS6).

Fig. 3.56. The U.S. Post Office issued two stamps for Lincoln's birthday February 12, 1923: (a) the $1 Lincoln Memorial stamp (Scott 571), and (b) the three-cent stamp (Scott 555). The rotary press example (Scott 584) debuted August 1, 1925. The Lincoln portrait after the $5 model is by John Eissler (BEP die no. P0713). The Lincoln Memorial was engraved by L.S. Schofield.

1924 JANUARY 21. The Rockett-Lincoln Film Company releases *The Dramatic Life of Abraham Lincoln,* starring George A. Billings (see fig. 3.46d). The producers were Al and Ray Rockett. The story and screenplay were by Frances Marion. Philip Rosen directed the movie, which was filmed at Sunland Park, Los Angeles. The film, which won a "Medal of Honor" from *Photoplay* magazine, was distributed by Associated First National Pictures.

1924. The Illinois Watch Company of Springfield, Illinois, publishes a small booklet, *The Book of A. Lincoln Watches.*

1924 FEBRUARY 1. The Honorable Oscar Edward Keller from the District of Columbia authors *Lincoln's Birthday a Holiday in the District of Columbia,* House Report number 140, which is committed to the Committee of the Whole House on the State of the Union and ordered to be printed. The report accompanies House Report 20. On May 21, 1924, Keller submits House Report number 799, *To Declare Lincoln's Birthday a Legal Holiday in the District of Columbia,* which also was ordered to be printed to accompany S.1641.

1924 FEBRUARY 12. The Illinois Watch Company institutes its "Lincoln Essay Contest To Increase Knowledge and Admiration of Lincoln Among School Children in the United States." The contest would be conducted nationwide by the company and local contest sponsors in this and successive years through 1928; winning essays were frequently published in local newspapers. Special award ceremonies were often held, at which winners and runners-up would read their essays aloud. The medals (shown at fig. 3.52b) were sculpted by Charles Louis Hinton, whom Volk himself had recommended. Space on the reverse was left to engrave the recipient's name. The sponsoring company's name was omitted from the design due to objections by Volk about commercializing Lincoln in that way. Hinton supported Volk's view. After the first year, the date was also removed from the die. The medals were produced by Whitehead & Hoag. At least 8,000 and perhaps more of these medals were stuck from 1924 to 1927. The company also issued a booklet to accompany the boxed medal.

1924 FEBRUARY. *The Numismatist* publishes Robert P. King's "Lincoln in Numismatics: A Descriptive List of the Medals, Plaques, Tokens and Coins Issued in Honor of the Great Emancipator" (fig. 3.59a). In

Fig. 3.57. (a) The State of Illinois issued small warrants for war "services rendered the United States of America," printed by Columbian Bank Note Co., Chicago, after the $5 currency model. Andrew Russel was state auditor of public accounts from 1917 to 1921. (b) Many collectors consider the Series 1923 $5 Silver Certificate (Friedberg-282), called the "Porthole Note" for obvious reasons, the most beautiful of the Lincoln $5 bills and one of the finest examples of U.S. currency in general. It features Charles Burt's iconic Lincoln portrait. The note face (BEP die no. MISC10797) is credited to Lyman F. Ellis and Harry P. Dawson.

Fig. 3.58. These three Roaring Twenties badges are patterned after the cent and $5 portraits: (a) 1924 Ladies of GAR badge; (b) circa 1920s Washington County, Ohio, Veterans Association badge; and (c) a controversial 1925 Pennsylvania Klan Reunion badge.

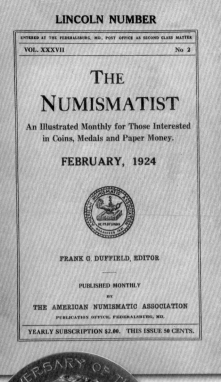

LINCOLN NUMBER

ENTERED AT THE FEDERALSBURG, MD., POST OFFICE AS SECOND CLASS MATTER

VOL. XXXVII   No 2

THE
NUMISMATIST

An Illustrated Monthly for Those Interested
in Coins, Medals and Paper Money.

FEBRUARY, 1924

FRANK G. DUFFIELD, EDITOR

PUBLISHED MONTHLY
BY
THE AMERICAN NUMISMATIC ASSOCIATION
PUBLICATION OFFICE, FEDERALSBURG, MD.

YEARLY SUBSCRIPTION $2.00.   THIS ISSUE 50 CENTS.

Fig. 3.60. Massachusetts governor Calvin Coolidge was a Lincoln fan. He established Lincoln's birthday observance in the commonwealth in 1919. On September 8, 1924, he hit the campaign trail with his vice presidential candidate, Charles Dawes, for a "Lincoln Tour across the country through 300 towns in 56 days." Their route paralleled much of the Lincoln Highway.

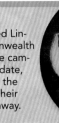

Fig. 3.61. Part of Lincoln's broad appeal is his rise from humble origins to achieve great success. Both (a) this circa 1920s "From Farm House to Whitehouse" cigar box label, and (b) the 1929 post card "The Earthly Pilgrimage of Abraham Lincoln" tap into that theme.

Fig. 3.59. (a) The American Numismatic Association journal *The Numismatist* dedicated its February 1914 issue as a "Lincoln Number," including Robert P. King's first listing "Lincoln in Numismatics" and other Lincoln articles. (b) Harry A. Gray suggested to Robert P. King that a medal be struck to mark the 1924 publication of King's catalog of Lincolniana in *The Numismatist*. The medal (King-912) was struck by Childs & Co., Chicago, and proceeds donated to the ANA.

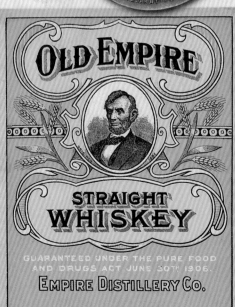

Fig. 3.62. The impact of the iconic Lincoln $5 bill image is witnessed by the likenesses on (a) a 1920s Old Empire Straight Whiskey label, and (b) a 1920s Old Abe cigars inner box label.

honor of this auspicious event, Boston numismatist Harry A. Gray has a medal struck by Childs, Chicago to celebrate the event.

1924 FEBRUARY 12. The first copy of *The Lincoln Library of Essential Information* appears. In February 1919, M.J. Kinsella, president of Frontier Press, had unveiled his plan to publish a concise, one-volume encyclopedia of useful information readily at hand that would provide a well-rounded education. Five years of research and an investment of $500,000 brought his dream to fruition. Through successive editions and multiple specialized references, the *Lincoln Library* series became a staple of reference sections and home study.

1924. *In the Footsteps of Abraham Lincoln,* an illustrated four-panel syndicated cartoon strip drawn by Russian émigré Nicholas Afonsky and edited by Ida M. Tarbell, debuts in newspapers as a teaching tool.

1924 APRIL 5. Lincoln cent designer Victor David Brenner dies.

1924 SEPTEMBER 8–NOVEMBER 3. Republican presidential and vice presidential candidates Calvin Coolidge and Charles Dawes hit the campaign trial on their (mostly) Lincoln Highway "Lincoln Tour" across the country through 300 towns in 56 days (fig. 3.60).

1924 SEPTEMBER 15. Sculptor Gaetano Cecere's bronze memorial to Lincoln is dedicated at Lincoln Memorial Bridge, Milwaukee.

1924 DECEMBER 12. The Lincoln Credit Union is chartered by the state of New York.

1925 AUGUST 20. Secretary of the Treasury Andrew W. Mellon appoints a committee to study currency design and production with a view to replacing the large-size notes with smaller bills. The committee recommends that Washington be on the $1 note "because his portrait was familiar to everyone and bills of this denomination had the greatest circulation." Similarly, the committee recommends "Lincoln for the $5s because he followed Washington in rank of American heroes and it seemed logical that Abe's likeness should appear on the denomination having the second largest circulation." In May 1927, Secretary Mellon approved the committee's recommendations.

1926 FEBRUARY. Dr. Carter G. Woodson launches Negro History Week, chosen to take place in the second week of February between the birthdays of Frederick Douglass and Abraham Lincoln; it evolved into Black History Month in 1976.

1926 MAY. The United States purchases the Oldroyd collection of about "3,000 authentic Lincoln mementos now on display in the historic Petersen House . . . [which] will preserve for future generations making pilgrimages to Washington a great store house of materials identified with Lincoln tradition."[11]

1926. M.E. Cadwallader privately publishes his poetically titled *Abraham Lincoln: The Friend of Man; His Life Was Another Drop in That Vat Where Human Lives, Like Grapes in God's Vintage, Yield the Wine That Strengthens the Spirit of Truth and Justice in the World.*

1926. The Prohibition Educational League publishes *Abraham Lincoln on Prohibition,* its first pamphlet.

1926 JULY 26. Robert Todd Lincoln dies.

1926. Carl Sandburg publishes *Abraham Lincoln: The Prairie Years,* which expresses "an intimacy with the familiar facts" and becomes a best-selling financial success for its author.

1926. For the U.S. Sesquicentennial Exposition in Philadelphia, BEP employees print a special set of silk handkerchiefs with nine vignettes. Six of these vignettes were unreported—including a Lincoln portrait, discovered by the present author in 2005. Most of the hankies depict the Liberty Bell, but others show Washington, Teddy Roosevelt, Woodrow Wilson, a Dreadnought battleship and eagle, and Trumbull's *Signing of the Declaration of Independence.* The vignettes were cataloged by Milt Friedberg in the July–August 2003 issue of *Paper Money.* The Reed specimen of the Lincoln hanky (ex Grinnell) is believed unique.

1927. Lt. Col. Charles Burnett, U.S. military attaché in Japan, prompts the America-Japan Society there to sponsor an Abraham Lincoln essay contest for Japanese schoolchildren. Winners would receive medals from the Lincoln Centennial Association and cash prizes from the America-Japan Society. The contest continued through 1930.

1927. Lyon G. Tyler, son of former president John Tyler, was president of William & Mary College. He also served as editor of the *William and Mary Quarterly* and "maintained a long campaign against Lincoln," in the words of Merrill Peterson.[12]

1927 APRIL. Robert P. King updates his "Lincoln in Numismatics" in *The Numismatist.*

1927. Thomas E. Brooks & Co. of Red Lion, Pennsylvania, files for a trademark for Old Abe Cigar: "Honest, True, Merit, Quality" (fig. 3.62b).

1927 JULY 3. Lorado Taft's sculpture portraying "Lincoln the Lawyer" is dedicated at Carle Park, Urbana, Illinois.

1928. Mrs. Robert Todd Lincoln presents to the Library of Congress the French gold medal that was originally a gift from the citizens of France to Mary Todd Lincoln.

1928. Lincoln National Life continues to prosper. "In 1928 [Arthur] Hall took the opportunity to repay the Lincoln family by creating the Lincoln Historical Research Foundation, dedicated to the life and legacy of Abraham Lincoln. The Foundation, under the leadership of Dr. Louis A. Warren, began to collect Lincoln-related material in 1928, published *Lincoln Lore* in 1929, and opened The Lincoln Museum to the public in 1931."[13]

1928. The Lincoln portrait chosen for $5 notes of all classes on the new series of standardized small-size currency is a cropped version of Charles Burt's engraving that first appeared on Series 1869 $100 large-size United States Notes. The Lincoln Memorial on the back was engraved by Joachim Benzing.

1928 APRIL 30. First delivery of Series 1928 $5 Federal Reserve Notes, with the new smaller Lincoln vignette on the face (fig. 3.64).

1928. Lincoln Caswell, a relation of his namesake for whom he bore a striking resemblance, performs on the Chatauqua circuit. His publicity claims that "while he lived Lincoln would not die."

1928. Whitehead & Hoag, Newark, New Jersey, builds a process exhibit "How Medals are Made," illustrated by examples of Hinton's Lincoln Essay Contest medal. The exhibit demonstrates the process from clay through several strikings to finished medal.

1928 SEPTEMBER 1. Bronze medallions marking the Lincoln Highway by Whitehead & Hoag (fig. 3.65) begin to be placed on 2,440 concrete markers by Boy Scout volunteers.

1929. American composer Robert Russell Bennett shares the RCA Victor competition prize, judged by Leopold Stokowski and others, for his "Abraham Lincoln: A Likeness in Symphony Form" (fig. 3.67).

1929. The Lincoln Centennial Association is renamed the Abraham Lincoln Association.

1929 FEBRUARY 11. Dr. Louis A. Warren publishes *Lincoln on Metal, Silk and Paper; Cultivating the Collective Instinct in Children.*

1929. The Abraham Lincoln Memorial Highway Association, Greenup, Illinois, publishes *Historic Proofs and Data in Support of the Lincoln Way, being the Route Traveled by the Thomas Lincoln Family in Coming from Indiana to Illinois in the Year 1830,* which it submits to the Governor of Illinois and the Department of Public Works and Buildings. The precise route was a matter of more than civic pride. To tie one's locality to the Lincoln tradition provided financial incentives, too!

Fig. 3.63. Circa 1920 Lincoln folk-art inlaid box.

Fig. 3.64. In 1928 as an economy measure, the U.S. switched from the old-size "saddle blanket" paper money to the currently used, small-size notes. Shown are a Series 1928 $5 Federal Reserve Note face (Friedberg-1950A) and a Series 1929 Federal Reserve Bank Note back (Friedberg-1850K).

Fig. 3.65. The Whitehead & Hoag bronze medallions that mark the Lincoln Highway.

Fig. 3.66. Navigating the Lincoln Highway was rough going in the early years. (a) The mud stretch was part of the highway through Nebraska in 1929. (b) The portal guarded the egress on the Colorado-Kansas state line in the 1920s. (c) The touring car at bottom reached the highway's terminus and rolled into the Pacific Ocean for good measure.

1929. S.M. Blunk also traces "The Lincoln Way." He describes the route traveled by Abraham Lincoln from his birthplace in Kentucky, through Indiana, to Springfield, Illinois, his final resting place, "to which spot thousands make yearly pilgrimages to pay homage to this great man."

1929 APRIL 15. First issue of *Lincoln Lore* is published. The weekly one-sheet was created by Dr. Louis A. Warren to spread the Lincoln "gospel" to the nation's press by supplying material suitable for publication. Over the years it grew in size and stature to encompass 1,894 issues (Winter 2008) at which time continuation of the publication became uncertain with the announced closing of the Lincoln Museum. Other Lincoln journals followed.

1929 MAY 30. A "Pilgrimage to the Tomb of Abraham Lincoln" is undertaken by Indiana school children under the auspices of the Kiwanis Clubs and school leaders from Indiana locations to Springfield, Illinois, via Wabash Railway.

1929 JULY 10. Lincoln and French's seated statue of Lincoln and Bacon's Lincoln Memorial appear on the back of Series 1928 U.S. Notes issued first this date.

1929 OCTOBER 15. Norman G. Flagg speaks on the "Lincoln-Douglas Debate" at Alton, Illinois, for the unveiling of a Memorial to the Seventh Lincoln-Douglas Joint Debate.

1930 FEBRUARY 8. *Collier's* cover shows Carroll M. Sexton's illustration of Gutzon Borglum's seated Lincoln cradling a Black infant with a story by Ida Tarbell on Lincoln and Ann Rutledge.

1930 FEBRUARY 12. Andrew O'Connor's granite bust of Lincoln is dedicated at Royal Exchange, London, England.

1930 JUNE 14. James Earle Fraser's nine-foot-tall seated figure of a beardless Lincoln is dedicated in Jersey City, New Jersey, on the Lincoln Highway. During the 1920s the city's Abraham Lincoln Association and school children had raised funds to build the monument. The young people came up with $3,500. Fraser also designed the

AMERICAN CLASSICS

ROBERT RUSSELL BENNETT

Abraham Lincoln: A Likeness in Symphony Form (1929)

Sights and Sounds (An Orchestral Entertainment) (1929)

Moscow Symphony Orchestra
William T. Stromberg

Fig. 3.67. In 1929 composer Robert Russell Bennett shared the RCA Victor competition prize, for his *Abraham Lincoln: A Likeness in Symphony Form*.

Fig. 3.68. Circa 1929 Sons of Veterans Lincoln badge.

Fig. 3.69. These two bonds were issued in 1929 before the stock-market crash. *(a)* The Lincoln Aircraft Co. stock, dated March 5, 1929, was printed by W.N. Perrin & Co., New York. *(b)* The Lincoln Gold Corporation stock, dated June 22, 1929, was printed on an anonymous stock form.

a
b

pediment. During the fund raising period, the statue was featured in articles in the *Jersey City Journal, Hoboken Observer,* and *Vanity Fair* magazine. Lincoln was one of Fraser's idols. They shared the same Western upbringing, physical prowess, and political philosophies. The sculptor was engaged in one Lincoln project or another frequently over a period of 40 years. Fraser "completed" his heroic-sized seated Lincoln figure for Jersey City in plaster in February 1930 (fig. 3.72). However, he was still tinkering with it the following month. News of his achievement spread like wildfire. Fraser and his wife, fellow sculptor Laura, who are considered "the First Family of American Sculpture," opened up their Greenwich Village studio in New York City to a host of dignitaries eager to view the Lincoln commission. Visitors included New York City's popular mayor Jimmy Walker, Teddy's son Archibald Roosevelt, Mrs. Edward Harriman, architect John Russell Pope, singer Al Jolson, sportswriter Grantland Rice, TR's secretary of state Elihu Root, painters, inventors, and a great many residents of Jersey City eager to see their statue. The following month Henry Ford and Arthur Hershey, founder of the chocolate company, came to Fraser's studio to view his Lincoln statue. Fraser described his statue of the pensive Lincoln in a letter to New Jersey officials: "His sad eyes set in their cavernous orbits, the troubled forehead and curiously twisted mouth, a face that bore in its expression the weight of worlds. His figure tall and slightly bent at the shoulders carried into his whole attitude what was depicted in his remarkable visage."[14] Later, in April, the statue was taken to Modern Art Foundry for casting in bronze. Placement of the Fraser statue was part of development of the trans-continental Lincoln Highway. At the time it was believed that Fraser's opus "End of the Trail" would be placed permanently at the western terminus of the Lincoln Highway in California. Laura Fraser recorded the dedication ceremony in her personal diary. After lunch with New Jersey governor Morgan F. Larson and other dignitaries, they proceeded to the ceremony. Members of the GAR unveiled the statue and laid a wreath, followed by many speeches. "Altogether the ceremony was impressive and Lincoln looks very beautiful," Mrs. Fraser recorded.[15]

1930 August 23. Leonard Crunelle's "The Captain" is dedicated at Dixon, Illinois, Ronald Reagan's boyhood home (1920–1937). Maybe the future president was there. The statue depicts Lincoln as a militia captain during the 1832 war against Chief Black Hawk (fig. 1.6).

1930. Engraver and printer Bernhardt Wall, Lime Rock, Connecticut, begins privately publishing his "Following Lincoln" portfolios, issued serially with release of "The Invitation to Gettysburg." Etching, printing, and binding are all done by Wall, who would create an impressive line of Lincoln works.

1931. Austin T. Hixon publishes *The Lincoln Highway through Davies County, Indiana.*

1931 February 12. Charter meeting of The Abraham Lincoln Fellowship at Berkeley, California. The meeting is attended by 10 San

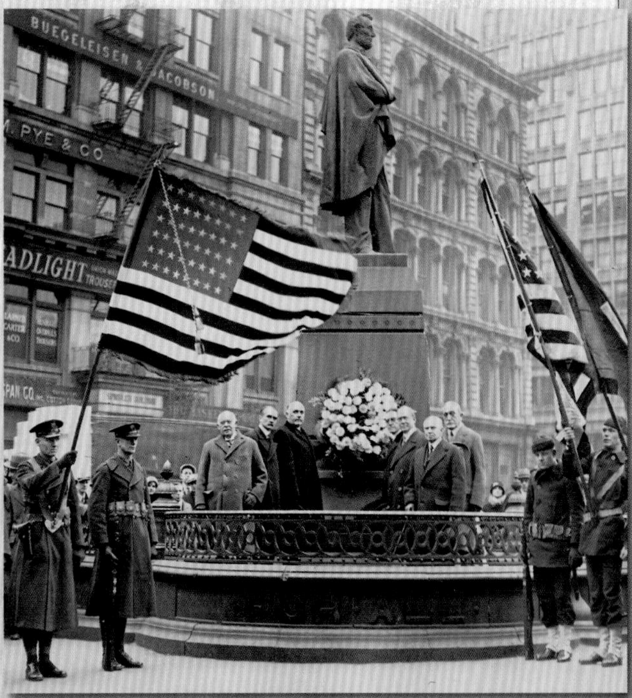

Fig. 3.70. Celebration of Lincoln's birthday at Henry Kirke Brown's statue, Union Square, New York City, 1929.

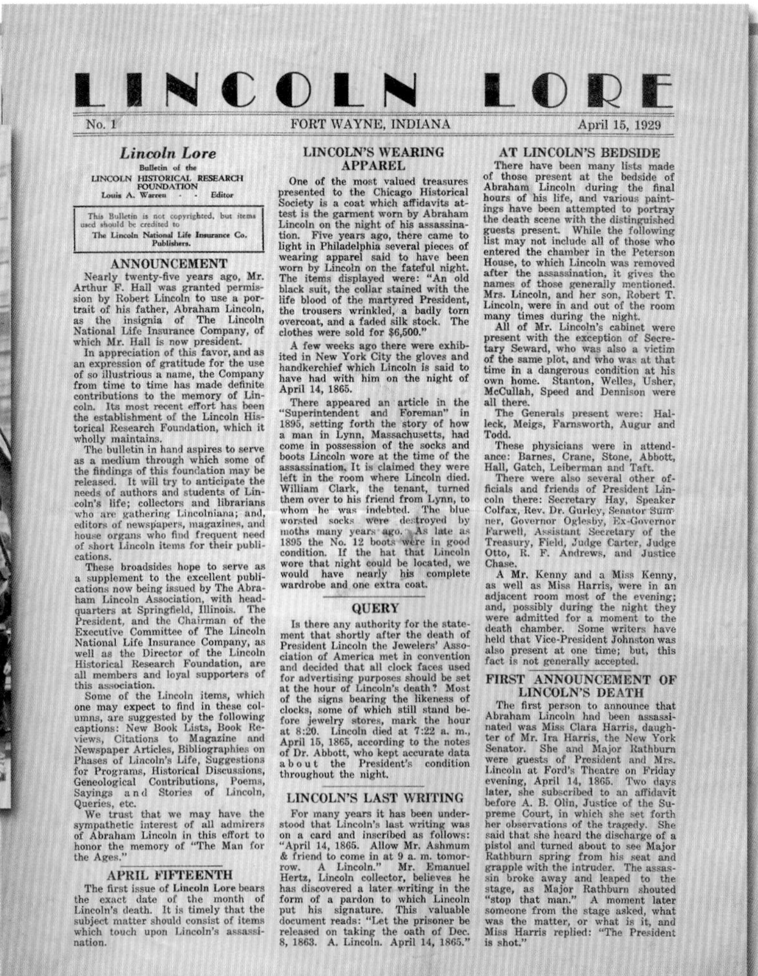

LINCOLN LORE

No. 1 | FORT WAYNE, INDIANA | April 15, 1929

Lincoln Lore
Bulletin of the
LINCOLN HISTORICAL RESEARCH FOUNDATION
Louis A. Warren - - Editor

This Bulletin is not copyrighted, but items used should be credited to
The Lincoln National Life Insurance Co.
Publishers.

ANNOUNCEMENT

Nearly twenty-five years ago, Mr. Arthur F. Hall was granted permission by Robert Lincoln to use a portrait of his father, Abraham Lincoln, as the insignia of The Lincoln National Life Insurance Company, of which Mr. Hall is now president.

In appreciation of this favor, and as an expression of gratitude for the use of so illustrious a name, the Company from time to time has made definite contributions to the memory of Lincoln. Its most recent effort has been the establishment of the Lincoln Historical Research Foundation, which it wholly maintains.

The bulletin in hand aspires to serve as a medium through which some of the findings of this foundation may be released. It will try to anticipate the needs of authors and students of Lincoln's life; collectors and librarians who are gathering Lincolniana; and, editors of newspapers, magazines, and house organs who find frequent need of short Lincoln items for their publications.

These broadsides hope to serve as a supplement to the excellent publications now being issued by The Abraham Lincoln Association, with headquarters at Springfield, Illinois. The President, and the Chairman of the Executive Committee of The Lincoln National Life Insurance Company, as well as the Director of the Lincoln Historical Research Foundation, are all members and loyal supporters of this association.

Some of the Lincoln items, which one may expect to find in these columns, are suggested by the following captions: New Book Lists, Book Reviews, Citations to Magazine and Newspaper Articles, Bibliographies on Phases of Lincoln's Life, Suggestions for Programs, Historical Discussions, Geneological Contributions, Poems, Sayings and Stories of Lincoln, Queries, etc.

We trust that we may have the sympathetic interest of all admirers of Abraham Lincoln in this effort to honor the memory of "The Man for the Ages."

APRIL FIFTEENTH

The first issue of **Lincoln Lore** bears the exact date of the month of Lincoln's death. It is timely that the subject matter should consist of items which touch upon Lincoln's assassination.

LINCOLN'S WEARING APPAREL

One of the most valued treasures presented to the Chicago Historical Society is a coat which affidavits attest is the garment worn by Abraham Lincoln on the night of his assassination. Five years ago, there came to light in Philadelphia several pieces of wearing apparel said to have been worn by Lincoln on the fateful night. The items displayed were: "An old black suit, the collar stained with the life blood of the martyred President, the trousers wrinkled, a badly torn overcoat, and a faded silk stock. The clothes were sold for $6,500."

A few weeks ago there were exhibited in New York City the gloves and handkerchief which Lincoln is said to have had with him on the night of April 14, 1865.

There appeared an article in the "Superintendent and Foreman" in 1895, setting forth the story of how a man in Lynn, Massachusetts, had come in possession of the socks and boots Lincoln wore at the time of the assassination. It is claimed they were left in the room where Lincoln died. William Clark, the tenant, turned them over to his friend from Lynn, to whom he was indebted. The blue worsted socks were destroyed by moths many years ago. As late as 1895 the No. 12 boots were in good condition. If the hat that Lincoln wore that night could be located, we would have nearly his complete wardrobe and one extra coat.

QUERY

Is there any authority for the statement that shortly after the death of President Lincoln the Jewelers' Association of America met in convention and decided that all clock faces used for advertising purposes should be set at the hour of Lincoln's death? Most of the signs bearing the likeness of clocks, some of which still stand before jewelry stores, mark the hour at 8:20. Lincoln died at 7:22 a. m., April 15, 1865, according to the notes of Dr. Abbott, who kept accurate data about the President's condition throughout the night.

LINCOLN'S LAST WRITING

For many years it has been understood that Lincoln's last writing was on a card and inscribed as follows: "April 14, 1865. Allow Mr. Ashmum & friend to come in at 9 a. m. tomorrow. A Lincoln." Mr. Emanuel Hertz, Lincoln collector, believes he has discovered a later writing in the form of a pardon to which Lincoln put his signature. This valuable document reads: "Let the prisoner be released on taking the oath of Dec. 8, 1863. A. Lincoln. April 14, 1865."

AT LINCOLN'S BEDSIDE

There have been many lists made of those present at the bedside of Abraham Lincoln during the final hours of his life, and various paintings have been attempted to portray the death scene with the distinguished guests present. While the following list may not include all of those who entered the chamber in the Peterson House, to which Lincoln was removed after the assassination, it gives the names of those generally mentioned. Mrs. Lincoln, and her son, Robert T. Lincoln, were in and out of the room many times during the night.

All of Mr. Lincoln's cabinet were present with the exception of Secretary Seward, who was also a victim of the same plot, and who was at that time in a dangerous condition at his own home. Stanton, Welles, Usher, McCullah, Speed and Dennison were all there.

The Generals present were: Halleck, Meigs, Farnsworth, Augur and Todd.

These physicians were in attendance: Barnes, Crane, Stone, Abbott, Hall, Gatch, Leiberman and Taft.

There were also several other officials and friends of President Lincoln there: Secretary Hay, Speaker Colfax, Rev. Dr. Gurley, Senator Sumner, Governor Oglesby, Ex-Governor Farwell, Assistant Secretary of the Treasury, Field, Judge Carter, Judge Otto, R. F. Andrews, and Justice Chase.

A Mr. Kenny and a Miss Kenny, as well as Miss Harris, were in an adjacent room most of the evening; and, possibly during the night they were admitted for a moment to the death chamber. Some writers have held that Vice-President Johnston was also present at one time; but, this fact is not generally accepted.

FIRST ANNOUNCEMENT OF LINCOLN'S DEATH

The first person to announce that Abraham Lincoln had been assassinated was Miss Clara Harris, daughter of Mr. Ira Harris, the New York Senator. She and Major Rathburn were guests of President and Mrs. Lincoln at Ford's Theatre on Friday evening, April 14, 1865. Two days later, she subscribed to an affidavit before A. B. Olin, Justice of the Supreme Court, in which she set forth her observations of the tragedy. She said that she heard the discharge of a pistol and turned about to see Major Rathburn spring from his seat and grapple with the intruder. The assassin broke away and leaped to the stage, as Major Rathburn shouted "stop that man." A moment later someone from the stage asked, what was the matter, or what is it, and Miss Harris replied: "The President is shot."

Fig. 3.71. Premiere issue of *Lincoln Lore.*

Francisco Bay area residents, aged 80 to 95, including former governor of California George C. Pardee. This club for those who "saw, heard, met, or knew Lincoln" was informally known as the "I knew Lincoln society." Membership reached 60.

1932 FEBRUARY 12. The Lincoln Museum is dedicated at Ford's Theatre, with the Oldroyd collection purchased by the U.S. earlier.

1932. Winfred Porter Truesdell, editor of the *Print Connoisseur*, publishes *Engraved and Lithographic Portraits of Abraham Lincoln*, which he projected as a multi-volume series. Unfortunately only Vol. 2 was published. At the time of his death, Truesdell also had on the table a project to compile and publish the photographs of general and president Ulysses S. Grant in a manner similar to Meserve's publication of Lincoln photographs. In three decades from 1902 on, he collected 98 photographs of Grant. Fortunately for collectors and historians, Truesdell's archives were purchased by historian Keya Morgan, who has spent more than a decade working on a monumental work titled "Grant in Photographs: Every Known Photograph," which at this writing is yet unpublished.

1932 FEBRUARY 12. The Lincoln Memorial Shrine is presented to the City of Redlands, California, by philanthropists Alma and Robert Watchorn. In addition to be a tribute to Lincoln, the memorial is dedicated to the memory of their son Emory Ewart, who had died from World War I injuries. Designed by architect Elmer Grey, the memorial houses George Grey Barnard's marble bust of Lincoln, murals by illustrator Dean Cornwell, letters, and thousands of items of Lincolniana.

1932. Dale Carnegie publishes *Lincoln the Unknown,* which remains in print in through several editions and often was autographed and presented by Carnegie to disciples of his self-improvement techniques.

1932 JUNE 2. Chicago Book & Art Auctions sells "Abraham Lincoln: The important collection of the late Henry M. Leland, Detroit MI." LeLand was the founder of Lincoln Motor Corp.

1932 SEPTEMBER 16. "Abraham Lincoln: The Hoosier Youth" (fig. 3.76). Paul Manship's heroic bronze statue is erected by Lincoln National Life Foundation, sponsored by The Lincoln National Life Insurance Company, Fort Wayne, Indiana. The statue is placed at the entrance plaza of the company.

1932 NOVEMBER. African-American voters abandon the "Party of Lincoln" and vote for Franklin D. Roosevelt, embracing his "New Deal" of social legislation.

1933 FEBRUARY. *Youth's Companion Combined With American Boy* publishes a classic illustration of Lincoln on a flatboat by Albin Henning, illustrator of numerous *Saturday Evening Post* covers and Western novels.

Fig. 3.72. Sculptor James Earle Fraser's love affair with Lincoln imagery spanned most of his productive, adult life. He is shown dwarfed by the plaster model for his contemplative, beardless Lincoln sitting on a rock. The statue was cast for Jersey City, erected along the Lincoln Highway, and dedicated on June 14, 1930.

Fig. 3.73. A 1930s Lincoln Highway 5¢ cigar label, which displays the route and connecting roads across the nation.

Fig. 3.74. Lincoln Memorial Celebration ticket, February 11, 1931.

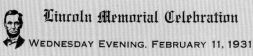

Lincoln Memorial Celebration
WEDNESDAY EVENING, FEBRUARY 11, 1931
ARSENAL
AT EIGHT O'CLOCK
RESERVED SEAT TICKET
RESERVED SEATS NOT OCCUPIED BY 8:00 P. M. WILL BE OPENED TO THE PUBLIC

1933 MARCH 11. First delivery of Series 1929 $5 Federal Reserve Bank Notes. Small-size Federal Reserve Bank Notes were issued in 1933 to pump more money into the Depression-ravaged U.S. economy.

1933 JUNE 1. Chicago's World's Fair, the "Century of Progress Industrial Exposition," has an impressive "Abraham Lincoln Exhibit Group" (fig. 3.79) next to a replica of Fort Dearborn. Included are replicas of Lincoln's birthplace cabin, Indiana cabin, New Salem store, Rutledge Tavern, and Chicago Wigwam. The host Illinois Building has a replica room from Lincoln's Springfield home and Lorado Taft's standing figure. Lincoln impersonator Lawrence Coghlan presented a show. A great many medals, bookmarks, banks, and even authenticated bits of rails split by Lincoln (fig. 3.80e) were sold as souvenirs.

1933 JULY 8. Rev. Dr. John Wesley Hill, Chancellor of the Lincoln Memorial University, presents a lecture "America Needs Today a Reincarnation of the Spirit and Principles of Lincoln." His address was reprinted in the "Congressional Record" January 26, 1934, by request of Hon. Kenneth McKellar of Tennessee.

1933 NOVEMBER 20. Lincoln impersonator Lincoln Caswell speaks at Gettysburg. The local paper says: "1863–1934, Seventy-one Years since the Gettysburg address, yet Abraham Lincoln speaks today!" Why the paper said "71" is not clear.[16]

Fig. 3.75. In 1932 Winfred Porter Truesdell published a monumental study of Lincoln images with a lovely original woodcut in five colors by Harry Cimino as the frontispiece.

Fig. 3.76. Sculptor Paul Manship is shown working on his *Hoosier Youth* for Lincoln National Life Insurance Co., dedicated in Fort Wayne, Indiana, on September 16, 1932.

LINCOLN TEA
Reg. U. S. Pat. Off.

Reg. U. S. Pat. Off.

ACTIVE INGREDIENTS
T. V. Senna leaves, Doggrass, Star Anise seed, Chamomile flowers, Licorice root, Fennel seed. Aniseed. Coriander seed.
Net Weight 2   oz. When Packed

LINCOLN PROPRIETARY COMPANY, FORT WAYNE, INDIANA
(Fort Wayne Drug Company, owners)

Fig. 3.77. Lincoln Proprietary Company, Fort Wayne, sold an herbal Lincoln Tea, circa 1930s.

Fig. 3.78. This "double Lincoln" small size Series 1929 $5 Lincoln National Bank of Lincoln, Illinois (Friedberg-S-2013) is a prize. The face die (BEP die no. NC13826) is credited to George L. Huber and Matthew D. Fenton.

Fig. 3.79. The 1933 Chicago World's Fair, "A Century of Progress International Exposition," included a lakefront "Lincoln Group" of structures. The German tourist who sent the postcard home said she had a good time seeing Lincoln's cabin.

Fig.3.80. (a) Shown is a replica of the Lincoln birthplace cabin at Chicago's Century of Progress International Expo. Souvenirs of CPIE included (b) this "Prosperity Coin" signed L.G. Cremona; two Lincoln cabin medals, (c) King-952 and (d) an unlisted type; and (e) a certified sliver of a rail originally split by Abe Lincoln, himself. Provenance documentation is enumerated and attested on the back of the plaque.

1934 JUNE 15. The City of Lincoln Park, Wayne County, Michigan, issues five month scrip with interest at five percent in denominations of $1, $5, and $10.

1934 DECEMBER 13. Lincoln impersonator Charles R. Miles (fig. 3.83) greets Christmas shoppers in Los Angeles following a highly successful tour of the Midwest giving presentations to schools and patriotic societies.

1935 FEBRUARY 12. The Abraham Lincoln Memorial Garden, Springfield, Illinois, opens, sponsored by the Garden Club of Illinois. This memorial was the brainchild of local civic leader Harriet Knudson. The goal was to set aside in Lincoln's memory a preserve of native plants that would have been familiar to Lincoln growing up in the Midwest. The city leased the land to the Lincoln Memorial Garden in perpetuity. Designs were furnished by Jens Jensen, and native trees, shrubs, and wildflowers were planted beginning the following year. The site was dedicated in 1939, financed in part by the family of drugstore magnate Charles Walgreen.

1936. American volunteers in the International Brigade fighting in the Spanish Civil War begin to organize near the French frontier in 1936. The Abraham Lincoln Brigade (one of two predominantly U.S. volunteer units; the other was the Washington Battalion) was formed in 1937. The recruits fought for the Spanish Republican forces against Gen. Francisco Franco's Nationalists. Many ALB volunteers were members of the Communist Party USA, or other left-leaning groups. The ALB swelled to about 450 soldiers and officers, but its record was undistinguished. Hundreds of U.S. nationals were killed during the war from 1936 to 1939. U.S. authorities considered some members to be communists, and handed down indictments.

1936 FEBRUARY 12. A Lincoln exhibition opens at the four-star Hotel Lincoln in New York City by Rufus Rockwell Wilson. Titled "The Life and Time of Abraham Lincoln," the historical and artistic display was mounted for the benefit of the Madison Square Boys' Club.

Fig. 3.81. A Lincoln portrait at the front of the 1930s schoolroom inspired the student's oration in this Emmett Watson illustration.

Fig. 3.82. During the Great Depression, scrip circulated in localized areas to stimulate commerce; several types issued in 1933 picture Lincoln: *(a)* Astor Auction scrip, Greenblatt's Market Grocery, 1S (unlisted); *(b)* Delaware Clearing House, no denomination proof (Shafer DE101); *(c)* Lewisburg (Ohio) Grain Elevators $5 (Shafer OH512-5); *(d)* Associated Merchants, Salt Lake City, Utah, $1 (Shafer UT170-1); and *(e)* Tenino (Washington) Chamber of Commerce 25¢ (Shafer WA410-25). The last piece is made of wood.

1936. The Works Progress Administration Illinois Arts Project presents the play *Abraham Lincoln.*

1936 OCTOBER 13. Lorado Taft's bronze monument to Lincoln and Douglas at Quincy, Illinois, is dedicated in Washington Park commemorating the debate between Abraham Lincoln and Stephen A. Douglas there on October 13, 1858.

1936. Lincoln scholar James G. Randall asks in an essay, "Is the Lincoln Theme Exhausted?" and concludes that it is not yet exhausted. [17]

1937 MARCH. University of Pennsylvania alumni launch a campaign to "promote" Lincoln from the cent to the nickel, according to an article in *The Numismatist.*

1937 JUNE 20. A ten-day Lincoln pilgrimage led by Dr. Louis A. Warren commemorates the 300th anniversary of the Lincoln family's landing in America. The tour is sponsored by the Filson Club, Louisville, Kentucky.

1937 SEPTEMBER 17. Lincoln's 60-foot tall head is dedicated on the 150th anniversary of the adoption of the U.S. Constitution at Mt. Rushmore National Memorial, "The Shrine of Democracy," in the Black Hills, South Dakota (fig. 3.89c). Five thousand attend.

1937 OCTOBER 10–12. Cuba issues the first foreign stamp bearing a likeness of Abraham Lincoln (fig. 3.90). The stamp is sold for only three days to benefit the Association of American Writers and Artists. During these three days no other stamps were sold in Cuba.

1937 DECEMBER 22. The Lincoln Tunnel is dedicated, connecting Manhattan with Weehawken, New Jersey, at a cost of $75 million (fig. 3.91).

1938 FEBRUARY. Lincoln Memorial University's quarterly the *Mountain Herald,* edited by Dr. Robert L. Kincaid, is rechristened the *Lincoln Herald* with its February issue.

1938 FEBRUARY 12. "Golden boy of American illustration" Joseph Christian Leyendecker creates a "Bronze Lincoln" for the *Saturday Evening Post.* Leyendecker did 138 *SEP* covers in all. This cover was reprised for its February 1976 issue.

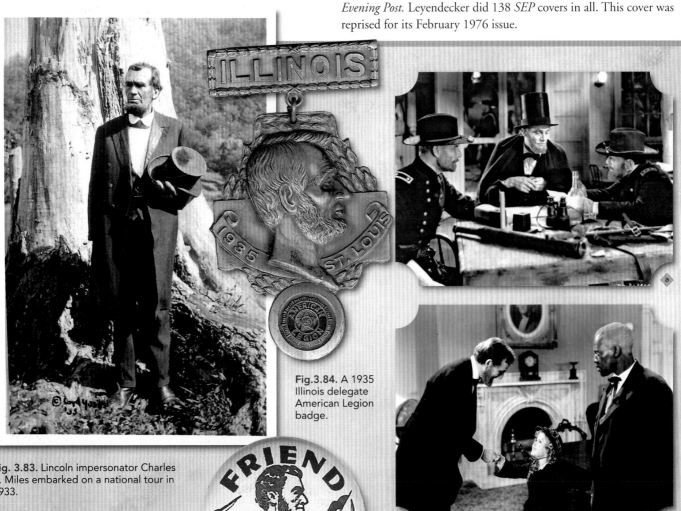

Fig.3.84. A 1935 Illinois delegate American Legion badge.

Fig. 3.83. Lincoln impersonator Charles R. Miles embarked on a national tour in 1933.

Fig. 3.85. American volunteers in the International Brigade fighting in the Spanish Civil War organized near the French frontier in 1936. The Abraham Lincoln was one of two principal units. The other was named for George Washington.

Fig. 3.86. Lincoln lit up the silver screen in the 1930s: (a) Lincoln (Walter Huston) strategizing with General Grant (Fred Warren) in D.W. Griffith's *Abraham Lincoln;* (b) Lincoln (Frank McGlynn Sr.) greets Virgie Cary (Shirley Temple) and Uncle Billy (Bill Bojangles Robinson) in *The Littlest Rebel,* 20th Century Fox, 1935.

1938. Robert E. Sherwood's *Abe Lincoln in Illinois* wins the Pulitzer Prize for Drama. Sherwood came by his historical inquisitiveness naturally. He was the grandson of a Civil War vet, numismatist, and antiquarian Thomas Addis Emmet (the younger, born 1828) who published the first catalog of Confederate currency in the *American Journal of Numismatics* two years to the day (May 1, 1865) that the last active trading date for Confederate notes had cast the exchange rate at 1,200 to 1.

1938. Massachusetts continues to observe Lincoln's birthday as a holiday by annual proclamations of its successive governors. Other state legislators acted to the same ends. By 1938 Lincoln's birthday was state holidays in 28 states: California, Colorado, Connecticut, Delaware, Illinois, Indiana, Iowa, Kansas, Kentucky, Massachusetts, Michigan, Minnesota, Missouri, Montana, Nebraska, New Jersey, New York, New Mexico, North Dakota, Ohio, Oregon, Pennsylvania, South Dakota, Tennessee, Utah, Washington, West Virginia, and Wyoming, as well as the territory of Alaska, and a federal holiday in the District of Columbia.

1938 APRIL 7. The Republic of San Marino issues a three-lire stamp commemorating the dedication of a bust of Lincoln by Raymond Barger the previous September 3, 1937.

1938 OCTOBER 20. A Lincoln 16-cent stamp (fig. 3.93a) is issued in the Presidential Series (Scott 821), which depicted U.S. presidents in the order of their terms of office on a series of graduated denominations, as well as Ben Franklin and Martha Washington. The designer was William Schrage, and the engraver was C.T. Arlt. The model was an 1862 marble bust of Lincoln by Sarah Ames Fisher in the Senate Wing of the U.S. Capitol. Sixteen cents was the airmail special delivery rate.

Fig. 3.87. Anarchist artist Jules Arceneaux also had a penchant for Abraham Lincoln. This circa 1930 ceramic is only one of his excellent depictions of Old Abe.

Fig. 3.88. (a) A 1936 Union Party Charter Membership certificate shows a Marshall-style Lincoln, no imprint. (b) That same year a United Republican Committee standee featured an American Bank Note Co. Litho image from its 1861 original design.

Fig. 3.89. (a) Mount Rushmore sculptor Gutzon Borglum was so enamored with Lincoln that he named his son Lincoln Borglum. Here he posed circa 1930s with a beardless Lincoln study for the great monument in the South Dakota's Black Hills. (b) Mt. Rushmore was still under construction in this circa 1936 stereoview. Note the scaffolding around the Roosevelt head. (c) A closeup of the Lincoln head reveals Borglum's desire to depict Abe in the process of emerging from the granite mountain.

1938. Nellie Verne Walker's bronze and limestone Lincoln Trail State Memorial to mark the location where, according to tradition, Abraham Lincoln entered Illinois with his family in March 1830 is dedicated. The frieze depicts three adults, two children, and an ox-pulled wagon guided by an angel.

1938. Ralph G. Newman renames his Chicago bookstore the Abraham Lincoln Book Shop (it opened in 1933 as Home of Books). This shop was frequented by Carl Sandburg and other notables.

1939. *Saturday Review* editor George Cooper Stevens considers whether best-sellers are born or made with publication of *Lincoln's Doctor's Dog* in several editions by G. Allen & Unwin and J.B. Lippincott Co.

1939 June 9. John Ford's *Young Mr. Lincoln* with Henry Fonda

in the role of the Illinois lawyer is released. Lamar Trotti's screenplay is nominated for an Academy Award. *Photoplay* editor Max J. Herzberg writes a guide to the film for school children titled *Abe Lincoln Grows Up,* which is recommended for secondary schools by the National Education Association.

1939. R.L. Parkinson issues "Lincoln: A Story in Poster Stamps."

1939 April 9. On Easter Sunday, African-American opera singer Marian Anderson performs an open-air concert at the Lincoln Memorial. Earlier Ms. Anderson had been barred from performing a concert at Constitution Hall by the Daughters of the American Revolution because she was Black; First Lady Eleanor Roosevelt resigned from the DAR over the flap. The concert at the Lincoln Memorial was sanctioned by President Franklin Roosevelt and Interior Secretary Harold Ickes. More than 75,000 people thronged to the free concert.

Fig. 3.90. In October 1937, Cuba issued a set of stamps honoring American writers and artists. The 8¢ value (Scott 350) depicts Lincoln.

Fig. 3.91. Julio Kileny's 1937 medal marking the opening of the Lincoln Tunnel between Manhattan and New Jersey.

Fig. 3.92. Supporters of the Abraham Lincoln Brigade marched in front of the Lincoln Memorial on Lincoln's birthday, February 12, 1938.

Fig. 3.93. (a) On October 20, 1938, the U.S. Post Office added a 16-cent stamp honoring Lincoln (Scott 821) to its presidential series. The Lincoln vignette was engraved by Carl T. Arlt, modeled on the bust by Sarah Fisher Ames.

(b) The BEP prepared this unadopted essay (Hessler-UE26) for a $5 note back with G.F.C. Smillie's engraving after the F.B. Carpenter–A.H. Ritchie *First Reading of the Emancipation Proclamation* design in the circa 1930s.

1939 APRIL 22. J. Henri Ripstra issues an aluminum Lincoln token for the first Central States Numismatic Society convention in Chicago using an original 1864 campaign token die and an original commemorative reverse engraved by him (fig. 3.96). That same day *Numismatic Scrapbook* issues wooden Lincoln cent flats. Ripstra was founder of the Lincoln Group of Chicago, and president of the American Numismatic Association.

1939 APRIL 30. The New York World's Fair opens, including a display of the steam locomotive operated by the New York Central and Hudson River Railroad that carried Lincoln to his inauguration in Washington, D.C.

1939. Carl Sandburg's four-volume *Abraham Lincoln: The War Years* is published, earning him the Pulitzer Prize in 1940.

1939 OCTOBER 19. A climactic scene in Frank Capra's wonderful film *Mr. Smith Goes to Washington* shows Congressman Jefferson Smith, played by James Stewart, consulting with Lincoln in the Lincoln Memorial in search of inspiration for his actions. The film concerns an idealistic if naïve political appointee who finds the going rough in the hardball political environment of Washington, D.C.

1939. President Franklin Delano Roosevelt accepts the donation of G.P.A. Healy's portrait of Lincoln for the White House. Roosevelt hangs it above the fireplace in the state dining room, where it remains to this day. During Theodore Roosevelt's time, a large moose head had hung there. F.D.R. had a quotation from John Adams, the White House's first chief resident, inscribed on the mantel beneath Lincoln's portrait: "I pray to Heaven," Adams had written, "to bestow the best of blessings on this house and on all that shall hereafter inhabit it. May none but honest and wise men ever rule under this roof." The state dining room is the larger of two dining rooms on the first (State) floor. It seats about 130 to 140 for state occasions. During the Kennedy presidency, conspicuous damage to the Healy Lincoln painting was restored.

Fig. 3.95. American-born contralto Marian Anderson performs at her famous 1939 Easter Sunday concert.

Fig. 3.94. In 1939 a Post cereal box had this premium commemorating the purported 100th anniversary of the invention of baseball by Abner Doubleday, a thesis now thoroughly discredited, but the box panel reported A.G. Spaulding's account of Lincoln's connection to the game, a highlight in baseball's history.

The obverse die of this token was used in 1864 to strike political tokens for Abraham Lincoln's second presidential campaign.

A souvenir of the Central States Numismatic Conference Chicago, April 22-23, 1939

Fig. 3.96. J. Henri Ripstra acquired the original 1864 Lincoln campaign medal die and restruck a commemorative in 1939.

Fig. 3.97. Raymond Massey appeared on Broadway as Abe Lincoln, and on the cover of the October 31, 1938, issue of *Life* magazine.

1940 JANUARY 28. Dr. Stewart W. McClelland delivers the sermon "Lincoln, the National Messiah" on the 50th anniversary of Lincoln Memorial University, Harrogate, Tennessee.

1940 FEBRUARY 12. A black-and-white film (in the era of *Gone With the Wind* Technicolor), *Abe Lincoln in Illinois* with Raymond Massey, based on the play by Robert E. Sherwood, is released. Massey, who had played the part on Broadway (fig. 3.97) is nominated for an Academy Award for best actor, but he's in fast company. Also nominated are Henry Fonda for *The Grapes of Wrath,* Charlie Chaplin for *The Great Dictator,* Laurence Olivier for Best Picture–winner *Rebecca,* and Jimmy Stewart, the ultimate winner, for *The Philadelphia Story.* Cinematographer James Wong Howe is also nominated for an Oscar, but again, Hitchcock's *Rebecca* takes the statuette.

1940 CIRCA. R. Walters publishes *The Lincoln National Memorial Trail and Shrines,* depicting the route the Lincoln family traveled and the Lincoln National Memorial Trail.

1940. Cooper Union institutes an annual Abraham Lincoln lecture series "Lincoln, Living Legend."

1940. *Abraham Lincoln Quarterly* is established.

1940 OCTOBER 20. A three-cent stamp marking the 75th anniversary of the adoption of the 13th Amendment to the U.S. Constitution (Scott 902) was issued October 20, 1940, at World's Fair Station at the New York World's Fair (fig. 3.100). William Roach designed it and C.T. Arlt was the engraver; 44,389,550 were issued.

1941 FEBRUARY. The *Instructor* magazine's cover features a reproduction of one of Douglas Volk's Lincoln paintings.

1942. Once again in wartime, the incumbent president F.D.R. claims the wartime legacy of Lincoln. Lincoln scholar Merrill Peterson said that F.D.R. "recognized the symbolic value of Lincoln in America and often spoke of Lincoln and manipulated the Lincoln symbol in American politics" in an interview with Brian Lamb, on C-SPAN's *Booknotes,* August 14, 1994.

1942. America is at war with the Axis Powers, and the U.S. needs funds for men and matériel. Some War Bonds carry Lincoln's image.

Fig. 3.98. Lincoln stories remained popular in Hollywood film fare. (a) Lincoln (John Carradine) listens to a soldier (Jimmy Stewart) in *Of Human Hearts,* Metro-Goldwyn-Mayer, which opened for Lincoln's birthday on February 11, 1938. If you haven't seen it you can catch the Stewart-Carradine dialog on YouTube. (b) Elsa Maxwell attends a Lincoln impersonator party with Ralph Bellamy and George Murphy (also note the sea of Lincolns in the background) in *Public Deb No. 1,* 20th Century Fox, 1940.

Fig. 3.99. 1940 Republican National Committee appointment by E.A. Wright Bank Note Co., Philadelphia.

The Treasury Department also issues an exciting War Bonds poster with a beardless Lincoln portrait by illustrator Boardman Robinson (fig. 3.103). Robinson was widely acclaimed for his World War I posters, and he originally created this Lincoln image in 1919. He signed it "BR19," which confuses those who think the poster was done by "B Rig." Robinson's vigorous Lincoln also appeared on the cover of the February 10, 1921, *Mid-Week Pictorial* special, "Lincoln Number."

1942 FEBRUARY 23. Cuba issues a three-cent, orange and brown stamp in its "Spirit of Democracy Series," (fig. 3.104) showing presidents Lincoln (U.S.), Maceo (Cuba), Bolivar (Columbia), and Juarez (Mexico).

1942 MAY. Library of Congress reprints "Lincoln Collections in the Library of Congress" from the December 1941 issue of *Abraham Lincoln Quarterly* as a pamphlet. They have reprinted it several times since.

1942 MAY 14. Aaron Copland's composition, *Abraham Lincoln Portrait,* debuts by the Cincinnati Symphony Orchestra.

1942 JUNE 8. Series 1934 $5 Federal Reserve Notes with HAWAII overprint are first delivered.

1942 JULY 7. In solidarity with a Free China, the U.S. issues a stamp marking the fifth anniversary of its fight against Japanese aggression. Sun Yat-Sen and Abraham Lincoln appear on the five-cent commemorative (Scott 906) with Lincoln's quote on democracy "Of the People, By the People, For the People," joint portraits, and map of China. The first day of issue was in Denver, Colorado. The stamp was designed by William Roach, and engraved by L.C. Kaufmann; 21,272,800 were issued (fig. 3.105a).

1942. The Civil War Round Table movement grows out of the first group meetings at the Abraham Lincoln Book Shop in Chicago. In summer 2008, that group held its 672nd meeting. In 1974 the Chicago CWRT instituted the Alan Nevins–Douglas Southall Freeman Award, named after two famous Civil War historians, for those furthering the movement.

Fig. 3.100. The U.S. Post Office commemorated the 75th anniversary of the 13th Amendment to the Constitution abolishing slavery with a three-cent commemorative stamp (Scott 902), issued October 20, 1940. The stamp depicts Thomas Ball's Emancipation group engraved by Carl T. Arlt.

Fig. 3.101. A patriotic cover for Lincoln's birthday on *Liberty* magazine, February 15, 1941.

Fig. 3.102. A World War II Railsplitter 84th Division Army patch.

1942 SEPTEMBER 4. Series 1934A $5 Silver Certificates for North Africa are first delivered.

1943 FEBRUARY 12. On Lincoln's birthday the BEP conducts a special press run of 1,000 twelve-subject sheets of Lincoln $5 Series 1935A HAWAII and Yellow Seal emergency notes for sale at face value to the public through the Treasury Department Cash Room. This work was authorized to be printed in this manner by Mr. G. Duncan, according to paper-money expert Peter Huntoon.

1942. In concert with the U.S. "V for Victory" postage stamp, Lincoln cents are privately overstruck with "V" for victory and a fastener attached to be worn as a pin (fig. 3.106).

1942 DECEMBER 23. The secretary of the Treasury sets the weight of a wartime steel Lincoln cent at 41.5 grains (later increased to 42.5 grains).

1943 FEBRUARY 12. Production of steel Lincoln cents begins at the Philadelphia Mint.

1943. Edward B. Marks Music Corp., Radio City, New York publishes "The Lincoln Penny" song, with words by Alfred Kreymborg and music by Elie Seigmeister, which includes the lyrics "Now when you see a penny, look at Lincoln's face! See how round and round again, Lincoln saved the race! Look at that small penny. Hold it close to you—And if you ever lose your way, Abe will lead you thru, Yes, Abe will come along with you." The poem first appeared in *Collier's* February 1942.

1943. The first volume of James Jay Monaghan's (ed.) Lincoln bibliography is printed; in 1945 the second volume was completed "and both were released" (Thomas Schwartz). Monaghan listed nearly 4,000 Lincoln works. Although not a definitive bibliography, this work became a handy check list for collectors and book sellers.

1944. Carl Sandburg and Frederick Hill Meserve publish *The Photographs of Abraham Lincoln.* Meserve had collected Lincoln photos since the early 1900s, and in 1917 privately published a book on the subject which sought to list every known Lincoln camera image.

Fig. 3.104. Cuba repeatedly honored Abraham Lincoln on its stamps. "Democracy in Americas" (Scott 369) was issued February 23, 1942.

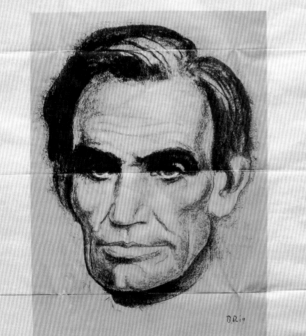

Fig. 3.103. Boardman Robinson's splendid 1919 beardless Lincoln portrait graced a 1943 Buy War Bonds poster.

Fig. 3.105. (a) The U.S. Post Office issued a United States–China commemorative stamp (Scott 906) on July 7, 1942, to show solidarity with the Nationalist Chinese struggle against Japanese aggression (BEP die no. P01125). The Lincoln portrait was engraved by L.C. Kaufmann. (b) On November 19, 1948, the Post Office issued a stamp marking the 85th anniversary of the Gettysburg Address (Scott 978). Lincoln was engraved by R.M. Bower.

1945. Harry and Bess Truman move a bed and furniture into Lincoln's old office, which since the construction of the West Wing had largely served as a presidential study, thereby creating the Lincoln bedroom. The Lincoln bedroom is one of a suite of three rooms (the others being the Lincoln sitting room and the Lincoln bathroom) on the second floor of the White House that had served as Abraham Lincoln's office during his presidency. What is now the Lincoln sitting room was secretary John Hay's office during the war. The cabinet met in Lincoln's office, and it was there that he first informed them of his intention to emancipate the slaves if the rebellious districts did not lay down their arms of insurrection. This suite of rooms has been remodeled several times. Lincoln never slept there.

1946 NOVEMBER 19. Congress's joint resolution designates November 19, 1946, "The Anniversary of Lincoln's Gettysburg Address, As Dedication Day."

1947 MAY 3. The Republic of San Marino marks the death of Franklin Roosevelt with an issue of one-lire and 50-lire stamps with F.D.R.'s reference to Lincoln's laudatory message to the country in 1861.

1947 JULY 26. The Lincoln papers (approximately 20,000 items) at the Library of Congress are released for public inspection. Items include Lincoln's drafts of his Emancipation Proclamation and second inaugural address.

1947 DECEMBER 24. The Republic of San Marino issues a series of stamps showing the historic U.S. stamps, including the Lincoln 90-cent issue of 1869.

1948. Illinois governor and future Democratic presidential candidate Adlai Stevenson embraces Lincoln. Stevenson's great-grandfather was Jesse Fell, a founder of the Republican party and Lincoln's campaign manager in his 1858 senatorial campaign. Stevenson is one of the distinguished Americans who narrated Aaron Copland's *Lincoln Portrait* in 1964.

1948 FEBRUARY 12. The Abraham Lincoln Friendship Train gathers farm produce for European relief in areas ravaged by the World War. It starts out from Lincoln, Nebraska, and crosses Iowa and Illinois en route to the Eastern seaboard. Along the way it stops at agricultural communities where individuals, companies, and school and other groups contribute cash and commodities. Donors could designate recipient organizations. Other friendship trains originated across the United States.

1948 FEBRUARY 14. *Collier's* magazine displays *Lincoln Sitting for Mathew Brady* by C.C. Beall, a fabulous illustrator and painter who did everything from the famous war bond poster showing Marines raising the flag at Iwo Jima to *MAD* magazine covers, and several excellent Lincoln historical paeans as well, including the *Collier's* cover of February 17, 1945.

1948 NOVEMBER 19. A three-cent stamp marking the 85th anniversary of Lincoln's Gettysburg Address (Scott 978) is issued at Gettysburg, Pennsylvania. The designer was C.R. Chickering, and the engraver was R.M. Bower; 63,388,000 were issued (fig. 3.105b).

1949 SEPTEMBER. *Fate* magazine's cover story asks whether Abe Lincoln was a "mystic."

1949. The Separatist Republic of Indonesia issues a 40-sen stamp with a portrait of Lincoln and Vice President Hatta.

1950 CIRCA. The Lincoln Heritage Trail, a route of 2,200 miles of interconnecting roads in Kentucky, Indiana, and Illinois, marks places that were significant in the life of Abraham Lincoln.

1950 FEBRUARY 12. *Philco Television Playhouse* airs "Ann Rutledge," starring Stephen Courtleigh as Lincoln and the future princess of Monaco, Grace Kelly, in the title role.

1951. The Lincoln Room at the University of Illinois, Urbana-Champaign, is founded with the donation of a large collection of books from Lincoln scholars Harlan Hoyt Horner and Henrietta Calhoun Horner. The donation marks the 50th anniversary of the Horners' 1901 matriculation. In 2001, 50 years later, the Lincoln Room merged with the school's Illinois Historical Survey. Harlan Horner was the author of *Lincoln and Greeley,* University of Illinois Press, 1953.

1951–1954. To call attention to the Cold War isolation of Berlin within the Communist bloc, West Germany issues a series of five stamps depicting the Freedom Bell in Berlin. On the rim of the bell is the phrase "a new birth of freedom" from Lincoln's Gettysburg Address. Successive issues show the bell clapper in varying positions as if it were actually pealing.

1951. The Illinois State Federation of Labor convention badge proclaims, "Labor Reveres Abraham Lincoln." There was a lot to like about Lincoln's employment record, which included stints as woodsman, flatboatsman, soldier, clerk, merchant, postmaster, lawyer, congressman, and president (fig. 3.107).

1952 AUGUST 11. A three-cent Mount Rushmore commemorative stamp (Scott 1011) is issued in Keystone, South Dakota. The designer was V.S. McCloskey Jr., and the engraver was M.D. Fenton; 116,255,000 were issued.

1952. Buffalo nickel designer, sculptor, and medalist James Earle Fraser designs prototypes for a proposed new Lincoln cent (fig. 3.108).

1953 JANUARY. The orchestral suite *Lincoln Portrait* by Aaron Copland is withdrawn from the Eisenhower inaugural celebration because of protests.

1953. The Abraham Lincoln Association publishes *The Collected Works of Abraham Lincoln,* including correspondence, speeches, and other writings.

Fig. 3.106. This 1942 Lincoln cent was embossed "V" for Victory and a pin mounted to its reverse to be worn as a badge during World War II.

Fig. 3.107. A 1951 Illinois State Federation of Labor delegate's badge, "Labor Reveres Abraham Lincoln." There was a lot for a laborer to admire about the rail-splitter.

Fig. 3.108. In anticipation of Lincoln's sesquicentennial in 1959, sculptor James Earle Fraser created this elegant cent design in 1952. It was one of his last accomplishments, as he unfortunately died the next year without seeing his vision come to fruition. Compare this design to new designs we will see in circulation if you dare!

Fig. 3.109. E.A. Wright Bank Note Co., Philadelphia, printed this 1952 Republican National Convention ticket.

Fig. 3.110. The Gulf, Mobile, and Ohio Railroad streamliner "Abraham Lincoln," circa 1950.

Fig. 3.111. Lincoln National Bank, Lincoln, Pennsylvania, stock certificate specimen by Security Bank Note Co. employs a likeness of the Marshall engraving.

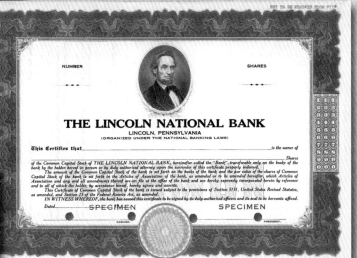

Fig. 3.112. Lincoln Lager Beer label, Merrill, Wisconsin, of indeterminate vintage.

Fig. 3.113.
(a) Lincoln Root Beer was popular in the 1950s.
(b) Lincoln Bank Bottle caps topped a variety of figural bottles that contained various flavors of punch and milkshake flavorings.

1953 AUGUST 29. The Lincoln, Illinois, centennial celebration begins, and is commemorated on a wooden nickel flat celebrating a "Century of Progress" (see fig. 1.27).

1953 NOVEMBER 29. Walter Cronkite hosts a *You Are There* episode titled "The Gettysburg Address."

1954. The Republican Party celebrates its centennial. Incumbent president Dwight D. Eisenhower and first GOP president Abe Lincoln share a commemorative medal, a Civil Rights brochure, and bronze centennial pins created for the occasion.

1954. During the year President Eisenhower, a recreational artist, paints a portrait of his White House predecessor, Abraham Lincoln. The portrait is used on his personal Christmas cards and reproduced on the cover of the *Chicago Sunday Times* magazine of February 9, 1958.

1954. *Collier's* reports the discovery of Alexander Hesler's Abraham Lincoln copy negatives. The cracked originals, which were damaged in the mail, are in the Smithsonian Institution.

1954 NOVEMBER 19. The Lincoln four-cent purple definitive stamp (Scott 1036) is issued as part of the Post Office's "Liberty Issue," which commemorates patriots and patriotic landmarks (fig. 3.115a). The stamp is issued in New York City. The designer was C.R. Chickering, and the engraver was R.M. Bower. The portrait was based on a painting by Douglas Volk in the National Gallery of Art, Washington, D.C.

1955. The Illinois General Assembly officially adopts the state slogan "Land of Lincoln." The U.S. Congress passes an act giving the state exclusive use of that slogan.

1955. Both *Guns Magazine* (April) and *Great Guns* magazine (July) feature cover stories about guns that killed U.S. presidents, including an illustration of the Booth derringer.

1955 APRIL 25. A Cuban stamp celebrates the Plaza de Fraternidad and the Lincoln monument there.

1955 DECEMBER 14. *Screen Director's Playhouse* airs the telefilm "Lincoln's Doctor's Dog," with Robert Ryan as Lincoln and Charles Bickford as Doc Stone, who gives a glum president a puppy to cheer him up during the dark days of the Civil War (fig. 3.117).

Fig. 3.114. U.S. Mint Chief Engraver Gilroy Roberts created the 1954 Republican Centennial medal with its conjoined portraits of Lincoln and Dwight D. Eisenhower. The reverse has quotations from Lincoln's second inaugural, and Eisenhower's speech summarizing Lincoln's philosophy at Lincoln Day, February 5, 1954. The medal was struck by Medallic Art Co.

Fig. 3.115. (a) The Lincoln four-cent postage stamp (Scott 1036) was issued on November 19, 1954. Lincoln's portrait was engraved by R.M. Bower based on the Douglas Volk painting (BEP die MISC16099). (b) The August 27, 1958, commemorative stamp (Scott 1115) honored the Lincoln–Douglas debates. The vignette was engraved by C.A. Brooks based on a painting by Joseph Boggs Hale.

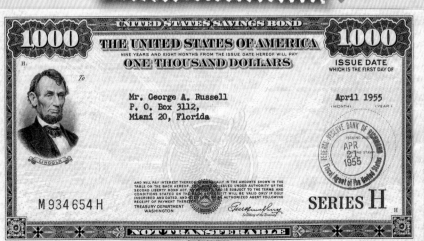

Fig. 3.116. Charles Burt's Lincoln portrait graced $1,000 Series H U.S. Savings Bonds from 1935. This bond was issued in 1955.

1956 APRIL 3. Monaco issues a three-franc stamp designed by Gaudan based on an Alexander Hesler photo to honor the Fifth International Philatelic Exhibition (FIPEX) in New York City.

1957 FEBRUARY 16. The *Saturday Evening Post* publishes an article on "The Lincoln Cult."

1957 FEBRUARY. Cuban president Fulgencio Batista, an ardent admirer of Lincoln, displays his Saint-Gaudens statue of Lincoln at Batista Library, Havana, to foreign press.

1958 JANUARY. *Classics Illustrated* issues a biographical number on Abraham Lincoln, showing a strapping youth squaring off in a wrestling match with Jack Armstrong. The issue is republished in various languages, including Greek.

1958. The centennial of the Lincoln-Douglas debates is marked by two bas-relief bronze plaques sculpted by Avard T. Fairbanks, which are installed at the Knox College Old Main building. The college was the site of the fifth Lincoln-Douglas debate.

1958 AUGUST 27. A four-cent Lincoln-Douglas debate centenary stamp (Scott 1115) has its first day of issue at Freeport, Illinois (see fig. 3.115b). Its designer was Ervine Metzl; its engraver, M.D. Fenton. In total, 114,860,200 were issued.

1958 NOVEMBER 6. Commission of Fine Arts (CFA) secretary L.R. Wilson forwards a design sketch for a new Lincoln Memorial cent reverse to commission members.

1958 NOVEMBER 12. CFA member Felix de Weldon complains that the Mint's proposed Lincoln Memorial cent design is too wordy and crowded.

1958 NOVEMBER 18. The CFA reviews the Mint-approved sketch by Frank Gasparro for the new Lincoln Memorial cent reverse.

1958 DECEMBER 8. CFA secretary L.R. Wilson reports to Mint director William Brett the commission's recommendation to simplify the proposed Lincoln Memorial cent design by removing the stars from the field and the name of the memorial.

1958 DECEMBER 20. President Eisenhower approves and announces the design change to the Lincoln Memorial cent reverse from the wheat ears reverse.

Fig. 3.117. A spate of films and TV programs touched on Lincoln in the mid-1950s: *(a)* Stanley Hall in *Prince of Players*, 20th Century Fox, 1955; *(b)* Mark Stevens in *Schlitz Playhouse of Stars* episode "Washington Incident," 1956; *(c)* Robert Ryan in *Screen Director's Playhouse* episode "Lincoln's Doctor's Dog," 1955; and *(d)* Richard Gaines in *TV Reader's Digest* episode "How Chance Made Lincoln President," 1955.

Chapter 4

Lincoln the Icon

1959-2009

I mages and representations of Lincoln have come to signify many things, including integrity, honesty, good value, sobriety, character, and thrift. Branding via icons seeks to appropriate an image for secondary purposes. Lincoln's venerated image has currency, as they say. This is not a new phenomenon. In Lincoln's own time, a city in Illinois claimed his name. Within weeks of his death another in Argentina did the same. Shortly thereafter Lincoln, Nebraska, became the capitol of that Western precinct. Lincoln's picture and identity were plastered on tobacco, paint, pens, and other commodities at a very early date. Lincoln understood this grafting phenomenon well. "Character is like a tree and reputation like its shadow," he wrote. "The shadow is what we think of it; the tree is the real thing."

Lincoln Memorial and Capitol Mall, Washington, D.C., August 28, 1963: "I have a dream . . ." *(a)* Martin Luther King's view, *(b)* Abraham Lincoln's view, and *(c)* God's view. This is arguably the most important date in the history of the Lincoln Memorial since its dedication in 1922.

A measure of the greatness of Lincoln's image is that it seems everyone wants a piece of his shadow. It's not just Republicans. Politicians of all stripes claim his legacy. Barack Obama is only the most recent Democrat to wrap himself in Lincoln's coattails. John Kerry, George McGovern, Mario Cuomo, Franklin D. Roosevelt, Woodrow Wilson, and others found Lincoln's progressive social message to their liking, and attempted to co-opt his favorable standing with the American public. The same is true of causes as divergent as the East is from the West, all seeking his anointing.

Advertising might be termed the artistic application of marketing science. To work successfully, it must strike a resonant chord in the viewing public. Americans are thoroughly inculcated with the universal image of Abraham Lincoln, his biography and character. The Lincoln icon is thus a shorthand symbol that advertisers can employ to quickly suppress viewer resistance and close a sale. Soda pop, beer, whiskey, football fields, playthings, autos, tombstones, thrift institutions, and comic books have all been christened with his brand. In becoming all things to all people, alas, Lincoln's salt has lost a good deal of its flavor.

The Lincoln cent was modernized for his birth sesquicentennial. Frank Gasparro's Lincoln Memorial design has served the Lincoln brand well for half a century now. Appropriately, introduction of the new cent brought Lincoln representations to both the obverse and reverse of the coin, which they had enjoyed on the $5 bill for several decades. But even in his memorial, Lincoln is not always the featured attraction. Crowds don't arrive at his temple solely to worship. The real action is often outside in the courtyard. The memorial stoop has become the country's front porch, where activity is directed not inward to the sanctum but outward toward the front lawn. No better symbol of this change in orientation could be offered than the drama that played out on August 28, 1963, arguably the second most important day in the Lincoln Memorial's existence since its dedication in 1922. Lincoln, the world, and the universe were merely witnesses to the human events of that day. In the years since, myriad protests and demonstrations have followed this pattern and unfolded at Lincoln's feet.

Although many still admire Lincoln, and he continuously ranks at or near the top of every poll of "best" or "most admired" U.S. presidents, he increasingly has become trivialized in the past half century. This dumbing-down of Lincoln has become a staple of pop culture. Dressed in drag, portrayed as a sex-craved buffoon on TV, or characterized as a melancholic insomniac in advertisements—such depictions are significantly divorced from Lincoln's prior idealized and idolized persona. During this period books by Lincoln detractors have also proliferated. Lincoln, originally the man of the people, was put on a pedestal only to be pulled off it and become commonplace once again.

In a less drastic way, this more irreverent approach to Lincoln is also evident on our paper money. Engraver Tom Hipschen's new "next generation" Lincoln portrait, which replaced the old $5 image, "reveals Lincoln with just a faint suggestion of merriment in his sparkling eyes, as though a smile were about to ignite his mask-like features." That's the description of the photographic model on which Hipschen based his image, according to Lincoln scholar Lloyd Ostendorf. Hipschen is one of the young lions of the Bureau of Engraving and Printing (BEP). The portrait is also more prominent, 180 percent as large as the old design. It offers a vibrant and exciting glimpse into the man many Americans feel was the greatest to hold the nation's highest office. This "twinkle-eyed" depiction offers up a Lincoln more like the man his contemporaries knew. The man with the weight of the world on his shoulders had his wry side, too. Its use is something of a déjà vu: this is the second time in U.S. currency history that a security engraving based on the "twinkle-eyed" Lincoln has graced the nation's paper money. But Hipschen's version is less straight-laced than Charles Burt's depiction, which appeared on $500 Gold Certificates over 120 years ago. This new image is a more modern Lincoln, in touch with our times.

1959 FEBRUARY 12. A joint session of Congress convenes for a commemorative observance to mark the 150th anniversary of Lincoln's birth, and to receive the report of the Lincoln Sesquicentennial Commission, chaired by Fred Schwengel.

1959 FEBRUARY 12. The Library of Congress opens an exhibition marking the 150th anniversary of Lincoln's birth, including more than 200 items from the Robert T. Lincoln, Jesse Weik, Oliver R. Barrett, and Alfred Whital Stern collections, and other items housed there. Included are manuscripts, the Volk life mask, the original glass negative on which the $5 bill portrait was based, Lincoln's letter to his cabinet expressing doubts of his reelection, and Lincoln's Second Inaugural Address in his own hand.

1959 FEBRUARY 12. The Lincoln Memorial cent (fig. 4.1) with Frank Gasparro's reverse design is released.

1959 FEBRUARY 12. The St. Louis Mercantile Bank celebrates "Lincoln Birthday in Downtown St. Louis" by distributing Uncirculated 1959 cents mounted on cards.

1959 FEBRUARY 12. The Lincoln Sesquicentennial one-cent stamp (Scott 1113, fig. 4.2b) is issued at Hodgenville, Kentucky. It was designed by Ervine Metzl and engraved by R.M. Bower; 120,400,200 were issued.

1959 FEBRUARY 14. Lincoln medal cataloger Robert P. King dies.

1959 FEBRUARY 18. The Commission of Fine Arts, the government watchdog over aesthetics in federal art matters, receives a critical review of the new Lincoln Memorial cent design from National Sculpture Society president Adlai S. Hardin, who calls the change "an act of desecration."

1959 FEBRUARY 27. The Lincoln Sesquicentennial three-cent stamp (Scott 1114, fig. 4.2c) is issued at New York City. It was designed by Ervine Metzl and engraved by A.W. Dintaman; 91,160,200 were issued.

1959 APRIL. *Civil War Times* magazine debuts with two illustrations of Lincoln on its cover.

Fig. 4.1. Frank Gasparro engraved the 1959 Lincoln Memorial cent design.

Fig. 4.2. Three more Lincoln Sesquicentennial stamps joined the Lincoln-Douglas issue of the previous year: (a) the four-cent stamp (Scott 1116), engraved by M.D. Fenton after a Fritz Busse drawing of the D.C. French Lincoln Memorial statue; (b) the one-cent (Scott 1113), engraved by R.M. Bower after a painting by G.P.A. Healy; and (c) the three-cent, (Scott 1114), engraved by A.W. Dintaman after Borglum's Lincoln bust in the U.S. Capitol.

Fig. 4.3. Lincoln Sesquicentennial medals included from left: (a) an unsigned 150th anniversary .900 fine gold medal with Lincoln birthplace cabin; (b) Medallic Art Co.'s Charles Calverley "With Malice Toward None" medal (King-987); (c) Lincoln National Life "He Held His Place" medal.

1959 MAY 30. The Lincoln Sesquicentennial four-cent stamp (Scott 1116, fig. 4.2a) with a close-up of Daniel Chester French's statue in the Lincoln Memorial is issued at Washington, D.C. It was designed by Ervine Metzl and engraved by C.A. Brooks; 126,500,000 were issued.

1959. King V. Hostick reprints Alexander Hessler's 1860 Lincoln portrait copy negatives for sale to collectors.

1959 JULY 17. Alfred Hitchcock's *North by Northwest* (fig. 4.4) debuts. The film's climax is an exciting chase scene taking place on the Mount Rushmore Monument.

1959 OCTOBER 18. The Lincoln Highway monument in Wyoming by sculptor Robert I. Russin (fig. 4.5) is dedicated at the nearly 9,000-foot summit of Lincoln Highway, 10 miles south of Laramie.

1959. Fidel Castro ousts Cuban president and Lincoln admirer Fulgencio Batista, shown in happier days at the Batista Library in Havana with a casting of Augustus Saint-Gaudens's Chicago statue (fig. 4.6).

1959. U.S. Assay Commission members receive medals with the George T. Morgan portrait bust of Lincoln (fig. 4.7).

1959 CIRCA. A group of scholars convenes under the watchful gaze of Lincoln (fig. 4.8). Books on the desk include *In Quest of Knowledge* (1955) and *Ideals of Life* (1954).

1960 MAY. "Error" Lincoln cents create a national mania. On the first cents of the year, the last two digits in the date were smaller than normal, and various die breaks and filled dies also occurred. So the Mint decided to remake the master dies, enlarging the last two digits to conform to earlier dates. This resulted in a scarcity: the 1960 Small Date cent. Mintage of the Philadelphia cents was believed to be only a few million. Denver-minted Small Dates were more plentiful. By June 1960, Philly Small Dates were fetching up to $5 each, setting off a national treasure hunt. The media had a field day with the commotion. Everybody jumped on the bandwagon, creating a much bigger event than had been caused by the 1955 Doubled Die cents five years earlier. Even concession stands at Little League ball fields in the northeast sported signs that said "small dates wanted."

Fig. 4.4. Mount Rushmore locale appears on poster of Alfred Hitchcock's *North By Northwest*, Metro-Goldwyn-Mayer, 1959.

Fig. 4.5. *(a)* Sculptor Robert I. Russin details his enormous Lincoln head for *(b)* the Lincoln Highway summit memorial, dedicated near Laramie, Wyoming, in 1959.

The price of a Proof set with a Small Date cent soared to over a hundred bucks. Dealers offered unsearched bags of pennies for treasure hunters, and sold sets of Philadelphia and Denver Large and Small Date coins in plastic holders like the one shown (purchased by the author in 1960), for about two dollars (fig. 4.9).

1959/1960. Foreign countries issuing commemorative stamps in Lincoln's honor include Argentina, Colombia, Ghana, Guatemala, Haiti, Honduras, Liberia, Nicaragua, San Marino, and Taiwan (fig. 4.10).

1960 APRIL 22. A 25-cent Lincoln air mail stamp (Scott C59, fig. 4.11) is issued in San Francisco, bearing Lincoln's phrase "Of the People / By the People / For the People" from his Gettysburg Address.

1960 MAY 14. USS *Abraham Lincoln* (SSBN-602) is launched at Portsmouth Naval Shipyard in Portsmouth, New Hampshire, as the U.S. Navy's fifth ballistic missile submarine (fig. 4.12). Its keel was laid November 11, 1958. Robert Todd Lincoln Beckwith, great-grandson of Abraham Lincoln, attended its commissioning on March 11, 1961. The *Lincoln* was 381 feet long, with a displacement of 5,900 tons. It packed 16 Polaris missile tubes and six torpedo tubes. The ship could accommodate 12 officers and 100 sailors. Propulsion came from a nuclear power plant and steam turbines. The ship was decommissioned on February 28, 1981, having logged nearly 450,000 nautical miles.

1960 SEPTEMBER 6. Presidential candidate John F. Kennedy holds a rally at the Lincoln statue in Spokane, Washington. Paraphrasing Lincoln, Kennedy says, "the world cannot exist half slave and half free—the election is about what course we take to move the world away from slavery and toward freedom."

1960 NOVEMBER 19. A quotation from Abraham Lincoln—"Those who Deny freedom to others Deserve it not for Themselves," from Lincoln's April 6, 1859, letter to Henry Pierce and others—graces a four-cent stamp (Scott 1143) issued as part of the Post Office Department's "American Credo" series of 1960–1961 (fig. 4.13). This stamp was designed by Frank Conley and engraved by R.J. Jones; 120,540,000 were issued.

Fig. 4.7. The 1959 U.S. Assay Commission Medal, (Julian-Keusch AC-103) utilized George Morgan's excellent Lincoln obverse. The 1943 and 1954 assay medals also used this obverse.

Fig. 4.6. Cuban president Fulgencio Batista was a Lincoln aficionado, and Saint-Gaudens's Lincoln decorated his Batista Library, Havana. He was overthrown by Fidel Castro.

Fig. 4.8. A group of scholars convene in Lincoln's presence in the late 1950s.

Fig. 4.9. 1960 P&D large and small date cents created a buzz.

1960 DECEMBER 19. Lincoln's home and tomb in Springfield, Illinois, are designated National Historic Landmarks.

1961 MARCH 4. A re-enactment of the first Lincoln presidential inauguration is held on the East Front Plaza of the U.S. Capitol. Actor John C. Collison plays the part of Lincoln.

1961 MARCH 23. *Coin World* announces the availability of its first medallic issue commemorating the U.S. Civil War, with busts of Abe Lincoln and Jefferson Davis (fig. 4.16). In the same issue, founding editor Dick Johnson's editorial laments the dearth of Civil War numismatic books. *Coin World* had been founded the previous year by J. Oliver Amos, who had inherited a local newspaper-publishing company established by his grandfather, Civil War general James Amos. The company also contract-printed a weekly stamp tabloid, and added a weekly numismatic tabloid to utilize excess press capacity and diversify the company. *Coin World* quickly became the largest-circulation periodical in its niche, attracting an array of numismatic talent including Johnson, Bob Obojski, Russ Rulau, Jay Guren, Courtney Coffing, David T. Alexander, Tom DeLorey, Bill Gibbs,

and the present author, who was staff writer and news editor there for six years beginning in the mid-1970s.

1961 APRIL. The Civil War centennial commemoration begins.

1961. Maine coin dealer Toivo Johnson issues a series of medals celebrating coin designers, including Victor David Brenner (fig. 4.17). His large, elaborate silver and bronze medals are manufactured by Coin Medals, Inc.

1961 APRIL 13. Lincoln artist and photo historian Lloyd Ostendorf's cover illustration appears on *Treasure Chest,* one of many such periodical illustrations over decades (fig. 4.18).

1962 APRIL 14. The Lincoln Society of Philately (fig. 4.19) is formed at the House Office Building. This group would issue commemorative Lincoln covers and publish *Lincoln Log* for about 15 years.

1962 SEPTEMBER 5. President John F. Kennedy signs Public Law 87–643, eliminating tin from the Lincoln cent and substituting zinc.

Fig. 4.10. Several countries marked Lincoln's sesquicentennial with postage. *(a)* Taiwan issued "Leaders of Democracy" stamps (Scott-1248/1249), depicting Sun Yat Sen and Lincoln, first day canceled December 25, 1959, at Puli; *(b)* Colombia's 20¢ stamp depicted D.C. French's statue (Scott 718); *(c)* Honduras's 12¢ stamp featured the Lincoln Memorial (Scott C294); and *(d)* San Marino issued a 15L stamp (Scott 435).

Fig. 4.11. U.S. 25-cent airmail stamp (Scott C59).

Fig. 4.12. The nuclear submarine USS *Abraham Lincoln* (SSBN-602) was commissioned March 8, 1961.

Fig. 4.13. Lincoln credo 4-cents stamp (Scott 1143).

The Lincoln Home in 1860

LINCOLN HOME NATIONAL HISTORIC SITE

FREE ADMISSION

ADMIT ONE -- HOME TOUR

JUL 21 '93 -1 45

Ten minutes before the above time, join the park ranger in front of the Lincoln Home. This ticket is valid only for the date and time stamped. Please exercise caution when walking within this restored nineteenth-century environment. Have a safe and enjoyable visit.

NO 214071

b

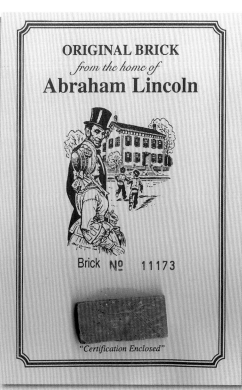

ORIGINAL BRICK
from the home of
Abraham Lincoln

Brick № 11173

"Certification Enclosed"

Fig. 4.14. *(a)* Lincoln's home in Springfield, Illinois, "the only home Lincoln ever owned," is a very popular tourist attraction administered by the National Park Service. *(b)* The ticket is from a 1993 visit by the author and his son. *(c)* Just in time for the Lincoln sesquicentennial, the Lincoln home underwent a spruce up, which included masonry work. Bits of the old brick that were replaced on the grounds have been sold with documentation attested by the contractor who performed the work.

Fig. 4.15. Lincoln National Life Insurance Co. medical draft.

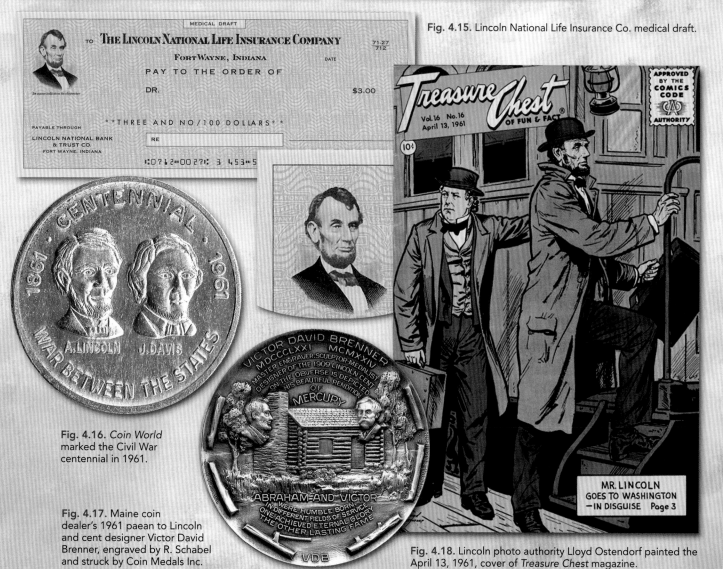

MEDICAL DRAFT

TO **THE LINCOLN NATIONAL LIFE INSURANCE COMPANY**

71-27
712

FORT WAYNE, INDIANA DATE

PAY TO THE ORDER OF

DR. $3.00

THREE AND NO/100 DOLLARS

PAYABLE THROUGH
LINCOLN NATIONAL BANK
& TRUST CO.
FORT WAYNE, INDIANA

RE

Fig. 4.16. *Coin World* marked the Civil War centennial in 1961.

Fig. 4.17. Maine coin dealer's 1961 paean to Lincoln and cent designer Victor David Brenner, engraved by R. Schabel and struck by Coin Medals Inc.

Fig. 4.18. Lincoln photo authority Lloyd Ostendorf painted the April 13, 1961, cover of *Treasure Chest* magazine.

1963. The 1,000-mile Lincoln Heritage Trail opens, with 3,000 markers. Author Andrew Ferguson cites Robert Newman, Illinois director of tourism in the 1960s, as saying, "the whole thing was cooked up by the marketing guys at the American Petroleum Institute. . . . They wanted to get people traveling. Get 'em into their cars, get 'em buying gasoline."[1] Actually Lincoln Trail treks had been organized since at least the 1930s to visit locations Lincoln had journeyed to. Scouting medals (such as the one shown in fig. 4.20) were awarded participants.

1963. The Hall of Fame for Great Americans at New York University issues Anthony de Francisci's Lincoln medal, designed after a bust by Augustus Saint-Gaudens (fig. 4.21). According to medallic expert Dick Johnson, Lincoln's "corpus of portrait medals was well served by de Francisci's HOF design."[2] Many medals (such as in fig. 4.22) mark the centennial of the Emancipation Proclamation and Gettysburg Address.

1963 FEBRUARY 9. The *New Yorker* features a cover illustration (fig. 4.23) by Aaron Birnbaum, whose economy of line renders an iconic image for all time. A tailor by profession, Birnbaum took up the brush in retirement and became a celebrated folk artist.

1963 MAY 10. *Time* magazine's 40th-anniversary issue is dedicated to "The Individual in America" with an unconventional cover portrait of Lincoln by Robert Vickrey (fig. 4.24). Lincoln was chosen, magazine editors said, as "the greatest, the classic, the archetypical individual in the American imagination."

1963 AUGUST 16. A five-cent stamp marking the centenary of Lincoln's Emancipation Proclamation (Scott 1233) is issued in Chicago (fig. 4.25). The designer was George Olden; 132,435,000 were issued.

1963 AUGUST 28. Dr. Martin Luther King delivers his famous "I have a dream" speech from the Lincoln Memorial steps as part of his civil rights march on Washington (shown on pages 224, 225). A crowd estimated at more than 200,000 hears Dr. King's stirring message, which concludes: "I have a dream that one day this nation will rise up and live out the true meaning of its creed: 'We hold these truths to be self-evident, that all men are

Fig. 4.19. Lincoln Society of Philately logo, 1962.

Fig. 4.20. This 1963 Lincoln Trail fob was awarded to Boy Scouts for participating in a Lincoln pilgrimage. For obvious reasons it is sometimes referred to as the "skull" medal.

Fig. 4.21. Anthony de Francisci created a vibrant Lincoln portrait for the Hall of Fame for Great Americans medal series, sponsored by Coin and Currency Institute, and struck by Medallic Art Co. in 1963.

Fig. 4.22. Lincoln's Emancipation Proclamation and Gettysburg Address were the subjects of numerous 1963 medals, including (a) "The Emancipator" and (b) "Lincoln's Gettysburg Address" by Philip Kraczkowski, struck by Robbins and (c) "Emancipation Proclamation" by Carl Ludwig Schmitz, struck by Medallic Art Co.

created equal.' . . . And when this happens . . . all of God's children . . . will be able to join hands and sing in the words of the old Negro spiritual: 'Free at last! Free at last! Thank God Almighty, we are free at last!'"

1963 NOVEMBER 22. With the assassination of President John F. Kennedy, the Associated Press immediately circulates a Kennedy photo showing him in front of the G.P.A. Healey portrait of Lincoln in the White House, and begins spreading accounts of the supposedly astounding personal coincidences between the two. Kennedy's funeral cortege would include the Lincoln caisson. Lists of the supposed coincidences become curios.

1963 NOVEMBER 23. Shock and sadness from the events in Dallas inspire Pulitzer Prize–winning *Chicago Sun-Times* editorial cartoonist Bill Mauldin's "Crying Lincoln" portrayal (fig. 4.26), one of the memorable images of the 20th century. A variety of Kennedy-Lincoln medals (fig. 4.27) are issued.

1964. Herbert C. Swim and O.L. Weeks receive rose patent number 2370 for the "Mr. Lincoln" rose, a red variety (fig. 4.28).

1964 FEBRUARY 12. The BEP begins printing $2 United States Notes with the motto "In God We Trust." Lincoln's birthday is chosen because both the class of

Fig. 4.23. Aaron Birnbaum's classic February 9, 1963, *New Yorker* cover.

Fig. 4.24. *Time* magazine called Lincoln the quintessential individual in its May 10, 1963, issue; cover by Robert Vickrey.

Fig. 4.25. Emancipation Proclamation stamp (Scott 1233).

Fig. 4.26. Pulitzer-prize-winning editorial cartoonist Bill Mauldin drew this iconic crying Lincoln illustration on the day John F. Kennedy was assassinated. It was first published in the November 23, 1963, *Chicago Sun-Times*. The autograph to the author dates to 1971.

Fig. 4.27. A number of medals were issued linking Lincoln to John F. Kennedy after the latter's assassination.

currency (U.S. notes) and the use of the motto "In God We Trust" (on two-cent coins) had commenced during Lincoln's administration a century earlier. On the same day, the BEP also begins producing $1 Federal Reserve Notes with the motto.

1964 MARCH. Alfred E. Neuman knocks Lincoln's hat off with a snowball on a Norman Mingo cover for the satiric humor magazine *MAD*. Alfred E. "What, Me Worry?" Neuman's cavalier attitude could serve as a metaphor for the revisionist approaches to Lincoln that began appearing, bringing the idolized figure down from his throne into the slush of everyday life. To complete the transition, Neuman, the everyman, symbolically Father Abraham as "Abraham Neuman" in a Spring 1971 issue of that publication (fig. 4.29).

1964 MARCH 2. The first $5 United States Notes with the motto "In God We Trust," Series 1963, are delivered.

1964 APRIL 10. President Lyndon Johnson participates in the dedication ceremony of the Lincoln monument in Ciudad Juarez, Chihuahua, Mexico.

1964 APRIL 22. The New York World's Fair opens and includes a Disney animatronic attraction called "Meet Mr. Lincoln," a full-featured robotic Lincoln impersonator (fig. 4.31) that would go on to be a featured attraction at Disney's theme parks. The Illinois "Land of Lincoln" pavilion at the fair issues medals (fig. 4.32). Chicago media giant WGN issues small plaques by MACO reprising Brenner's 1907 opus.

1964 SEPTEMBER 16. The first $5 Federal Reserve Notes with the motto "In God We Trust," Series 1963, are delivered.

Fig. **4.28.** In 1964 Herbert C. Swim and O.L. Weeks patented the "Mr. Lincoln Rose."

Fig. **4.29.** *(a)* Alfred E. Neuman takes it to the icon on the cover of the March 1964 issue of *MAD* magazine, delightfully drawn by ace illustrator Norman Mingo. *(b)* Meanwhile, the "what, me worry?" scamp becomes the Lincoln-everyman Abraham Neuman. In February 1957 Neuman joined Mount Rushmore.

Fig. **4.30.** During the mid-1960s General Motors Technical Center, Warren, Michigan, attempted to interest the U.S. Mint is a high-capacity roller press. Several experimental pieces were struck, including this pseudo-Lincoln cent design with its Manufacturing Development Staff reverse, circa 1964, Pollock-unlisted.

Fig. **4.31.** Walt Disney animatronics captured body language in an elegant way in the lavish popular history production "Great Moments with Mr. Lincoln," offering stirring excerpts from Lincoln's speeches in a dramatic setting. The presentation debuted at the 1964 New York World's Fair, and then was staged at Disney theme parks.

1965. The Lincoln Academy of Illinois is established as a non-profit, nonpartisan corporation to recognize outstanding contributions made by living Illinois natives or residents "toward the social, cultural, and technological progress of mankind, and thereby to encourage greater dedication to such progress by all citizens of Illinois." Individuals are recognized as laureates at an annual ceremony and given the Order of Lincoln medallion, the highest award given by the State of Illinois. Nominations are received in 11 fields of endeavor. Recipients have included historian Michael Bechloss and author Gary Wills. The organization also honors one senior from each of the four-year degree-granting institutions of higher learning in Illinois.

1965. United States Banknote Corporation "Integrity" ads depict the Gettysburg Lincoln. Its Security-Columbian Banknote Company division utilizes the vignette on Lincoln First Group stock certificates (fig. 4.33).

1965 APRIL. The centenary of Lincoln's death sparks an outpouring of commemorative stamps around the world (fig. 4.34), including issues from Central African Republic, Chad, Congo, Cuba, Dahomey, Dominican Republic, Gabon, Ghana, Guatemala, India, Liberia, Mali, Mauritania, Niger, Ras al-Khaimah (United Arab Emirates), Rwanda, Surinam, Togo, Upper Volta, and Venezuela.

1965 APRIL 9. Lincoln's phrase "With Malice Toward None" from his second inaugural address appears on a five-cent stamp (Scott 1182) issued to mark the 100th anniversary of the end of the Civil War.

1965 APRIL 23. Die cutter J. Henri Ripstra's silver, bronze, and aluminum Abraham Lincoln medal sets commemorating the end of the

Fig. 4.32. (a) For the 1964–1965 New York World's Fair, Illinois' Lincoln Pavilion distributed several different fiber Lincoln medals manufactured by Stafford Manufacturing Co., Brooklyn. (b, c) Chicago super station WGN distributed special presentation plaques, featuring a reduction of the Brenner Lincoln plaque by Medallic Art. Co.

INTEGRITY has always been a keynote of United States Banknote Corporation. Dedication to the ideals of quality and service.
The intaglio prints and lithographic representations of our hand engraved vignettes embody this dedication to artistic endeavor.
These striking prints are offered in a variety of sizes; in Black or Sepia tone on 100% rag, Neutral Ph paper.
Unique additions to any collection.

UNITED STATES BANKNOTE CORPORATION

Fig. 4.33. (a) United States Banknote Corporation stressed "Integrity," exemplified by the "Gettysburg Lincoln" image, in its 1965 advertising literature. (b) Its Security-Columbian Banknote Co. division printed stock for Lincoln First Group Inc. with the same vignette, issue date November 14, 1969.

Civil War sell for $15 at the Central States Numismatic Society convention in Chicago.

1965 JULY 18. Disneyland celebrates its 10th anniversary with the opening of the "Great Moments with Mr. Lincoln" exhibition in the park's Opera House. To encourage children to become "personally" acquainted with Abe, admission is complimentary.

1965 NOVEMBER 19. A black four-cent Lincoln stamp in the "Prominent Americans" series is issued (Scott 1282).

1966 APRIL 15. A Lincoln statue is dedicated in Mexico City by President Lyndon Johnson.

1967 CIRCA. Vietnam-era military patches include the 84th Airborne "Rail-splitter" Division patch (fig. 4.35) and the Illinois National Guard patch (fig. 4.36a).

1967 FEBRUARY 12. San Francisco rock promoter Bill Graham throws an "Abe Lincoln's Birthday Party" benefit concert (fig. 4.37) at Fillmore Auditorium, headlined by the Grateful Dead.

1967 OCTOBER 27. *Time* magazine's cover story reports on antiwar demonstrations, showing marchers at the Lincoln Memorial, which increasingly has become a rallying point for protesters. The Black Panthers would stage a rally there in 1970 (fig. 4.38).

1968 JANUARY 30. The restored Ford's Theatre, where Lincoln was shot, is reopened.

1968 FEBRUARY 12. James Earle Fraser's original plaster model for his Lincoln statue in Jersey City, New Jersey, is unveiled at the National Cowboy Hall of Fame and Western Heritage Center in Oklahoma City, Oklahoma. The museum acquired the piece from the Fraser estate in 1968 for its special gallery entitled the Fraser Studio Collection. "My apprehensions about the cost of the plaster model were overridden by my unswerving belief that the Lincoln statue was vital to the exhibition, and, except for *End of the Trail*,

more important than any other single work in the Studio Collection," museum director Dean Krakel recalled.[3] The plaster model was restored and placed on a new base. More than 300 invited guests attended the unveiling. The Lincoln statue was originally part of a separate gallery (fig. 4.39) devoted to the work of Fraser and his wife, sculptor Laura Gardin Fraser, but due to museum expansion it is presently located at the east end of the main museum corridor.

1968 APRIL 4. Martin Luther King is fatally shot. Countries honoring King and Lincoln on stamps include Ajman, Manama, Ras al-Khaimah, Sharjah, and Khor Fakkan (United Arab Emirates); Paraguay; and Yemen.

1969 MARCH 7. In *Star Trek*'s third-season episode entitled "The Savage Curtain," the crew of the Starship *Enterprise* meets Abraham Lincoln in deep space. Lincoln enlists Captain Kirk and Mr. Spock in a battle of good against evil, with villains who include Genghis Khan. Lee Bergere played Lincoln (see fig. 4.40).

1969 MAY 16. Lloyd E. Wagaman rolls Lincoln-portrait Jefferson nickels at the Indiana State Numismatic Association convention.

1969. The world's largest Lincoln statue (72 feet) is erected at the Charleston, Illinois, Speedway campground.

1969. South Dakota senator Karl Mundt introduces bill S. 71 to place Mount Rushmore on the back of the $1 note (fig. 4.41). Unfortunately, several months later Mundt had a stroke, and his bill never passed.

1970 FEBRUARY 1. Equatorial Guinea issues .900 fine gold 500 pesetas and .999 fine silver 75 pesetas depicting "Abramo Lincoln" (fig. 4.42).

1970. The Lincoln Mint's "Life of Lincoln" medal series debuts, designed by Lloyd Ostendorf.

1970. The annual Abraham Lincoln National Rail-splitting Contest is inaugurated at Lincoln, Illinois (fig. 4.43).

Fig. 4.34. Many nations marked the centennial of Lincoln's death in 1965, including (a) the Congo with its 90f stamp (Scott C35) and (b) Central African Republic with its 50f souvenir sheet (Scott C28).

Fig. 4.35. Vietnam War–era 84th Airborne Rail-splitter Division patch.

Fig. 4.36. *(a)* Vietnam War–era Illinois National Guard patch. *(b)* The State of Illinois also awards its "Distinguished Service" medal to members of the Illinois National Guard.

Fig. 4.37. The 1967 poster by Hank Lebo that advertised Abe Lincoln's birthday bash, rock style.

Fig. 4.38. In 1970 the Black Panther Party staged a demonstration at the Lincoln Memorial.

Fig. 4.39. James Earle Fraser's contemplative Lincoln plaster model as it appeared during the 1970s at National Cowboy Hall of Fame and Western Heritage Center, Oklahoma City, Oklahoma.

1970. From 1970 to 1975, the BEP and American Bank Note Co. print purple $5 food coupons with the familiar Lincoln vignette from the $5 bill (fig. 4.44).

1970. Medallic Art Co. produces Lincoln Heritage Trail medals in silver (fig. 4.45) and bronze using the Calverley portrait with modeling by Joseph Di Lorenzo.

1970 APRIL 10. The Manama Dependency of Ajman issues the round 60-DH Abraham Lincoln "gold coin" stamp.

1971 MARCH 17. The new Walt Disney film *The Barefoot Executive* concerns a mail clerk at a fictional broadcasting company who pitches a project entitled *Abraham Lincoln's Doctor's Dog* (ALDD or "Aldy" for short) to studio executives. The clerk (played by Kurt Russell) asserts that TV shows about Lincoln, doctors, and dogs are popular, and thus ALDD will be a hit. Studio programming director Francis X. Wilbanks (Joe Flynn) rejects the idea. But see the entry for December 14, 1955 (page 218).

1972. Lincoln Memorial University issues a 75th anniversary medal executed by Italian-American sculptor Albert d'Andrea from an inventive Lloyd Ostendorf design (fig. 4.46).

1973 CIRCA. Experimental notes are printed in Germany on Giori presses (fig. 4.47), and in Geneva, New York, on Magna presses, which simulate designs from U.S. currency (fig. 4.48). Magna presses were first employed by the BEP in 1976.

1973. U.S. biomedical engineer Leon D. Harmon publishes a research article on the "Abraham Lincoln Effect," in which a pixilated (degraded) image (block portrait) can be more recognizable at a distance than when viewed up close. The phenomenon is so named by Harmon because he chose to use a portrait of Lincoln to construct his first block portrait, on which he published a technical report in 1971. (See the entry "1974 and 1976" for more.)

1974 JANUARY 2. A 26-cent airmail stamp showing Mount Rushmore is issued (Scott C88).

Fig. 4.41. South Dakota Senator Karl Mundt introduced S-71 in 1969 to place Mount Rushmore on the back of $1 note. Unfortunately, several months later Mundt had a stroke, and his bill never passed. Mount Rushmore had been considered for the back of the $2 bill earlier (Hessler-UE17).

Fig. 4.40. Lee Bergere as Lincoln in an episode of *Star Trek*.

Fig. 4.43. Lincoln, Illinois, Railsplitting Contest patch.

Fig. 4.44. Series 1970 $5 food coupon with the familiar Lincoln money image. Engravers were Kenneth C. Wiram and Howard F. Sharpless, (BEP die no. MISC17845).

Fig. 4.42. In 1970 Equatorial Guinea stuck (a) a gold 500 pesetas (KM-24) and (b) a silver 75p (KM-10.1), depicting the "Gettysburg Lincoln" image.

1974 FEBRUARY 12. At the height of the Watergate scandal, Richard Nixon's speech at the Lincoln Memorial analogizes his critics to those who plagued Lincoln. Nixon goes on to say that Lincoln stood firm and he would too.

1974. To cut costs from rising copper prices, the Mint produces aluminum cent trial strikes (fig. 4.51), which are distributed to Congress and staff and then recalled. One example is now at the Smithsonian, and a second specimen was offered but withdrawn by an auction company.[4]

1974 AND 1976. Salvador Dali paints two versions of *Gala Contemplating the Mediterranean Sea Which at Twenty Metres Becomes the Portrait of Abraham Lincoln,* depicting his nude muse, a small portrait of Abe based on the $5 note pose, and a cruciform. Dali employed the "Lincoln Effect" in his homage, which morphs as an optical illusion into a larger Lincoln portrait with distance. Compare this great modern artist's cerebral rendering to the simple portrait of

Lincoln created for this book by the present author to illustrate the "Lincoln Effect" (fig. 4.52).

1976 FEBRUARY 12. The Library of Congress unseals a box containing Lincoln's personal possessions from the time of his assassination. It reveals that Lincoln had a Confederate $5 note in his brown billfold when assassinated. A photo released by the LOC at the time showed that he also had a linen handkerchief, two pairs of spectacles, a lens polisher, a pocketknife, several newspaper clippings, a watch fob, and miscellaneous other items. The Confederate note depicts the CSA capitol at Richmond and Confederate Treasury secretary Christopher G. Memminger. It is not known how Lincoln obtained the Confederate note or why he was carrying it. In 2004, indie rock band Rainer Marie recorded the song "The Contents of Lincoln's Pockets" for their *Anyone in Love With You (Already Knows)* album. The song describes the pocket contents accurately, and paints an impressionistic scene of "Lincoln struck at the back of the head" falling forward onto the floor. It asks, "you've never been hit before,

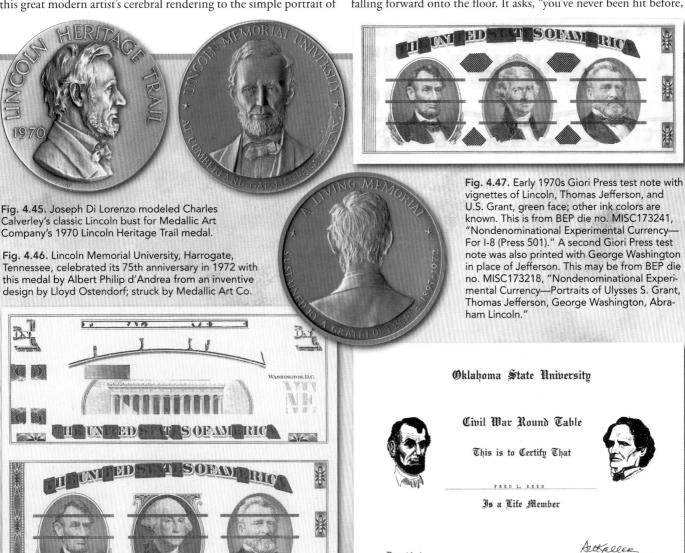

Fig. 4.45. Joseph Di Lorenzo modeled Charles Calverley's classic Lincoln bust for Medallic Art Company's 1970 Lincoln Heritage Trail medal.

Fig. 4.46. Lincoln Memorial University, Harrogate, Tennessee, celebrated its 75th anniversary in 1972 with this medal by Albert Philip d'Andrea from an inventive design by Lloyd Ostendorf; struck by Medallic Art Co.

Fig. 4.47. Early 1970s Giori Press test note with vignettes of Lincoln, Thomas Jefferson, and U.S. Grant, green face; other ink colors are known. This is from BEP die no. MISC173241, "Nondenominational Experimental Currency—For I-8 (Press 501)." A second Giori Press test note was also printed with George Washington in place of Jefferson. This may be from BEP die no. MISC173218, "Nondenominational Experimental Currency—Portraits of Ulysses S. Grant, Thomas Jefferson, George Washington, Abraham Lincoln."

Fig. 4.48. A 1973 Magna Press test note with vignettes of Lincoln, George Washington, and U.S. Grant, green obverse; other ink colors are known. This likely was produced from BEP die no. MISC17956, "Experimental for Non-Security Die," engraved by Robert G. Culin Sr. in 1972.

Fig. 4.49. The author's Civil War history mentor, awarding-winning author Dr. LeRoy Fischer, signed this Lincoln-Davis Civil War Round Table certificate in 1974.

how can you deal with that kind of information?" The group has since disbanded.

1976 JULY 5. The *New Yorker* Bicentennial cover (fig. 4.53) is an inventive typographical portrait of Lincoln by Lou Myers, comprised of famous quotes relating to America's past. These include items from Capt. John Smith, Sam Adams, George Washington, Thomas Jefferson, James Russell Lowell, Carl Schurz, Susan B. Anthony, Booker T. Washington, Felix Frankfurter, Wendell Wilkie, and others. Lincoln's contribution to the discourse is "As I would not be a slave, so I would not be a master. This expresses my idea of democracy." This expression is not from any of Lincoln's speeches or letters. It was written on a scrap of paper that Lincoln's widow gave to a Chicago judge, and attributed conjecturally to circa August 1, 1858.[5]

1977 FEBRUARY 12. Wooden nickels with Lincoln black four-cent stamps mounted on one side are issued and postmarked at the Pearl Harbor, Hawaii, Memorial Station as souvenirs.

1977 JUNE 4. The Abraham Lincoln Library and Museum of Lincoln Memorial University in Harrogate, Tennessee, is dedicated. Construction was financed in part by a half-million-dollar donation by trustee Col. Harland Sanders, of Kentucky Fried Chicken fame.

1977 APRIL. The cover of the *National Lampoon* shows a mesmerized Lincoln seated on his memorial throne, a beer can in his left hand and a portable TV with rabbit ears balanced precariously in his lap between his knees (fig. 4.54a). Lincoln spoofs have become increasingly prevalent in recently years.

1977. Log Cabin Republicans form to combat an anti-gay initiative in California. The group takes its name from the fact that Lincoln, a reformer, was born in a log cabin.

1978 OCTOBER. *MAD* magazine publishes "Exclusive: New Ballistic Test Proves Booth Did Not Shoot Lincoln."

1980 SEPTEMBER 26. Singer Bette Midler's concert film *Divine Madness,* which opens in limited release on this date, is advertised in posters incorporating her image into Mount Rushmore in place of Jefferson, and seated on the Lincoln Memorial throne as a mermaid

Fig. 4.51. Copper price mania drove the U.S. Mint to strike experimental 1974 aluminum cents (Pollock-2084), but then abandon the project when the copper price chilled.

Fig. 4.50. Paraguay issued a 150 guaranies Lincoln silver coin (KM-107) in 1974.

Fig. 4.52. *(a)* Alexander Gardner's "Gettysburg Lincoln" (Ostendorf-77), manipulated by the author to illustrate the Abraham Lincoln effect. *(b)* Salvador Dali's 1974 "Gala Contemplating the Mediterranean Sea which at Twenty Metres Becomes the Portrait of Abraham Lincoln" makes artistic use of the Abraham Lincoln effect.

Fig. 4.53. Illustrator Lou Myers created a memorable U.S. Bicentennial cover for the July 5, 1976, issue of *The New Yorker*.

(fig 4.54c). This relaxed spoofing is the kind of spirited whimsy that made *MAD* magazine, *National Lampoon,* and *Saturday Night Live* perennial favorites with youthful audiences.

1981 APRIL 1. *The Lincoln Cent* by Stephen G. Manley is published.

1981. The Ford's Theatre Lincoln medal is established to honor those who "exemplify by their body of work the lasting legacy and character of our most beloved president, Abraham Lincoln."

1982 APRIL 14. The Quarterman Publishing reprint of Robert King's *Lincoln in Numismatics* is copyrighted.

1982 DECEMBER 16. The *New York Times* article "Statue Stirs Controversy" reports: "The statue depicting Abraham Lincoln and a freed slave in Boston's Park Square might be moved to an out-of-sight location because some blacks are said to be offended by it. Thomas Ball created the bronze statue, entitled *Emancipation,* in 1877. The Boston Art Commission is expected to rule next month on a new site." The statue remained put.

1984. Gore Vidal's *Lincoln: A Novel* is published by Random House. A raft of criticism from Lincoln scholars greets his treatment, which intensifies when a made-for-TV movie based on the book and starring Sam Waterston is released four years later.

1984 APRIL 16. Lincoln and Washington profiles appear on a 20-cent stamp (Scott 2081) marking the 50th anniversary of the National Archives (fig. 4.55a).

1984 OCTOBER 16. The U.S. Postal Service issues its "A Nation of Readers" 20-cent stamp (Scott 2106), based on the familiar photo of Lincoln and Tad perusing what is actually a photo album, not a book (fig. 4.55a). For a better representation of the photo see fig. 1.164a.

1985 MARCH 29. A 22-cent stamp with the flag over the Capitol and a quote from Lincoln's Gettysburg Address is issued.

1985 OCTOBER 7. Art Buchwald publishes a parody, *You Can Fool All the People All the Time,* with Art on the cover as Abe.

1986 MAY 22. At the AMERIPEX '86 stamp show, the U.S. Postal Service releases a 22-cent Lincoln stamp (Scott 2217g) as part of a set of sheets of stamps showing the U.S. presidents (fig. 4.55c).

Fig. 4.54. Making light with Old Abe has replaced the reverence exhibited towards him formerly, at least to some degree. Pictured are: (a) *National Lampoon,* April 1977; (b) *MAD* magazine, January, 1994; (c) Bette Midler's *Divine Madness* poster, The Ladd Co., 1980; (d) *National Lampoon's Senior Trip,* New Line Cinema, 1995; (e) Burger King's Lincoln Muggle by TM&C Vinyl, 1992; (f) Hard Rock Cafe Washington, D.C., pin, 1990s; (g) Hard Rock Hotel, Las Vegas, "5" chip, 1990s.

1987 NOVEMBER 12. The BEP souvenir card for the Hawaii State Numismatic Association convention features a Series 1923 Lincoln Porthole $5 Silver Certificate face.

1988 FEBRUARY 13. The USS *Abraham Lincoln* (CVN-72), the U.S. Navy's fifth Nimitz-class supercarrier, is launched. Newport News Shipbuilding had received a contract to build the carrier December 27, 1982. She would be commissioned on November 11, 1989. The carrier was nearly 1,100 feet long, displaced approximately 97,000 tons, and was powered by nuclear reactors and steam turbines. It had a capacity of 20,000 persons. Her first deployment was during Operations Desert Shield / Desert Storm. The ship and crew were also involved in humanitarian missions in the Philippines and Somalia. The *Abe* was the first carrier to integrate female aviators into its crew after laws against women doing combat duty were changed. The *Abraham Lincoln* has since been deployed to the Persian Gulf in support of U.S. operations in the Middle East. Planes off the carrier's desk led the air strikes in Operation Iraqi Freedom. Some 16,500 sorties were flown (fig. 4.56).

1988 MARCH 27. NBC broadcasts *Lincoln,* based on Gore Vidal's novel, with Sam Waterston in the title role. Historical inaccuracies chafe the Lincoln community, leading to somewhat heated public exchanges between the author and the scholars on the nature of historical "facts" and the purposes of literature.

1988 DECEMBER. The movie *Watchers* features a super-intelligent golden retriever that can recognize pictures, such as the one of Lincoln on the cover of *TV Guide* (from February 1988).

1988 CIRCA. In trade press ads, the Fulfillment Corporation of America asks a telling question: "Is this man pretty enough to be President today?" recommending itself to customers as working harder and smarter without pretense, just like Abe (fig. 4.57). Lincoln affiliation—often with humor—is a hallmark of contemporary advertising, notable recently with Rozerem and Burger King.

1989 MARCH 16. A World Stamp Expo '89 postage stamp is issued by the USPS. It reprises the 1869 carmine and black Lincoln 90-cent stamp and touts the show in Washington, D.C., that fall.

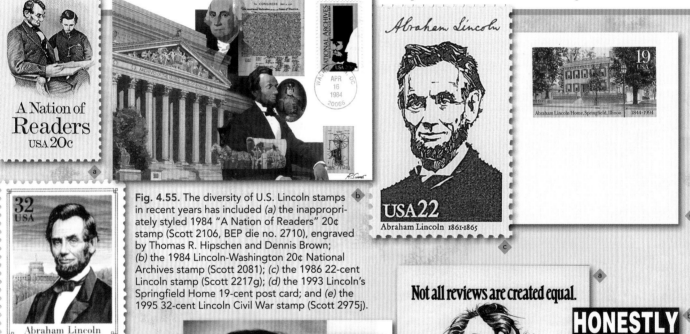

Fig. 4.55. The diversity of U.S. Lincoln stamps in recent years has included (a) the inappropriately styled 1984 "A Nation of Readers" 20¢ stamp (Scott 2106, BEP die no. 2710), engraved by Thomas R. Hipschen and Dennis Brown; (b) the 1984 Lincoln-Washington 20¢ National Archives stamp (Scott 2081); (c) the 1986 22-cent Lincoln stamp (Scott 2217g); (d) the 1993 Lincoln's Springfield Home 19-cent post card; and (e) the 1995 32-cent Lincoln Civil War stamp (Scott 2975j).

Fig. 4.56. The USS *Abraham Lincoln* (CVN-72) is a Nimitz-class supercarrier, with a distinguished service record on humanitarian and military missions for the U.S. Navy over the past two decades. Shown is the obverse of one of the "challenge coins" connected with the ship.

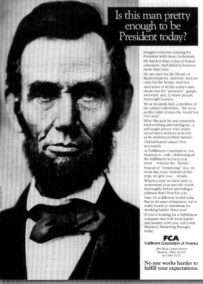

Fig. 4.57. Fulfillment Corporation of America's Lincoln ad from the late 1980s.

Fig. 4.58. Lincoln's legacy and historical character traits have become an advertising shorthand, as in (a) this *PC World* ad, 1988, or (b) in this furniture store come on, circa 1990.

When the WSE89 opened the Post Office released a souvenir sheet depicting the original stamp and three trial color proofs.

1989 NOVEMBER 22. *Back to the Future Part II* opens in wide release. For the film ace Hollywood prop master John Zemansky creates a very original, futuristic prop $5 bill (Reed UB80), which uncannily presages the style adopted in the next decade by the U.S. Treasury (fig. 4.59).

1990. Association of Lincoln Presenters is formed to preserve Abraham and Mary Lincoln's legacy, words, and works by dressing and acting the part. Organization members number in the hundreds.

1990. The Lincoln Prize is established by Richard Gilder and Lewis Lehrman of the Gilder-Lehrman Institute, and Gabor Boritt of Gettysburg College, as "the nation's most generous award in the field of American history," currently $50,000 annually. The field of interest is, of course, Lincoln and the Civil War.

1990 MAY 23. Gallup Poll reveals 62 percent of Americans want to retain the Lincoln cent. General Accounting Office tells Congress it favors continuation of the one-cent coin too.[6] In testimony before the House subcommittee on Consumer Affairs and Coinage, GAO representative L. Nye Stevens tells Congressmen there is "limited public demand for elimination of the penny."

1990. Cook Islands' $50 coin with Lincoln and the Capitol anticipates "500 Years of America, 1492–1992" (fig. 4.60a).

Fig. 4.59. *Back to the Future II,* Universal Pictures, 1989, made nearly $350 million worldwide. Here's $5 that got away.

Fig. 4.60. Non-circulating legal tender coins are struck for collectors and sold with high markups to make a profit for the issuer. They are coins only in the sense that the issuing country says they are coins. In the 1990s, NCLTs with Lincoln images included: *(a)* 1990 Cook Islands Lincoln and Capitol $50 (KM-48); *(b)* 1991 U.S. Mount Rushmore $5 gold (KM-230); *(c)* 1991 Mt. Rushmore $1 silver (KM-229); *(d)* 1991 Mt. Rushmore 50¢ copper-nickel (KM-228); and *(e)* 1993 Cuba 10 pesos silver (KM-375.1).

Fig. 4.61. In 1991 tests were undertaken of web-fed presses to increase productivity of BEP press rooms. Shown is *(a)* a Security Columbian web press test note, plate 16804 in green (other colors known); *(b)* an Alexander Hamilton Web Press test note in yellow (also known in purple); and *(c)* a web test die 16648 in blue. *(d)* Also shown is a photo of the rotary press test plate drum, flopped so it is oriented like the notes.

1991. The U.S. Mint coins a trio of Mt. Rushmore commemorative coins to mark the 50th anniversary of the monument. The gold $5 shows an eagle in flight, while the dollar and half dollar are pretty pedestrian (figs. 4.60b-d).

1991. Hamilton Stevens Group test-prints web press notes under BEP supervision (fig. 4.61). Web presses produced $1 Federal Reserve Notes the following year.

1991 MARCH 29. A stamp depicting a flag over Mount Rushmore (Scott 2523) is issued.

1991 DECEMBER 7. *Austin American-Statesman* reports pending legislation pressed by Senator Alan Cranston urging the replacement of the Lincoln Memorial on the cent reverse with a theme from the Bill of Rights. No action was taken.

1993. Castro's Republic of Cuba marks the 130th anniversary of the Emancipation Proclamation with a .999 fine silver 10-peso coin (fig. 4.60e).

1994 FEBRUARY. *Scientific American* pairs old Abe and a zesty Marilyn Monroe as a cover to illustrate William Mitchell's investigation into photo manipulation, "When Is Seeing Believing?" "Digital forgery can create photographic evidence for events that never happened," the publication warns (fig. 4.62).

1994 FEBRUARY 12. As part of the "Historic Preservation" series, a 19-cent U.S. postal card (Scott UX174) shows Lincoln's Springfield home (fig. 4.55d).

1995 JUNE 29. A 32-cent Lincoln stamp (Scott 2975j) appears in a set of 20 setenant Civil War commemorative stamps (fig. 4.55e).

1994 CIRCA. A laid-back approach to Lincoln has even shown up in Springfield, Illinois, "the town that Lincoln loved," as witnessed by the impish figure on the city's visitor literature. Meanwhile Lincoln scholarship seems lacking there too, as the city's visitor's bureau literature sports an anachronistic image of Lincoln based on a photo taken years after he left for the East (fig. 4.63).

1995 SEPTEMBER 8. *National Lampoon's Senior Trip,* a comedy about a group of slackers journeying to meet the president, debuts. Publicity centers around posters and paraphernalia similar to the magazine cover 18 years earlier (see fig. 4.54d). French's Lincoln Memorial figure is wearing shades, clutching a beverage can, and sporting a protest button.

1997 APRIL. In a poll conducted by the present author on Abraham Lincoln Online, three in four preferred Ostendorf-77 ("Gettysburg Lincoln") as the model for the new $5 bill portrait.

1998 MAY. *Life* magazine inducts Lincoln into its Hall of Heroes.

1998 JUNE. In anticipation of new $5 note designs with an enlarged portrait, the present author exhibits several suggested face and back designs at the Memphis International Paper Money Show (fig. 4.66).

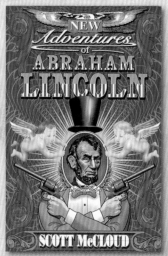

Fig. 4.62. A stodgy Abe and a vivacious Marilyn Monroe arm-in-arm were the cover illustration for an article on photo manipulation in the February 1994 issue of *Scientific American.* The illustration works, of course, because it is startlingly fresh and unexpected.

Fig. 4.64. *George* magazine was the brainchild of John F. Kennedy Jr. An early issue featured actor Harrison Ford dressed up as Honest Abe, August 1997.

Fig. 4.65. Graphic novelist and artist Scott McCloud turned a bizarre plot involving fake and real Lincolns into a cult success in his *New Adventures of Abraham Lincoln,* published in February 1998.

Fig. 4.63. *(a)* Lincoln had a beard for all of two months that he lived in Springfield, Illinois, but the anachronistic image the Springfield visitors bureau chose in 1993 for its town guide in based on a photo taken in 1864 (Ostendorf-84). *(b)* Somebody with a sense of humor in Lincoln's hometown remembered "Kilroy was here," and executed a graphical tour de force in throwing out the welcome mat to the world.

1998 SEPTEMBER. Lincoln cries at the demise of superhero Captain America. Largely fictionalized narratives in which the Lincoln character is one of an ensemble cast have proliferated in comic books during the last four decades (fig. 4.67). Often these "time travel" dramas involve superheroes who sometimes alter Lincoln's personal history.

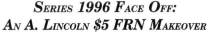

Fig. 4.66. Anticipating the new $5 notes following release of the Series 1996 $100 Federal Reserve Notes in March 1996, the present author exhibited several proposed Lincoln designs at the June 1998 Memphis International Paper Money show. The exhibit was titled "Series 1996 Face Off: An A. Lincoln $5 FRN Makeover." Shown is an example of a proposed new design carrying over the Charles Burt Lincoln portrait and watermark, and another and favored design with Lorenzo Hatch's handsome circa 1902 engraving based in the "Gettysburg Lincoln" as the vignette and watermark.

Fig. 4.67. Lincoln characters and characterizations have become de rigueur components of comic book fiction during the last generation, bending space-time and historical consistency. A citizen on the 19th century would hardly recognize the fellow named Lincoln that they'd find in most stories Lincoln has appeared in, among others, (a) *Mysteries of Unexplored Worlds*, May 1964; (b) *M.A.R.S. Patrol*, August 1968; (c) *The Flash*, November 1971; (d) *Scooby-Doo*, December 1977; (e) *The Incredible Hulk*, September 1979; (f) *Weird Western Tales Starring Scalphunter*, March 1979; (g) *Unexpected*, December 1981; (h) *Legends*, January 1987; (i) *Captain America*, September 1988; (j) *Detective Comics*, November 1988; (k) *Bill & Ted's Excellent Adventure*, 1989; (l) *Bill & Ted's Excellent Comics*, December 1991; (m) *Bill & Ted's Excellent Comic Book*, October 1992; (n) *Guy Gardner Warrior*, February 1995; and (o) *Batman*, December 1998.

1999 OCTOBER 5. UPN television network debuts the short-lived, controversial series *The Secret Diary of Desmond Pfeiffer*, about a card cheat who serves as Lincoln's butler at the White House during the Civil War. Lincoln is played for laughs by Dann Florek (fig. 4.68m, with Christine Estabrook, who plays Mary) as a character who much more resembles then-incumbent Bill Clinton. Other recent portrayals of Lincoln of stage and screen are also shown.

1999 OCTOBER 6. Comedian and satirist Jon Stewart publishes *Naked Pictures of Famous People.* The cover of the first edition has a nude Lincolnesque figure in stove pipe hat, eyes blacked out, self-consciously covering his private parts with his hands.

1999 OCTOBER 8. In the film *Fight Club,* Tyler Durden (Brad Pitt) tells the narrator (Edward Norton) that his favorite historical character to fight would be Abraham Lincoln because "Big guy, big reach. Skinny guys fight 'til they're burger." Lincoln's physical prowess is something of legend. In 1998, he was commemorated on a "Heroes of Wrestling" card (fig. 4.70).

1999 NOVEMBER 16. The BEP unveils V. Jack Ruther's adopted face and back designs for the Series 1999 $5 Federal Reserve Notes (fig. 4.71). This includes a new, larger Lincoln image by portrait engravers William Fleishell III and Thomas R. Hipschen. This portrait is a much freer interpretation than Charles Burt rendered from the same model 130 years earlier. The BEP also unveils a new, streamlined view of the Lincoln Memorial to appear on the new notes engraved by Thomas R. Hipschen, with lettering by Dixie March. Because of its size and shading, the seated Lincoln figure within the memorial is much more easily seen.

1999 DECEMBER 1. Feature cartoonist Howard Shoemaker creates his humorous illustration of Lincoln window-shopping for a red propeller-cap as a gift for the present author (fig. 4.72). A similar image by Shoemaker appeared in a men's magazine.

2000 FEBRUARY 25. Public Law 106-173, amended by an Act of July 24, 2001, creates the Abraham Lincoln Bicentennial Commission. Lincoln scholar Harold Holzer, Sen. Richard Durbin (D-IL), and Rep. Ray LaHood (R-IL) are co-chairs.

Fig. 4.68. Reportedly Steven Spielberg is developing a Lincoln movie based on Doris Kearns Goodwin's *Team of Rivals* for release in 2010. Rumors have run rife speculating on the project. Recent screen and stage depictions of Lincoln include: *(a)* Barry Atwater in 1960, *(b)* F. Murray Abraham in 1966, *(c)* Fred Gwynne in 1972, *(d)* Arthur Hill in 1975, *(e)* Hal Holbrook in 1974, *(f)* John Anderson in 1977, *(g)* Gregory Peck in 1982, *(h)* Sam Waterston in 1988, *(i)* Robert Barron in 1989, *(j)* Jason Robards in 1991, *(k)* Lance Henriksen in 1998, and *(l)* Dann Florek in 1998.

2000 MAY 21. Commenting on the new Lincoln visage to appear on the $5 bill, humor columnist John Breneman complained "our currency is simply not tall enough to accommodate Lincoln's prodigious and distinctive headgear."

2000. The Republic of Liberia issues silver $5 and $20 coins depicting Lincoln. Additional gold $25 coins portraying Lincoln and Mount Rushmore were issued in 2001 and 2002 (fig. 4.73).

2000 MAY 24. New Series 1999 Lincoln $5 notes are shipped to banks, and officially introduced at a Lincoln Memorial ceremony that same day.

2000. New, large portraits on U.S. paper money invite editing, and the art of "refacing" becomes popular. This Lincoln $5 caricature (fig. 4.74) was created for this book by Fred L. Reed IV.

2000 SEPTEMBER 23. "Picturing Lincoln: the Changing Image of America's 16th President" featuring the Jack L. Smith collection opens at the Northern Indiana Center for History of Indiana Historical Society.

2002 APRIL 13. Illinois governor George Ryan announces five finalists from among 6,000 design suggestions for the state's quarter dollar. Proposals were reviewed by a committee of 14, comprised of state officials, school teachers, and members of the public—including a coin dealer, Harlan J. Berk. Finalist designs included Abraham Lincoln, the Sears Tower, and prairie flora and fauna. "Kansas and Nebraska have prairies, but only Illinois has Lincoln," said renowned Chicago numismatist Berk (author of *100 Greatest Ancient Coins*).

2002 MAY 17. The U.S. Secret Service releases findings supporting genuineness of the purported 1959-D Lincoln cent with Wheat Ears reverse (fig. 4.75). This cent is "one of the most controversial coins to appear on the market in decades," according to coin expert Ron Guth. Authorities are at a loss to explain its existence. Some experts feel the coin is a fake, but if so it is so perfect that it has fooled the U.S. Secret Service. According to a report by writer Paul Gilkes in the trade publication *Coin World*, the coin was given a clean bill of health by the feds after "optical and scanning electron microscopic examinations."[7] The coin was slated to be sold at a September 22 and 23, 2002, auction by

Fig. 4.69. Limited edition bimetallic $10 chip from the Plaza hotel and casino, Las Vegas.

Fig. 4.70. *(a)* Artist Jason McCorkle put a celebrated image to Tyler Durden's *Fight Club*. *(b)* Lincoln's Asics 1998 "Heroes of Wrestling" card.

Fig. 4.71. New Series 1999 Lincoln $5 Federal Reserve Note with larger Lincoln portrait by William Fleishell III and Thomas R. Hipschen (BEP die no. MISC19827-3) was engraved in 1998. Back of the new Lincoln $5 note has a more open, streamlined Lincoln Memorial by Hipschen, with lettering by Dixie March.

Fig. 4.72. When cartoonist Howard Shoemaker sent this delightful original drawing and his compliments to the author, he suggested it might dress up a future work. Now's the time; this is the place. Thanks, Howard!

Ira and Larry Goldberg Coins & Collectibles, but was removed from the sale after convicted forger and murderer Mark Hofmann claimed to have made the coin. Investigation of Mr. Hofmann's claims failed to be substantiated. The coin was then listed in the Goldbergs' February 24 and 25, 2003, sale. It eventually sold for $45,000.

2002 JUNE 24. The Abraham Lincoln Bicentennial Commission endorses a series of new cent reverses for 2009 observance.

2002 OCTOBER 8. Illinois governor George H. Ryan unveils the selection for the "Land of Lincoln" state quarter design. "I am proud that Lincoln is standing boldly in the center of the design. His resolve and example mean a great deal to people in Illinois and throughout the world," Ryan said in announcing the design from among the 6,000-plus ideas his office received. The design was inspired by artwork submitted to the governor by Thom Cicchelli of Chicago. In addition to the state's motto "Land of Lincoln," the Lincoln figure is modeled from *The Resolute Lincoln,* a statue by Avard Fairbanks. "It is meant to reflect a turning point in Lincoln's career and the changes that Lincoln went through during the six years he spent in New Salem, where he resolves to put down the ax and pick up the book,"

according to the governor's official announcement. The statue was dedicated in 1954 as a gift to the State of Illinois from the National Society of the Sons of Utah Pioneers. It is located in New Salem State Historic Site.

2003 JANUARY 2. The Illinois state quarter is released to the public. (fig. 4.76) The design was engraved by Mint sculptor/engraver Donna Weaver. Official mintage was 463,200,000.

2003 APRIL 5. The dedication of a statue to Abraham Lincoln in Richmond, Virginia, former capital of the Confederate States of America, stirs up a predictable hornet's nest.

2003 MAY 1. President George W. Bush is greeted by a controversial "Mission Accomplished" sign on board USS *Abraham Lincoln* as the commander-in-chief welcomes the ship's crew back from deployment.

2003 MAY 1. On that same day but flying under the international news radar, Pasadena, California, mayor Bill Bogaard calls Lincoln "a source of inspiration to our national values" at his "Mayor's Prayer Breakfast" speech entitled "A New Commitment to National Values."

Fig. 4.73. The Republic of Liberia struck more non-circulating legal tender coins honoring Lincoln in the new century: (a) 2000 Liberia $5 silver (Bruce-X17); (b) 2000 Liberia $20 silver (KM-479); (c) 2001 Liberia $25 Lincoln Memorial gold (KM-666); (d) 2001 Liberia $25 Mt. Rushmore gold (KM-667); (e) 2002 Liberia $25 Lincoln and Memorial gold (KM-669).

Fig. 4.74. The new larger Lincoln portrait and the power of the internet sprung forth a groundswell of "re-facing" opportunities like that of Fred L. Reed IV shown here.

2003. The Republic of Liberia strikes Lincoln $10 and $20 commemorative coins, followed by further issues in 2004 and 2006 (fig. 4.77).

2003 SEPTEMBER 8. The inaugural game is played at Lincoln Financial Field in Philadelphia—Eagles vs. Tampa Bay Buccaneers.

2003 DECEMBER 15. The National Archives exhibits the Gettysburg Address to inaugurate a special exhibition of the documents voted by the American public as the most important in our country's history. Lincoln's two minutes and "few appropriate remarks" was voted as the eighth most influential document in American history. It had not been seen by the public since 1999.

2004 JANUARY 19. National Archives special display of the most influential documents in U.S. History concludes with the exhibition of Lincoln's Emancipation Proclamation, which was voted the sixth most important.

2004. National Parks Service purchases Wills House, Gettysburg, where Lincoln made final edits to his Gettysburg Address, for use as a museum (fig. 4.78).

2004 JUNE. In anticipation of further currency redesign (before the feds announced they would not colorize the $5 denomination), Memphis International Paper Money Show exhibitor Fred Reed offers some suggestions (fig. 4.80).

2004 SEPTEMBER 7. Illinois Republican Rep. Ray LaHood introduces the *Abraham Lincoln Bicentennial 1-cent Coin Redesign Act.*

2004 SEPTEMBER 21. Illinois Democrat Sen. Richard Durbin introduces the *Abraham Lincoln Bicentennial 1-cent Coin Redesign Act.*

2004 NOVEMBER 24. Bonhams and Butterfields auction the Lloyd Ostendorf collection of Lincolniana, including the original glass plate negative of the photo engraved by Charles Burt for Lincoln 50-cent Fractional Currency.

2004. New York City gallery owner Keya Morgan purchases the majority of the Lloyd Ostendorf collection of Lincoln photographs, adding them to the Herbert Wells Fay collection of Lincoln photographs that he had purchased in the 1990s. Mr. Morgan says he plans a book on Lincoln photographs to update the work of his mentor Lloyd Ostendorf.

Fig. 4.75. The U.S. Secret Service announced on May 17, 2002, that a 1959-D Wheat Ears cent mule, claimed to have been made by convicted murderer and forger Mark Hoffman, was a genuine U.S. Mint product and could be legally sold. The coin is believed unique.

Fig. 4.76. 2003 Illinois state quarter.

Fig. 4.77. Liberia is a small country with a big appetite for collectors' dollars. More recent noncirculating legal tender collector issues featuring Lincoln include: *(a)* 2003 Liberia $10 Lincoln and Memorial, copper-nickel (KM-824); *(b)* 2003 Liberia $20 Mary Todd Lincoln-Abraham Lincoln silver (KM-825); *(c)* 2004 Liberia $20 Emancipation Proclamation silver (KM-826); *(d)* 2006 Liberia $10 copper-nickel (KM-827).

2005 FEBRUARY 10. Congressman Ray LaHood (R-IL) introduces the *Abraham Lincoln Bicentennial 1-cent Coin Redesign Act* (H.R. 767). Illinois Democrat Sen. Richard Durbin introduces the *Abraham Lincoln Bicentennial 1-cent Coin Redesign Act* (S. 341).

2005 APRIL 15. Senator Richard Durbin (D-IL) introduces S. 811, calling for a Lincoln birth bicentennial silver dollar.

2005 APRIL 19. The Lincoln Presidential Library and Museum, which bills itself as the "center of gravity for all things Lincoln," is dedicated (fig. 4.81). Constructed for $115 million, it is the largest presidential library complex in the nation. The Library has 46,000 Lincoln documents and artifacts, including nearly 1,500 documents signed or written in Lincoln's hand. These include holographic copies of the Gettysburg Address and Lincoln's Second Inaugural Address. In its first two years of operation, more than a million visitors entered its portals.

2005 APRIL 27. The House passes bill 422-6 marking Lincoln's birth bicentennial with four commemorative cent reverses; the same day the House passes the Presidential dollar bill which calls for commemorative dollars for all presidents, including, of course, Lincoln once again. On December 22, 2005, President George Bush signs S. 1047, the Presidential $1 Coin Act of 2005, which also authorizes $50 American bison bullion coin, and four reverse designs for the 2009 Lincoln cent.

2005. The state of Illinois institutes the Commemorative Medallions Program.

2005 JUNE 8. Congressman Ray LaHood (R-IL) introduces H.R. 2808, calling for a Lincoln birth bicentennial silver dollar.

2005 JULY 4. A special issue of *Time* magazine features the cover story "Uncovering the Real Abe Lincoln" (fig. 4.82).

2005 AUGUST 17. The Abraham Lincoln Medal of Freedom is filed with the Illinois secretary of state to honor Illinois National Guard members mobilized for the war on terrorism, which had been established through executive order by governor Rod R. Blagojevich. The medal embodied Lincoln's "militia spirit" as a member of the Illinois Militia during the Blackhawk War, the governor said. The award rec-

Fig. 4.78. The David Wills House in downtown Gettysburg, Pennsylvania, where Lincoln is said to have polished his Gettysburg Address the night before, is on the National Register of Historic Places, and now administered by the National Parks Service. This advance admission ticket is probably from the 1960s.

Fig. 4.79. Stock certificate for "The Original" Lincoln Logs Ltd., printed by ABNCo, dated May 5, 2004.

Fig. 4.80. In 2004 before the Treasury announced it would not colorize the $5 bills, the present author revived his crusade to get the feds to use the "Gettysburg Lincoln" on the new bill. He staged another "Face Off" display at the June 2004 Memphis International Paper Money Show. Shown is (a) a Series 2004 colorized $5 with the then current likeness, and (b) another with the preferable Gettysburg likeness, based on the circa 1902 engraving of Lorenzo Hatch.

Fig. 4.81. April 19, 2005, was the date of the official dedication ceremony of the Abraham Lincoln Presidential Library and Museum in Springfield.

ognizes the service of members of the Illinois Army and Air National Guard.

2005 SEPTEMBER 6. The House passes H.R. 2808, calling for a Lincoln birth bicentennial silver dollar.

2005 SEPTEMBER 12. CivilWarToken.net announces a $21,500 private-treaty record sale of a Civil War token employing the desirable "Lincoln" REDEEMED and hunting dog brass-button die, Fuld 134/184. For a look at this so-called loose "Lincoln" portrait see figure

1.159. This eclipsed the previous record price ($14,500) for a patriotic Civil War token, established by the private-treaty sale in 1999 of the unique Fuld 226A/322A discovered by Fred Reed in the 1960s.

2005. Souvenir gag "Lincoln Bedroom" towels (fig. 4.83) appear in the wake of reports that well-connected donors could buy their way into overnight stays. Lincoln's identity is also connected to things as disparate as red roses (see fig. 4.28); to license plates (fig. 4.84); to Lincoln Rock (fig. 4.85) a natural formation near Seymour Canal, Alaska; and to the author's personal bookplate (fig. 4.86).

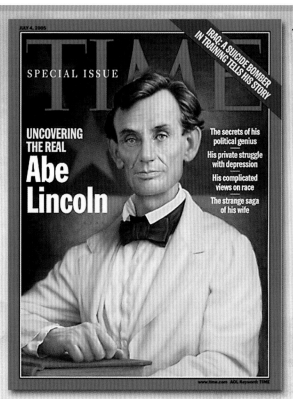

Fig. 4.82. For July 4, 2005, *Time* magazine published a "special issue," billed as "Uncovering the Real Abe Lincoln" with suggestive cover blurbs to spur newsstand sales.

Fig. 4.83. The Lincoln bedroom at the White House is a suite of three rooms on the second floor of the mansion that served as Lincoln's office, cabinet room, and secretaries' office. A novelty Lincoln bedroom towel states "compliments of your stay at the White House."

Fig. 4.84. Illinois and South Dakota still like to tout their Lincoln pride on their auto license plates: (a) 1983 South Dakota, (b) 1985 Illinois, (c) 2003 Illinois, (d) 1984 Illinois Lincoln Fest, (e) 2001 Illinois Automobile License Plate Collectors Assn. Convention, and (f) 2006 South Dakota.

Fig. 4.85. Lincoln Rock, Seymour Canal, Alaska, is one geographical feature said to look like Old Abe. Lincoln Rock near Tenino, Washington, and Mount Lincoln, near Lawton, Oklahoma, are others.

Fig. 4.86. In 2006 the author had customized bookplates printed after consulting with legendary numismatist Dr. George Fuld. Fuld's bookplate features a Washington medallion, emblematic of his long-standing interest and research in the field of Washingtonia. The author's personal ex libris employs the 50-cent fractional currency likeness against a field containing the text of the Gettysburg Address.

2005 September 27. The Citizens Coinage Advisory Committee nixes recommendation for a 2009 Abraham Lincoln commemorative coin. CCAC rejects a Lincoln 2009 commemorative coin in favor of "commemorative coins other than Lincoln." One year to the day later, President Bush signed legislation authorizing the coin.

2006 July. An enigmatic print and television advertising campaign for the sleep aid Rozerem shows Lincoln and a beaver in absurdist situations, but captures public attention and sparks Internet chatter (fig. 4.87).

2006 April 28. Heritage Numismatic Auctions sells a 1999 Lincoln cent-dime mule on a cent planchet, the discovery coin, at its CSNS sale for $138,000. This type of coin is dubbed a "mule" because it is the offspring of two different species of coinage dies, a Lincoln cent obverse die, and a Roosevelt dime reverse die. The slightly smaller reverse die caused some deformation at the periphery of the obverse strike. How such coins (*pièces de merde,* in Walter Breen's phraseology) escape the U.S. Mint is problematical, yet such Mint errors—whether by accident or design—are highly prized by many collectors. More recently, similar discoveries have been made of 1993-D cent/dime on a cent planchet and 1995 cent/dime on a dime planchet mules. The 1999 mule shown (fig. 4.88) was purportedly discovered in a bank-wrapped cent roll in 1999 in Erie, Pennsylvania. The finder sold the coin to a local jewelry store, Dempsey & Baxter. Four years later the firm sold the piece to a private collector who specializes in such exotic items, who then consigned it to the Heritage sale in 2006.

2006 June. Thomas Schwartz, interim director of the Abraham Lincoln Presidential Library and Museum, says "the era of a heroic Lincoln is over"; emphasis today is on the personal Lincoln. Having a personal relationship with the small "l" Lincoln has long been part of the American experience, witness: (1) the three little tow-headed girls in the wagon clutching their Lincoln banks in 1929; or (2) the youthful Lincoln in his 1953 Halloween costume, or (3) the 1950 family portrait where a group snuggles up to Borglum's seated Lincoln statue and share Old Abe's bench in Newark, New Jersey (fig. 4.89).

2006 June 29. The U.S. Treasury, Federal Reserve, and U.S. Secret Service announce new colorful $5 Lincoln Federal Reserve Notes will be introduced in 2008, reversing their previous position (fig. 4.90). The decision is due to the large quantities of $100 counterfeits printed on genuine $5 notes, whose ink had been removed, and which passed most standard examination techniques because security features were in similar places on both denominations.

2006 June 29. Senate unanimously passes S. 811, *Abraham Lincoln Commemorative Coin Act,* calling for up to a half million Lincoln birth bicentennial silver dollars in 2009.

2006 September 8. The Senate passes the House version of legislation calling for a Lincoln birth bicentennial silver dollar by unanimous consent.

2006 September 27. President George W. Bush signs legislation (PL 109–285) authorizing up to 500,000 silver dollars honoring Abraham Lincoln's birth bicentennial.

2006 September 28. The first PCGS-graded MS-70 (absolutely perfect) circulation-strike Lincoln cent, a 1973 coin, brings $15,120 in a Teletrade Internet auction.

2006 October 5. Stack's (ANR) auctions the original Lincoln portrait die created by Charles Burt in March 1861 (ABNCo die #141) from ABNCo archives, which had been used on $10 Demand Notes and $10 Legal Tender Notes. This die is shown on page 27. The die and attendant documentation are purchased by Lincophile Fred Reed. The same collector also later purchases the ABNCo cylinder roller die by which Burt's image from die #141 was transferred for use on currency plates (see page 27, fig. 1.70).

2006 November 13. The South Dakota state quarter debuts at Rushmore National Memorial Amphitheater, with a Mount Rushmore design (fig. 4.92). On July 11, 2004, the Web site www.sdquarter.com went online seeking citizen participation in the project to design the state's quarter. On September 21, 2004, the Citizens Coinage Advisory Committee had weighed in against a Mount Rushmore design due to Native American resentment of the memorial's location on sacred tribal grounds. When the motif was adopted, *Coin World* columnist Q. David Bowers labeled the Mount Rushmore design "a tired, overdone motif."[8]

2007 February 11. *New York Times* op-ed writer David Margolik advocates abandoning the Lincoln cent and placing Lincoln's portrait on a new $2 or $5 coin.

2007 March. At a Portland, Oregon, "peace" rally, the city's Abe Lincoln monument is defaced with graffiti when "Abe wants Peace" is scrawled on it.

2007 April 19. In Springfield, Illinois, organizers announce, "The rally will begin at 12:00 pm in front of the Lincoln Statue and will end between 12:30 pm and 12:45 pm"; instructions are duplicated on April 10, 2008. Rallying for various causes at the Lincoln statue outside city hall in San Francisco is also popular, and has been since the civil rights demonstrations of the 1960s (fig. 4.94). Back east, in March 2008 a Jersey City peace rally similarly met up at Fraser's Lincoln statue there.

2007 May. Lincoln Springs Resort, Ashmore, Illinois, opens with the gangly 72-foot-tall "ugly" Lincoln statue, the world's tallest.

2007 May 5. The National Inventors Hall of Fame medal is first presented. The medal was designed by former Mint sculptor-engraver Thomas Rogers. It depicts Thomas Edison and Abraham Lincoln (fig. 4.95). The institution is located in Akron, Ohio, to recognize and foster "the spirit and practice of invention—the innate human impulse that drives social and economic progress." The HOF was originally founded in 1973 by the U.S. Patent and Trademark Office and the National Council of Intellectual Property Law Associations. Its Hall of Fame building opened in 1995. Edison's inventions are well known. Of course, as recorded here earlier, Lincoln is the only U.S. president to secure a U.S. patent. "The medal features Edison because he was the nation's most prolific inventor and Lincoln because he was a staunch supporter of the patent system and also an inventor," Hall of Fame public relations director Rini Paiva reported. "You'll have noticed on the medal that the quote on the outer edge is a Lincoln quote: 'The patent system added the fuel of interest to the fire of genius.'"[9] An inventor must hold a U.S. patent to be considered for induction into the Hall of Fame. "Selection committees decide whether the invention is significant enough to have moved society forward and impacted it in a positive way, changing our lives in the process," the spokesperson added.

2007 MAY 16. The Illinois Department of Military Affairs solicits bidders on $60,000 contract to produce the Abraham Lincoln Medal of Freedom.

2007 AUGUST 18. The Lincoln Financial Group distributes free bobble-head Lincoln figurines at the Washington Nationals baseball game.

2007 SEPTEMBER 20. The Commission of Fine Arts recommends designs for four 2009 circulating Lincoln cent reverses.

2007 SEPTEMBER 20. A new Abe Lincoln colorized $5 bill design is unveiled digitally online by the Bureau of Engraving and Printing.

2007 SEPTEMBER 25. The Citizens Coinage Advisory Committee rejects all seven Mint-proposed designs for the commemorative cent to mark "Aspect 4" covering Lincoln's presidency.

2007 OCTOBER 31. Reps. Peter Roskam (R-IL) and Michael Castle (R-DE) introduce H.R. 4036, requiring change in the content of the Lincoln cent, after the Mint complains cents cost more than face value to produce due to increases in copper prices.

2007 NOVEMBER 13. The Citizens Coinage Advisory Committee recommends 1865 portrait / the Gettysburg Address designs for 2009 Abraham Lincoln bicentennial silver dollar.

Fig. 4.87. Lincoln and a beaver became a 2006 advertising odd couple pitching Rozerem, a sleep aid.

Fig. 4.88. In 2006 collectors learned about the odd 11-cent piece, the 1999 cent-dime mule, then a raft of other dates of equally curious parentage sprang forth, leading to bemusement and excoriation.

Fig. 4.89. Growing up with Lincoln can take all kinds of turns, like (a) the three little blonde girls with Abe banks and wagon in 1929 or (b) the young lad who trick or treated as Abe in 1953 or (c) the family that settled in with Abe at Borglum's Newark statue in 1950.

Fig. 4.90. (a) Before the feds debuted the colorized notes, they printed 400 million Series 2006 non-colorized $5 Federal Reserve Notes. (b) Then they introduced the colorized notes again as Series 2006. This is the first time in U.S. paper money history that two notes of the same denomination and class but with different designs have the same Series year designation.

2007 NOVEMBER 15. The Commission of Fine Arts reviews designs for the Lincoln bicentennial silver dollar, and recommends a bust based on the Daniel Chester French Lincoln Memorial statue.

2007 DECEMBER 21. The movie *National Treasure: Book of Secrets* takes history sleuth Ben Gates (Nicholas Cage) into the bowels of Mount Rushmore in search of the lost City of Gold.

2008. Barack Obama claims the progressive Lincoln legacy, exhibiting the affectations of several previous Democratic presidential aspirants, who also invoked Lincoln's blessings on their political careers: Woodrow Wilson, Franklin Roosevelt, George McGovern, and John Kerry (fig. 4.98).

2008 JANUARY 16. Library of Congress unveils three photo negatives—long mislabeled—taken of the crowd that witnessed Abraham Lincoln's second inaugural at the U.S. Capitol on March 4, 1865.

2008 FEBRUARY. The Token and Medal Society announces a new book updating Robert P. King's *Lincolniana,* by Paul A. Cunningham, Kathie Lawrence, David Schenkman, and Fred Reed, is in preparation.

2008 MARCH 3. The Lincoln Museum in Ft. Wayne, Indiana, announces in will close its doors at the end of June because of a downturn in attendance. A spokesperson for Lincoln Financial Foundation, which operated the museum, said it was yet to be determined what would be done with the archival material. Reports indicated

Fig. 4.91. The September/October 2006 issue of *Paper Money,* bimonthly journal of the Society of Paper Money Collectors, examined various aspects of Lincoln portrayals on U.S. currency.

Fig. 4.92. 2006 South Dakota state quarter.

Fig. 4.94. Civic demonstrations in San Francisco often take place at City Hall in front of Abe Lincoln, and have for more than a generation. This is a May 27, 1963, San Francisco Civil Rights Freedom March.

Fig. 4.93. WWLD mirrors the success of the "What Would Jesus Do?" movement. "What Would Lincoln Do?" is a question that editorial writers and bloggers have been asking a lot of late. This indicates that many still think Lincoln is relevant.

Fig. 4.95. Former U.S. Mint sculptor-engraver Thomas Rogers created the National Inventors Hall of Fame medallion first awarded in 2007, depicting famous inventors Thomas Alva Edison and Lincoln.

that the Library of Congress and Ford's Theatre Museum, among other groups, were interested.

2008 MARCH 9. Lincoln scholar Harold Holzer addresses the impending closing of the Lincoln Museum in an op-ed piece published in the Fort Wayne *Journal Gazette:* "This must be how people felt the first time Lincoln was assassinated," he wrote.

2008 MARCH 13. The first of the colorized, next-generation Lincoln $5 bills to enter circulation is spent at the gift shop of President Lincoln's Cottage at the Soldiers' Home in Washington, D.C. These notes are designated Series 2006, the same series designation as the non-colorized $5 bills also bearing the signatures of Treasury Secre-

tary Henry Paulson Jr. and Treasurer Anna Escobedo Cabral. Thus two notes of the same denomination and same class of currency, but with different designs have the same series designation for the first time in the history of U.S. currency.

2008 MARCH 30. San Francisco dedicates a 40-foot-long, 8-foot-high public monument to members of the Abraham Lincoln Brigade.

2008 JUNE 3. The Medford, Oregon, *Mail Tribune* reports that the Abe Lincoln statue in Lithia Park, Ashland, Oregon, has been decapitated for a fifth time. Previously, Lincoln had lost his head in 1958, 1967, 1973, and 2005. According to the report, damage is estimated at $1,200, but park officials "have no idea if they will restore the statue now or not."

Fig. 4.96. Why not a Lincoln sucker? The purveyors of Lincoln Head Pops no doubt think their product is wonderful.

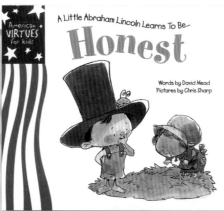

Fig. 4.97. What we have here is a difference of opinion. Is he or isn't he . . . honest, that is? (a) Author David Mead thought so in his 2003 *A Little Abraham Lincoln Learns to be Honest.* (b) Author Thomas J. DiLorenzo and the Ludwig von Mises Institute think not.

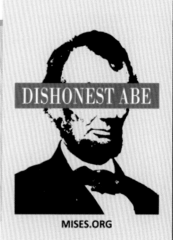

Fig. 4.98. Democratic presidential candidates have gravitated to Lincoln for a variety of reasons: (a) his honesty (1974), (b) his greatness (2004), (c) his egalitarianism (2008). For presidential candidate Barack Obama, the third time proved to be the charm.

Fig. 4.100. Buffing up took a whole new meaning in the Library of Congress' inventive public service announcement "are you history buff?"

Fig. 4.99. Kentucky was so enthusiastic about getting out their message for the upcoming bicentennial of Lincoln's birth at Hodgenville, that the author obtained this 2009 Kentucky "Birthplace of Lincoln" license plate in early 2008.

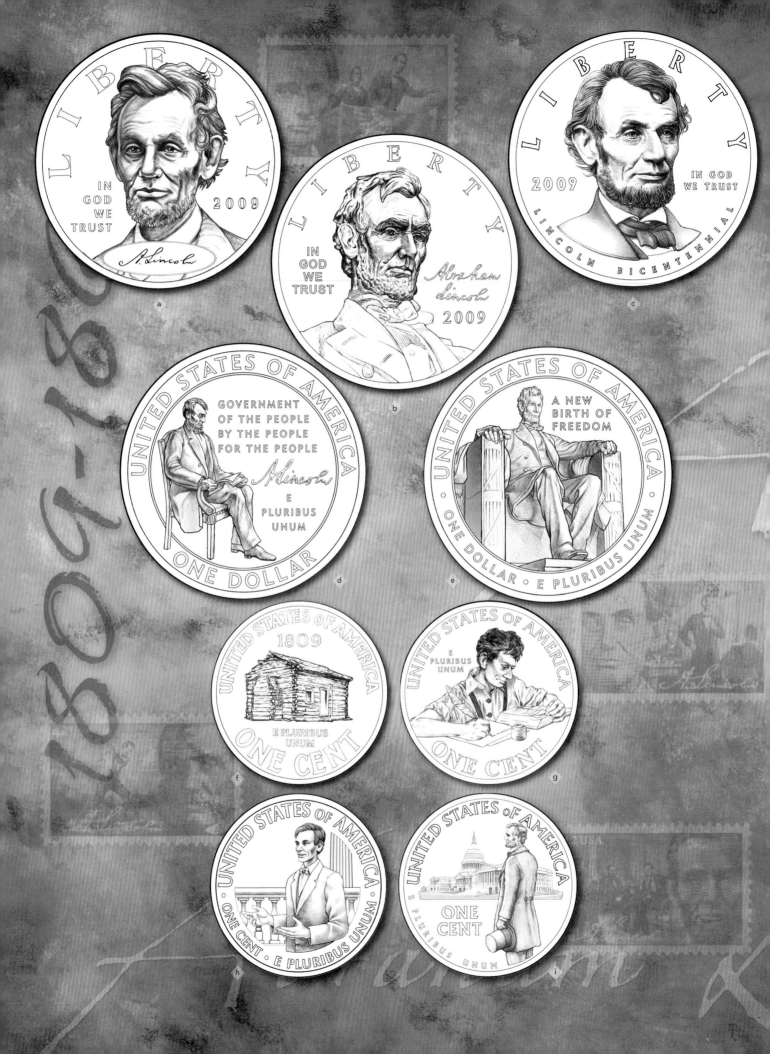

Chapter 5

Lincoln, the Irrelevant?

2009-future

For years, a banner hung from Lincoln and Herndon's former law-office building, reading "He Lives in the Hearts of the People." Is the memory of Lincoln still enshrined in the hearts of the people, and will it continue thus forever? The answer depends on whom one listens to. Recently a news weekly posed the question, "Who is more important, Lincoln or Darwin?" The question arose because they were both born on the same day and were both about to be honored on the 200th anniversary of their birth. *Newsweek* editors examined the question and chose Lincoln, but scientists might have chosen Darwin. So much the better for Lincoln aficionados, but the periodical's choice sparked a firestorm on the Internet. Outraged science-minded types lacerated the choice. One called Lincoln "irrelevant," especially outside the United States.

The question of Lincoln's relevancy to 21st-century Americans calls forth strong passions. Richard Lawrence Miller, author of the two-volume *Lincoln and His World,* posed just such a question in an Internet chat room. "Is Lincoln relevant any more?" Miller wrote. "I've begun to wonder." He continued, "Our world is changing in so many ways since I began writing about Lincoln. He ultimately united Americans, but now we are as divided as in the 1850s. What guidance does Lincoln's experience give us?"

Responses varied from a hearty "Yes, now more than ever," because of his humanistic values, strong leadership, and moral strength, to replies that he was a fascist whose relevance is that he should be avoided. Lincoln detractors have certainly had a field day of late. But the venom and spleen shown by modern-day Lincoln-haters wouldn't have surprised Lincoln at all. He heard worse during his own lifetime.

Author John Patrick Diggins's *On Hallowed Ground: Abraham Lincoln and the Foundations of American History* put a floor under the discussion. Lincoln believed the principles of the Declaration and the Constitution, and put those principles into action. "What should render Lincoln relevant to different people everywhere is his conviction that America's political ideals transcend differences of race, class, gender, religion, and ancestry. He believed that all of humanity possesses certain qualities and endowments," Diggins wrote.

While this approach appeals to high principles, another recent Lincoln author, journalist Andrew Ferguson, reported in his delightful *Land of Lincoln: Adventures in Abe's America* that Lincoln's relevance today increasingly depends on his averageness, his similarity to the man on

Suggested Mint designs for the obverse of the Lincoln bicentennial commemorative silver dollar included *(a)* a bust based on a February 5, 1865, Alexander Gardner photo (Ostendorf-116); *(b)* a sketch of D.C. French's Lincoln memorial statue head; and *(c)* a portrait based on the old-style $5 bill model, Anthony Berger's February 9, 1864, photo (Ostendorf-92).

Suggested Mint designs for the reverse of the Lincoln bicentennial dollar included *(d)* Lincoln seated in a chair, similar to the February 9, 1864, Anthony Berger photo of Lincoln and Tad examining a photo album at Brady's Gallery (Ostendorf-93); and *(e)* a drawing of Lincoln seated on his Lincoln Memorial throne by Daniel Chester French.

Designs under consideration for the 2009 Lincoln bicentennial cent program were required to represent one of four phases of Lincoln's life. Pictured *(f–i)* are some contenders. See fig. 5.1 for the final designs.

Fig. 5.1. The Mint revealed the 2009
Lincoln cent designs on September
22, 2008. The coins will depict, in
order of their release, (a) a log cabin,
representing his birth and early life in
Kentucky; (b) a young Lincoln educating himself while working as a rail-
splitter in Indiana; (c) Lincoln as a young
professional in front of the Illinois
state capitol; and (d) the half-finished
U.S. Capitol dome, representing his
presidential years in Washington.

the street. Lincoln, Ferguson found, has been humanized, demystified. His relevance today rests on the fact that average Americans can see themselves in him.

Such a turn of affairs shouldn't be too surprising, even to Lincoln enthusiasts. The last century has had a way of tipping golden idols over on their feet of clay. But bringing Abe down off the pedestal is not the same as bringing him down to size. After all, he was six feet four. He cast a long shadow even when his feet were firmly planted on the ground with his fellows. For many years Lincoln's humanity was clothed in the robes of perfection; today's cynical crowd wants to shout "the emperor has no clothes." A recent "humor" book cover depicted Lincoln naked and embarrassed.

The year 2009 marks the 200th anniversary of Abraham Lincoln's birth, and an opportunity for Americans to reexamine his words, deeds, and relevancy. Congress set up a Lincoln Bicentennial Commission, authorized commemorative coins, planned a rededication of the Lincoln Memorial, and scheduled a special ceremony at the U.S. Capitol for February 12. Individuals and organizations across the country are making Lincoln relevant to their local communities, as well. The events calendar on the Library of Congress Lincoln Bicentennial Web site shows one or more scheduled programs most days in the months leading up to February 2009. Programs include a Lincoln Bicentennial playwriting contest, Lincoln walking tours, Lincoln-Douglas debate cele-brations, patriotic concerts, the Abraham Lincoln National Rail-Splitting Contest, sculpture ded-ications, symposia, and dedication of the Lincoln Memorial Garden in Lincoln City, Indiana.

Numismatically, the Lincoln bicentennial celebration promises a lot of heat. Under provisions of Public Law 109-145, dated December 22, 2005, four new cent reverses will honor Abraham Lincoln. Plans call for release of these new cents into circulation at intervals throughout the year— January 1, April 1, July 1, and October 1. The designs focus on different stages or aspects of Lin-coln's life. The cent obverse will restore Brenner's historical Lincoln profile, which has weathered some over the years. In addition to these new Lincoln cents for circulation, Congress mandated a numismatic issue of "pennies with the same metallic content as the 1909 penny"—that is, 95 percent copper, 5 percent tin and zinc.

In addition to authorizing the Lincoln Bicentennial cents, Congress also passed "The Abraham Lincoln Commemorative Coin Act," Public Law 109-285, September 27, 2006. It provides for the issue of up to 500,000 legal-tender dollar coins composed of 90 percent silver, "in commem-oration of the bicentennial of the birth of Abraham Lincoln." These NCLT (non-circulating legal tender) numismatic coins will be the size of the old silver dollar, 1.5 inches in diameter, and not the size of the "golden" mini-dollars. Both Proof and Uncirculated editions will be coined, but only at one minting facility per "particular quality of the coins minted under this Act." A sales surcharge of $10 per coin will be paid to the Abraham Lincoln Bicentennial Commission to further its work. Coins may be issued by the Treasury for one year, starting January 1, 2009.

Congress acted against the express wishes of the Citizens Coinage Advisory Committee (CCAC), which had nixed a proposed Lincoln commemorative coin at its September 27, 2005, meeting. Meeting precisely one year to the date before the Lincoln silver dollar measure was enacted, the CCAC "voted against recommending a commemorative coin for the 200th anniver-sary of Abraham Lincoln's birth," according to reporter Bill McAllister, writing in the numismatic trade publication *Coin World.* The panel hoped "that Congress [would] decide that four com-memorative cents are enough to honor the 16th president."

Exact designs for the several cents were left to the discretion of the secretary of the Treasury, subject to suitable specified mottos, consultation with the Abraham Lincoln Bicentennial Com-mission and the Commission of Fine Arts, and review by the CCAC. In September 2007 the Commission of Fine Arts (CFA) weighed in on the matter. Choosing from among a plethora of designs suggested by the Mint, CFA recommended reverses having a Kentucky log cabin, a pair of hands with a quill signing a document, Lincoln in front of the Illinois Statehouse, and a view of the incomplete U.S. Capitol. About the same time, the CCAC picked a different Kentucky cabin, a youthful Lincoln inscribing a paper, and Lincoln standing at a table holding a document. It rejected all the suggested "aspect 4" designs for Lincoln's presidential years, and urged a design that more overtly evoked Lincoln's role during the war. On January 15, 2008, the CCAC met to reconsider additional design candidates for the fourth reverse.

The design-selection process in general, and for the Lincoln commemorative cents in partic-ular, has drawn fierce criticism. *Coin World* editor Beth Deisher pointed out that the "designs don't fit [a] small coin canvas." She went on to add, "Artists preparing designs for the four com-memorative reverses for the 2009 Lincoln cents . . . appear to have had larger coins in mind. . . . Virtually all of the 38 candidate designs . . . would be better on coins with larger diameters such as quarter dollar, half dollar, or dollar coins."[1]

Designs are composed as black-and-white line and wash drawings eight inches in diameter; a Lincoln cent, however, is only about three-fourths of an inch in diameter. As a result, Deisher charged, the proposed designs are cluttered. She expressed the need for simpler, cleaner approaches, instead of the elaborate illustrations Mint artists had concocted. "Presenting one element that can convey the message of many words is what distinguishes artist wannabes from great artists and sculptor/engravers," she wrote. Since Lincoln was a great president, she continued, "To commemorate the bicentennial of his birth with less than great designs would be a travesty."[2]

Deisher's views were seconded by a U.S. Mint insider, T. James Ferrell, who was sculptor/engraver at the U.S. Mint when the statehood quarters were launched. He said, "Many of [the state quarters] were stuffed with almost mural-sized concepts on a small size. They're hard to read now, but wait until they get some wear." Specifically, on the proposed cent designs, Ferrell wrote that "the imagery [suggested] is too small for a cent. . . . Designs rendered as large black-and-white images may not translate to small bas-relief sculpture."[3]

Both Ferrell and founding *Coin World* editor Dick Johnson say that the problem is that the artists presently designing U.S. coins like the new Lincoln cent reverses are graphic artists, who work in two dimensions (as opposed to sculptors, who work in three). Their flat medium requires a great deal of detail to bring up the design. But since coins are three dimensional and small, less is better.

Designer of the Kentucky cabin cent is Richard Masters, Jim Licaretz, sculptor; the Indiana cent was designed and sculpted by Charles Vickers; the Illinois cent was designed by Joel Iskowitz and sculpted by Don Everhart; and the cent representing Lincoln's presidency was designed by Susan Gamble and sculpted by Joseph Menna.

On October 30, 2008, the United States Postal Service revealed four designs for Lincoln commemorative stamps that will be released in 2009. Springfield, Illinois, was chosen as the first-day-of-issue city, with that day scheduled for February 9. The chosen stamp designs are shown in figure 5.2.

As if this were not enough good news for Lincoln enthusiasts, three additional new Lincoln coins are also scheduled for 2010. Yet another new reverse design to replace the Lincoln Memorial is scheduled to appear on the cent reverse that year. Congress mandated that this design be "emblematic of President Lincoln's preservation of the United States of America as a single and united country." How long the new cent reverse will last is uncertain, as is the composition of the coin due to increases in materials and manufacturing costs. The Mint has asked for standby authority to change the cent's composition.

In 2010, the fourth year of the Presidential $1 coin series will wrap up in mid-November with the release of the Abraham Lincoln golden mini-dollar in that series. At about the same time, the Mary Todd Lincoln First Spouse $10 gold coin (one-half ounce, .9999 fine) is scheduled to be released.

Over the years many unsuccessful attempts were made in Congress to have Lincoln's birthday observed as a national holiday. A century ago, on the eve of the Lincoln birth centennial, Congress did authorize President Theodore Roosevelt to declare February 12, 1909, a national holiday. Roosevelt did so, but in the words of late Lincoln scholar Louis A. Warren, "It would appear that the lateness of the proclamation could have had little effect in causing the day to be observed generally."

Lincoln's birthday was at one time generally observed as a legal state holiday outside the South. By 1928 it was observed in 28 states and the territory of Alaska, and as a federal holiday in the District of Columbia. The observance of President's Day as a federal holiday on the third Monday in February resulted from a proclamation by President Richard Nixon in 1971. State observances of Lincoln's birthday began to dwindle, although it is still a legal holiday in 16 states. Another seven states observe a Washington-Lincoln day. Congress could act on this matter beginning with the observance of February 12, 2009. That would, at least in some ways, solve any question of Lincoln's relevance to America in the 21st century.

Fig. 5.2. Available February 9, 2009, these four commemorative U.S. postage stamps illustrate aspects of Lincoln's life: *(a)* the rail splitter includes the earliest known photograph of Lincoln, taken by N.H. Shepherd in 1846, and depicts Lincoln as a youth splitting a log; *(b)* the lawyer includes Abraham Byers's 1858 photograph of Lincoln and an image of Lincoln in an Illinois courtroom; *(c)* the politician has the Cooper Union photo taken by Mathew Brady in February 1860 and an illustration of Lincoln in one of his famous 1858 debates with Stephen A. Douglas; *(d)* and the president shows the "Gettysburg Lincoln" November 1863 photo by Alexander Gardner and an image of Lincoln and generals Ulysses S. Grant and William T. Sherman, based on a painting by George P.A. Healy. The stamp art was created by Mark Summers.

Notes

CHAPTER 1

1. Lincoln, *Collected Works,* vol. 3.
2. *Journal of the Abraham Lincoln Association* 11 (1990).
3. Mrs. P.A. Hanaford, *Abraham Lincoln: His Life and Public Services* (Boston: B.B. Russell & Co., 1866), 31.
4. *Lincoln Lore,* no. 259.
5. Lincoln, "Second Lecture on Discoveries and Inventions" (delivered before the Young Men's Association of Bloomington, IL, April 6, 1858).
6. *The Lincoln Log: a daily chronology of the life of Abraham Lincoln.*
7. Raymond, *Life and Public Services,* 100.
8. Holzer, *Lincoln at Cooper Union,* 98.
9. *New York Times,* April 14, 1895.
10. *New York Times,* July 30, 1860.
11. Richard Hershberger to author, April 5, 2008.
12. Richard Hershberger to author, December 10, 2007.
13. Orville Browning, quoted in *The Lincoln Log.*
14. Lincoln, *Papers at the Library of Congress.*
15. Ibid.
16. Boyd, *Memorial Lincoln Bibliography,* 115.
17. Lincoln, *Collected Works,* vol. 4.
18. See O-40 in Hamilton and Ostendorf, *Lincoln in Photographs,* 67.
19. Holzer, Boritt, and Neely, *The Lincoln Image,* 31.
20. Ibid.
21. Ibid.
22. Lincoln, *Papers at the Library of Congress.*
23. Hamilton and Ostendorf, *Lincoln in Photographs,* 80.
24. Boyd, *Memorial Lincoln Bibliography,* 143, 158.
25. William H. Beach, *The First New York Lincoln Cavalry* (New York: The Lincoln Cavalry Association, 1902), 22.
26. New York State Military Museum and Veterans Research Center, "1st Cavalry Regiment, Civil War," http://www.dmna.state.ny.us.
27. *Lincoln Lore,* no. 1188.
28. "The Work of Thomas U. Walter, Architect," in *Glenn Brown's History of the United States Capitol,* GPO Access, http://www.gpoaccess.gov.
29. Lincoln, *Papers at the Library of Congress.*
30. Bowers, *Obsolete Paper Money,* 415.
31. Lincoln, *Papers at the Library of Congress.*
32. Ibid.
33. Ibid.
34. *Congressional Globe,* Library of Congress.
35. http://archiver.rootsweb.ancestry.com/th/read/INJENNIN/2002-07/1026578144
36. Lincoln, *Papers at the Library of Congress.*
37. *New York Times,* February 8, 1862; Knox, *United States Notes,* 118.

38. Act of February 12, 1862, HR 182, *Congressional Record; New York Times,* January 5, 1862; January 8, 1862; and January 22, 1862.
39. Act of February 12, 1862, HR 182, *Congressional Record; New York Times,* January 9, 1862, and January 23, 1862.
40. *New York Times,* January 17, 1863.
41. Gilfillan, *Annual Report,* 455.
42. Lincoln, *The Lincoln Log.*
43. *New York Times,* March 31, 1862.
44. Lincoln, *Collected Works,* vol. 7.
45. For more on this, see the author's *Civil War Encased Stamps: The Issuers and Their Times* (BNR Press, 1995; revised second edition in press).
46. Tainter, "History of Types"; Knox, *United States Notes,* 137.
47. Boyd, *Memorial Lincoln Bibliography,* 133.
48. Alfred L. Sewell, "The Veteran Eagle; and What the Children Did," *The Little Corporal,* December 1866, 88–90.
49. See Boyd, *Memorial Lincoln Bibliography,* 95.
50. Julian, *Medals of the United States Mint,* 58.
51. Boyd, *Memorial Lincoln Bibliography,* 150.
52. Ibid.
53. Lincoln, *Papers at the Library of Congress.*
54. Knox, *United States Notes,* 139.
55. Lincoln, *Papers at the Library of Congress.*
56. Ibid.
57. Matt Rothert, "Unusual Aspects of U.S. Fractional Currency," *The Numismatist* 77 (August 1964): 1030.
58. Dauer and Dauer, *American History as Seen Through Currency,* 185.
59. Lincoln, *Collected Works, vol. 7.*
60. Ibid.
61. Ibid., vol. 6.
62. Ibid.
63. *Lincoln Lore,* no. 1188.
64. Fuld and Fuld, *Patriotic Civil War Tokens,* 178.
65. Boyd, *Memorial Lincoln Bibliography,* 109.
66. Silvestre Reyes, "Counting Our Blessings," wwwc.house.gov/reyes/news_detail.asp?id=723.
67. Library of Congress, "Emancipation Proclamation on Display," www.loc.gov /loc/lcib/9803/emanc.html.
68. Hamilton and Ostendorf, *Lincoln in Photographs,* 145.
69. Lincoln, *Papers at the Library of Congress.*
70. Gabor Boritt, "In Lincoln's Hand," *Wall Street Journal,* November 16, 2006, WSJ Opinion Archives, http://www.opinionjournal.com/la/?id=110009250.
71. Lincoln, *Papers at the Library of Congress.*
72. Lincoln, *Ibid.*
73. Lincoln, *Collected Works, vol. 7.*
74. Lincoln, *Papers at the Library of Congress.*
75. *New York Times,* March 18, 1864.

76. Raymond, *Life and Public Services,* 728.

77. Lincoln, *Papers at the Library of Congress.* A Library of Congress note says: "Carpenter finished the painting in July [August] and Derby's firm acquired the rights to distribute prints of the work."

78. Lincoln, *Papers at the Library of Congress.*

79. Ibid.

80. Lincoln, *Ibid.*

81. Ibid.

82. *Harper's Weekly,* January 10, 1863.

83. Lincoln, *Papers at the Library of Congress.*

84. Ibid.

85. *New York Times,* January 4, 1864.

86. C.G. Memminger to Major General Whiting, January 19, 1864, Confederate Treasury correspondence.

87. Lincoln, *Papers at the Library of Congress.*

88. Hessler and Chambliss's *Comprehensive Catalog* does not list this note, but in *Paper Money of the United States,* Arthur and Ira Friedberg state that two examples are known. Official records confirm this issue.

89. Gilfillan, *Annual Report.*

90. Harry E. Pratt, *The Personal Finances of Abraham Lincoln* (Springfield, IL: Abraham Lincoln Association, 1943), 183–184.

91. *Harper's Weekly,* July 9, 1864, 447.

92. *Harper's Weekly,* September 24, 1864.

93. Lincoln, *Papers at the Library of Congress; Collected Works, vol. 8.*

94. Lincoln, *Collected Works,* vol. 8.

95. Everett K. Cooper, "Counterfeiter or Collaborator?" *Paper Money,* no. 34 (Summer 1970).

96. Lincoln, *Collected Works,* vol. 8, 545.

97. Gilfillan, *Annual Report, 457.*

98. Holzer, Boritt, and Neely, *The Lincoln Image,* 102–110, fig. 52.

99. Boyd, *Memorial Lincoln Bibliography,* 114–115; see *Harper's Weekly* ads.

100. Lincoln, *Papers at the Library of Congress.*

101. Holzer, Boritt, and Neely, "Francis Bicknell Carpenter 1830–1900: Painter of Abraham Lincoln and His Circle," *American Art Journal* 16, no. 2 (1984): 75.

102. *New York Times,* September 23, 1864.

103. Julian, *Medals of the United States Mint,* 101.

104. Lincoln, *Papers at the Library of Congress.*

105. Ibid.

106. Ibid.

107. Lincoln, *Collected Works,* vol. 8.

108. Lincoln, *Papers at the Library of Congress.*

109. *An Act for the punishment of counterfeiting the current coin of the United States; and for other purposes,* 9th Cong., 1st sess. (April 21, 1806), *U.S. Statutes at Large,* 404, chap. XLIX.

110. *New York Times,* August 11, 1864.

111. Lincoln to Attorney General James Speed, December 22, 1864, pardoning John Lawson, a.k.a. John Lassano, on account of Lawson's "reputation for honesty," in *Collected Works,* vol. 8; see also Darcy Andries, "The Most Controversial Presidential Pardons Ever," Associated Content, http://www.associatedcontent.com/article/302424/the_most_controversial_presidential.html?cat=75.

112. See P.S. Ruckman Jr., "Stink-Bomb Pardons," June 25, 2007, http://libbypardon.net/2007/06/stink-bomb-pardons.html.

113. Lincoln, *Collected Works,* vol. 8.

114. *Lincoln Lore,* no. 1170.

115. Smithsonian Institution, National Portrait Gallery, "Abraham Lincoln," http://www.npg.si.edu/exh/travpres/lincs.htm.

116. Boyd, *Memorial Lincoln Bibliography,* 112.

117. Julian, *Medals of the United States Mint,* 254.

118. *Lincoln Lore.*

119. Fite and Reese, *An Economic History of the United States* (Boston: Houghton Mifflin, 1959).

CHAPTER 2

1. *Harper's Weekly,* April 22, 1865.

2. *New York Times,* October 23, 1865.

3. Raymond, *Life and Public Services,* 728.

4. Boyd, *Memorial Lincoln Bibliography,* 110.

5. Ibid., 132.

6. Ibid., 103.

7. Ibid., 151.

8. Kirk Savage, *Standing Soldiers, Kneeling Slaves: Race, War, and Monument in Nineteenth-Century America* (Princeton, NJ: Princeton University Press, 1999), 101.

9. Boyd, *Memorial Lincoln Bibliography,* 106.

10. Raymond, *Life and Public Services,* 738.

11. F.B. Carpenter, quoted in Raymond, *Life and Public Services,* 733.

12. Raymond, *Life and Public Services,* 728.

13. Ibid., 726.

14. Julian, *Medals of the United States Mint,* 254.

15. Holzer, Boritt, and Neely, *Changing the Lincoln Image,* 21.

16. *Utica Morning Herald,* February 12, 1866.

17. Boyd, *Memorial Lincoln Bibliography,* 145.

18. Ibid., 161.

19. *New York Times,* December 23, 1866.

20. Lincoln, *Papers at the Library of Congress.*

21. Jennifer L. Bach, "Acts of Remembrance: Mary Todd Lincoln and Her Husband's Memory," *Journal of the Abraham Lincoln Association* 25, no.2 (2004).

22. Mary Todd Lincoln to Alexander Williamson, July 21, 1866, quoted in Bach, "Acts of Remembrance."

23. Boyd, *Memorial Lincoln Bibliography,* 26.

24. Savage, *Standing Soldiers, Kneeling Slaves,* 99.

25. Boyd, *Memorial Lincoln Bibliography,* 172.

26. Ibid., 173.

27. *San Francisco Alta California,* May 3, 1868, reported in the *New York Times,* May 29, 1868.

28. Boyd, *Memorial Lincoln Bibliography,* 132.

29. Library of Congress.

30. Gilfillan, *Annual Report,* 455.

31. 1847 USA, "Postage Stamps of the United States First Issued in 1869," http://www.1847usa.com/identify/19th/1869.htm.

32. *New York Times,* November 17, 1869.

33. Claudia Dickets to the author, May 27, 2008.

34. *Brooklyn Daily Eagle,* September 4, 1869.

35. *New York Times:* August 27, 1869; September 5, 1869; and September 8, 1869.

36. Boyd, *Memorial Lincoln Bibliography,* 174–175.

37. Laban Heath, *Heath's Infallible Counterfeit Detector at Sight,* 1878 edition.

38. Boyd, *Memorial Lincoln Bibliography,* 173.

39. Ibid.

40. *Brooklyn Daily Eagle,* October 27, 1871.

41. Julian, *Medals of the United States Mint,* 239.

42. *Lincoln Lore,* no. 1363.

43. Jay Monaghan, *Lincoln Bibliography, 1839-1939,* vol. 1, edited by Paul M. Angle (Springfield, IL: Illinois State Historical Library, 1943), 238.

44. Boyd, *Memorial Lincoln Bibliography,* 174.

45. *Decatur Republican,* March 2, 1876.

46. U.S. Senate Art & History page, article on Francis Bicknell Carpenter's painting *First Reading of the Emancipation Proclamation of President Lincoln,* http://www.senate.gov/artandhistory/art/artifact/Painting_33_00005.htm.

47. Julian, *Medals of the United States Mint,* 86.

48. Earliest date used: July 16, 1890.

49. *Lincoln Lore,* no. 978.

50. *New York Times,* February 13, 1898.

51. Dick Johnson, communications to the author, 2008.

52. Joe Hartwell, "The History of the USS *President Lincoln* During WWI," http://freepages.military.rootsweb.ancestry.com/~cacunithistories/USS_President_Lincoln.html.

53. British Wreck Commissioner's Inquiry, Day 20, Testimony of Edward Wilding, Titanic Inquiry Project, http://www.titanicinquiry.org/BOTInq/BOTInq20Wilding02.php.

54. *Coin World,* April 2, 2007.

55. *Lincoln Lore,* no. 1363.

56. Gene Hessler, *U.S. Essay, Proof and Specimen Notes* (Port Clinton, OH: BNR Press, 1979), 206.

CHAPTER 3

1. 1847 USA, "Postage Stamps of the United States First Issued in 1909," http://www.1847usa.com/identify/YearSets/1909.htm.

2. Breen, *Walter Breen's Complete Encyclopedia,* 225–226.

3. See Andrew W. Pollock III, *United States Patterns and Related Issues* (Wolfeboro, NH: Bowers & Merena Galleries, 1994), 378.

4. *New York Times,* February 7, 1914.

5. *Barnard's Lincoln: The Gift of Mr. and Mrs. Charles P. Taft to the City of Cincinnati* (Cincinnati: Steward & Kidd Co., 1917).

6. Quoted in William Pederson and Frank L. Williams, eds., *Franklin D. Roosevelt and Abraham Lincoln: Competing Perspectives on Two Great Presidents* (N.p.: M.E. Sharpe, 2003), 141.

7. *New York Times,* November 2, 1922.

8. *New York Times,* July 15, 1922.

9. John Curry, "The Mall of Fame," *Atlantic Monthly,* July 1997, 14–18.

10. John Hoffmann, "Lincoln Essay Contests, Lincoln Medals, and the Commercialization of Lincoln," *Journal of the Abraham Lincoln Association* 24, no. 2 (2003).

11. *Washington Post,* May 2, 1926.

12. C-SPAN interview with Brian Lamb, August 14, 1994.

13. Lincoln Library & Museum cited on www.lincolnarchives.us/index.php?act=otherresources.

14. Quoted in Freundlich, *The Sculpture of James Earle Fraser,* 198.

15. Krakel, *The End of the Trail,* 43.

16. The University of Iowa Special Collections reports this item from the *Harrisburg Telegraph,* November 20, 1933, but why it reads 1863–1934, and 71 years is unclear. See www.lib.uiowa.edu/spec-coll/MSC/ToMsc100/MsC36/monaghan-pamphlets.htm

17. James G. Randall spoke at the December 28, 1934, meeting of the American Historical Association. His subject was "Has the Lincoln theme been exhausted?" His essay was later published in the January 1936 issue of *The American Historical Review.*

18. Thomas Schwartz, "James Jay Monaghan's Lincoln Bibliography, 1839–1939: A History," *Journal of the Abraham Lincoln Association,* Winter 1993.

CHAPTER 4

1. Ferguson, *Land of Lincoln,* 201.

2. D. Wayne Johnson, "Abraham Lincoln on Coins, Medals and Tokens: A Complete List of Lincoln Items by Known Artists," unpublished manuscript.

3. Krakel, *The End of the Trail,* 78.

4. Pollock, 392–393.

5. Lincoln, *Collected Works,* vol. 2.

6. *Numismatic News,* October 4, 2005.

7. *Coin World,* June 25, 2002, and September 30, 2002.

8. *Coin World,* December 5, 2005.

9. Rini Paiva to Fred Reed, June 10, 2008.

CHAPTER 5

1. Beth Deisher, "Editorial Opinion: Designs don't fit small coin canvas," *Coin World,* October 15, 2007, 14.

2. Ibid.

3. T. James Ferrell, "Bad Designs," *Coin World,* November 5, 2007, 15.

❧ Select Bibliography ❧

For a more complete listing please consult www.WhitmanBooks.com/AbeBook.

Abraham Lincoln Association. *The Abraham Lincoln Quarterly,* various issues.

Abraham Lincoln Association. *Journal of the Abraham Lincoln Association,* Springfield, IL. Champagne: University of Illinois Press, various issues.

Abraham Lincoln Library and Museum, Harrogate, TN, research collections.

Abraham Lincoln Presidential Library & Museum, Springfield, IL, www.alplm.org.

Ackerman, Donald L., ed., and Jonathan H. Mann, publisher. *The Rail Splitter* 1–13 (1995–present).

American Historical Auctions. *Historical Images and Manuscripts,* June 28, 1998.

American Numismatic Association. *The Numismatist,* various issues.

American Numismatic and Archaeological Society. *American Journal of Numismatics,* various issues.

American Numismatic Society, collections, database.

American Topical Association. *Topical Time,* various issues.

American Topical Association, ATA Americana Unit. *Americana Philatelic News,* various issues.

Anderson, Dwight G. *Abraham Lincoln: the Quest for Immortality.* New York: Alfred A. Knopf, 1982.

Bancroft, George. *Memorial Address on the Life and Character of Abraham Lincoln. . . the 12th of February, 1866.* Washington: Government Printing Office, 1866.

Bank Note Reporter, various issues.

Bartlett, D.W. *The Life and Public Services of Hon. Abraham Lincoln . . . [and] a biographical sketch of Hon. Hannibal Hamlin,* Authorized Edition. New York: A.B. Burdick, 1860.

Boritt, Gabor S., ed. *The Historian's Lincoln: Pseudohistory, Psychohistory, and History.* Urbana and Chicago: University of Illinois Press, 1988.

Boritt, Gabor, ed. *The Historian's Lincoln: Rebuttals, What the University Press Would Not Print.* Gettysburg, PA: privately printed, 1988, 43 pp., erratum sheet.

Boritt, Gabor, ed. *The Lincoln Enigma.* New York: Oxford University Press, 2001.

Boritt, Gabor S., Mark E. Neely Jr., and Harold Holzer. "The European Image of Abraham Lincoln," *Winterthur Portfolio* 21 (Summer/Autumn 1986): 153–183.

Bowers, Q. David. *A Guide Book of Lincoln Cents.* Atlanta: Whitman Publishing, LLC, 2008.

Bowers, Q. David. *Obsolete Paper Money Issued by Banks in the United States, 1782–1866.* Atlanta: Whitman Publishing, LLC, 2006.

Bowers, Q. David, and David M. Sundman. *100 Greatest American Currency Notes,* Atlanta: Whitman Publishing, LLC, 2006.

Boyd, Andrew. *Memorial Lincoln Bibliography: Being an Account of Books, Eulogies, Sermons, Portraits, Engravings, Medals, etc.* Albany, NY: Andrew Boyd, Directory Publisher, 1870.

Breen, Walter. *Walter Breen's Complete Encyclopedia of U.S. and Colonial Coins.* New York: Doubleday, 1988.

Bullard, F. Lauriston. *Lincoln in Marble and Bronze.* A publication of The Abraham Lincoln Association, Springfield, Illinois. New Brunswick, NJ: Rutgers University Press, 1952.

Burdette, Roger W. *Renaissance of American Coinage, 1909–1915.* Great Falls, VA: Seneca Mill Press, 2007.

Carnegie, Dale. *Lincoln the Unknown.* New York: Pocket Books, 1932, 1952.

Carpenter, F.B. *Six Months at the White House with Abraham Lincoln. The Story of a Picture.* New York: Hurd and Houghton, 1867.

Chambliss, Carlson R. *U.S. Paper Money Guide and Handbook.* Port Clinton, OH: BNR Press, 1999.

Chandler, Robert J. "San Francisco: The Lincoln Monument That Was," *The Rail Splitter* 7, no. 1-2 (Summer/Fall 2001): 22–23.

Chicago Evening Journal, 1861–1865.

Christie's, New York. Various sales catalogs, 1990–2007.

Cincinnati Daily Enquirer, 1861–1865.

Civil War Token Society. *Journal of the Civil War Token Society* (also *Copperhead Courier*), 1967–date.

Craughwell, Thomas J. *Stealing Lincoln's Body.* Cambridge, MA: Harvard University Press, 2007.

Cuhaj, George, ed. *Standard Catalog of United States Paper Money,* 25th ed. Iola, WI: Krause Publications, 2006.

Cuomo, Mario M. *Why Lincoln Matters Today More than Ever.* New York: Harcourt, Inc., 2004.

Dauer, Edward A. and Joanne C. Dauer. *American History as Seen Through Currency.* Fort Lauderdale, FL: printed privately, 2003.

Dennett, Tyler, ed. *Lincoln and the Civil War in the Diaries and Letters of John Hay.* New York: Da Capo Press, Inc., 1939, 1988.

Deutsch, Kenneth L., and Joseph R. Fornieri, eds. *Lincoln's American Dream, Clashing Political Perspectives.* Washington, DC: Potomac Books, 2005.

DiLorenzo, Thomas J. *The Real Lincoln: a New Look at Abraham Lincoln, His Agenda, and an Unnecessary War.* Roseville, CA: Prima Publishing, 2002.

Donald, David, ed. *Inside Lincoln's Cabinet: the Civil War Diaries of Salmon P. Chase.* New York: Longmans, Green & Co., 1954.

Donald, David Herbert. *Lincoln.* New York: Touchstone Books, 1995.

Doty, Richard. *America's Money, America's Story: a Comprehensive Chronicle of American Numismatic History.* Iola, WI: Krause Publications, 1998.

Edison, Hank. "What Would Lincoln Do?" Common Dreams News Center, September 25, 2007, www.commondreams.org.

Fairbanks, Eugene F., comp. *Abraham Lincoln Sculpture Created by Avard T. Fairbanks.* Bellingham, WA: Fairbanks Art and Books, 2002.

Ferguson, Andrew. *Land of Lincoln: Adventures in Abe's America.* New York: Atlantic Monthly Press, 2007.

Fischer, Roger A. *American Political Ribbons and Ribbon Badges, 1825–1981.* Lincoln, MA: Quarterman Publications, 1985.

Fite, Gilbert C. and Jim E. Reese. *An Economic History of the United States.* Boston: Houghton Mifflin, 1959.

Frank Leslie's Illustrated Weekly, 1860–1865.

Friedberg, Arthur L., and Ira S. Friedberg. *A Guide Book of United States Paper Money.* Atlanta: Whitman Publishing, LLC, 2005.

Friedberg, Arthur L., and Ira S. Friedberg. *Paper Money of the United States,* 18th ed. Clifton, NJ: The Coin and Currency Institute, 2006 (and various editions).

Friedberg, Milton R. *The Encyclopedia of United States Fractional & Postal Currency.* Rockville Centre, NY: Numismatic and Antiquarian Service Corporation of America, 1978.

Fuld, George, and Melvin Fuld. *U.S. Civil War Store Cards.* N.p.: Civil War Token Society, 1982.

———. *Patriotic Civil War Tokens,* 4th ed. Iola, WI: Krause Publications and Civil War Token Society, 1982.

Freundlich, A.L. *The Sculpture of James Earle Fraser.* N.p.: Universal Publishers, 2001.

Gilfillan, Jas. *Annual Report on the State of the Finances,* December 7, 1881. Washington: Government Printing Office, 1881.

Goode, James M. *The Outdoor Sculpture of Washington, D.C.: A Comprehensive Historical Guide.* Washington, DC: Smithsonian Institution Press, 1974.

Grant, Robert W. *The Handbook of Civil War Patriotic Envelopes and Postal History,* vol. 1. Hanover, MA: printed privately, 1977.

Halliday, E.M. "Carving the American Colossus," *American Heritage* 28 (June 1977): 19–27.

Hamilton, Charles and Lloyd Ostendorf. *Lincoln in Photographs: An Album of Every Known Pose.* Dayton, OH: Morningside Press, 1985.

Harper's Weekly, 1860–1865, and various issues thereafter.

Harkness, David J. "Lincoln on Stage, Screen, and Radio," *Lincoln Herald* 7 (March 1941): 15–18.

Harris, Gordon L. *New York State Scrip and Private Issues.* N.p.: printed privately, 2001.

Hatcher, James B., ed. *Scott Specialized Catalogue of United States Stamps,* 75th ed. New York: Scott Publishing Co., 1978.

Haxby, James A. *Standard Catalog of United States Obsolete Bank Notes, 1782–1866,* 4 vols. Iola, WI: Krause Publications, 1988.

Hepburn, A. Barton. *A History of Coinage and Currency in the United States and the Perennial Contest for Sound Money.* New York: The Macmillan Co., 1903.

Hepburn, A. Barton. *A History of Currency in the United States.* New York: The Macmillan Company, 1924.

Herndon, William H. and Jesse William Weik. *Herndon's Lincoln: the True Story of a Great Life,* 3 vols. Springfield, IL: The Herndon's Lincoln Publishing Co., 1921.

Hessler, Gene. *The Engraver's Line: an Encyclopedia of Paper Money & Postage Stamp Art.* Port Clinton, OH: BNR Press, 1993.

———. *An Illustrated History of U.S. Loans, 1775–1898.* Port Clinton, OH: BNR Press, 1988.

———. *U.S. Essay, Proof and Specimen Notes.* Port Clinton, OH: BNR Press, 1988.

Hessler, Gene, and Carlson Chambliss. *The Comprehensive Catalog of U.S. Paper Money,* 7th ed. Port Clinton, OH: 2006.

Hewitt, Robert. *The Lincoln Centennial Medal . . .* New York: G.P. Putnam's Sons The Knickerbocker Press, 1908.

Hill, Frederick Trevor. "The Lincoln-Douglas Debates, Fifty Years After," *The Century Magazine* 77 (November 1908): 3–19.

Hoffman, John. "Lincoln Essay Contests, Lincoln Medal, and the Commercialization of Lincoln," *Journal of the Abraham Lincoln Association* 24 (Summer 2003): 36ff.

Holzer, Harold, ed. *Abraham Lincoln Portrayed in the Collections of the Indiana Historical Society,* compiled by Emily Castle and Barbara Quigley. Indianapolis: Indiana Historical Society Press, 2006.

Holzer, Harold. *Lincoln at Cooper Union, the Speech that made Abraham Lincoln President.* New York: Simon & Schuster Paperbacks, 2004.

Holzer, Harold. *Washington and Lincoln Portrayed: National Icons in Popular Prints.* Jefferson, NC: McFarland & Co., Inc., 1993.

Holzer, Harold and Mark E. Neely Jr. *Mine Eyes Have Seen the Glory: the Civil War in Art.* New York: Orion Books, 1993.

Holzer, Harold, Gabor Boritt, and Mark Neely. *Changing the Lincoln Image.* Fort Wayne, IN: Louis A. Warren Lincoln Library and Museum, 1985.

Holzer, Harold, Gabor Boritt, and Mark Neely. *The Lincoln Image: Abraham Lincoln and the Popular Print.* New York: Charles Scribner's Sons, 1984.

Homren, Wayne. "Reed Promotes New Lincoln Portrait for U.S. $5 Bill," *E-Sylum,* vol. IX, November 19, 2006.

Illinois Watch Company. *The Book of A. Lincoln Watches.* Springfield, IL: Illinois Watch Co., 1924.

Jeffrey, Gary, and Kate Petty. *Graphic Nonfiction: Abraham Lincoln, the Life of America's Sixteenth President.* New York: Rosen Publishing Group, 2005.

Jones, Malcolm. "Who Was More Important: Lincoln or Darwin?" *Newsweek* 112 (July 7, 2008), pp. 30–34.

Julian, R[obert] W. *Medals of the United States Mint: The First Century, 1792–1892.* El Cajon, CA: Token and Medal Society, 1977.

Julian, R[obert] W., and Ernest E. Keusch. *Medals of the United States Assay Commission, 1860–1977.* Lake Mary, FL: Token and Medal Society, 1989.

Katz, D. Mark. *Witness to an Era, the Life and Photographs of Alexander Gardner.* New York: Viking, 1991.

King, Robert P. *Lincoln in Numismatics.* N.p.: Token and Medal Society, 1966.

Knox, John Jay. *United States Notes: A History of the Various Issues of Paper Money by the Government of the United States.* London: T. Fisher Unwin, 1885.

Krakel, Dean. *End of the Trail: The Odyssey of a Statue.* Norman: University of Oklahoma Press, 1973.

Krause, Chester L., and Clifford Mishler. *Standard Catalog of World Coins, 1901–Present.* Iola, WI: Krause Publications, 2003.

Kunhardt, Dorothy Meserve, and Philip B. Kunhardt Jr. *Mathew Brady and His World.* Alexandria, VA: Time-Life Books, 1977.

Kunhardt, Philip B. Jr., Philip B. Kunhardt III, and Peter W. Kunhardt. *Lincoln: an Illustrated Biography.* New York: Alfred A. Knopf, 1992.

Kunkel, Mabel. *Abraham Lincoln: Unforgettable American.* Charlotte, NC: Delmar Co., 1976.

Lincoln, Abraham. *Autobiography of Abraham Lincoln.* N.p.: Americanization Department, Veterans of Foreign Wars of the United States, n.d.

———. *Abraham Lincoln Papers at the Library of Congress,* Microfilm Collection. Washington, DC: Library of Congress, 1947.

———. *The Collected Works of Abraham Lincoln,* 8 vols. Edited by Roy P. Basler. New Brunswick, NJ: Rutgers University Press, 1953.

———. *The Speeches of Abraham Lincoln, Including Inaugurals and Proclamations.* New York: Lincoln Centenary Association, 1908.

———. *The Works of Abraham Lincoln,* vol. 7. New York: The University Society, Inc., 1908.

Lincoln Fellowship of Wisconsin. *The Lincoln Ledger,* various issues.

Lincoln Lore, nos. 1–1894 (April 15, 1929–Winter 2009). Luce, Henry L., ed. "The Individual in America . . . Lincoln and Modern America: The Heritage of a Free Choice in an Organized Society," *Time,* May 10, 1963, 20–25.

Luftschein, Susan. *One Hundred Years of American Medallic Art, 1845–1945.* Catalog of the John E. Marqusee Collection, Herbert F. Johnson Museum of Art, Cornell University, Ithaca, NY, 1995.

Marcovitz, Hal. *American Symbols and Their Meanings: The Lincoln Memorial.* Philadelphia: Mason Crest Publishers, 2003.

McClure, R.B. *The Abraham Lincoln Portfolio of Photogravures from the Famous McClure Collection.* New York: R.B. McClure, 1909.

McMurtry, R. Gerald. *Beardless Portraits of Abraham Lincoln.* Fort Wayne, IN: Public Library of Fort Wayne and Allen County, 1962.

———. "A Great Lincoln Collection," *Lincoln Herald* 43 (March 1941): 2–8.

———. "Lincoln Poster Stamps," *Lincoln Herald* 43 (March 1941): 9, 13.

Mead, David, and Chris Sharp. *A Little Abraham Lincoln Learns to be Honest.* San Marcos, CA: Virtue Books, 2003.

Mearns, David C. *Lincoln Collections in the Library of Congress,* 2nd ed. Washington: Library of Congress, 1943.

Mellon, James. *The Face of Lincoln.* New York: Bonanza Books, 1979.

Meserve, Frederick Hill, and Carl Sandburg. *The Photographs of Abraham Lincoln.* New York: Harcourt, Brace and Co., 1944.

Mihm, Stephen. *A Nation of Counterfeiters: Capitalists, Con Men, and the Making of the United States.* Cambridge, MA: Harvard University Press, 2007.

Milgram, James W. *Abraham Lincoln Illustrated Envelopes and Letter Paper, 1860–1865.* Northbrook, IL: Northbrook Publishing Co., 1984.

Miller, Francis Trevelyan. *Portrait Life of Lincoln.* Springfield, MA: The Patriot Publishing Co., 1910.

Miller, William Lee. *Lincoln's Virtues: an Ethical Biography.* New York: Alfred A. Knopf, 2002.

Moffatt, Frederick C. *Errant Bronzes: George Grey Barnard's Statues of Abraham Lincoln.* Newark: University of Delaware Press, 1998.

Monaghan, Jay. *Lincoln Bibliography, 1839–1939,* 2 vols. Collections of the Illinois State Historical Library, vols. XXXI and XXXII. Edited by Paul M. Angle, State Historian.

Moran, Michael F. *Striking Change: the Great Artistic Collaboration of Theodore Roosevelt and Augustus Saint-Gaudens.* Atlanta: Whitman Publishing, LLC, 2008.

Morris, Melvin (ed.). *Abraham Lincoln on Worldwide Stamps.* American Topical Association Handbook #135. Tucson, AZ: American Topical Association, 1998.

Neely, Mark E. Jr. *The Abraham Lincoln Encyclopedia.* New York: Da Capo Press, 1982.

Neely, Mark E. Jr. *The Last Best Hope of Earth: Abraham Lincoln and the Promise of America.* Cambridge, MA: Harvard University Press and the Huntington Library and Illinois State Historical Library, 1993.

New Orleans Bee, 1861–1865, various issues.

New York Times, 1860–1865, and various issues thereafter.

Nicolay, John, and John Hay. "Abraham Lincoln: Premier or President?" N.d., 18. pages.

Oates, Stephen B. *Abraham Lincoln: The Man Behind the Myths.* New York: Harper & Row, 1984.

Ostendorf, Lloyd. "Abraham Lincoln at Independence Hall, Philadelphia, February 22, 1861," *Saturday Evening Post,* January–February 1976.

———. *Lincoln and His Photographers.* Historical Bulletin No. 27. Madison, WI: Lincoln Fellowship of Wisconsin, 1972.

———. *Lincoln's Photographs: A Complete Album,* Dayton: Rockywood Press, 1998. 3rd edition

———. "Signed Lincoln Photographs," *Incidents of the War,* vol. 1 (Summer 1986), 20–23.

Paper Money, various issues.

Peterson, Merrill D. *Lincoln in American Memory.* New York: Oxford University Press, 1994.

Pierand, Richard V. and Robert D. Linder. *Civil Religion & The Presidency.* Grand Rapids, MI: Academie Books, 1988.

Pratt, Harry E. *Abraham Lincoln Chronology, 1809–1865.* Springfield, IL: Illinois State Historical Library, 1957.

Pratt, Harry E. *Lincoln's Inner Circle.* Springfield, IL: Illinois State Historical Society, 1955.

Pritzker, Barry. *Mathew Brady.* New York: Crescent Books, 1992.

Randall, James G. and David Herbert Donald. *The Civil War and Reconstruction.* Lexington, MA: Heath, 1969.

Raymond, Henry J. *The Life and Public Services of Abraham Lincoln.* New York: Derby and Miller, 1865.

Reed, Fred L. *Civil War Encased Stamps: the Issuers and their Times.* Port Clinton, OH: BNR Press, 1994, 1995; revised 2nd edition in press.

Reinfeld, Fred. *The Story of Civil War Money.* New York: Sterling Publishing Co., 1959.

Reinhart, Mark S. *Abraham Lincoln on Screen, a Filmography, 1903–1998.* Jefferson, NC: McFarland & Co., 1999.

Richmond Inquirer, 1861–1865, various issues.

Rockett, Al, and Ray Rockett. *The Dramatic Life of Abraham Lincoln.* San Francisco: Souvenir Book Publishing Co., 1924,

Rose, Jon. *United States Postage Stamps of 1869.* Sidney, OH: Linn's Stamp News, 1996.

Rothert, Matt. *A Guide Book of United States Fractional Currency.* Racine, WI: Whitman Publishing Co., 1963.

———. "Unusual Aspects of U.S. Fractional Currency," *The Numismatist,* vol. LXXVII (August 1964), pp. 1027–1031.

Rulau, Russell. *Standard Catalog of United States Tokens, 1700–1900,* 4th ed. Iola, WI: Krause Publications, 2004.

Saad, Lydia. "Lincoln Resumes Position as Americans' Top-Rated President," February 19, 2007, www.galluppoll.com.

Sandburg, Carl. *Abraham Lincoln, the War Years,* vol. 3. New York: Harcourt, Brace & Co., 1939.

Schingoethe, Herb, and Martha Schingoethe. *College Currency: Money for Business Training.* Port Clinton, OH: BNR Press, 1993.

Schuckers, J.W. *The Life and Public Services of Salmon Portland Chase.* New York: D. Appleton and Co., 1974.

Schneider, Stuart. *Collecting Lincoln with Values.* Atglen, PA: Schiffer Publishing Ltd., 1997.

Schwartz, Barry. *Abraham Lincoln and the Forge of National Memory.* Chicago: University of Chicago Press, 2000.

———. "Iconography and Collective Memory: Lincoln's Image in the American Mind," *Sociological Quarterly,* 32, no. 3 (1991): 301–319.

———. "Lincoln at the Millennium," *Journal of the Abraham Lincoln Association,* vol. XXIV (Winter 2003), pp. 1–31.

Shaw, Albert. *Abraham Lincoln: His Path to the Presidency, a Cartoon History.* New York: The Review of Reviews Corp., 1930.

Shaw, Albert. *Abraham Lincoln: The Year of His Election, a Cartoon History.* New York: The Review of Reviews Corp., 1930.

Shenk, Joshua Wolf. "The True Lincoln," *Time,* June 26, 2005, www.time.com.

Sherwood, Robert E. *Abe Lincoln in Illinois.* New York: The Playwrights' Co., December 25, 1939 .

Sloan, Richard, ed. *The Lincoln Log* 2–7 (October/November 1977–January, 1981).

Spaulding, Elbridge Gerry. *A Resource of War: The Credit of the Government Made Immediately Available. . . .* Buffalo, NY: Express Printing Co., 1869.

Speer, Bonnie Stahlman. *The Great Abraham Lincoln Hijack, 1876 attempt to steal the body of President Lincoln.* Norman, OK: Reliance Press, 1990.

Stahl, Alan M., ed. *The Medal in America.* Coinage of the Americas Conference at the American Numismatic Society, New York, Sept. 26-27, 1987. New York: American Numismatic Society, 1988.

Staudenraus, P.J., ed. *Mr. Lincoln's Washington: the Civil War Dispatches of Noah Brooks,* New York: Thomas Yoselof, 1967.

Steers, Edward Jr. *Lincoln Legends: Myths, Hoaxes, and Confabulations Associated with our Greatest President.* Lexington, KY: University Press of Kentucky, 2007.

Stevens, George. *Lincoln's Doctor's Dog and Other Famous Best Sellers.* New York: J.B. Lippincott, 1938, 1939.

Stevenson, Augusta. *Abraham Lincoln, the Great Emancipator.* New York: Macmillan Publishing Co., 1932, 1959, 1986.

Stickler, Harry D. *Trails and Shrines of Abraham Lincoln.* Chicago: Lincolniana Art and Book Association of America, 1934.

Sullivan, Edmund B. *American Political Badges and Medalets, 1789–1892.* Lawrence, MA: Quarterman Publications, 1981.

———. *Collecting Political Americana.* Hanover, MA: The Christopher Publishing House, 1991.

Sullivan, George. *Picturing Lincoln: Famous Photographs that Popularized the President.* New York: Clarion Books, 2000.

Swiatek, Anthony, and Walter Breen. *The Encyclopedia of United States Silver & Gold Commemorative Coins, 1892–1954.* New York: ARCO Publishing, 1981.

Taft, Horatio Nelson. *Washington during the Civil War: The Diary of Horatio Nelson Taft, 1861–1865,* 3 vols. Manuscript Division, Library of Congress, Washington, DC, 1,240 pages.

Taft, Lorado. *The History of American Sculpture,* new edition. New York: The Macmilliam Co., 1924.

Taft, Robert. *Photography and the American Scene: A Social History 1839–1939.* New York: Dover Publications, 1938, 1964.

Tainter, J[ohn] S. "History of the Types of United States Paper Currency," *The Numismatist* 66 (August, 1953).

Taxay, Don. *An Illustrated History of U.S. Commemorative Coinage.* New York: ARCO Publishing Co., 1967.

Taxay, Don. *The U.S. Mint and Coinage.* New York: ARCO Publishing Co., 1966.

Taylor, Tom (Mark Lemon). *Punch, or the London Charivari,* 1861–1865.

Thomas, Benjamin P. *Abraham Lincoln,* with an introduction by Stephen W. Sears. New York: Book-of-the-Month Club, Inc., 1986.

Thomas, Christopher A. *The Lincoln Memorial and American Life.* Princeton, NJ: Princeton University Press, 2002.

Thompson, Frank. *Abraham Lincoln Twentieth-Century Popular Portrayals.* Dallas: Taylor Publishing Co., 1999.

Tice, George. *Lincoln.* New Brunswick, NJ: Rutgers University Press, 1984.

Truesdell, Winfred Porter. *Engraved and Lithographed Portraits of Abraham Lincoln,* vol. 2., Champlain, NY: Privately printed at the Trousdale Press, 1933.

Turner, George T. *Essays and Proofs of United States Internal Revenue Stamps.* Arlington, MA: Bureau Issues Association, 1974.

Turner, Justin G., and Linda Levitt Turner. *Mary Todd Lincoln: Her Life and Letters.* New York: Alfred A. Knopf, 1987.

Waldsmith, John. *Stereo Views: An Illustrated History and Price Guide.* Radnor, PA: Wallace-Homestead Book Co., 1991.

Walsh, William S., ed. *Abraham Lincoln and the London Punch.* New York: Moffat, Yard and Co., 1909.

Ward, Geoffrey C., Ric Burns, and Ken Burns. *The Civil War, an Illustrated History.* New York: Alfred A. Knopf, 1990.

Warren, Louis A. "Unlimited Field of Lincolniana Collecting," *Hobbies,* 42(October 1940), 1–6.

Wells, Samuel R. "Abraham Lincoln, Portrait, Character, and Biography," *American Phrenological Journal and Life Illustrated,* vol. XL (October 1864), pp. 97–98.

Westbrook, Robert A. *An Illustrated Catalogue of Early North American Advertising Notes.* New York: R.M. Smythe, 2001.

White, Charles W. "The Lincoln Cult," *Saturday Evening Post,* February 16, 1957, 36–37, 90, 92.

Wills, Garry. "Lincoln, the Power of Words in Times of War, an essay," *Life,* February 1991.

Wilson, Douglas L. *Honor's Voice: The Transformation of Abraham Lincoln.* New York: Vintage Books, 1998.

Wilson, Rufus Rockwell. *Lincoln in Caricature.* New York: Horizon Press, 1953.

Wilson, Rufus Rockwell. *Lincoln in Portraiture.* New York: The Press of the Pioneers, 1935.

Wright, A.M. *The Dramatic Life of Abraham Lincoln.* New York: Grosset & Dunlap, 1925.

Yeoman, R.S. *A Guide Book of United States Coins,* 12th ed. Racine, WI: Whitman Publishing, 1958 (and other editions).

Zabriskie, Andrew C. *A Discriptive Catalogue of Political and Memorial Medals Struck in Honor of Abraham Lincoln.* New York: privately printed, 1873.

About The Author

Photo by Rebecca Taylor, www.rebeccataylor.net

A lifelong journalist, Fred Reed is the author or editor of more than a dozen books and has written hundreds of articles. His work has won him numerous literary awards from the American Numismatic Association, the Society of Paper Money Collectors, the Numismatic Literary Guild, and other organizations. These include, from the SPMC, two Nathan Gold Lifetime Achievement Awards, two Awards of Merit, and the Forrest Daniel Literary Award; from the ANA, the first-place Heath Literary Award and the Wayte and Olga Raymond Memorial Literary Award; and from the NLG, "Best Specialized Book" in both World Paper Money, and Tokens and Medals categories. Reed is a recipient of a National Gold Ink Award, and a gold vermeil medal from the International Philatelic Decentennial Expo PACIFICA '97. He has been editor/publisher of the Society of Paper Money Collectors' award-winning bi-monthly journal *Paper Money* for nearly a decade, and is a regular columnist for *Coin World, Bank Note Reporter,* and *Coins* magazine. His Lincoln research has been published in the *Lincoln Herald, The Numismatist,* and *Paper Money,* among other publications. His award-winning *Civil War Encased Stamps: the Issuers and Their Times* is being prepared for a second edition.

Bank Note Reporter has published many Lincoln articles by Mr. Reed, including "Presidential pardons of counterfeiters further irk Republican Congress" (August 2008), "Desperate Treasury approved photographic detectors" (July 2008), "Early efforts against fakers proved spotty" (April 2008), "Feds ramped up enforcement to foil fakers" (March 2008), "Bogus $10 U.S. Notes proliferated; solutions, few" (February 2008), "Auctions bring new ABNC die use to fore" (January 2008), "Federalizing didn't solve counterfeiting problems" (December 2007), "ABNC die 141 has distinguished heritage" (September 2007), "Lincoln currency portrait family tree traced" (August 2007), and "State bank note issuance grew despite problems" (April 2006).

In *Coins Magazine,* Mr. Reed has published articles on Old Abe, including "Original Greenbacks: Patent Anti-Counterfeiting Ink Proved a Bust" (September 2008), "A Noble Experiment: Dividend Checks Remain from Failed Freedman's Bank" (January 2008), "Zero in on Old Abe: Porthole Note Famous, Valuable & Aptly Named" (August 2007), "Take a wooden nickel: 'paper' collectibles include these diverse woods" (June 2007), "Your Share in America: Savings Bonds Allow Little Guy to Take Stock in America," (April 2007), "Let's Get It Right: Treasury's about face provides golden face-change opportunity" (January 2007), and "Hometown Bank Notes: Relic of Civil War, Killed Off By Great Depression" (June 2006).

His articles featured in *Coin World* on the Great Emancipator include "Artistic violation: James Earle Fraser researcher believes reuse of designs of Indian Head 5¢ betrays them" (October 8, 2001), "Emancipation Proclamation: BEP should use G.F.C. Smillie's engraving" (March 26, 2001), "Emancipation Proclamation: Lincoln's edict led directly to his appearance on fractional currency" (March 19, 2001), "An icon for the ages: Cities, business schools depict president on notes" (July 24, 2000), "Abraham Lincoln: Lincoln's portraits on paper money help establish federal government image" (July 10, 2000), "Lincoln the Icon: Private banks and businesses use presidential portraits on paper money" (July 17, 2000), "New Lincoln Portrait Based on photo taken on his 55th birthday" (December 6, 1999), "Vision and Artistry: James and Laura Frasers' revitalization of U.S. coinage an international success" (January 19, 1998), "Meet the Frasers . . . Married collaborators left their mark on the nation's coinage in remarkable ways" (January 5, 1998), "Abraham Lincoln: Money shapes how Americans view the 16th President" (four-part series: February 10, 17, 24, and March 3, 1997), "Lincoln Popular Subject for Medallic Art: Commemorative Medals Frequently Use Universal Image" (March 28, 1990), "Lincoln Photos Fill Public's Need for Image: Universal Image Most Acceptable Photo of Martyred President" (March 21, 1990), "Advertising, Hollywood Use Lincoln Portrait: Legendary Honesty Wins Lincoln Place on Checks, Advertisements" (March 14, 1990), "Advertisers Quick to Use Lincoln Image: Sought to Use Portrait of 'Honest Abe' to Suggest Honesty" (March 7, 1990), "Lincoln Portrait Appears on Many Items: Early 19th Century Books Feature Illustrations Based on Portrait," (February 28, 1990), "Berger-Burt Image of Lincoln Wide-Ranging: 'Universal Lincoln' Appearances Range from Stamps to Cards" (February 21, 1990), "Lincoln: Face of Lincoln an American Institution" (February 14, 1990), and "Face Value: Lincoln Features Have Always Attracted Interest" (February 11, 1987).

Lincoln-related articles appearing in *Paper Money* include "New Nex-Gen colorized $5 FRNs are unprecedented," (July-August, 2008), "Did Abraham Lincoln's icon image on money influence his public perception-Part II?" (March-April, 2008), "Civil War Change Shortage Gave Rise to Curious Makeshifts" (January-February 2005),

In addition to publishing books and articles, Mr. Reed has displayed large exhibits on Lincoln at several Memphis International Paper Money Shows: *Abraham Lincoln on Non-Federal Currency,* 1999, 2007; *A Checklist of Abraham Lincoln on Checks,* 2002; *nextGen, smecksGen, get with it Treasury; give us the Gettysburg Lincoln on our new $5 Federal Reserve Notes,* 2004; and *Series 1996 Face-Off: An A. Lincoln $5 FRN Makeover,* 1998; *Series 2004 Face Off: An A. Lincoln $5 FRN Makeover,* 2003.

He's written about Lincoln for E-Sylum with "Even More on Lincoln and Chase," June 8, 2008, and "More on Salmon P. Chase and Abraham Lincoln," May 25, 2008. He has Lincoln entries at www.wikicoins.com: "FR 93 $10 Legal Tender Note," "FR 282 Porthole note," and "FR 1800-1 Series 1929 $5 National Bank Note."

Additional articles Mr. Reed has penned on this subject include "Did Abraham Lincoln's icon image on money influence his public perception," *The Lincoln Herald,* Winter 2007; "Emergency Money Fulfills Civil War Needs," *Civil War Token Society Journal,* Spring–Fall 1977; "'Honest Abe' Lincoln: Privately issued 19th century U.S. paper money offers many different portraits of Lincoln," *Paper Money Values,* Spring 2006; "In the 'Twinkle of an Eye': Once Popular Lincoln Photo Returns as Lincoln Icon for the 21st Century," *2000 Coin Almanac,* 1999; "New $5 Note Spiffs Up Lincoln Image," November 19, 1999, www.collectors.com; "Pliny Chase," *Journal of the Civil War Token Society,* Summer 1975; "Sculptor Fraser models proposed Lincoln cent and nickel," *Heritage Insider,* December 1999; "Shades of the Blue and Grey," *The Blue and the Grey,* October 1964–February 1965; "Shades of the Blue and Grey," *Linn's Weekly Stamp News,* April 26, 1965; and "A Very Brady Bank Note: One, well-executed photograph helped define America's 16th President, influenced scores of portraits and was adapted for a contemporary $5 bill," *The Numismatist,* February 2008.

Photo Credits

All images except those listed below are from the collection of the author.

Donald Ackerman: 1.149a

Joel Anderson: 1.81a

David Beach: 2.164a, 2.164b, 2.200a

Q. David Bowers: 1.91b, 1.92, 1.117, 1.133, 1.156a, 1.159, 1.163, 1.168c, 2.16a

Jonathan Brecher: 3.14a

Terry Bryan: 1.1

Bureau of Engraving and Printing Historical Resource Center: 3.4

Chicago History Museum (Chicago Historical Society): 2.8

Ed Dauer: 1.81b, 1.89, 1.112

Daniel Dolfi: 2.115

C. John Ferreri: 1.59b

Ira Goldberg: 4.75

Heritage Auctions: 1.32, 1.38, 1.42a, 1.42c, 1.47, 1.48c, 1.69b, 1.83c, 1.85d, 1.91a, 1.114a, 1.114b, 1.122, 1.127, 1.129b, 1.129c, 1.142b, 1.146, 1.148, 1.15, 1.157a, 1.157b, 1.169b, 1.175, 2.3b, 2.7b, 2.7c, 2.17, 2.57, 2.65, 2.85a, 2.86, 2.92, 2.100a, 2.100c, 2.107, 2.148, 2.159b, 2.174, 2.196, 3.3a, 3.3b, 3.28, 3.32, 3.41, 3.64 (face), 4.3a, 4.3, 4.37, 4.88

Ray Herz: 4.7

Gene Hessler: 1.71, 1.88, 2.183, 3.93b

Katie Jaeger: 1.48a, 1.54

D. Wayne Johnson: 2.209

Bob Kerstein, scripophily.com: 2.106c

Robert Kvederas Jr. and Robert Kvederas Sr.: 4.61c, 4.61d

H. Joseph Levine, Presidential Coin and Antique Co.: 3.58c, 3.103

Library of Congress: 1.19, 1.25a, 1.35, 1.50a, 1.52a, 1.52b, 1.64, 1.67, 1.78a, 1.78b, 1.78c, 1.84c, 1.94c, 1.99, 1.101, 1.105a, 1.110a, 1.118, 1.123, 1.132a, 1.132b, 1.137b, 1.147, 1.151, 1.152, 1.154a, 1.154b, 1.155a, 1.162, 1.168a, 1.172, 1.173a, 1.173b, 2.2b, 2.6, 2.20a, 2.22, 2.24b, 2.27a, 2.27b, 2.27c, 2.3, 2.39, 2.59a, 2.59b, 2.59c, 2.6, 2.62, 2.73, 2.74, 2.76, 2.77, 2.87b, 2.106a, 2.106b, 2.113, 2.156a, 2.176, 2.180a, 2.180b, 2.194, 3.36, 3.52a, 4.38

Robert Laper: 1.33a

Joe Lepczyk: 3.108

Dana Linett, Early American History Auctions: 1.164b, 2.7a, 2.44, 2.128, 2.129

Mastro Auctions: 2.25b

Steve Morawiec, Dolphin Photos: 3.89c

National Cowboy and Western Heritage Museum: 3.72

National Inventors Hall of Fame: 4.95

New York Public Library: 2.156b

Chris Nelson: 1.72b, 1.153a, 2.11, 2.12a

Lloyd Ostendorf: 2.61a

Art Paradis: 1.93a

Daniel E. Pearson: 1.16

Princeton University: 1.140b

Rail Splitter: 1.46, 2.162a

Fred L. Reed IV: 4.74

Sergio Sanchez: 2.11

Fred Schwan: 2.134

Peter Schwartz: 2.97

Austin Sheheen: 1.129a

Howard Shoemaker: 4.72

Siegel Auction Galleries: 3.55

Smithsonian Institution: 2.149, 4.51

Spink-Smythe: 2.132

Stack's: 1.56, 1.108b, 1.156b, 3.34b

Saul Teichmann: 2.68

U.S. Army Signal Corps: 3.39b

U.S. Mint: Chapter 5 opening art

U.S. Navy: 4.12

U.S. Patent Office: 1.26

U.S. Patent Office: 2.98

U.S. Postal Service: 5.2

University of Wyoming: 4.5a

Mark VanWinkle: 3.14b

Delbert Wallace: 2.38

Alan Weinberg: 1.36a, 1.36b, 1.42d, 1.43, 1.44, 1.104, 1.141, 1.158a, 1.158b, 2.15a, 2.15b, 2.35, 2.67, 2.122, 2.159a, 2.202

Whitman Image Archives: 5.1

Scott Winslow: 1.34, 1.36c

❧ Index ❧

A. Lincoln watch, 143, 170, 182, 186, 199

Abe Lincoln Grows Up (Herzberg), 211

Abe Lincoln in Illinois: film, 4, 6, 7, 12, 18, 24, 213; play, 10, 210, 212

Abraham Lincoln (Classics Illustrated), 219

Abraham Lincoln: film, 6, 91, 194, 209; play, 193–195, 209

Abraham Lincoln (train), GM&O, 217

Abraham Lincoln: A Likeness in Symphony Form, 202, 203

Abraham Lincoln Association: Jersey City, 124, 157, 203; Springfield, 202, 216

Abraham Lincoln Bicentennial 1-Cent Coin Redesign Act, 245, 246

Abraham Lincoln Bicentennial Commission, 242, 244, 254

Abraham Lincoln Bicentennial silver dollar, 246, 247, 248, 249, 250, 252–253, 254

Abraham Lincoln Birthplace Memorial, 168

Abraham Lincoln Book Shop (Chicago, Illinois), 211, 214

Abraham Lincoln Brigade (battalion), 208, 209, 211, 251

Abraham Lincoln Centennial Association, 176, 184, 201, 202

Abraham Lincoln Commemorative Coin Act, 248

Abraham Lincoln effect, 234, 235, 236

Abraham Lincoln Exhibit Group, 206, 207

Abraham Lincoln Fellowship (Berkeley, California), 204–205

Abraham Lincoln Friendship Train, 216

Abraham Lincoln High School (San Francisco, California), 83

Abraham Lincoln Lecture Series, Cooper Union, 213

Abraham Lincoln Library & Museum (Harrogate, Tennessee), 162, 236

Abraham Lincoln Medal of Freedom, 246–247, 249

Abraham Lincoln Memorial Garden, 208

Abraham Lincoln Memorial Highway Association, 202

Abraham Lincoln National Rail-Splitting Contest, 232, 234, 254

Abraham Lincoln Papers, Library of Congress, 195, 216

Abraham Lincoln pen, 131, 132

Abraham Lincoln Presidential dollar coin, 246, 255

Abraham Lincoln Presidential Library & Museum, 98, 246, 248

Abraham Lincoln Sesquicentennial Commission, 223

Abraham Lincoln's Doctor's Dog, 234

Alan Nevins–Douglas Southall Freeman Award, 214

American Bank Note Co., 2, 23, 27, 31, 34, 37, 45, 49, 117, 119, 128, 134, 135, 136, 141, 145, 147, 148, 149, 157, 158, 160, 163, 168, 210, 234, 246, 248

American Bond Detector, 48

American Journal of Numismatics, 210

American Numismatic & Archaeological Society (American Numismatic Society), 99, 116, 118, 119, 145, 159, 177, 179

Ames, Sarah Fisher, 140, 210, 211

Anderson, Marion, 211, 212

Anthony, Susan B., 236

Arlt, Carl T., 210, 211, 213, 214

Association of Lincoln Presenters, 186, 239

Bacon, Henry, 196, 197, 203

Baldwin, George D., 26, 33, 145

Baldwin, Marcus W., 162, 166, 167, 169, 177, 178, 184, 191

Ball, Thomas, 125, 129, 148–149, 150, 185, 214, 237. *See also* Lincoln Freedom Monument, D.C.

Bancroft, George, 13, 99, 118, 119

Barber, William, 116, 131, 144, 152

Barnard, George Grey, 184, 189, 190–191, 192–193, 195, 205

Barron, Robert, 242

baseball (townball), 16, 19, 21, 43, 212

Batista, Fulgencio, 219, 224, 225

Beckwith, Robert Todd Lincoln, 225

Beecher, Henry Ward, 13, 97

Bellew, Frank, 81, 83

Berger, Anthony, 55, 56, 59, 78, 80, 84, 117, 135, 138, 139, 253

Billings, George A., 6, 7, 8, 10, 84, 91, 194, 199

Black History Month, 201

Black Panther Party, 232, 233

Bolen, John Adams, 83, 87

Booth, John Wilkes, 82, 86, 89, 99, 101, 103, 118, 218

Borglum, Gutzon, 14, 15, 171, 172, 184, 185, 186, 193, 203, 210, 223, 248, 249

Borglum, Lincoln, 186, 210

Boritt, Gabor, 239

Boutwell, George S., 36, 102, 134, 137, 139

Bovy, Hugues, 112

Boy Scouts, 195–196, 202, 228

Boyd, Andrew, 5, 27, 143, 145

Brady, Mathew, 13, 15, 24–25, 56, 64, 66, 68, 69, 70, 84, 216, 255

Breckinridge, John C., 19–20, 21

Brenner, Samuel H., 173

Brenner, Victor David, 170, 173, 175, 180, 183, 191, 201, 226, 227, 230

Brooks, Noah, 107, 157

Brown, Henry Kirke, 5, 137, 138, 139, 186, 204

Bryant, William Cullen, 41, 99, 188

Buchanan, James, 12, 24, 26, 42

Buchwald, Art, 237

Burt, Charles, 2, 3, 27, 31, 36, 37, 49, 59, 86, 94, 117, 135, 138, 139–140, 143, 147, 148, 152–153, 162, 168, 173, 176, 198, 199, 201, 218, 222, 241, 242, 245, 248

Bush, George W., 244, 246, 248

Buttre, John Chester, 17, 18, 88, 105, 117, 180, 134

Calhoun, John C., 69, 107, 108

Calverley, Charles, 162, 159, 223

Carnegie, Dale, 205

Carpenter, Francis B., 41, 54, 55, 59, 71, 75–77, 94, 113, 117, 120, 121, 131, 136, 139, 150, 164, 165, 211

Caswell, Lincoln, 202, 206

Cathedral of St. John the Divine, 197, 198

Century of Progress Industrial Exposition, 206, 207

Charnwood, Lord, 176, 188, 191, 195

Chase, Salmon P., 1, 14, 26, 31, 36, 41, 49, 55, 64, 66, 68, 82, 114, 118

Chicago World's Fair (see World's Columbian Exposition)

Citizens Coinage Advisory Committee, 248, 249, 254

Civil War Campaign Medal (badge), 169–170

Civil War Round Table, 214, 235

Civil War Times (periodical), 223

Cochrane, John, 61, 62, 64

Colfax, Schuyler, 101–102, 118

Colored People's Educational Monument Association, 109, 111, 113, 114, 128

Columbian Bank Note Co., 199

Commission of Fine Arts, 191, 219, 223, 249, 250, 254

Compound Interest Treasury Notes, 48, 49, 62, 69, 119, 145

"Contents of Lincoln's Pockets, The" (song), 235–236

Continental Bank Note Co., 45, 116, 128, 134, 135, 140, 141, 148

Coolidge, Calvin, 193, 200, 201

Coolidge-Dawes Lincoln Highway Tour, 200, 201

Cooper Union, 213

Cooper Union photograph, 13, 14, 15, 17, 18, 21, 22, 23, 28, 132

Copeley, Humphrey, 79

Copperheads, 38

Copland, Aaron, 214, 216

counterfeiting, 36, 37, 57, 58, 62, 68, 82, 122, 134–135, 136, 137–138, 139, 144, 150, 151, 153, 248

Crunelle, Leonard, 4, 204

cult of Lincoln, 193, 219

Currier & Ives, 16, 17, 18, 19, 21, 47, 60, 64–65, 73, 76, 100, 105, 107, 108

Dali, Salvador, 235, 236

Davis, Jefferson, 29, 32, 38, 54, 71, 74, 102–103, 118

Demand Notes, 2, 31–32, 33–34, 35, 36, 37, 54, 147, 248

Dintaman, A.W., 223

Douglas, Stephen A., 5, 12, 14, 19, 20, 21, 171, 255

Douglass, Frederick, 86, 114, 149

Drake, John B., 14, 23

Dramatic Life of Abraham Lincoln (film), 6, 7, 8, 10, 84, 91, 194, 199

Drane, Samuel Dade, 183, 194

Drinkwater, John, 193–195

Durbin, Richard, 242, 245, 246

Duthie, James, 49, 55

E.A. Wright Bank Note Co., 213, 217

Eastman, Harvey Gridley, 14, 15

Educational Lincoln Monument Association, 109, 111, 113, 114, 128

Eisenhower, Dwight D., 216, 218, 219

Ellis, Salathiel, 21, 28, 42, 43

Emancipation Monument. *See* Lincoln Freedom Monument, D.C.

Emancipation Proclamation, 33, 36, 43, 44, 46, 51, 51, 54, 55, 60, 71, 72, 115, 125, 129, 135, 143, 144, 149, 177, 216, 228, 229, 240, 245; first reading of, 41, 55, 120, 121, 131, 139, 150–151, 165, 211

Emerson, Ralph Waldo, 18, 101, 164

Fay, Herbert Wells, 245

Federal Reserve Bank Notes, 139, 188, 202, 206

Federal Reserve Notes, 139, 165, 188, 202, 214, 230, 240, 242, 243, 244, 248, 249, 251

Fell, Jesse W., 3, 216

Ferris, J.L.G., 9, 190

films portraying Lincoln, 4, 5, 6, 7, 8, 10, 11, 12, 18, 24, 84, 91, 182, 194, 199, 209, 211, 213, 219, 237, 238

First National Bank of Idaho, 118

Fischer, LeRoy, 235

Flannery, Lot, 129–130, 197

Fleishell, William III, 242, 243

Fonda, Henry, 5, 6, 7, 10, 11, 176, 211, 213

Ford's Theater, 86, 90, 93, 162, 205, 232, 237, 251; Lincoln medal, 237

Fort Abraham Lincoln (Dakota Territory), 144

Fort Lincoln (Washington, D.C.), 29–30

Fortress Monroe, 71

Fractional Currency, 43, 72, 94, 117, 135–136, 139–140, 144, 245

Fraser, James Earle, 15, 124, 184, 203–204, 205, 216, 217, 232, 233, 248

Freedman's Bureau, 127

Freedman's Savings & Trust Co., 84

Freedmen's Aid Society, 168

Freedom Memorial Monument. *See* Lincoln Freedom Monument, D.C.

Fremont, John C., 12, 38, 61, 62, 64, 77, 114

French, Daniel Chester, 186, 196, 197, 203, 223, 224, 226, 240, 250, 253

Gage, David A., 14

Gage, George W., 14, 16, 98

Gardner, Alexander, 24–25, 43, 52, 70, 84, 89, 117, 158, 236, 255

Garfield, James A., 119, 150, 152, 153, 157, 159, 164, 165

Gasparro, Frank, 219, 222, 223

Gault, John, 36, 64, 66, 68

German, Christopher S., 1, 13, 23, 26, 34, 45, 128

Gettysburg Address, 52, 152, 180, 189, 215, 216, 218, 225, 228, 237, 245, 246, 249; memorial, 161, 186

Gettysburg College, 239

Gettysburg National Military Park, 143, 186

Gilder-Lehrman Institute, 239

Gold Certificates, 79, 94, 139, 143, 148, 152, 153, 173, 222

Gore Vidal's Lincoln (film), 237, 238

Grand Army of the Republic (GAR), 118–119, 143, 155, 164, 171, 176–177, 179, 204

Grand Old Party (GOP), 133, 167

Grant, Ulysses S., 51, 52, 59, 79, 82, 86, 118, 119, 129, 133, 136, 137, 139, 146, 147, 148, 150, 153, 155, 159, 160, 162, 163, 164, 166–167, 171, 205, 235, 255

Gray, Harry A., 200, 201

Great Central Fair (Philadelphia), 54, 64

Gugler, Henry, 138, 139, 153, 157, 173, 176

Gumey, Jeremiah, 75, 76, 101, 103

Hall of Fame for Great Americans, 164–165, 198, 228

Hall, Arthur, 168, 201

Halpin, Frederick, 59, 117, 121, 136

Hamilton Bank Note Co., 187

Hamilton Stevens Group, 240

Hamlin, Hannibal, 17, 18, 20, 21

Hannaford, Mrs. P.A., 111

Harding, Warren G., 196, 197

Harper's Weekly, 17, 20, 21, 22, 24, 28, 35, 38, 41, 44, 61, 62, 68, 74, 77, 82, 92, 93, 98, 102, 107, 109, 131, 133, 137, 166

Hartford Wide Awakes, 14, 15

Hatch, Lorenzo, 158, 241, 246

Hawthorne, Nathaniel, 18

Hay, John, 14, 50, 83, 93, 154, 158, 216

Healy, G.P.A., 131, 212, 223, 229

Hearst, William Randolph, 168, 197

Heath Counterfeit Detector, 139

Hepburn v. Griswold, 82

Herndon, William H., 5–7, 16, 93, 154, 157, 253

Hessler, Alexander, 17, 151–152, 218, 219, 224, 253

Hewitt, Robert, 171, 177

Hilton, Winthrop E., 62, 68

Hinton, Charles Louis, 197, 199

Hipschen, Thomas R., 222, 238, 242, 243

Holzer, Harold, 15, 242, 251

Homer Lee Bank Note Co., 1, 158

Hosmer, Harriet, 128, 129

Howard, O.O., 127, 162

Howells, William Dean, 18, 162

Huntington, Charles R., 180

Huston, Walter, 6, 91, 176, 209, 194

Illinois commemorative medallions, 246

Illinois Lincoln Fest, 247

Illinois National Guard, 232, 233, 246

Illinois state quarter, 243, 244, 245

Illinois Watch Co., 143, 170, 182, 186, 187, 197, 198, 199

"In God We Trust" motto, 229–230

In the Footsteps of Abraham Lincoln (cartoon), 201

Interest-Bearing Treasury Notes, 48, 49, 55, 119, 145

"Is the Lincoln Theme Exhausted?" (Randall), 209

Isham, Mary Lincoln, 198

John A. Lowell Bank Note Co., 182

Johnson, Andrew, 62, 64, 66, 68, 69, 71, 72, 102–103, 110, 118, 120, 134, 141

Kelly, Grace, 6, 216

Kennedy, John F., 212, 225, 226, 229

Kennedy, John F. Jr., 240

Key, William H., 64, 71, 116
Kileny, Julio, 211
Kimmel & Forster, 107, 115
Kincaid, Robert L., 209
King, Martin Luther Jr., 222, 223, 228–229, 232
King, Robert P., 199, 200, 201, 223, 237, 250
LaHood, Ray, 242, 245, 246
Lambert, William Henry, 162, 164
"Land of Lincoln" (motto), 218, 230, 244, 247
Lawson, John (a.k.a. John Lassano), 82
Lee, Robert E., 50, 86, 166
Leech, Edward O., 180
Legal Tender Notes, 2, 33, 34, 36, 37, 43, 44, 48, 54, 57, 82, 94, 104, 117, 122, 131, 132, 134–135, 137–139, 148, 153, 165, 173, 201–202, 248. *See also* United States Notes
Lehrman, Lewis, 239
LeLand, Henry M., 196, 205
license plates: Illinois, 247; South Dakota, 247
Life magazine "Hall of Heroes," 240
Life of Lincoln medal series, 232
Lincoln, Argentina (city), 114, 115
Lincoln, Illinois (city), 11–12, 218
Lincoln, Nebraska (city), 132, 148, 186, 197, 216
Lincoln nickel electrotrial, 184, 185
Lincoln quarter, 54, 113
"Lincoln Redeemed" token die, 79, 247
Lincoln $3 gold pattern, 123
Lincoln Academy of Illinois, 231
Lincoln Aircraft Co., 203
Lincoln Bank Bottle, 217
Lincoln bedroom, 216, 247
Lincoln Birthday Association of Buffalo, 154
Lincoln Birthplace Memorial, 179, 188, 189
Lincoln cabin, 159, 160
Lincoln Cavalry (First N.Y. Cavalry Regt.), 28
Lincoln cent, 167, 175, 176, 180, 180, 182, 184, 186, 191, 198, 209, 215, 217, 219, 222, 223, 224–225, 226, 235, 236, 239, 240, 245, 248, 249, 252–253, 254, 255; aluminum, 236; mule with dime, 248, 249; proposed new, 216, 217; roller, 230; superstitions concerning, 186; V for Victory, 215, 217
Lincoln Centennial March, 177
Lincoln Centennial medal (Hewitt), 171
Lincoln Chapter No. 147 RAM, 144
Lincoln Christ statues (Barnard), 195
Lincoln Club, 171; of Cincinnati, 157, 159
Lincoln cork-faced horse collars, 151
Lincoln Credit Union (New York), 201
"Lincoln Cult, The" (article), 193, 219
Lincoln Douglas Square (Alton, Illinois), 173

Lincoln essay contests, 179, 180, 197, 198, 199, 201, 202
Lincoln exhibitions, 154, 159, 162, 164, 177, 188, 208
Lincoln Farm Association, 168, 170, 182, 188
Lincoln Fellowship of New York, 171
Lincoln Financial Field, 245
Lincoln Financial Foundation, 250
Lincoln Financial Group, 249
Lincoln First Group, Inc., 231
Lincoln folk art, 172, 202
Lincoln Freedom Monument, Washington, D.C. (National Freedom Memorial), 125, 128–129, 148–149, 150, 185, 214
Lincoln Fund Insurance Co., 131
Lincoln Gold Corp., 203
Lincoln Grammar School (San Francisco), 83, 115
Lincoln Group of Chicago, 212
Lincoln Gun, 71
Lincoln Head pops, 251
Lincoln Herald, 162, 209
Lincoln Heritage Trail, 216, 228, 234, 235
Lincoln High School (Lincoln, Nebraska), 186
Lincoln Highway (D.C.–Gettysburg) Memorial, 186
Lincoln Highway (transcontinental), 166, 187, 191, 202, 203, 204, 205, 224
Lincoln Highway Association, 187
Lincoln Highway Commission, 188
Lincoln Hirelings, 38, 151
Lincoln Historical Research Foundation, 201
Lincoln Hospital (Washington, D.C.), 127
Lincoln impersonators, 186, 202, 206, 208, 209, 239
Lincoln in Numismatics (King), 199–201, 237, 250
"Lincoln in Seeds," 167
Lincoln Institute: Jefferson City, Missosuri, 121; Lincoln Ridge, Kentucky, 183–184
Lincoln Lager beer, 217
Lincoln Legion, 166, 172, 193
Lincoln Library of Essential Information, 201
Lincoln Log (periodical), 226
Lincoln Logs, 195, 196, 246
Lincoln Lore (periodical), 10, 201, 203, 204
Lincoln Magazine, 167–168
Lincoln Memorial (Washington, D.C.), 187, 196–197, 198, 202, 203, 211, 219, 222, 223, 222, 223, 226, 228, 232, 235, 236–237, 240, 242, 243, 244, 245, 250, 254, 255
Lincoln Memorial Bridge (Milwaukee), 201
Lincoln Memorial Club of Cincinnati, 145
Lincoln Memorial Collection exhibition, 154
Lincoln Memorial Commission, 197

Lincoln Memorial Garden (Lincoln City, Indiana), 254
Lincoln Memorial Hall (Hodgenville), 2
Lincoln Memorial Ladies Citizens Committee, 197
Lincoln Memorial Shrine (Redlands, California), 205
Lincoln Memorial University, 162, 206, 209, 213, 234, 235, 236
Lincoln Mint, 232
Lincoln Monument Association: Washington, D.C. (*see* National Lincoln Monument Association); Philadelphia, 165
Lincoln Motor Co., 196
Lincoln Museum: Chicago, 159; Fort Wayne, 201, 203, 250–251; Washington, D.C., 167, 205
Lincoln National Bank: Lincoln, Illinois, 207; New York City, 152, 168; Pennsylvania, 217
Lincoln National Life Foundation, 205
Lincoln National Life Insurance Co., 168, 173, 201, 205, 206, 223, 227
Lincoln National Memorial Trail, 213
Lincoln nickel pattern, 119–120
Lincoln Paint & Color Co., 195
Lincoln Park Chapter no. 177 RAM, 150
Lincoln parks: Chicago, 115, 155, 156, 171, 177; Washington, D.C., 150; Jersey City, 124; Michigan, 208; San Francisco, 187
"Lincoln Penny, The" (song), 215
Lincoln Prize, 239
Lincoln Proprietary Co., 206
Lincoln Pure White Lead, 121
Lincoln Railsplitter U.S. Army Division, 190, 214, 232
Lincoln Record Corp., 195
Lincoln Rock, 247
Lincoln room, University of Illinois, 216
Lincoln root beer, 217
Lincoln Society of Philately, 226, 228
Lincoln Square (Washington, D.C.), 127
Lincoln statue controversy (Barnard), 190–191, 192–193, 195
Lincoln Subscription (label), 140
Lincoln syrup, 196
Lincoln tea, 206
Lincoln Temperance Association, 128
Lincoln Temperance Society, 127
Lincoln Territory: Oklahoma, 124, 126, 127; South Dakota, 151; Wyoming, 130
Lincoln the Unknown (Carnegie), 205
Lincoln Tower (London), 148
Lincoln Trail, 228; *see also* Lincoln Heritage Trail
Lincoln Trail State Memorial (Illinois), 211

Lincoln Tree (Sequoia National Park), 161
Lincoln Tribute Book (Hewitt), 177
Lincoln Tunnel, 209, 211
Lincoln Union, 139
Lincoln, Abraham: apotheosis, 104, 106, 107; assassination, 86, 91–93, 143; athletic prowess, 5, 10, 219, 242, 243; attempted theft of corpse, 150; autobiography, 3, 5; birthplace, 1, 2, 3, 169, 170, 181, 202, 203; birthday as legal holiday, 145–146, 167, 170–171, 176–177, 193, 196, 199, 210, 255; birthplace replica, 2, 3, 169, 206, 207, 223, 253; Black Hawk War, 3, 4, 204, 246; burial, 104; campaign biographies, 17–18, 68, 71; in campaign songs, 19; and Christianity, 7; collected works, 216; and Confederate $5 bill, 86, 91, 235; Cooper Union address, 13–14, 184; depicted as Christ, 193; education, 3, 5, 8; exposure to slavery, 7, 8; expresses doubts on reelection, 73; films depicting, 4, 5, 6, 7, 8, 10, 11, 12, 18, 24, 84, 91, 182, 194, 199, 209, 211, 213, 219, 237, 238; First Inaugural reenactment, 226; funeral, 96–97, 104; funeral car, 98, 159, 160; funeral train, 97–98, 100, 212; honorary citizenship of San Marino, 31; honesty, 10, 17, 19, 21; inaugural trip, 23, 24–26; Indiana cabin, 8, 206, 207; legal career, 3, 11–12, 16, 17, 82, 253, 255; life mask, 14, 15, 83–84, 223; member of Congress, 3; name misspelled, 17, 22, 105; nominated for presidency, 14, 16, 62; patent, 11, 23; phrenology, 36, 78–79, 105; plays depicting, 10, 193–195, 209, 210, 212; postmaster, 10; purchase of U.S. bonds, 36, 50, 54; rail splitter, 5, 6, 8, 9, 10, 14, 19, 20, 21, 207; second inaugural address, 86, 87, 104, 138, 169, 178, 216, 223, 231, 246, 250; shredded currency, 172; spoofs of, 230, 237, 240; Springfield home, 153, 155, 161, 168, 226, 227, 238, 240; tomb, 133, 166, 203
Lincoln, Abraham, depictions of in postwar South, 141, 144, 148
Lincoln, Abraham, depictions of outside United States: in Argentina, 114–115; in Belgium, 111; in Brazil, 124; in Cuba, 211, 209, 219, 224; in England, 29, 113, 119, 157, 158, 180, 188, 193–195, 197, 203 (see also *Punch*); in France, 109, 111, 122–123, 180, 201; in Germany, 28, 29, 111, 112, 118, 125; in Greece, 111, 113, 219; in Italy, 111; in Mexico, 114, 230, 232; in Norway, 175, 187; in Scotland, 159, 161; in Switzerland, 112

Lincoln imagery: on advertising scrip, 126; on bonds, 46; on carpetbagger scrip, 141, 144, 148; on casino tokens, 237, 243; on checks, 86, 128, 137, 144, 153, 163, 168, 227, 52, 71, 122, 133; , on comic books, 241; on commercial products, 121, 130–131, 132, 146, 147, 149, 153–154, 155, 157, 158, 159, 160, 166, 168, 183, 193, 195, 196, 200, 203, 205, 206, 207, 208; on Cook Islands coins, 239; on corporate bonds, 246; on corporate stocks, 203, 231, 246; on county scrip, 148; on Cuban coins, 239, 240; on Depression scrip, 208; earliest extant photo, 11; on Ecuatorial Guinea coins, 232, 234; imagery, on experimental U.S. currency, 234, 235, 239, 240; on foreign bonds, 114; on foreign stamps, 2, 4, 169, 209, 210, 214, 215, 216, 218, 219, 225, 226, 231, 232, 234; on Liberian coins, 243, 244, 245; on Liberty Loan bonds, 191; on Liberty Loan bonds poster, 189, 190; on license plates, 247, 251; on merchant scrip, 41–42, 43, 44, 148; on Paraguay coins, 236; on prop money, 239; on scrip, 135, 139, 141, 161; on state bank notes, 23, 33, 46, 58; on state bonds, 27; on U.S. bonds, 26–27, 48, 127, 191, 213, 214, 215; on U.S. coins, 119–120, 167, 175, 176, 180, 182, 184, 185, 186, 191–192, 198, 209, 215, 217, 219, 222, 223, 224–225, 226, 235, 236, 239, 240, 243, 248, 249, 252–253, 254, 255; on U.S. Food Coupons, 139, 234; on U.S. paper money, 27, 31, 36, 37, 49, 55, 58, 52, 69, 94, 131, 135–140, 144, 145, 148, 153, 161–162, 163, 173, 176, 187, 188, 195, 198, 199, 201–202, 206, 214, 215, 222, 229–230, 238, 240, 241, 242, 243, 244, 245, 246, 248, 249, 251; on U.S. postal cards, 145, 184, 188, 240; on U.S. revenue stamps, 110, 111, 117, 125, 142, 143, 148, 149, 151; on U.S. savings bonds, 218; on U.S. stamps, 93–94, 119, 120, 132–133, 134, 135, 139, 140, 143, 157, 161, 164, 166–167, 177, 178, 184, 198, 210, 211, 213, 214, 215, 216, 218, 219, 223, 225, 226, 228, 231, 232, 237, 238–239, 240; on U.S. war bonds, 214, 215; on U.S. war savings stamps, 198
Lincoln, Abraham, mourned outside United States: in Argentina, 124; in Brazil, 124; in China, 124; in England, 124; in Switzerland, 124
Lincoln, Immortal American, 5, 10
Lincoln, Mary Todd, 7, 10, 21, 55, 92, 122, 123, 153, 159, 193, 236, 239, 245, 255

Lincoln, Mrs. Robert Todd, 201
Lincoln, Nancy Hanks, 3, 8
Lincoln, photographs of, 11, 13, 15, 16, 17, 18, 20, 23, 24, 31, 32, 33, 34, 35, 43, 52, 53, 54, 55, 56, 64, 66, 67, 68, 70, 83, 85, 84, 94, 223, 224, 226, 245, 250, 253, 255
Lincoln Portrait (Copland), 214, 216
Lincoln, Robert Todd, 13, 48, 50, 152, 155, 157, 168, 171, 190, 195, 197, 201, 223
Lincoln, Thaddeus (Tad), 84, 86, 88, 89, 109, 110, 237
Lincoln, Thomas, 3, 8, 182, 202
Lincoln, Willie, 97
Lincoln: A Novel (Vidal), 237, 238
Lincoln-Alliance Bank, 196
Lincoln-Douglas debates, 12, 14, 18, 171, 173, 203, 209, 218, 219, 223, 254, 255
Lincoln-Illinois half dollar, 191–192
Lincoln-Lee Legion, 166
Lincoln's Clemency (film), 182
Lincoln's Doctor's Dog, 211, 218
Lincoln's Doctor's Dog (telefilm), 219
Lindsay, Vachel, 186
Littlefield, John H., 138, 139, 157, 176
Log Cabin maple syrup, 196
Log Cabin Republicans, 236
Log Cabin syrup, 157
Logan, John A., 119, 171, 196
Punch (London periodical), 38–39, 44, 46, 82, 107–108, 109
Lovett, George H., 32, 78, 102
Lowell, James Russell, 18, 114, 236
Lyman School for Boys, 184
Magnus, Charles, 29, 35, 44, 95, 106
Marshall, William Edgar, 122, 123, 154, 168, 182, 183, 217
Mary Lincoln candies, 193
Massey, Raymond, 4, 6, 7, 10, 12, 18, 24, 176, 212, 213
Masters, Richard, 255
Mauldin, Bill, 229
Maxwell, Elsa, 213
Mayer, Eugene Jr., 171
Mayer, Ferd., 42
McAdoo, William Gibbs, 191
McClees, James E., 33
McClellan, George B., 32, 35, 43, 44, 64, 73, 74, 75, 76
McClellan, George B. Jr., 177, 178
McClelland, Stewart W., 213
McClure's magazine, 161, 162
McCulloch, Hugh, 82, 86, 122
McGlynn, Frank Sr., 47, 209
McGovern, George, 222, 250, 251
McKinley, William, 119, 164, 165
McLellan, Charles W., 164

McRae, John Chester, 47, 105

Mead, Larkin G., 109, 122, 123, 137, 146

Meade, M.A., 48, 49

Medallic Art Co., 172, 173, 177, 179, 223, 228, 231, 234, 235

Meet Mr. Lincoln, 230, 232

Mendel, Ed, 42, 51

Merriam, Joseph, 19, 37, 83, 123

Meserve, Frederick Hill, 179, 188, 205, 215

Mezzara, Pietro, 83, 115–116

Middleton, Strobridge & Co., 42, 82, 157

Miles, Charles R., 208, 209

Mills, Clark, 83–84, 134, 135

Mills, Fisk, 134, 135

Monaghan, Jay, 145, 215

Monroe, Marilyn, 240

Morgan, George T., 154, 155, 178, 191, 192, 224, 225

Mount Rushmore National Memorial, 171, 186, 209, 210, 216, 224, 232, 234, 236, 239, 240, 243, 244, 248, 250

Muller, L.G., 144–145, 173, 184

Mundt, Karl, 232, 234

Nast, Thomas, 44, 45, 83, 92, 93, 102

National Association for the Advancement of Colored People (NAACP), 179

National Bank Note Co., 2, 26–28, 31, 33, 34, 37, 45, 48, 49, 55, 62, 94, 117, 118, 119, 120, 127, 128, 134, 135, 136, 137, 140, 143, 144, 145, 151

National Bank Notes, 122, 207

national banks, 82, 118

National Cowboy Hall of Fame and Western Heritage Center, 232, 233

National Freedom Memorial, 125, 128–129, 148–149, 150, 185, 214

National Inventors Hall of Fame, 11, 248–249, 250

National Lincoln Monument Association: Springfield, 109, 123, 130, 137, 146, 148, 161; Washington, D.C., 93, 124, 126–127, 128

National Parks Service, 227, 245, 246

Negro History Week, 201

New Salem State Historic Site, 244

New Salem, IL, 168, 197

Newman, Ralph G., 211

Nicolay, John G., 59, 75, 93, 154, 158, 168

Ninger, Emanuel, 153

Nixon, Richard M., 235, 255

Northwestern Sanitary Fair (Chicago), 39, 51, 52, 86, 88, 113

Numismatic & Antiquarian Society of Philadelphia, 141

Oak Ridge Cemetery (Springfield), 133, 146, 148

Oakleaf, Joseph Benjamin, 164, 173

Obama, Barack, 222, 250, 251

O'Connor, Andrew, 191, 192, 203

Old Abe (bald eagle), 38–39, 156

Old Abe Soda & Ginger Ale, 169

Oldroyd, Osborn Hamiline, 153, 161; collection of Lincolniana, 198, 201, 205

Order of Lincoln medallion, 231

Ostendorf, Lloyd, 226, 227, 232, 234, 245

Ourdan, Joseph, 45, 94, 120, 134, 140, 143

Paquet, Anthony C., 74, 77, 78, 86, 88, 113, 116, 143

Parkinson, R.L., 5, 10, 211

Perine, George E., 61, 70, 105

Perrine, George H., 118

Petersen House, D.C., 161, 162, 201

Piccirilli Brothers, 197

Pickett, Byron, 144, 173, 184

plays depicting Lincoln, 10, 193–195, 209, 210, 212

"Poetical Cult of Lincoln, The" (Van Doren), 193

postal-currency envelope, 134, 135

Prang, Louis, 44, 69, 82, 84, 106

Pratt, Bela Lyon, 177, 178

President Lincoln (ocean liner), 168–169, 190, 191

President Lincoln's Cottage, 251

Preston, Robert, 183

Prohibition Educational League, 201

Randall, James G., 209

Raymond, Henry J., 71, 113

Reagan, Ronald, 204

Ream, Vinnie, 121, 122, 142, 143

Reed, Fred L. IV, 243, 244

Republican Club of the City of New York, 151, 157, 162, 179, 184

Republican National Committee, 213, 217

Rice, M.P., 158

Ripstra, J. Henri, 212, 231

Ritchie, Alexander Hay, 68, 120, 121, 131, 139, 150, 165, 211

Robinson, Boardman, 214, 215

Rodman, Thomas Jackson, 71

Rogers, John, 129

Roine, Jules Edouard, 172, 176, 177, 178, 179

Roosevelt, Franklin D., 205, 211, 212, 213, 216, 222, 250

Roosevelt, Theodore, 167, 168, 173, 175, 176–177, 179, 184, 190, 201, 210, 212, 255

Russin, Robert I., 224

Ruther, V. Jack, 242

Rutledge, Ann, 5, 6, 10, 203, 216

Saint-Gaudens, Augustus, 84, 154, 155, 156–157, 177, 181, 188, 192, 195, 196, 198, 219, 224, 228

Sandburg, Carl, 1–2, 36, 176, 201, 211, 212, 215

Sandburg's Lincoln (film), 11

Sanders, Harlan, 236

Sarmiento, Domingo Faustino, 114–115

Sartain, John, 69, 71, 105, 106, 107, 121, 139

Sartain, Samuel, 5, 24, 105

Schurz, Carl, 28, 236

Schwartz, Thomas, 248

Schwengel, Fred, 223

Scott, Winfield, 1, 29, 32, 35, 145

Sealey, Alfred, 23

Security Bank Note Co., 217

Security-Columbian Banknote Co., 231, 239

Seward, William H., 14, 29, 41, 55, 59, 69, 103, 124, 126, 143

Shepherd, N.H., 11, 255

Sherman, John, 124, 128, 146

Sherman, William Tecumseh, 51, 128, 146, 255

Sherwood, Robert E., 210, 213

Shreve & Co., 179

Siegel, Emil, 116, 118, 119

Silver Certificates, 139, 161–162, 163, 167, 187, 198, 199, 215, 238

Smillie, George F.C., 162, 163, 165, 167, 198, 211

Soldiers' Fair (Springfield, Massachusetts), 83

Soldiers' National Cemetery (Gettysburg, Pennsylvania), 52, 113

Soldiers' National Monument (Gettysburg, Pennsylvania), 152

South Dakota state quarter, 248, 250

Southern Illustrated News, 57

Speed, James, 124

Speed, Lucy, 32–33

Spinner, Francis E., 36, 48, 79, 127, 128

spoofs on Lincoln, 230, 237, 240

Spooner, J.C., 64

SS *President Lincoln* (U.S. troop carrier), 190, 191

Stanton, Edwin M., 59, 68, 91, 101, 129, 136, 139, 140

Stephens, Henry Louis, 36, 60

Studley, R.P., 135, 144, 148

Sun Yat-Sen, 214, 226

Taft, Charles P., 184, 189

Taft, Lorado, 201, 206, 209

Taft, William Howard, 180, 184, 189, 190, 196–197

Tarbell, Ida, 93, 161, 162, 166, 195, 201, 203

Taylor, Tom (Mark Lemon), 107–108

Tenniel, John, 39, 81, 107, 109

Thanksgiving Day Proclamation, 52

Thayer, William M., 111, 113, 140–141

tobacco products, named for Lincoln: A. Lincoln Segars (*sic*), 130; Abe Lincoln Honest

Long Cut tobacco, 153–154; Great Liberator cigars, 159; Honest Old Abe cigars, 132; Lincoln Bouquet cigars, 155; Lincoln Highway cigars, 205; Old Abe cigars, 130, 132, 200, 201

Towle, Patrick J., 157, 196

Townsend, George Alfred, 69, 110

Tremont House, 12, 14, 16, 21, 23

True, Benjamin F., 19, 21

Truesdell, Winfred Porter, 2, 205, 206

Truth, Sojourner, 161

Union League, 50, 71, 78, 97, 98, 187; New York, 98; Philadelphia, 50, 71, 187

Union Party, 210

United Republican Committee, 210

U.S. Assay Commission, 224, 225

United States Banknote Corp., 114, 231

United States Notes, 229–230. *See also* Legal Tender Notes

U.S. paper money, refacing of, 243, 244

U.S. Secret Service, 82, 243, 245, 248

Upham, Samuel C., 41, 55, 62, 63, 106

USS *Abraham Lincoln*: (CVN-72), 238; (SSBN-602), 225, 226

Volck, Adalbert, 24, 36, 46, 47, 108

Volk, Douglas (Stephen A. Douglas), 196, 197, 198, 199, 213, 218

Volk, Leonard Wells, 14, 15, 16, 17, 84, 144, 152, 154, 155, 223

Wall, Bernhardt, 204

Warren, Henry F., 86

Warren, Louis A., 144, 177, 201, 202, 203, 209, 255

Washington, Booker Taliaferro, 179, 236

Washington, George, 26, 52, 104, 106, 107, 108, 114, 119–120, 133, 134, 136, 139, 145, 147, 152, 155, 159, 160, 164, 176, 177, 188, 189, 198, 201, 235, 236

Weaver, Donna, 244

Weik, Jesse W., 5, 188, 223

Weinman, Adolph A., 180, 181, 186

Welles Gideon, 2, 14

Wells, John G., 50

Wells, Samuel R., 78–79, 105

Western Bank Note & Engraving Co., 137, 176

Western Sanitary Commission, St. Louis, 149, 150

"What Would Lincoln Do?" 250

Whig party, 3, 5, 12

White, John H., 62, 68

Whitehead & Hoag, 177, 179, 189, 197, 198, 199, 202

Whitman, Walt, 18, 104, 116, 117, 127, 151, 155, 156, 157

Wills House (Gettysburg, Pennsylvania), 245, 246

Willson, Joseph, 42, 43

Wilson, Rufus Rockwell, 208

Wilson, Woodrow, 139, 188, 189, 201, 222, 250

World's Columbian Exposition, 159, 160

Wright, John Lloyd, 195, 196

Young Mr. Lincoln (film), 5, 6, 7, 10, 11, 211

Zabriskie, Andrew C., 145, 159

Zearing, Henry, 160

Zemansky, John, 239

The U.S. Mint unveiled the design for the Abraham Lincoln bicentennial silver dollar on November 19, 2008, the 145th anniversary of Lincoln's delivery of his Gettysburg Address. The obverse was created by U.S. Mint Artistic Infusion Program Master Designer Justin Kunz and sculpted by U.S. Mint sculptor-engraver Don Everhart. Symbolic of Lincoln's strength and resolve, the image was inspired by Daniel Chester French's famous sculpture of the president that sits inside the Lincoln Memorial in Washington, D.C. The coin's reverse was designed and executed by U.S. Mint sculptor-engraver Phebe Hemphill. The inscription bears Lincoln's immortal words—the final 43 words of the Gettysburg Address—and his signature.

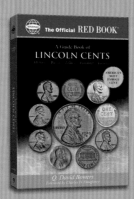

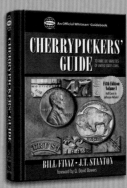
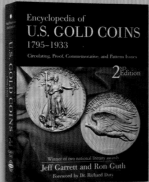
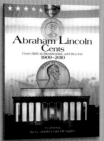

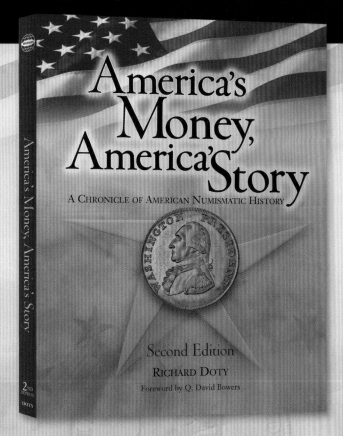